Special Relationship in the Malay World

ISEAS YUSOF ISHAK
INSTITUTE

Special Relationship in the Malay World

Indonesia and Malaysia

Ho Ying Chan

 YUSOF ISHAK
INSTITUTE

First published in Singapore in 2018 by
ISEAS Publishing
30 Heng Mui Keng Terrace
Singapore 119614

Email: publish@iseas.edu.sg
Website: bookshop.iseas.edu.sg

The responsibility for facts and opinions in this publication rests exclusively with the author and his interpretations do not necessarily reflect the views or the policy of the publisher or its supporters.

ISEAS Library Cataloguing-in-Publication Data

Ho, Ying Chan.
    Special Relationship in the Malay World : Indonesia and Malaysia.
    1. International relations.
    2. Balance of power.
    3. Indonesia—Foreign relations—Malaysia—History.
    4. Malaysia—Foreign relations—Indonesia—History.
    5. National security—Indonesia.
    6. National security—Malaysia
    7. ASEAN.
    8. Southeast Asia—Foreign relations.
    I. Title.
DS640 M3H67   March 2018

ISBN 978-981-4818-17-9 (soft cover)
ISBN 978-981-4818-19-3 (Ebook PDF)

Typeset by International Typesetters Pte Ltd
Printed in Singapore by Markono Print Media Pte Ltd

"Sometimes I see Malaysia as my brother;
sometimes I see it as my enemy."

An Indonesian Senior Researcher

CONTENTS

LIST OF FIGURES

LIST OF TABLES

ACKNOWLEDGEMENTS

This book originated from my concern over the impacts of culture/ identity on politics. To what extent does the factor of culture — especially common identities — shape the ties between states? The book is built on my PhD thesis, which I had completed at the University of New South Wales (UNSW) at the Australian Defence Force Academy (ADFA) in April 2015. It is the revised and updated version of the thesis. I am deeply indebted to the support of many people without which the completion of this study would not have been possible.

First of all, I would like to thank Professor Clinton Fernandes for his excellent supervision. I am indeed very fortunate to be able to develop my thesis under Clinton's supervision. Clinton has been a great source of inspiration and a dedicated supervisor. I thank him specifically for thoroughly reading through my chapters, offering both encouragement and incisive criticism, while also pointing out my technical mistakes. Clinton's supervision throughout had assisted me in clarifying my ideas and had made me want to improve the quality of my thesis. I express my deepest gratitude for Clinton's guidance and his firm support for the publication of this book.

I am also very grateful to the kind support I had received from the School of Humanities and Social Sciences (HASS) of UNSW at ADFA. My special thanks go to Professor David Lovell, the former Head of School, for his help in securing partial financial support from UNSW for my PhD study at the university. This financial support had been crucial in allowing me to have peace of mind throughout my

PhD study. I thank Associate Professor Jian Zhang for his kind advice and support. I would also like to thank Associate Professor Craig Stockings, the then Research Coordinator, and the administrative staffs for ensuring strong administrative support for my research. Bernadette McDermott, Marilyn Anderson-Smith and Shirley Ramsay had never hesitated to assist me when I needed their help in solving administrative matters that I encountered.

I, meanwhile, would like to express my deep gratitude to my employer in Malaysia — Universiti Tunku Abdul Rahman (UTAR) — for partially sponsoring my PhD study at UNSW. I am deeply indebted to Professor Chuah Hean Teik, President of UTAR. Professor Chuah was indeed the very first person that had discerned the academic qualities in me, and had since strongly encouraged me to develop my intellectual capacity through a PhD study. Professor Chuah together with Professor Lee Sze Wei, Professor Ewe Hong Tat and Dr Stephen Leong Mun Yoon from UTAR had provided me their invaluable support and encouragement throughout my study in Australia. I owe special gratitude to them.

My earnest appreciation goes to the interviewees of this study, who had been very patient in sharing with me their knowledge, experience and insights on Indonesia–Malaysia relations. The analysis of the bilateral ties in this study has surely benefited from these interviews. I too extend my thanks to Perdana Library of Perdana Leadership Foundation (Malaysia), ISEAS Library (Singapore), and Ali Alatas Library of the Ministry of Foreign Affairs of the Republic of Indonesia, for their generosity in sharing with me their materials related to this study.

I express my sincere gratitude to Mr Ng Kok Kiong, Head of ISEAS Publishing, and Ms Sheryl Sin Bing Peng, the book's editor, for their generous assistance during the preparation for this publication. Besides, many thanks are due to the three anonymous reviewers. Their valuable comments and suggestions have helped make the manuscript a better one.

I am also thankful to all my friends for their care and support. In particular, I would like to thank Dr Huang Chia-Yu, who had been supportive in my four years of PhD study in Australia; Ms Lee Kar Hui, who had been kind in assisting me during my fieldwork; and Ms Samantha Cheah Pei Wen, who had selflessly helped me to design the cover of this book.

Finally, I dedicate this book to my parents, Ho Yew Kee and Tan Sook Ha, and my two sisters, Ho Key Kuen and Ho Pui Kuen. Their love, patience, encouragement and understanding make this book possible.

Ho Ying Chan
May 2018

ABBREVIATIONS

AMDA	Anglo-Malayan Defence Agreement / Anglo-Malaysian Defence Agreement
APEC	Asia-Pacific Economic Cooperation
ASA	Association of Southeast Asia
ASEAN	Association of Southeast Asian Nations
Bendera	Benteng Demokrasi Rakyat (The People's Democratic Front)
CPM	Communist Party of Malaya
CPOPC	Council of Palm Oil Producing Countries
DPR	Dewan Perwakilan Rakyat (People's Representative Council)
EAEC	East Asia Economic Caucus
EAEG	East Asian Economic Group
EC	European Community
FAO	Food and Agriculture Organization of the United Nations
FPDA	Five Power Defence Arrangement
GAM	Gerakan Aceh Merdeka (Aceh Independence Movement)
GATT	General Agreement on Tariffs and Trade

GBC	General Border Committee
GDP	Gross Domestic Product
G-15	Group of Fifteen
ICJ	International Court of Justice
Maphilindo	Malaysia–Philippines–Indonesia Confederation
MASOC	Malaysia SEA Games Organising Committee
MOU	Memorandum of Understanding
MPR	Majelis Permusyawaratan Rakyat (People's Consultative Assembly)
MPRS	Provisional People's Consultative Assembly
NAFTA	North American Free Trade Agreement
NAM	Non-Aligned Movement
NATO	North Atlantic Treaty Organisation
NIC	Newly Industrializing Country
NORAD	North American Air Defense Agreement
OECD	Organization for Economic Co-operation and Development
OIC	Organisation of Islamic Cooperation
OPEC	Organization of the Petroleum Exporting Countries
OPSUS	*Operasi Khusus* (Special Operations)
PJBD	Permanent Joint Board on Defence
PKI	Partai Komunis Indonesia (Communist Party of Indonesia)
PRB	Partai Rakyat Brunei
PRRI	Pemerintah Revolusioner Republik Indonesia (Revolutionary Government of the Republic of Indonesia)

RELA	Jabatan Sukarelawan Malaysia (The People's Volunteer Corps)
SAF	Singapore Armed Forces
SEAFET	Southeast Asia Friendship and Economic Treaty
SEATO	Southeast Asia Treaty Organization
SESKOAD	Sekolah Staf Komando Angkatan Darat (Army Staff and Command College of Indonesia)
TAC	Treaty of Amity and Cooperation in Southeast Asia
TNKU	North Kalimantan National Army
TPDA	Three Power Defence Arrangement
UMNO	United Malays National Organisation
UN	United Nations
UNESCO	United Nations Educational, Scientific and Cultural Organization
USSR	Union of Soviet Socialist Republics
ZOPFAN	Zone of Peace, Freedom and Neutrality

1

INTRODUCTION

The term "special relationship" has been used by many states to characterize a specific set of their bilateral ties with other states: for example, the ties between the United States and the United Kingdom; the United States and Canada; the United States and Israel; France and the Sub-Saharan African states; and Spain and the Latin American states. The meaning of a special relationship is centred on the term "special". It usually means a quality that is exceptional in a positive sense. Consequently, a special relationship between two states is generally being understood as a close friendship.

The concept of a special relationship remains under-defined and under-conceptualized. A large part of the meaning of this concept has been introduced by politicians, which often entails sentimental expressions. British Prime Minister Margaret Thatcher reiterated her understanding of the Anglo-American special relationship during her speech in Washington in 1985: "[i]t is Special. It just is. And that's that!"[1] she asserted. Margaret Thatcher's assertion reflects politicians' instinctive

---

[1] Margaret Thatcher's Speech at British Embassy, Washington, 20 February 1985, available at <http://www.margaretthatcher.org/document/105971> (accessed 15 March 2011).

understanding of the concept of a special relationship. Such instinctive tendency contributes to the opacity of the concept. Feldman has pointed out that an obvious reason for the absence of a definition of a special relationship is "the brevity with which journalists are forced to write or with which politicians and government are obliged to speak".[2] Systematic disentangling of what has been said about a special relationship, therefore, is necessary in order to establish an understanding of the concept which best reflects its real meaning.

The essence of a special relationship is reflected by its association with close friendship. As Aristotle had noted, "no one can have complete friendship with many people".[3] A friendship fundamentally means a relationship that is different from other relations. Friendships are commonly understood as "a relationship satisfying cognitive and emotional needs and characterized by reciprocity, trust, openness, honesty, acceptance, and loyalty".[4] In other words, a friendship is an intimate relationship that is "necessarily exclusive".[5]

The intimate nature of a friendship means that friends depend on each other for creating "a stable sense of Self", in which they constantly confirm and adapt their ideas of order.[6] Berenskoetter has pointed out that throughout history, "friendships have been identified as being capable of both strengthening and undermining order".[7] For example, the United States and the United Kingdom had jointly created and are leading the

---

[2] Lily Gardner Feldman, *The Special Relationship Between West Germany and Israel* (Boston: George Allen & Unwin, 1984), p. 4.

[3] Aristotle, NE, Book VIII, 6 and Book IX, 10, quoted in Felix Berenskoetter, "Friends, There Are No Friends? An Intimate Reframing of the International", *Journal of International Studies* 35, no. 3 (2007): 668.

[4] Ibid., p. 649.

[5] Laurence Thomas, "Friendship and Other Loves", in *Friendship: A Philosophical Reader,* edited by Neera Kapur Badhwar (Cornell: Cornell University Press, 1993), pp. 48–64. Marilyn Friedman, *What Are Friends For?* (Ithaca: Cornell University Press, 1993), quoted in Berenskoetter, "Friends, There Are No Friends? An Intimate Reframing of the International", p. 649.

[6] Berenskoetter, "Friends, There Are No Friends? An Intimate Reframing of the International", pp. 672–73.

[7] Ibid.

Western World; likewise, France and Germany have been working together to forge European integration. The dynamics of friendships indicate that a special relationship — which is a friendship between two states — is a force that has a tendency to fashion order.

However, conflicts are discernible in a special relationship. As Kissinger has noted, the close Anglo-American special relationship at times experiences "mutual exasperation".[8] Reynolds, meanwhile, argues that the unique feature of U.S.–UK special ties is that both cooperation and competition have equal weight in the relationship.[9] He observes that Anglo-American relations are woven with "complex strands of interest, ideology and emotion", and describes it as "a relationship of competitive cooperation".[10]

The tendency of two states sharing a special relationship to establish their common vision of the world, coupled with the conspicuous presence of conflicts in such a relationship, implies that the relationship might generate impacts on international politics. Viewed in this light, the concept of a special relationship deserves a detailed study.

The association of a special relationship with close friendship means that the relationship is intertwined with peaceful qualities. A relationship between two states is close only when there is a desire for peace between them. For example, the mutual wish for friendly ties between the United States and the United Kingdom since the 1890s had given rise to a special relationship between the two states in the 1910s. Similarly, the desire for rapprochement between France and Germany since the end of the Second World War had led to the close ties between all levels of societies of the two states under the framework of the Franco–German Friendship Treaty.[11]

---

[8] Henry A. Kissinger, "Reflections on a Partnership: British and American Attitudes to Postwar Foreign Policy", *International Affairs* 58, no. 4 (1982): 575.

[9] David Reynolds, "Rethinking Anglo-American Relations", *International Affairs* 65, no. 1 (1989): 98.

[10] David Reynolds, *The Creation of the Anglo-American Alliance 1937–41: A Study in Competitive Co-operation* (London: Europa Publications Limited, 1981), pp. 293–94.

[11] Feldman, *The Special Relationship Between West Germany and Israel*, pp. 284–85.

The peaceful characters of a special relationship imply that it has the qualities of a pluralistic security community. A pluralistic security community is a transnational region comprised of sovereign states whose people maintain dependable expectations of peaceful change. Dependable expectations of peaceful change means the ability of the actors concerned to know that neither of them would prepare or even consider to use violence as a means to resolve their disputes. The peaceful nature of a pluralistic security community coincides with the traits of peace in a special relationship. In this sense, there is an inseparable link between a special relationship and a pluralistic security community.

Yet, while a special relationship has the qualities of a pluralistic security community, it is not necessarily a pluralistic security community. The United States and Britain continued to engage in their rivalries for naval supremacy throughout the 1920s even though they had begun to share a special relationship since the 1910s. The United States and Canada each continued to develop war plans directed at each other well into the late 1930s despite the existence of special ties between them since the 1910s. The fact that a special relationship is not necessarily a pluralistic security community denotes that certain conditions need to be in place before the relationship can become such a community. This observation brings about the central question of this study: under what circumstances could a special relationship lead to the emergence of a pluralistic security community?

Through addressing the central question, this study aims to establish an understanding of a special relationship, its dynamics and its transformation into a pluralistic security community. A theoretical framework based on constructivist theory has been developed to address the central question. By reviewing the existing literature on special relationships and security communities, the framework establishes an appreciation of the essence of a special relationship as well as its links with a pluralistic security community. Various evidences in international relations, especially the histories of Anglo–American and U.S.–Canada relations from the 1850s to the 1960s, have been used by the framework to substantiate its arguments. The basic idea of the framework is as follows:

A state's survival essentially concerns its existence of self. The will to survive of a state hence is rooted in its awareness of self. States' understandings of self shape, and are shaped by, their identities and power, namely, material capacities, in the form of identifications with one another.

A state's understanding of self is the basis for its intersubjective understandings. Intersubjective understandings of states are a stable set of identities and interests which are founded on their understandings of self.[12] States apprehend the world through the lenses of their intersubjective understandings.[13] Intersubjective understandings are essentially the cognitive collective knowledge of states, yet they are experienced as having an independent and real existence, hence confront the states as social reality.[14]

This study reveals that two states share a special relationship when two sources of closeness — that of the two states' common identities and common strategic interests — coexist between them. It argues that a special relationship produces substantial cooperation and substantial conflicts between the two states involved. In other words, a special relationship is distinguished by its double-edged effects. This study points out that a special relationship constitutes a security regime. Two states in a special relationship — a security regime — are bound by their shared commitment to avoid an armed conflict between them. Built on a special relationship's existing function as a security regime — this study argues — the relationship will transform into a pluralistic security community when power imbalance exists between the two states involved.

The theoretical framework of this study is being tested through the examination of Indonesia–Malaysia relations from 1957 to 2017. It is a common recognition that Indonesia and Malaysia share a special relationship since the two states are bound by their common cultural

---

[12] Alexander Wendt, "Anarchy is What States Make of It: The Social Construction of Power Politics", *International Organization* 46, no. 2 (1992): 397–99.

[13] Ibid., pp. 396–97. Also see Jeffrey T. Checkel, "The Constructivist Turn in International Relations Theory", *World Politics* 50, no. 2 (1998): 326.

[14] Wendt, "Anarchy is What States Make of It", p. 399. Also see Emanuel Adler, "Seizing the Middle Ground: Constructivism in World Politics", *European Journal of International Relations* 3, no. 3 (1997*b*): 327.

identities. By developing a theoretical framework of a special relationship, this study aims at advancing better appreciation of Indonesia–Malaysia relations — which is to explain the bilateral ties through the lens of the interplay of power and common identities in the relationship. In particular, this study seeks to address a long-standing puzzle in Indonesia–Malaysia relations: why conflicts between Indonesia and Malaysia are rather obvious even though both allegedly are close to each other? That said, this study is not a comprehensive historical account of Indonesia–Malaysia relations. It is rather an attempt to better understand the bilateral ties by examining it using the theoretical framework of this study.

Indonesia–Malaysia relations, in the meantime, provide a strong test of this study's theoretical framework. The notion of a special relationship is originated from the West. Also the most studied special relationships in international politics are those formed by Western and developed states, such as the Anglo–American and the U.S.–Canada special relationships. These are the reasons why this study has decided to incorporate the histories of Anglo–American and U.S.–Canada relations into its theoretical framework. The examination of Indonesia–Malaysia relations, therefore, will reveal whether this study's hypothesis is able to predict the forming of a special relationship, its dynamics, and its transformation into a pluralistic security community, considering that Indonesia and Malaysia share common identities, yet they are neither Western nor developed states. In other words, if the theoretical arguments of this study apply to Indonesia–Malaysia relations, the arguments' ability to predict will be significantly proven, hence could be generalized as a theory of a special relationship.

This book consists of two major parts: (1) Theoretical Framework of a Special Relationship and (2) History of Indonesia–Malaysia Relations, 1957–2017. Chapters 2 to 4 — the first part — constitutes the theoretical framework. Chapter 2 identifies the essence of a special relationship, the relationship's expressions, and the circumstances in which such a relationship will emerge. It also confirms that a special relationship and a pluralistic security community are essentially interlinked, and that such a relationship can transform into a pluralistic security community. Chapter 3 based on the findings of the previous chapter discusses the key conceptual components of a special relationship, followed by Chapter 4 which explains the dynamics of such a relationship and its transformation into a pluralistic security community.

The second part — Chapters 5 to 7 — tests the theoretical arguments of this study by examining Indonesia–Malaysia relations from 1957 to 2017. Chapter 5 argues that there was no special relationship between Indonesia and Malaya/Malaysia from 1957 to 1965. Chapter 6 — Indonesia–Malaysia relations from 1966 to 1984 — explains that the two states began to share a special relationship shortly after the fall of the Sukarno regime. Chapter 7 — Indonesia–Malaysia relations from 1985 to 2017 — reveals the double-edged effects of the Indonesia–Malaysia special relationship, and shows that the relationship is not a security community but remains as a security regime owing to the absence of power imbalance between Indonesia and Malaysia.

Chapter 8 — the conclusion — discusses the key findings of the study as well as the insights on Indonesia–Malaysia relations brought forth by this study.

Part I

Theoretical Framework of a Special Relationship

2

MAKING SENSE OF A SPECIAL RELATIONSHIP

This chapter reveals that a special relationship between two states is founded on their two sources of closeness — that of the two states' common identities and shared strategic interests. It subsequently discusses about the expressions of a special relationship. This chapter then brings to light the understanding that two states bound by common identities each needs to own a necessary amount of power before they could share a special relationship. After defining a security community, this chapter demonstrates that a special relationship and a pluralistic security community are basically different from each other, yet they are essentially interlinked — the two concepts each represents a relationship of common identities as well as power between two sovereign states. Finally, the chapter reveals that certain conditions need to be in place before a special relationship can transform into a pluralistic security community.

THE CONCEPT OF A SPECIAL RELATIONSHIP

The Coming About of the Conception of a Special Relationship

The concept of a special relationship is generally being understood as a closer friendship between two states when compared to their other bilateral relations, where such a relationship is founded on the two states' closely shared interests and their sentimental assertion of shared identities. The idea of a "special relationship" entered into the discussion of international relations when the term was coined by Winston Churchill in his "iron curtain" speech at Fulton, Missouri in March 1946. Churchill in his speech warned that permanent peace would not be achieved without "the fraternal association of the English Speaking People. This means a special relationship between the British Commonwealth and Empire and the United States."[1]

The notion of a special relationship between Britain and the United States was a century in the making, amid the ripening of their friendship since the late eighteenth century. The sense of closeness between the two states was naturally and consistently generated by their common identities, rooted in the two states' shared culture, common language, historical ties and shared political values and institutions. In 1782, after it was reminded by Britain of the possibility of French pursuing deceptive tactics, the United States had decided to ignore its treaty with France, which obliged them not to make separate peace with other states.[2] It went ahead to conduct separate negotiations with Britain to end the American Revolutionary War.[3] Such an incident demonstrated the dynamics of common identities, which produced positive associations between the United States and Britain, even at a time when Britain had suffered a grave military defeat in its war against the United States a year earlier. As observed by Allen, the two states pursued "the practice of playing off doubtful friends against open enemies"; the Frenchman, on the other hand, acknowledged "the unusual character of the Anglo-American relationship".[4]

The mutual sense of closeness, which derived from their shared identities, was openly expressed by the political leaders from the United

---

[1]   Randolph S. Churchill, ed., *The Sinews of Peace, Post-War Speeches by Winston S. Churchill* (London: Cassell, 1948), pp. 98–99.
[2]   Harry C. Allen, *Great Britain and the United States: A History of Anglo-American Relations (1783–1952)* (New York: St. Martin's Press Inc., 1955), pp. 253–56.
[3]   Ibid.
[4]   Ibid.

States and the United Kingdom during the 1780s. On 5 December 1782, King George III in the House of Lords said, "Religion, language, interests and affection may, and I hope will, yet prove a bond of permanent union between the two countries."[5] On the other hand, the first American Minister to Britain, John Adams, when first met with King George III in 1785 said, "I shall esteem myself the happiest of men if I can be instrumental...restoring...the old good-nature and the old good-humour between people who, though separated by an ocean and under different governments, have the same language, a similar religion and kindred blood."[6]

However, common identities-induced positive identifications between the United States and Britain alone, did not result in substantial friendship between them. At the turn of nineteenth century, the brief existence of the two states' common strategic interests had shown that substantial friendship between them nearly came into being, when common identities and shared strategic interests almost coexisted in their relationship. In the late 1790s to early 1800s, there had been talks of forging an Anglo-American alliance to face the common threat exerted by the culturally different other — France.[7] The natural bonds between the United States and the United Kingdom underpinned by their common identities, led them to look to each other for help when they were threatened by states of different culture.

Britain realized the value of American friendship amidst its war against France. As a war between the United States and France had become increasingly likely in the late 1790s, Britain began to explore possible collaborations with the United States to confront France. Such collaborations, however, did not materialize; America and France soon achieved peace in 1801. Nonetheless, not long after that, Thomas Jefferson, then U.S. President, made no secret that the United States would seek for the assistance from Great Britain if necessary, in order to quash France's desire to expand its power in North America following France's acquisition

---

[5] Robert Balmain Mowat, *Americans in England* (U.S.: Houghton Mifflin Company, 1935), p. 54.
[6] Allen, *Great Britain and the United States*, p. 266.
[7] Ibid., pp. 304–6.

of Louisiana from Spain in 1800.[8] Yet, such strategic consideration quickly evaporated in 1803, when Napoleon proposed to sell Louisiana to the United States.[9] America swiftly accepted the offer as it deemed Louisiana was the key to its future.[10] The coexistence of common identities and shared strategic interests in U.S.–UK relations did not eventually come into place; firm Anglo-American friendship therefore had yet to surface.

Similar dynamics of possible cooperation between the United States and Britain re-emerged in the 1820s. The French invasion of Spain in April 1823 had raised talks of Anglo-American cooperation to prevent France from acquiring Spanish colonies in Latin America. Such cooperation, however, did not take place as the two states held fundamentally different strategic concerns. The United States, with its prime aim of preventing European powers from interfering in American continent's affairs, hence its fear of Britain's intention to annex Spanish colonies in America, requested Britain to recognize the independence of Spanish American colonies, before the two states could cooperate to contain France.[11] Britain, on the other hand, rejected such demand as it deemed the revolutions of the Spanish American was contradictory to its political system of monarchy, and it had recently been an ally of Spain.[12] Above all, Britain was fearful of American annexation in Latin America, especially the Spanish lands of Texas and Cuba.[13] Once again, the divergence of their respective strategic interests prohibited the two states from forging substantial friendship between them, despite sharing common identities.

Since the 1850s, the U.S. power had grown consistently. Henry Adams observed, "The revolution since 1861 was nearly complete, and, for the first time in history, the American felt himself almost as strong as an Englishman."[14] The growing American power spawned structural

---

[8]   Ibid., p. 306.
[9]   Ibid.
[10] Ibid.
[11] Ibid., pp. 359, 366, 372–75.
[12] Ibid., pp. 366–67, 374–75.
[13] Ibid., p. 369.
[14] Henry Adams, *The Education of Henry Adams* (U.S.: Sentry Edition, 1961), p. 235.

changes in the U.S.–UK relations. Allen wrote, "Anglo-American friendship grew in strength almost exactly in proportion as American world interests expanded."[15] The increasingly powerful United States found itself in growing need of British friendship while it was expanding its power abroad in the 1890s.[16] Britain — a world power — on the other hand, was in strong desire for American friendship as it was increasingly conscious of its isolation in international affairs, especially in the face of the threats from Russia and Germany.[17] In short, both the United States and the United Kingdom needed each other to preserve their respective interests overseas. The growing of American power, matched with Britain's existing power, produced their mutual need for strategic cooperation between them. The perceived mutual strategic dependence had its roots in the two states' mutual sense of closeness, derived from their common identities. Mahan — then a former U.S. navy admiral — wrote in 1897,

> When we begin really to look abroad, and to busy ourselves with our duties to the world at large in our generation — and not before — we shall stretch out our hands to Great Britain, realizing that in unity of heart among the English-speaking races lies the best hope of humanity in the doubtful days ahead.[18]

The coexistence of shared identities and common strategic interests in Anglo-American relations during the 1890s, intensified positive identifications between them. As a consequence, their friendship grew substantially. The two states' policymakers during this period advocated the idea of "Anglo-American understanding". Mahan in his first published work in 1890 avowed a "cordial understanding with Britain".[19] Then U.S. Secretary of State, John Hay, proclaimed, "As long as I stay here no action shall be taken contrary to my conviction

---

[15] Allen, *Great Britain and the United States*, p. 562.
[16] Ibid., p. 568.
[17] Ibid., pp. 425, 525, 568.
[18] A.T. Mahan, *The Interest of America in Sea Power: Present and Future* (London: Sampson Low, Marston & Company, Limited, 1897), pp. 258–59.
[19] Allen, *Great Britain and the United States*, p. 563.

that the one indispensable feature of our foreign policy should be a friendly understanding with England. But an alliance must remain, in the present state of things, an unattainable dream."[20] The idea of "understanding", according to Allen, meant the United States and the United Kingdom held "a tone of general agreement on broad principles", but avoided concrete cooperation, let alone the forming of an alliance between them.[21]

Britain's and America's policies during the Spanish-American War in 1898, and the Boer War in 1899, exemplified the idea of Anglo-American understanding. The British government adhered to the policy of benevolent neutrality, when the United States was at war with Spain in 1898. While such policy meant the absence of concrete cooperation between the United States and Britain, it actually reflected British friendly approach towards America. As British did not share the anti-American feeling of other European states, it practically protected the United States from the threats exerted by hostile European powers, since it was Great Britain that controlled the seas.[22] On the other hand, British neutrality enabled the effective blockade in the Atlantic battle area by the United States during the war.[23] After America had won the war, Britain welcomed its annexation of Spanish colonies in the Pacific and the Caribbean, as America's expansion would check the power of Britain's potential enemies, hence allowed Britain to concentrate on other more vital danger areas.[24] Likewise for the Boer War in 1899, the practice of the policy of impartial neutrality by the U.S. government, in effect served as a crucial force to hamper other powers from interfering in this war. Without American participation, no effective interference could be possible.[25] Such policy came as an important assistance to

---

[20] Robert Balmain Mowat, *The Diplomatic Relations of Great Britain and the United States* (London: Edward Arnold & Co, 1925), p. 284.

[21] Allen, *Great Britain and the United States*, pp. 549, 581.

[22] Ibid., p. 575.

[23] Ibid., pp. 576–77.

[24] Ibid., pp. 581–83.

[25] Ibid., pp. 592–93.

Britain. It essentially allowed Britain to decisively defeat the Boer Republics at a time when Britain was isolated in Europe.[26]

At the turn of the twentieth century, because of the steadily growing strength of the United States, mutual strategic dependence between America and Britain continued to solidify, hence friendship between them consistently intensified.[27] In the early 1900s, British policy of friendship with America had become the essential complement of Anglo-Japanese Alliance and Anglo-French Entente Cordiale.[28] The United States, on the other hand, was determined to maintain an intimate understanding with Britain.[29] A letter sent by then U.S. President, Theodore Roosevelt, to Spring-Rice, a British diplomat, during this period reflects the friendly sentiment between the two states in the early 1900s,

> I feel so perfectly healthy myself and the Americans and Englishmen for whom I care…seem so healthy, so vigorous and on the whole so decent that I rather incline to the view of my beloved friend, Lieutenant Parker… whom I overheard telling the Russian naval attaché at Santiago that the two branches of Anglo-Saxons had come together, and "together, we can whip the world, Prince".[30]

Having understood the true extent of American power, British realized the benefits of pursuing American friendship and the disastrous outcome of provoking American enmity.[31] The increasing number of culturally different great powers during the early 1900s, led Britain to view American friendship as the promising answer to its international problems.[32] Meanwhile, the supremacy of British navy, and the emergence of America's naval power, gave birth to the mutual complementary functions

---

[26] Ibid., pp. 590, 593.
[27] Ibid., p. 549.
[28] Ibid., p. 607.
[29] Ibid., p. 610.
[30] Forrest Davis, *The Atlantic System: The Story of Anglo-American Control of the Seas* (London: George Allen & Unwin Ltd., 1943), p. 142.
[31] Allen, *Great Britain and the United States*, pp. 441, 581.
[32] Ibid., pp. 607–8.

of their navies, particularly in addressing the two states' shared fear of Germany, which looked set to construct a great fleet.[33]

In the late 1900s, the Anglo-American friendship had become an indispensable factor in each of their foreign policy.[34] The mutual strategic dependence of the two states in international affairs led them to realize the increasing importance of maintaining a good understanding between them. Spring-Rice, after visiting the United States in 1905, where he represented Britain to discuss with the United States on the settlement of Russo–Japanese War in the Far East, said,

> In England, of course, as Chamberlain told me very earnestly, every thinking man is convinced of the absolute necessity for England of a good understanding with America…[35]

Roosevelt in his letter to King Edward VII in 1905 wrote,

> I absolutely agree with you as to the importance, not only to ourselves but to all the free peoples of the civilized world, of a constantly growing friendship and understanding between the English-speaking peoples.[36]

The mutual good understanding engendered the two states' parallel actions in international politics. Both states sided with Japan during its war with Russia in the Far East; both supported the Open Door Policy in China. Then British Foreign Secretary, Lord Lansdowne, assured Washington in 1903 that Britain was "prepared to follow the United States step by step up to any point that may be necessary for the protection of our common interests in China".[37] When, in 1905, asked by the Japanese if America would join the Anglo–Japanese alliance, Lansdowne replied, "…I should expect to find them moving upon parallel lines with us, I doubted whether they were likely to do more."[38]

---

[33] Ibid., pp. 560, 601, 607–8.
[34] Ibid., p. 614.
[35] Ibid., p. 616.
[36] Lionel M. Gelber, *The Rise of Anglo-American Friendship: A Study in World Politics, 1898–1906* (London, New York and Toronto: Oxford University Press, 1938), p. 185.
[37] Ibid., p. 167.
[38] Allen, *Great Britain and the United States*, p. 619.

Turning into the 1910s, the policy of American friendship, according to Allen, had become the traditional foreign policy of Britain.[39] Such a tradition was especially obvious, when Britain's strategic dependence on the United States turned salience during the First World War. As America's power had the deciding impact on the outcome of the war, Britain was determined to ensure its friendship with the United States.[40] Then British Prime Minister, Herbert Henry Asquith, said to the U.S. Ambassador to Britain, Walter Hines Page, "Mr. Page, after any policy or plan is thought out on its merits my next thought always is how it may affect our relations with the United States. That is always a fundamental consideration."[41] Meanwhile, the presence of the threat exerted by the culturally different hostile power — German during the war, intensified the common identities-induced positive identifications between Britain and the United States. Spring-Rice, the British Ambassador, reported to the British government of his conversation with then U.S. President, Woodrow Wilson,

> I knew that you believed the hope and salvation of the world lay in a close and cordial understanding between the free nations, more especially between those who were of the household of our language...we could almost endure with equanimity all the horrors of this terrible struggle if they led in the end to a close, sure and permanent understanding between the English-speaking peoples. If we stood together we were safe. If we did not stand together nothing was safe.[42]

Wilson in other occasions said, "if Germany won it would change the course of our civilization and make the United States a military nation...", "England is fighting our fight."[43]

---

[39] Ibid., p. 637.

[40] Ibid., pp. 630, 637.

[41] Burton J. Hendrick, *The Life and Letters of Walter H. Page Volume II* (London: William Heinemann Ltd., 1923), p. 169.

[42] Stephen Gwynn, ed., "From April 1917 to January 1918", in *The Letters and Friendships of Sir Cecil Spring Rice: A Record, Volume II* (New York: Books For Libraries Press, 1972a), p. 425.

[43] Edward Mandell House, *The Intimate Papers of Colonel House Volume I: Behind the Political Curtain, 1912–1915* (London: Ernest Benn Limited, 1926), p. 299. Also see Horace C. Peterson, *Propaganda for War: The Campaign Against American Neutrality, 1914–1917* (U.S.: Kennikat Press, 1968), p. 181.

Underpinned by the coexistence of their shared identities and common strategic interests arose since the end of nineteenth century, Anglo-American relations evolved into a bilateral relationship with special characters in the 1910s. Policymakers and government officials of the two states during this period shared an understanding that their friendship was closer than their other bilateral ties. Walter Hines Page, then U.S. Ambassador, described his relationship with then British Foreign Secretary, Edward Grey, "Now the relations that I have established with Sir Edward Grey have been built up on frankness, fairness and friendship. I can't have relations of any other sort nor can England and the United States have relations of any other sort."[44] Recounted on his friendship with then U.S. Secretary of State, William Jennings Bryan, the British Ambassador, Spring-Rice wrote, "whatever may be said of the relations, politically speaking, of England and America, one thing is absolutely certain — in no other country can an Englishman make such friendships."[45] Allen observed, by 1910s, Britain understood America deeper than it understood any other power of the time; its understanding of America was hitherto the deepest in history.[46]

Meanwhile, Anglo-American economic interdependence had grown extensively in the 1910s. The economic links between America and Britain during this period were far stronger than those either state had with any other state. On the other hand, while the United States joined the Allies as an "Associated Power", not an ally, to fight against Germany during the First World War, the Anglo-American military cooperation was, nonetheless, intimate. The two states' navies which were commanded by the British Admiral Bayley were operated in the chain of command based on seniority, not nationality, "the same courts of inquiry were shared", and the admiral "flew his flag indifferently" in either state's ships.[47] In sum, by the 1910s, America and Britain, in substance, shared a special relationship.

---

[44] Burton J. Hendrick, *The Life and Letters of Walter H. Page Volume I* (London: William Heinemann Ltd., 1923a), p. 382.

[45] Stephen Gwynn, ed., "The End of Service", in *The Letters and Friendships of Sir Cecil Spring Rice*, p. 432. Also see Allen, *Great Britain and the United States*, p. 634.

[46] Allen, *Great Britain and the United States*, p. 654.

[47] Ibid., p. 693.

As the relationship continued to evolve into the 1920s, the British survival at sea had become essentially depended on its good relations with the United States — a newly emerged world power.[48] Britain had accepted its naval equality with the United States and the superiority of America's economy.[49] The policy of American Friendship since then, became the fundamental basis of British foreign policy.[50]

The friendship between the United States and Britain eventually gave birth to the alliance between them in the Second World War. It was a time where Anglo-American friendship reached its climax. Ties between them during the war were far stronger than any alliance, and unprecedented in the history of war.[51] The catastrophic threat of Nazi Germany amplified the combination of common identities and shared strategic interests in Anglo-American relations. Both states became the "sole bastion of Western civilization against the onslaughts of Nazi might", thus depended on each other for survival.[52] Then British Prime Minister, Winston Churchill, said in Parliament on 18 June 1940,

> I expect that the Battle of Britain is about to begin. Upon this battle depends the survival of Christian civilization...Hitler knows that he will have to break us in this Island or lose the war...if we fail, then the whole world, including the United States, including all that we have known or cared for, will sink into the abyss of a new Dark Age...[53]

Churchill's speech made plain the mutual strategic dependence between Britain and America in defending the existence of their common civilization. The United States also understood that defending Britain against Nazi Germany concerned the very survival of America and its way of life.

The Anglo-American friendship during the war became exceptionally special. The two states together established a unique common machinery

---

[48] Ibid., p. 728.
[49] Ibid., p. 723.
[50] Ibid., p. 728.
[51] Ibid., p. 835.
[52] Ibid., p. 781.
[53] Winston S. Churchill, *The Second World War Volume II: Their Finest Hour* (London: Cassell & Co. Ltd., 1949), pp. 198–99.

for conducting the war, especially the creation of the Combined Chiefs of Staff Committee.[54] It was a joint body responsible to the U.S. President as Commander-in-Chief, and to the British Prime Minister as Minister of Defence; in which it served to ensure the unity of command during the war. Amidst the establishment of this committee, then U.S. President, Franklin D. Roosevelt, rejected a proposal for an Inter-Allied Supreme War Council, which would involve other allied powers; for he deemed that "only Britain and the United States could really frame the strategy of the war and execute it".[55] So close was their relationship where in McNeill's words, "After 1942 it would have been almost beyond the power of either nation to disentangle itself from the alliance with the other, even had anyone considered such a step desirable."[56]

The decades of growing closeness between the United States and Britain, which was bolstered by their common struggle against the deadly Axis in the Second World War, nurtured the idea of special associations with the United States among British policymakers. In July 1940, amid facing the greatest threat ever from Nazi Germany, then British Foreign Secretary, Lord Halifax, wrote in an official letter "the possibility of some sort of special association" between the United States and Britain.[57] Such an idea was later adopted by then British Prime Minister, Winston Churchill. In September 1943, he "instructed postwar planners that nothing should prejudice 'the natural Anglo-American special relationship'"; in February 1944, he told the Foreign Office, "It is my deepest conviction that unless Britain and the United States are joined in a special relationship…another destructive war will come to pass."[58]

---

[54] Allen, *Great Britain and the United States*, pp. 837–38.

[55] Ibid.

[56] William Hardy McNeill, *America, Britain, & Russia: Their Co-operation and Conflict, 1941–1946* (New York and London: Johnson Reprint Corporation, 1970), p. 17.

[57] Halifax to Hankey, 15 July 1940, FO 371/25206, W8602/8602/49, quoted in David Reynolds, "Rethinking Anglo-American Relations", *International Affairs* 65, no. 1 (1989): 94.

[58] Telegram of 24 September 1943, quoted in Elisabeth Barker, *Churchill and Eden at War* (London: Macmillan, 1978), p. 199. Also see Churchill, minute M. 125/4, 16 February 1944, PREM 4/27/10, quoted in Reynolds, "Rethinking Anglo-American Relations", p. 94.

The term "special relationship" went public when Churchill, while addressing the House of Commons in November 1945, advocated the need to preserve Britain's "special relationship" with the United States over the atomic bomb.[59] The persistent contemplation of special ties with America culminated in Churchill's decision to elaborate publicly the notion of Anglo-American special relationship in his "iron curtain" speech in the United States in 1946.

Since then, "special relationship" becomes a notable term in international politics. Policymakers use this term to describe close ties between states. Former U.S. President, Jimmy Carter, claimed, "We have a special relationship with Israel."[60] Former German Ambassador to Israel said, "Germany's relationship to Israel was never as normal as its ties to any other country. Relations were always special."[61] Former Canadian Prime Minister, Stephen Harper, said, "The United States remains Canada's most important ally, closest friend and largest trading partner and I look forward to working with President Obama and his administration as we build on this special relationship."[62]

The Anglo-American special relationship emerged through the ripening of their generations of growing friendship. Yet, such an evolution was triggered, buttressed and sustained by two underlying sources of closeness — that of the coming together of common identities and shared strategic interests in the relations. There was no substantial friendship between Britain and the United States, despite their constant sense of closeness towards one another, which was induced by their

---

[59] Winston S. Churchill, "The Anglo-American Alliance, November 7, 1945, House of Commons", in *Winston S. Churchill: His Complete Speeches, 1897–1963 Volume VII 1943–1949,* edited by Robert Rhodes James (New York and London: Chelsea House Publishers, 1974a), p. 7248.

[60] Bernard Reich, "Reassessing the United States–Israel Special Relationship", *Israel Affairs* 1, no. 1 (1994): 65.

[61] Welt am Sontag, 6 January 1980, quoted in Lily Gardner Feldman, *The Special Relationship Between West Germany and Israel* (Boston: George Allen & Unwin, 1984), p. 176.

[62] Stephen Harper, Statement on the Inauguration of Barack Obama as the 44th President of the United States of America, 20 January 2009, available at <http://www.pm.gc.ca/eng/media.asp?category=3&id=2391> (accessed 7 March 2012).

common identities. Substantial friendship between the two states began to emerge with the emergence of their common strategic interests in the late nineteenth century. The perceived mutual strategic dependence of the United States and the United Kingdom, in the meantime, had its origin in the common identities of the two states. It is the coexistence of the two sources of closeness that establishes intimacy between the United States and the United Kingdom, and produces cooperation between them. Thus, for a special relationship to exist, the coexistence of common identities and shared strategic interests in the ties of the two states involved appears to be necessary.

The Two Sources of Closeness in a Special Relationship

Most of the policymakers and scholars, who have discussed the concept of a special relationship, acknowledge the existence of the twin sources of closeness, namely, two states' common identities and shared strategic interests. Common identities of two states are derived from their shared culture, common language, historical ties or shared political values and institutions. Common strategic interests of two states, on the other hand, mean the two states rely on each other's material presence for survival. A state's strategic interest means a material presence which is fundamental to its survival.

Churchill's conception of a special relationship was founded on the "fraternal association" between the United States and Britain, coupled with the strategic calculation where such partnership would strengthen "shared security interests and interlinked global economic interests".[63] Former British Prime Minister, Tony Blair, argued, Britain should remain an ally of the United States, not simply because it is powerful, "but because we share their values".[64] His assertion explains that, while the special ties with the United States are essential for Britain's

---

[63] Churchill, ed., *The Sinews of Peace, Post-War Speeches by Winston S. Churchill*, pp. 98–99. Also see Patrick Porter, "Last Charge of the Knights? Iraq, Afghanistan and the Special Relationship", *International Affairs* 86, no. 2 (2010): 358.

[64] Samuel Azubuike, "The 'Poodle Theory' and the Anglo-American 'Special Relationship'", *International Studies* 42, no. 2 (2005): 132.

security, such an association is also a result of their shared values.[65] Former U.S. President, Bill Clinton, in a speech to both houses of the British Parliament in November 1995 said,

> Today the United States and Britain glory in an extraordinary relationship that unites us in a way never before seen in the ties between two such great nations…our relationship with the United Kingdom must be at the heart of our striving in this new era, because of the history we have lived, because of the power and prosperity we enjoy…[66]

Clinton's speech indicates that the U.S.–UK special relationship is vital for both states' survival, owing to their historical ties, combine with the amount of power that each of them possesses.

Kissinger, in his article "Reflections on a Partnership: British and American Attitudes to Postwar Foreign Policy" later suggested that common values and geopolitical consideration were complementary elements in U.S.–UK relations.[67] Reynolds argues that Anglo-American relation is a "relationship of culture as well as power", and that its special quality is derived from the two states' common interests, shared values and close personal ties "in the face of common threat".[68] Dumbrell, on the other hand, argues that the combination of inertia, gluing effect of shared culture and the refashioning of interests serve to ensure the sustainability of the U.S.–UK special relationship.[69] The refashioning of

---

[65] Former British Foreign Secretary, Ernest Bevin once contented, "Now is the time to build up the strength of the free world, morally, economically and militarily with the United States, and at the same time to exert sufficient control over the policy of the well-intentioned but inexperienced colossus on whose co-operation our safety depends…" See Reynolds, "Rethinking Anglo-American Relations", p. 97.

[66] *Public Papers of the Presidents – 1995, Vol. 2*, Remarks to the Parliament of the United Kingdom in London, 29 November 1995, quoted in Steve Marsh and John Baylis, "The Anglo-American 'Special Relationship': The Lazarus of International Relations", *Diplomacy & Statecraft* 17, no. 1 (2006): 184.

[67] Henry A. Kissinger, "Reflections on a Partnership: British and American Attitudes to Postwar Foreign Policy", *International Affairs* 58, no. 4 (1982): 587.

[68] Reynolds, "Rethinking Anglo-American Relations", p. 104. Also see David Reynolds, "A 'Special Relationship'? America, Britain and the International Order since the Second World War", *International Affairs* 62, no. 1 (1985–86): 5–6.

[69] John Dumbrell, "The US–UK 'Special Relationship' in a World Twice Transformed", *Cambridge Review of International Affairs* 17, no. 3 (2004): 448.

interests entails the changing of their common threat from the Nazism in the Second World War, Soviet communism in the Cold War, to terrorism in the War on Terror; coupled with their continued mutual reliance in achieving respective basic strategic needs.[70]

The discussions of other so-called special relationships also see a combination of identities and strategic drivers. Former U.S. Secretary of State, Warren Christopher, while describing the U.S.–Israel relations in 1993 said, "...the relationship between the United States and Israel is a special relationship for special reasons. It is based upon shared interests, shared values, and a shared commitment to democracy, pluralism and respect for the individual."[71] A former French government official described France's special ties with its ex-colonies in Africa as "the partner closest historically, closest geographically and culturally, surest sentimentally, and — last but not least — in the medium term, the most useful economically".[72] Such a statement highlights the combination of shared identities and common strategic interests as the reasons for the France–Sub-Saharan Africa special relationship.

Reich in his article "Reassessing the United States–Israel special relationship" contends that the U.S.–Israel special relationship is founded on "ideological, emotional and moral pillars and on a commitment to democratic principles buttressed by strategic and political factors".[73] Both states view each other as a truly reliable strategic asset in preserving the peace and stability in the Middle East.[74] Haglund and Dickey hold similar understanding of the U.S.–Canada special relationship. Both respectively contends that the relationship is rooted in the two states'

---

[70] Ibid., pp. 438, 444–45, 449.
[71] Reich, "Reassessing the United States–Israel Special Relationship", p. 64.
[72] Jacques Ferrandi, "*La politique africaine de la France et la Communaut'e'economique europ'eenne*'", in *La France et l'Afrique: quelle politique africaine pour la France?* edited by Jacques Baumel (Paris: La Foundation du Futur, 1985), p. 52, quoted in Alison Brysk, Craig Parsons, and Wayne Sandholtz, "After Empire: National Identity and Post-Colonial Families of Nations", *European Journal of International Relations* 8, no. 2 (2002): 282.
[73] Reich, "Reassessing the United States–Israel Special Relationship", p. 65.
[74] Ibid., pp. 66, 69–72.

historical ties, geographical proximity and close security and economic ties.[75] Both notice the demographic intermingling between the two states, and their unparalleled interdependence in homeland security and in economy.[76] Feldman, on the other hand, attributes the West Germany–Israel special relationship to historical intertwining between Germany and the Jewish people, coupled with their mutual strategic dependence.[77] Israel needed West Germany for economic assistance, and West Germany needed acceptance from Israel to affirm its clean break with old Nazi Germany.[78]

While examining the Canada–Commonwealth Caribbean special relationship, Momsen maintains that the relationship is founded on their common resistance to "British imperialism and American economic hegemony", shared histories and geographical proximity.[79] Both Canada and the Commonwealth Caribbean are "two British Commonwealth members in the western hemisphere", both have "long-standing trade links, colonial traditions and similar political systems".[80] Brysk, Parsons and Sandholtz, in their article "After Empire: National Identity and Post-Colonial Families of Nations" argue that "only identity" explains why the European states like France, Spain and Britain sustain special relationships with their ex-colonies.[81] Nevertheless, the authors do acknowledge the existence of strategic considerations in these relationships. For example, France maintains special ties with its former

[75] David G. Haglund, "The US–Canada Relationship: How 'Special' is America's Oldest Unbroken Alliance?" in *America's 'Special Relationships': Foreign and Domestic Aspects of the Politics of Alliance*, edited by John Dumbrell and Axel R. Schafer (London and New York: Routledge, 2009), pp. 61–69. Also see John Sloan Dickey, *Canada and the American Presence: The United States Interest in an Independent Canada* (New York: New York University Press, 1975), p. 180.

[76] Ibid.

[77] Feldman, *The Special Relationship Between West Germany and Israel*, pp. 1–28.

[78] Ibid.

[79] Janet Henshall Momsen, "Canada–Caribbean Relations: Wherein the Special Relationship?" *Political Geography* 11, no. 5 (1992): 501.

[80] Ibid.

[81] Alison, Parsons and Sandholtz, "After Empire: National Identity and Post-Colonial Families of Nations", p. 268.

colonies in Africa so as to "bolster itself strategically against other great powers".[82] For Britain, the continuation and strengthening of its ties with the Commonwealth has its "great potential future value".[83] And from Spain's perspective, the importance of Spain at the international level rests on its role as a "bridge between the EU and Western hemisphere", as well as the status of its former colonies in Latin America.[84]

A few scholars who have attempted to conceptualize the notion of a special relationship confirm the existence of the two sources of closeness in such a relationship. According to Feldman, "historical intertwining" and/or "intense history of mutual preoccupation" "constitute an essential background" for a special relationship's creation.[85] She claims that "a major catalyst for the creation of a special relationship is the existence, for both partners, of a specific need that both perceive only the other country capable of fulfilling."[86] Somewhat differently, Liow maintains that

> the concept of "special relationships" describes relations between states whose populations share historical and sentimental bonds, and whose leaders impute meaning into their relations on the back of these bonds. Such relationships warrant an almost immutable belief (on the part of their leaders and populations) that they, at least in theory, are meant to share a relationship driven by more than purely material factors.[87]

Feldman and Liow respective observation indicates that the intertwining of two states' mutual material needs and shared identities spawns the emergence of a special relationship between them.

The Expressions of a Special Relationship

Literature on special relationships also demonstrates the characters of such relations in terms of their expressions. The sentimental expressions of closeness are apparent in a special relationship. British policymakers'

---

[82] Ibid., p. 278.
[83] Ibid., p. 295.
[84] Ibid., pp. 285, 288.
[85] Feldman, *The Special Relationship Between West Germany and Israel*, p. 262.
[86] Ibid., p. 265.
[87] Joseph Chinyong Liow, *The Politics of Indonesia–Malaysia Relations: One Kin, Two Nations* (London and New York: Routledge, 2005b), p. 11.

response to September 11 terror attacks exhibits their emotional bonds with the United States. In April 2002, former British Foreign and Commonwealth Office Minister, Denis MacShane, stressed, September 11 "was an attack on us all…It was an attack on our shared values and a test of our integrity."[88] At the same month, then British Prime Minister, Tony Blair, asserted,

> When America is fighting for those values, then, however tough, we will fight with her. No grandstanding, no offering implausible but impractical advice from the comfort of the touchline, no wishing away the hard choices on terrorism and WMD, or making peace in the Middle East, but working together, side-by-side.[89]

Later when he addressed the U.S. Congress in July 2003, Blair pledged, "our job is to be there with you".[90] An additional example of the sentimental expressions in a special relationship is that existing between the United States and Israel. Israeli Prime Minister, Benjamin Netanyahu, while addressing U.S. President, Barack Obama, on the issue of Iranian nuclear threat in March 2012, said, "…we are you, and you are us, we are together…Israel and America stand together."[91]

The sentimental expressions of closeness in a special relationship are stemming from the common identities of the two states involved. As for Anglo-American relations, Marsh and Baylis observe, the "Churchillian rhetoric of the fraternal association" between the two states is imbued with "a natural, reflexive, and unique emotional underpinning".[92] Wallace and Phillips argue, the sentimental assertions in the U.S.–UK special

---

[88] Statement by FCO Minister, Denis MacShane, Westminster Hall, London, 25 April 2002, available at <www.britainusa.com>, quoted in Marsh and Baylis, "The Anglo-American 'Special Relationship'", p. 188.

[89] Former British Prime Minister, Tony Blair's Speech at the George Bush Senior Presidential Library, 7 April 2002, available at <www.fco.gov>, quoted in Marsh and Baylis, "The Anglo-American 'Special Relationship'", p. 188.

[90] David Coates and Joel Krieger, *Blair's War* (Cambridge: Polity Press, 2004), p. 9.

[91] The U.S. President Barack Obama and Israeli Prime Minister Benjamin Netanyahu, Press Conference at the White House, Washington, United States, 5 March 2012, available at <http://www.whitehouse.gov/photos-and-video/video/2012/03/05/president-obama-s-bilateral-meeting-prime-minister-netanyahu-israe>.

[92] Marsh and Baylis, "The Anglo-American 'Special Relationship'", p. 173.

relationship are derived from their shared values.[93] Reich, on the other hand, maintains, "shared ideals and values sustain a strong psychological bond between American and Israeli peoples".[94] In a more general sense, Feldman contends the "historical intertwining and/or intensity" between two states which share a special relationship results in their mutual "psychological resonance".[95]

The sentimental associations between two states sharing a special relationship, combine with their mutual positive identifications arising from their common strategic interests, give rise to the two states' mutual understanding that they share a special relationship, which means a relationship that is *closer* than other bilateral relations either of them enjoys. Haglund has argued, "special" denotes a distinctive normative judgement in positive sense.[96] The functioning of a special relationship begins with both states involved sharing such normative understanding, in which it necessarily entails the comparisons with their other bilateral ties, in order for the two states to apprehend the distinctiveness of their relationship. As Danchev maintains, "special" is "a matter of comparison" and "evaluation makes reference to others".[97] Two states' shared perception of having a special relationship is exemplified by Dobbs's observation on the U.S.–UK relations in facing the issue of Iraq War in 2003. He writes, "For us to be on the other side of Britain on an issue like Iraq would be very hard for an American president. It is one thing for France and Germany to be on the other side, but if Britain was on the other side, that would create doubts among the American people."[98] Such a remark demonstrates the understanding of the American people, in which the U.S.–UK relationship is closer than

---

[93] William Wallace and Christopher Phillips, "Reassessing the Special Relationship", *International Affairs* 85, no. 2 (2009): 263.

[94] Reich, "Reassessing the United States–Israel Special Relationship", p. 65.

[95] Feldman, *The Special Relationship Between West Germany and Israel*, pp. 264–65.

[96] Haglund, "The US–Canada Relationship: How 'Special' is America's Oldest Un-broken Alliance?", p. 61.

[97] Alex Danchev, "On Specialness", *International Affairs* 72, no. 4 (1996): 744.

[98] Michael Dobbs, "Old Alliance, New Relevance", *Washington Post*, 30 January 2003, quoted in Azubuike, "The 'Poodle Theory' and the Anglo-American 'Special Relationship'", p. 136.

their other bilateral ties, owing to the special associations between the two states.

The shared understanding held by two states with special ties, in turn, stirs up their respective *expectation* that their relationship *should be* closer than their other bilateral ties. As Danchev has argued, the "specialness" in a relationship is "a process of interaction, laced with *expectation*".[99] Also he maintains, "A special relationship is never fully achieved. At any given moment it is not as pliant or as potent — not as special — as one partner would wish."[100] His observation reflects that a special relationship is suffused with the dynamics of expectation. Reynolds's examination of Anglo-American relations in the late 1930s confirms the expectation dynamics. He discerns the two states' relationship was mainly characterized by British "tendency to expect assistance in the long term and in time of war" from the United States.[101] The sense of closeness towards the United States prompted Britian to believe that it could count on America for effective cooperation.[102] Churchill had admitted, one of the most powerful forces which sustained him during the early period of the Second World War was his expectation that the United States would come to rescue Britain from the onslaught of Nazi Germany.[103]

The *expectations* in a special relationship lead to a *higher intensity of interactions* between the two states concerned as compared with that of their other bilateral ties. As Reich observes, "relationships between friends and allies vary in quality and intensity".[104] Since the quality of a bilateral relationship is built upon the intensity of their interactions, therefore, the closeness of a special relationship which distinguishes it from other bilateral relations is first illustrated by its *higher intensity of interactions*, instead of deeper quality of interactions. This observation

---

[99] Danchev, "On Specialness", p. 748.

[100] Alex Danchev, *On Specialness: Essays in Anglo-American Relations* (Great Britain: Macmillan Press Ltd., 1998), p. 154.

[101] David Reynolds, *The Creation of the Anglo-American Alliance 1937–41: A Study in Competitive Co-operation* (London: Europa Publications Limited, 1981), p. 10.

[102] Ibid., p. 12.

[103] Allen, *Great Britain and the United States*, p. 725.

[104] Reich, "Reassessing the United States–Israel Special Relationship", p. 78.

is confirmed by Brysk's, Parsons's and Sandholtz's understanding, in which they monitor the intimacy of the special relationships between the European states and their former colonies in terms of the intensity of their interactions.[105] More often than not, preferential treatments are the expression of such a higher *intensity of interactions*. Feldman observes, a special relationship is frequently associated with the pursuit of preferential policies in a bilateral relationship.[106] In her survey of characterizations of the Anglo-American special relationship, Feldman notes that prominent commentators, Churchill, Kissinger, Bell and Turner, all view the pursuit of preferential policies as the concrete expression of a special relationship.[107] Preferential treatments are a state's policies interlace with substantial benefits which only offer to a particular other state. For example, Britain enjoys uniquely privileged access to U.S. nuclear technology; no other America's allies could have similar access. France's, Spain's and Britain's respective national foreign aid directed to their ex-colonies greatly exceed the Organisation for Economic Co-operation and Development (OECD) states' average level of aid to these destinations.

The *intensity of interactions* between two states can be measured in terms of the *extent* and the *degree* of interactions. As Reynolds writes, the closeness of the Anglo-American special relationship can be gauged in terms of the degree and the extent of their cooperation against the relationships between the United States and its other close allies.[108] In a special relationship, its *higher intensity of interactions* means the *extent* of interactions between the two states involved is *wider*, and/or the *degree* of their interactions is *deeper*, than those in their other bilateral relationships. The *deeper degree* of interactions indicates the existence of preferential treatments in such a relationship. For example, when compared to their other bilateral relationships, the special

---

[105] Brysk, Parsons and Sandholtz, "After Empire: National Identity and Post-Colonial Families of Nations", p. 296.
[106] Feldman, *The Special Relationship Between West Germany and Israel*, p. 4.
[107] Ibid., pp. 247–52.
[108] Reynolds, "A 'Special Relationship'? America, Britain and the International Order since the Second World War", p. 4.

relationship between the United States and the United Kingdom has a *wider extent* of interactions, ranging from deep economic cooperation, to close consultative relationship between the two bureaucracies, intimate global division of labour in signals intelligence, close collaboration between the military forces, and unparalleled nuclear technology sharing. And the relationship has a *deeper degree* of interactions, in which the depth of intimate collaborations between the two states could not be matched by other America's allies. Likewise, the U.S.–Israel special relationship has a *higher intensity of interactions*, when compared to their other bilateral relations in the Middle East, with a *wider extent* of interactions covering the area of defence, economics, science and technology, cultural exchange, and diplomatic support; and a *deeper degree* of interactions evidenced by the United States being Israel's "principal arms supplier" to ensure Israel "a qualitative military edge over its neighbors", and by Israel's privileged access to U.S. President and other senior American officials.

Special Relationship — An Intersubjective Understanding

In the literature, there are two schools in explaining the nature of a special relationship — the realist school and the identity school. The realist school argues, the concept of a special relationship is a tool used by either of the two states involved to pursue their respective strategic needs, in which their common identities, encapsulate in the term of a special relationship, have been the facilitator for achieving such aims. Reynolds and Baylis are among the scholars in this school.

Reynolds maintains, the notion of the Anglo-American special relationship has been "a deliberate British creation — a 'tradition' invented as a tool of diplomacy".[109] In realists' view, Britain manipulates its common culture and close historical ties with the United States in the name of "special relationship", to try harness America's massive power, so as to serve British interests, in particular, to manage its

---

[109] Ibid., p. 2.

decline in power.[110] Similarly, in an article written by Baylis and Marsh, both maintain that the U.S.–UK special relationship is the product of Britain's purposive cultivation by consistently reclaiming their shared roots, especially the common experience of the Second World War.[111] Such cultivation, they contend, is due to Britain's determination to remain as a global actor, and its realization of America's power, which combine culminates in its belief that, to best promote British interests, it is to closely align with the United States.[112]

Dickie, on the other hand, argues that, while sentiment has been employed in moulding the relations, the U.S.–UK special relationship is essentially founded on the two states' common strategic interest, namely, their mutual reliance in facing the Communist threat.[113] In his view, with the collapse of the Soviet Union, the fundamental reason for Anglo-American intimate friendship thus vanishes, and the relationship, as a consequence, becomes "'Special' no more".[114] As Dickie writes, "[w]hen there was no longer a Communist threat requiring Britain to be the alliance standard-bearer in Europe for the Americans, the principal *raison d'être* of that relationship had gone."[115] Similarly, Elie maintains, amid the manipulation of their natural affinity, strategic interests have been the root for Anglo-American special relationship, in which he describes the relations as "a valuable tool of foreign policy for both partners".[116] Both states need each other in international politics. From facing the common threats of then Nazi Germany, Communist Russia and now international terrorism, to

---

[110] Ibid. Also see Reynolds, "Rethinking Anglo-American Relations", pp. 95–96, 98, 111; and John Baylis, "The 'Special Relationship': A Diverting British Myth?" in *Haunted by History: Myths in International Relations,* edited by Cyril Buffet and Beatrice Heuser (Oxford: Berghahn Books, 1998), pp. 119–20, 134.

[111] Marsh and Baylis, "The Anglo-American 'Special Relationship'", pp. 174, 201.

[112] Ibid., pp. 174, 200–1.

[113] John Dickie, *'Special' No More — Anglo-American Relations: Rhetoric and Reality* (London: Weidenfeld & Nicolson, 1994), pp. x, xiv, 257.

[114] Ibid., p. 276.

[115] Ibid., p. xiv.

[116] Jerome B. Elie, "Many Times Doomed But Still Alive: An Attempt to Understand the Continuity of the Special Relationship", *Journal of Transatlantic Studies* 3, no. 1 (2005): 77.

serving their respective basic political needs.[117] In his view, Britain maintains special ties with the United States to serve its real aim of preserving the UK's status as a prominent power on international stage.[118] The United States, on the other hand, values the strategic importance of the assets possessed by Britain.[119] As a UN Security Council permanent member, an important player in North Atlantic Treaty Organisation (NATO), the staunchest ally of the United States, coupled with its geostrategic location in Europe, Britain's support has been crucial for the United States' policies on the world stage, as a source of legitimacy, in particular, as the guardian of America's interests in the European integration process.[120] Meanwhile, the United States cherishes British friendship, owing to its "military, intelligence and diplomatic capabilities and expertise".[121]

The identity school disagrees with realists' argument. In their view, common identities are central in a special relationship; instead of merely facilitating the two states involved towards achieving their real aim — that of the fulfillment of respective strategic needs, as realists argue.

Dawson and Rosecrance describe the Anglo-American Alliance: "[h]istory, tradition, affinity have been crucial to the alliance, rather than peripheral".[122] They argue, "[t]he relationship is special in one notable sense: the theory of alliances does not explain it..."[123] In their view, although it seems apparent that common interests are the basis for Britain and America to maintain their special bonds, yet such an assumption does not address the fundamental question — why the two states believe the connection is "logical" and "necessary" as "it is to learn that they deemed it so".[124]

---

[117] Ibid., pp. 65, 72, 77.
[118] Ibid., pp. 66, 77.
[119] Ibid., pp. 71–73, 77.
[120] Ibid., pp. 72, 76–77.
[121] Ibid., pp. 71, 77.
[122] Raymond Dawson and Richard Rosecrance, "Theory and Reality in the Anglo-American Alliance", *World Politics* 19, no. 1 (1966): 51.
[123] Ibid.
[124] Ibid., pp. 47–48.

For identity school, a special relationship is the natural consequence of cultural affinities, historical ties as well as common political traditions shared by the two states involved. Churchill had put it, "the natural Anglo-American Special Relationship", "the fraternal association of the English Speaking People".[125] Such natural harmony, according to identity school, set U.S.–UK relations "apart from 'normal' relations between states in the international system".[126]

Similarly, Brysk, Parsons and Sandholtz maintain, it is the shared historical bonds that lead France, Spain and Britain to maintain special ties with their respective ex-colonies.[127] Material calculation does not explain such motivations.[128] They observe, the common historical ties between these former imperial powers and their ex-colonies result in third party states acknowledging the special associations among them.[129]

Both realist and identity schools respectively does not adequately explain the essence of a special relationship. The realist's argument of such a relationship being a strategic tool for the two states involved, necessitates the understanding of why states perceive certain material interest as strategic/fundamental to them. If states view material interest in pure material terms, then the realist school exhibits its limitation in explaining why the Anglo-American special relationship continues to survive in the post-Cold War era, since the fundamental rationale of their partnership, as some realists have argued — the Soviet threat — no longer exists. Also realist school is unable to convincingly explain why time and again, the promising United States' partnership with other states could not ultimately prevail over its special ties with the United Kingdom, even though these alternative partnerships seemed

---

[125] Telegram of 24 September 1943, quoted in Barker, *Churchill and Eden at War*, p. 199. Also see Churchill, ed., *The Sinews of Peace, Post-War Speeches by Winston S. Churchill*, pp. 98–99.

[126] John Baylis, ed., *Anglo-American Relations since 1939: The Enduring Alliance* (Manchester and New York: Manchester University Press, 1997), p. 9.

[127] Brysk, Parsons and Sandholtz, "After Empire: National Identity and Post-Colonial Families of Nations", pp. 268, 270–71.

[128] Ibid., p. 271.

[129] Ibid., pp. 270–71.

to assure greater material benefits for America. For example, the prospect of friendship between the two superpowers — America and Russia — in the 1940s, did not eventually occur; although for the United States, its friendship with Russia appeared to be materially more valuable than its partnership with Britain, owing to their vast power that constituted the foundation of world affairs.[130] Similarly, the emergence of a united Germany as a powerful European state at the end of the Cold War, attracted the United States to view Germany as its main European partner, which was portrayed as "partnership in leadership".[131] Yet, such a possible better alternative to Britain friendship again did not come into existence.[132]

As such, the material existence itself does not explain whether it is a state's strategic interests. The realist school's assertion — states utilize a special relationship to pursue their strategic interests — is credible; yet its inability to explain why those material interests are "strategic" for them, reveals the theory's problematic interpretation of a special relationship. Constructivist theory seems able to fill in this gap.

Two fundamental principles underpin constructivism. First, people react to the reality based on the meanings that the reality has for them; which means humans apprehend the world through the lenses of their intersubjective understandings.[133] Actors' intersubjective understandings denote a stable set of identities and interests which are founded on their conceptions of self.[134] Such understandings are fundamentally

---

[130] Allen, *Great Britain and the United States*, pp. 875–79. Also see Reynolds, "Rethinking Anglo-American Relations", p. 106; and Elie, "Many Times Doomed But Still Alive", p. 74.

[131] John Dumbrell, *A Special Relationship: Anglo-American Relations from the Cold War to Iraq* (New York: Palgrave, 2006), pp. 123–24. Also see William Wallace, "The Collapse of British Foreign Policy", *International Affairs* 82, no. 1 (2005): 54; and Elie, "Many Times Doomed But Still Alive", p. 74. Also see Dumbrell, "The US–UK 'Special Relationship' in a World Twice Transformed", p. 439.

[132] Elie, "Many Times Doomed But Still Alive", p. 74.

[133] Alexander Wendt, "Anarchy is What States Make of It: The Social Construction of Power Politics", *International Organization* 46, no. 2 (1992): 396–97. Also see Jeffrey T. Checkel, "The Constructivist Turn in International Relations Theory", *World Politics* 50, no. 2 (1998): 326.

[134] Wendt, "Anarchy is What States Make of It", pp. 397–99.

the cognitive collective knowledge of actors, namely, "a function of what actors collectively 'know'"; yet they are experienced as having an independent and real existence, hence confront individuals as social fact.[135] Second, intersubjective understandings, namely, the normative structure, emerge out of mutually constitutive interactions among actors and their intersubjective understandings.[136]

Constructivist insights therefore point out that, actors apprehend the material presence based on the meanings furnished by their intersubjective understandings. As such, it is a state's intersubjective understandings that inform them why certain material interests are "strategic"; in which the knowledge of strategic interests is originated from a state's identities, as intersubjective understandings are founded on actors' conceptions of self. The United States' understanding of strategic interest confirms the observation.

America defines its strategic interests based on the core ideas of its nationhood — that of the principles of liberty.[137] Central to American idea of liberty is "anticollectivism — the independent individual can be a republican".[138] The liberty notion is "connected with the very concept of modernity", in which the United States believes that the only way of becoming modern is the American way — "to 'liberate' productivity and innovation from 'ancient' cultures and ideologies".[139] For America,

---

[135] Ibid., p. 399. Also see Emanuel Adler, "Seizing the Middle Ground: Constructivism in World Politics", *European Journal of International Relations* 3, no. 3 (1997*b*): 327.

[136] Wendt notes that constructivists "share a cognitive, intersubjective conception of process in which identities and interests are endogenous to interaction". See Wendt, "Anarchy is What States Make of It", pp. 394, 399, 403. Also see Checkel, "The Constructivist Turn in International Relations Theory", p. 326; Michael Barnett, "Social Constructivism", in *The Globalization of World Politics,* edited by John Baylis and Steve Smith (New York: Oxford University Press, 2005), p. 267; Adler, "Seizing the Middle Ground", p. 330; Alexander Wendt, "The Agent-Structure Problem in International Relations Theory", *International Organization* 41, no. 3 (1987): 350; and Brysk, Parsons and Sandholtz, "After Empire: National Identity and Post-Colonial Families of Nations", p. 269.

[137] Odd Arne Westad, *The Global Cold War: Third World Interventions and the Making of Our Times* (Cambridge: Cambridge University Press, 2005), pp. 10, 17.

[138] Ibid., p. 11.

[139] Ibid., pp. 11, 12.

defending its own liberty means safeguarding its survival.[140] Therefore, any material existence which could support its freedom is of strategic importance to the United States; any which undermines it presents as a strategic threat to the U.S.

America protects the capitalist world system, as it is an extension of the principles of liberty, and for fear that the international market might be taken over by other ideologies which ultimately threaten the American liberty.[141] The United States fought in the two world wars, and confronted the Soviet Union in the Cold War, all with one aim — to defeat the alternative forms of modernity, promised by German imperialism, Nazism, Japanese militarism and Soviet Communism, which America interpreted as threatening its very survival, namely, its way of life, if left unchecked.[142]

America's example shows that a state's identities, in the form of intersubjective understandings, inform its appreciation of whether a material presence has strategic value for them. As identity gives birth to one's strategic apprehensions, therefore, common identities shared by two states produce their similar understanding of strategic interests. The British felt betrayed by the United States when it waged a war against the United Kingdom in 1812, as Britain during that time was in the midst of fighting another war against France, which the British deemed that they were fighting the similar cause of America — to defend "the liberty of mankind against the very real menace of Napoleonic tyranny".[143] In the 1940s, Americans discerned more similarities between British and U.S. values than their differences in a world with a powerful presence of "totalitarianism".[144] "Both were liberal, capitalist democracies, sharing common beliefs in the rule of law and the principle of peaceful change."[145] Likewise, the shared values of the United States and Israel breed their similar strategic vision of a Middle East with

---

[140] Ibid., pp. 8, 11, 16, 20–21.

[141] Ibid., pp. 12, 15.

[142] Ibid., pp. 17–19, 20–21, 25.

[143] Allen, *Great Britain and the United States*, p. 301.

[144] Reynolds, "A 'Special Relationship'? America, Britain and the International Order since the Second World War", p. 5.

[145] Ibid.

political order that coincides with the interests of Western democracy.[146] Shared historical and cultural bonds between the European states and their respective former colonies also bring about their analogous strategic thinking. Former French Minister of Cooperation, Jacques Godfrain said, "At the United Nations, thanks to Africa, we carry more weight than our population, our land area or our GDP...Our small country, with its small strengths, can move the planet because we have relations of amity and intimacy with fifteen or twenty African countries."[147] Such a remark reflects that both France and its ex-colonies in Africa similarly view the support from the counterpart as important in international politics. Likewise, for Spain and its former colonies in Latin America, the alike strategic mindset is shown by both parties' assumption of Spain's position as a bridge between Europe and the Western hemisphere, and where cooperation between them is vital to balance against U.S. dominance.[148]

The realist scholar, Baylis, has indeed acknowledged the ability of common identities in generating similar strategic outlook of the states involved. For Anglo-American relations, he writes, "...there is little doubt that ideological affinity has been an asset of some importance which has contributed to the common perception of security problems..."[149] As such, common identities is not the facilitator in a special relationship, as realists have argued; instead, they are crucial in such a relationship. Common identities result in two states bound by a special relationship sharing similar strategic understandings.

However, similar appreciation of strategic interests does not necessarily mean the two states involved share "common" strategic interests. Although the shared identities of Britain and the United States gave rise to their alike strategic apprehensions, yet both states did not view each other as

---

[146] Reich, "Reassessing the United States–Israel Special Relationship", pp. 66, 72, 80–81. Also see Westad, *The Global Cold War*, pp. 127–28, 197.

[147] Jacques Godfrain, *L'Afrique, notre avenir* (Paris: Lafon, 1998), p. 15, quoted in Brysk, Parsons and Sandholtz, "After Empire: National Identity and Post-Colonial Families of Nations", p. 283.

[148] Ibid., pp. 286–88.

[149] John Baylis, "The Anglo-American Relationship and Alliance Theory", *International Relations* 8, no. 4 (1985): 378.

sharing common strategic interests up until the late nineteenth century, which subsequently led to the emergence of their special relationship. Likewise, despite sharing a similar vision of political order in the Middle East, which is informed by their shared identities, the United States did not see the strategic value of Israel right after its independence in 1948, up until Israel had decisively defeated its Arab foes in the 1967 Six-Day War.[150] Thereafter, the United States forges special ties with Israel.[151] These historical evidences indicate that, apart from sharing similar strategic understandings, which stem from their common identities, certain element needs to be in place in order for the two states involved to share common strategic interests, which will subsequently gives rise to a special relationship between them. Therefore, contradictory to the identity school's argument, common identities are crucial in a special relationship, but not certainly central.

Two states sharing common identities each needs to own a certain amount of power, namely, material capacity, in order to shape their similar strategic outlook into their "common" strategic interests. As discussed in earlier section, America saw its mutual strategic dependence with Great Britain only after the United States had emerged as a major power in the late nineteenth century. Both states, because of the necessary amount of material capacity that each possesses, need each other to preserve their similar vision of order in international politics. The U.S.–Israel relations present the same evidence. Before 1967, the United States' policy in the Middle East was dominated by its strategy of rallying the support of the Arab states to confront the Soviet Union, and to secure its access to Middle Eastern oil. Israel, as a consequence, had been generally excluded, and the United States had restrained itself

---

[150] Reich, "Reassessing the United States–Israel Special Relationship", pp. 66, 68–69. Also see Westad, *The Global Cold War*, pp. 127–28; and Mitchell G. Bard and Daniel Pipes, "How Special is the US–Israel Relationship?" *Middle East Quarterly* (June 1997): par. 6–7, available at <http://www.meforum.org/349/how-special-is-the-us-israel-relationship>.

[151] Reich, "Reassessing the United States–Israel Special Relationship", pp. 66, 68–72. Also see Bard and Pipes, "How Special is the US–Israel Relationship?", par. 6–7.

from entangling in the Arab–Israeli conflict to prevent provoking the Arabs' anger. The growing of Israel's material capacity prompted a fundamental change in the United States' Middle East policy. Through its astounding victory in the 1967 Six-Day War, Israel had demonstrated to the United States that it is capable of imposing its strength in the Middle East, thus able to fashion an order in the region which is parallel with the U.S.'s strategic interests. The strategic value of Israel was particularly salient in the late 1960s, a time when America, due to its defeat in Vietnam, was in need for partners which could check the spread of Soviet influence in the Middle East. Henceforth, the United States needs the support of Israel — a powerful state in the Middle East — to maintain a strategic landscape in the region which both similarly prefer, and Israel deepens its need for America's power to ensure its survival.

The necessity for two states with similar strategic understanding deriving from their common identities, to own a certain amount of power, in order to produce their common strategic interests hence creating a special relationship between them, indicates that power plays a crucial role in such a relationship. Once again, constructivist theory seems able to explain the role of power in a special relationship.

As Adler has explained, "[c]onstructivism is the view that the manner in which the material world shapes and is shaped by human action and interaction depends on dynamic normative and epistemic interpretations of the material world".[152] Actors' intersubjective understandings inform their appreciation of the material existence, in turn, the material world shapes and is shaped by their conceptions of self. As such, founded on their similar understanding of strategic interests, which is perceived through their intersubjective understandings, when power owned by each of the two states involved has reached to a certain level, it produces the two states' mutual strategic dependence, and therefore, generates positive identifications between them.

Viewed in this light, a special relationship is not a tool with common identities of the two states involved being the facilitator of this relationship.

---

[152] Adler, "Seizing the Middle Ground", p. 322.

It is also not the natural consequence of the two states' common identities. A special relationship between two states is produced, as the two states' common identities-induced mutual sense of closeness, coupled with their mutual positive identifications stemming from their appreciation of sharing common strategic interests, give birth to their understanding that the two states share a closer relation than their other bilateral ties. The two states' common strategic interests are founded on their similar strategic outlook rooted in their common identities, and created by their necessary amount of power. That said, a special relationship is an intersubjective understanding.

THE CONCEPT OF A SECURITY COMMUNITY AND ITS LINKS WITH A SPECIAL RELATIONSHIP

Defining a Security Community

A security community, according to Deutsch, "is a group of people which has become *integrated*".[153] By integration he means "the attainment, within a territory, of a *sense of community* and of institutions and practices strong enough and widespread enough to assure, for a *long* time, dependable expectations of *peaceful change* among its population".[154] In this sense, a group of people is integrated whenever they are bound by a shared sense of community which induces dependable expectations of peaceful change among them.[155] Dependable expectations of peaceful change means the ability of the actors concerned to know that neither of them would prepare or even consider to use violence as a means to resolve their disputes.[156]

---

[153] Karl W. Deutsch, Sidney A. Burrell, Robert A. Kann, Maurice Lee, Jr., Martin Lichterman, Raymond E. Lindgren, Francis L. Loewenheim, and Richard W. Van Wagenen, *Political Community and the North Atlantic Area: International Organization in the Light of Historical Experience* (Princeton, NJ: Princeton University Press, 1957), p. 5.

[154] Ibid.

[155] Ibid., pp. 32, 84.

[156] Ibid., pp. 5, 56–57. Also see Emanuel Adler and Michael Barnett, "A Framework for the Study of Security Communities", in *Security Communities,* edited by Emanuel Adler and Michael Barnett (Cambridge: Cambridge University Press, 1998a), p. 34.

Deutsch explains that sense of community is "a matter of mutual sympathy and loyalties; of *we-feeling*, trust, and consideration; of at least partial identification in terms of self-images and interests; of ability to predict each other's behaviour and ability to act in accordance with that prediction".[157] Sense of community, therefore, denotes an understanding of collective-self. Each of the actors involved views the other as part of self. They can understand each other just as they understand themselves.[158] As a consequence, sense of community, when reaches to a certain degree, generates dependable expectations of peaceful change among the actors involved. Because they understand each other in collective terms, actors involved identify each other's needs, goals and fate as those of their very own; hence, they view violent conflict between them as unthinkable, for waging a war against each other means threatening their own identity.[159]

The integration of a group of people, Deutsch explains, can be categorized into two different types. A security community is *amalgamated* when two or more previously independent political communities formally merge into a single political entity and achieve integration among them.[160] The United States is an example of amalgamated security communities.[161] On the other hand, it is *pluralistic*, when two or more states constitute a security community while retaining their respective independence and sovereignty.[162] The relationship between the United States and Canada is an example of pluralistic security communities.[163]

---

[157] Deutsch et al., *Political Community and the North Atlantic Area*, p. 129.

[158] Ibid., p. 57.

[159] Adler and Barnett, "A Framework for the Study of Security Communities", p. 47. Also see Michael Barnett and Emanuel Adler, "Studying Security Communities in Theory, Comparison, and History", in *Security Communities,* p. 434; and Emanuel Adler, "Imagined (Security) Communities: Cognitive Regions in International Relations", *Journal of International Studies* 26, no. 2 (1997a): 264.

[160] Deutsch et al., *Political Community and the North Atlantic Area*, p. 6.

[161] Ibid.

[162] Ibid., p. 6. Also see Emanuel Adler and Michael Barnett, "Security Communities in Theoretical Perspective", in *Security Communities,* p. 5; and Amitav Acharya, *Constructing a Security Community in Southeast Asia: ASEAN and the Problem of Regional Order* (London and New York: Routledge, 2001), p. 16.

[163] Deutsch et al., *Political Community and the North Atlantic Area*, p. 6.

This study is concerned with pluralistic security communities which are formed by two sovereign states. According to Adler and Barnett, a pluralistic security community is "a transnational region comprised of sovereign states whose people maintain dependable expectations of peaceful change".[164] As such, the key distinguishing feature of a pluralistic security community is not the absence of conflict in the community *per se*, but rather its members' ability to manage disputes within the group without resort to violence or contemplate to use any such means.[165]

There are two reasons that necessitate this research to focus on bilateral pluralistic security communities. First, the earliest emergences of pluralistic security communities are those of bilateral, which include the security community between U.S.–Canada since the 1870s; U.S.–UK since the 1890s; Denmark–Sweden and Denmark–Norway since the 1900s; Norway–Sweden since 1907; Britain–Norway, Britain–Denmark, and Britain–Sweden since the 1910s; Britain–Belgium and Belgium–Netherlands since 1928; Britain–Netherlands; France–Belgium.[166] These historical evidences show that pluralistic security communities are originated from the bilateral relations of two sovereign states.

Second, bilateral pluralistic security communities form the basis of a multilateral one. For example, although the transatlantic states constitute a multilateral pluralistic security community, it is in fact preceded by a cluster of bilateral ones, which include the above mentioned bilateral pluralistic security communities.[167] Meanwhile, Deutsch's definition of a security community, which requires at least two political units to constitute such a community, reflects that bilateral relations of two political entities

[164] Adler and Barnett, "A Framework for the Study of Security Communities", p. 30.

[165] Acharya, *Constructing a Security Community in Southeast Asia*, p. 16.

[166] Deutsch et al., *Political Community and the North Atlantic Area*, pp. 29–30, 65–66.

[167] Ibid., pp. 10, 29–30, 65–66, 118. Also see Ole Waever, "Insecurity, Security, and Asecurity in the West European Non-War Community", in *Security Communities*, pp. 69–70, 79, 81, 104; Emanuel Adler, "Seeds of Peaceful Change: The OSCE's Security Community-Building Model", in *Security Communities*, pp. 119–20; and Vincent Pouliot, "Security Community In and Through Practice: The Power Politics of Russia–NATO Diplomacy", PhD dissertation, University of Toronto, 2008, pp. 46–47.

serve as the fundamental fabric of any security community.[168] As a pluralistic security community, either bilateral or multilateral, is essentially spawned by the bilateral ties of two states, the examination of the concept of pluralistic security communities, therefore, should necessarily begin with those of bilateral, particularly with regard to the emergence of such a community.

Security Community — An Intersubjective Understanding

The central tenet of a security community is that the political units involved share a sense of community — that of an understanding of self in collective terms. Actors involved view each other as part of self. That said, the conception of self entails the dynamics of identification with one another. Such a phenomenon demonstrates the limitation of realism and liberalism in explaining the concept of a security community.

Both the theories are founded on a fundamental principle, that is — an actor's conception of self is constant and exogenously given.[169] Through the lenses of realism and liberalism, actors invariably view self in egoistic terms, consequently, they merely change their behaviour, but not identities and interests.[170] Therefore, both the theories explain only the behaviour of actors; exclude the possibility where appreciations of self are endogenous to interactions that allow actors to identify with each other, and may result in certain actors sharing a collective-self understanding.

The constructivist theory, on the other hand, explains the phenomenon where actors' conceptions of self are endogenous to interactions. As outlined in earlier section, constructivism observes that actors perceive the world through the lenses of their intersubjective understandings, in which such understandings are founded on their appreciations of

---

[168] Deutsch et al., *Political Community and the North Atlantic Area*, pp. 6, 122.

[169] Wendt, "Anarchy is What States Make of It", p. 391. Also see Alexander Wendt, "Collective Identity Formation and the International State", *The American Political Science Review* 88, no. 2 (1994): 384.

[170] Wendt, "Anarchy is What States Make of It", pp. 391–92. Also see Wendt, "Collective Identity Formation and the International State", p. 384; and Adler and Barnett, "Security Communities in Theoretical Perspective", p. 11.

self, and are emerged from the mutually constitutive interactions among actors and their intersubjective understandings. As such, constructivism essentially recognizes that actors' conceptions of self are socially constructed, hence are subjected to the dynamics of identification among actors; consequently allow for the possibility of the emergence of an understanding of collective-self shared by the actors involved.

Collective-self, an understanding which produces a security community, indicates that such a community is, in essence, an intersubjective understanding shared by the political units involved. As explained in earlier section, actors' intersubjective understandings denote a stable set of identities and interests which are founded on their conceptions of self. However, a pluralistic security community should be distinguished from a special relationship, which is also an intersubjective understanding shared by two states. Even though both the concepts represent intersubjective understandings which entail positive identifications between the states concerned, they are basically different from one another.

A special relationship denotes two states sharing an understanding that their relationship is *closer* than their other bilateral ties. A closer relation, however, does not necessarily mean both the states concerned share a collective-self understanding. While two states perceive a close relation among themselves, they could, at the same time, entrench in a situation where they apprehend each other in egoistic terms. For instance, in the 1910s, although the United States and Britain had begun to share a relationship with special characters, they, during this period, continued to hold egoistic understanding of one another, thus pursued competitive politics between them. In the late 1910s, the two states were engaged in rivalry for naval supremacy, and were suspicious of each other's maritime power. The United States was apprehensive of British supreme naval power, which they perceived could threaten their national interests anytime.[171] The United Kingdom was anxious with America's naval expansion, as this would challenge Britain's maritime superiority which had guaranteed its greatness for three centuries.[172]

---

[171] Allen, *Great Britain and the United States*, pp. 701, 704–5, 733–34.
[172] Ibid., pp. 703–5, 733, 743.

Viewed in this light, a special relationship should not be assumed as tantamount to the two states concerned sharing a collective-self understanding, namely, a security community; nevertheless, the two states at least intersubjectively recognize that their relation is closer, when compared to other bilateral ties either state enjoys.

The Two Elements that Breed a Pluralistic Security Community

A pluralistic security community, as a socially constructed phenomenon, emerges out of the interactions among states. Yet, interaction itself is not adequate to explain how certain states would share a collective-self understanding. In the literature of security communities, apart from states' interactions, two elements have been pointed out as crucial in spawning the emergence of a pluralistic security community — that of the material capacity, namely, power, of the states involved; and their common identities.

Deutsch has pointed out, the material capabilities and the compatibility of major values of the states involved, play vital roles in forging a pluralistic security community between them.[173] He defines major values

---

[173] Deutsch outlines three crucial conditions for the establishment of a pluralistic security community, namely, the material capabilities of the states concerned, the compatibility of their major values, and mutual predictability of behaviour shared among them. According to Deutsch, mutual predictability of behaviour is first based on familiarity of the states concerned on each other's conduct, and could eventually founded on their collective-self understanding. In other words, states sharing mutual predictability of behaviour could mean they constitute a security community. As such, mutual predictability of behaviour should be first understood as an outcome of the interactions of the states concerned; owing to the fact that mutual predictability of behaviour is the states' *shared understanding* produced by their interactions. Based on this first understanding, mutual predictability of behaviour can subsequently be understood as an element that shape and be shaped by the interactions of the states involved, just like the other two conditions. Therefore, mutual predictability of behaviour should not be viewed as one of the crucial conditions that breed a pluralistic security community. It is, in fact, fundamentally an outcome spawned by the material capabilities and the compatibility of major values of the states concerned amid the mutually constitutive dynamics between these two elements and the states' social interactions. See Deutsch et al., *Political Community and the North Atlantic Area*, pp. 38, 46–49, 56–58, 66–67, 70, 118, 123–29.

as values which are important within each of the political units concerned, and are also important for the relations among them.[174] In other words, major values are those which the political units involved respectively owns, and collectively share; namely, their common identities. Similarly, Adler and Barnett observe, states' power and their cognitive structures form the structural girders for the development of a pluralistic security community.[175] Cognitive structure, according to them, is a regional system of meanings which is made up of people who share common identities.[176] For example, Australia and Canada, the English-speaking states, constitute a cognitive region/structure.[177]

The elements of power and common identities shape and are shaped by social interactions among states, which amid such mutually constitutive dynamics, engender the rise of a pluralistic security community.[178]

In terms of power, Deutsch discerns that, a pluralistic security community grows around a group of powerful states, in which they constitute the core area of the community.[179] He writes, "larger, stronger, more politically, administratively, economically, and educationally advanced political units were found to form the cores of strength around which in most cases the integrative process developed".[180] For example, France and Germany, two of the most powerful states in the European Union, together has been the engine for the integration process of this security community.[181] Likewise, the North Atlantic security

---

[174] Ibid., p. 123.

[175] Adler and Barnett, "A Framework for the Study of Security Communities", pp. 39–41.

[176] Ibid., pp. 40–41. Also see Adler, "Imagined (Security) Communities", pp. 252–55.

[177] Adler, "Imagined (Security) Communities", p. 254.

[178] Adler and Barnett, "A Framework for the Study of Security Communities", pp. 38–39. Also see Deutsch et al., *Political Community and the North Atlantic Area*, pp. 38, 70.

[179] Deutsch et al., *Political Community and the North Atlantic Area*, pp. 37–39.

[180] Ibid., p. 38.

[181] Douglas Webber, "Introduction", in *The Franco–German Relationship in the European Union,* edited by Douglas Webber (U.S. and Canada: Routledge, 1999), p. 1. Also see David P. Calleo, "Introduction", in *Europe's Franco–German Engine,* edited by David P. Calleo and Eric R. Staal (Washington, D.C.: Brookings Institution Press, 1998), p. 1; Gisela Hendriks and Annette Morgan, *The Franco–German Axis in European Integration* (UK and U.S.: Edward Elgar Publishing Limited, 2001), pp. 4–7; and Adler, "Seeds of Peaceful Change", pp. 119–20.

community had emerged around its core state — the superpower, America.[182] Meanwhile, according to Deutsch, founded on their existing material capacities, the further growth of power owned by the strong political units too will be making major contributions to the establishment of a security community.[183] He observes, the developments of pluralistic security communities are usually accompanied by the substantial increases in the power of the states involved.[184] In sum, Deutsch notices that a strong state's power has the attractive effects, which brings together a group of states towards forming a security community.

Adler and Barnett confirm Deutsch's observation of power. They argue that, because of its attractive effects, power can be a magnet.[185] Adler explains, "powerful states, or cores of strength, are necessary for the development of security communities because, like a magnet, they attract weaker states that expect to share the security and welfare associated with them."[186] Magnetic power, according to them, is "the authority to determine shared meaning that constitutes the 'we-feeling' and practices of states and the conditions which confer, defer, or deny access to the community and the benefits it bestows on its members."[187] The magnetic pull effects of strong states' power thus indicate that, power leads to the weaker states to identify positively with the powerful ones; consequently, allows for the possibility of the emergence of a collective-self understanding shared among them.

In the realm of common identities, the Kantian school's liberal interpretation of the Deutschian notion of a security community is rather inaccurate. Deriving from Deutsch's study which chooses the North Atlantic area, for it covers all major powers of the free world, as the case to examine his concept of a security community, the Kantians advocate

---

182 Josef Joffe, "Europe's American Pacifier", *Foreign Policy*, no. 54 (1984): 64–69, 81–82. Also see Adler, "Seeds of Peaceful Change", pp. 119–20; and Adler, "Imagined (Security) Communities", p. 256.

183 Deutsch et al., *Political Community and the North Atlantic Area*, pp. 38–41.

184 Ibid.

185 Adler and Barnett, "A Framework for the Study of Security Communities", pp. 39–40.

186 Adler, "Imagined (Security) Communities", p. 276.

187 Adler and Barnett, "A Framework for the Study of Security Communities", p. 39.

liberal democracy as a necessary condition for the establishment of such communities.[188] This misunderstands Deutsch's study. Deutsch does not regard liberal democracy *per se* as essential to produce a security community; rather, he sees it as "an example" of common identities shared by certain political units, which, in his view, shared identities are crucial for them to constitute a security community. In short, Deutsch is referring to political entities' common identities, not democracy.

In his study, Deutsch deliberately refrains from adopting a definition of North Atlantic area which only includes the democracies located within this region.[189] He makes it clear that such an attempt is to avoid the conclusion where democracy is a requirement for the forming of a security community.[190] Deutsch instead views North Atlantic area as a region constituted by the non-Soviet-dominated states situated in this territory, which hence includes the then two non-democracies in the area — Portugal and Spain.[191] That said, Deutsch intends to examine the effects of "common political values" shared by certain political units in spawning a security community, not democratic values specifically. The conclusion of Deutsch's study vindicates his attempt to look at political communities bound by common political values.

As mentioned earlier in this section, Deutsch concludes that compatibility of major values of the states concerned is essential in engendering a security community among them; in which such values are those they individually own and collectively share. That said, major values, according to Deutsch's definition, are common values of the political units concerned; and that he views "basic political ideology" as one of the elements of such values, namely, common political values.[192] Thus, for the case of North Atlantic area, "democracy and

---

[188] Deutsch et al., *Political Community and the North Atlantic Area*, p. 9. Also see Christopher B. Roberts, "ASEAN's Security Community Project: Challenges and Opportunities in the Pursuit of Comprehensive Integration", PhD dissertation, The University of New South Wales, 2008, p. 22; and Amitav Acharya, "Collective Identity and Conflict Management in Southeast Asia", in *Security Communities*, pp. 198–99.

[189] Deutsch et al., *Political Community and the North Atlantic Area*, pp. 9–10.

[190] Ibid.

[191] Ibid., pp. 9–10, 126.

[192] Ibid., pp. 123–24.

non-communist economics" have been outlined by Deutsch as the two crucial common political values shared by the political units within this region.[193] Deutsch subsequently assesses the region in terms of the compatibility of major values which, with the presence of the two common values, the North Atlantic area rates high.[194] As such, Deutsch's emphasis on non-Soviet-dominated states in his definition of North Atlantic area, his definition of major values, and his attempt to appraise the North Atlantic area in terms of its compatibility of major values, make plain that the Deutschian concept of a security community stresses the essentiality of political units' common identities in such communities. Democracy is an example of common identities.

Adler's and Barnett's understanding of states' common identities coincides with Deutsch's observation. Adler discerns that, "people who are territorially and politically organized into states, owe their allegiance to states, and act on their behalf", will also at the same time, bound by a transnational cognitive structure/region which is constituted by them sharing common identities.[195] A cognitive region transcends states' boundaries and any territorial base.[196] Because of their shared identities, people within a cognitive region identify positively with one another thus preserve the existence of this regional intersubjective understandings.[197] Under certain circumstances, according to Adler, a cognitive structure/region will foster a collective-self understanding shared by states within the region, hence forge a security community among them.[198] In other words, a pluralistic security community is founded on the common identities shared by the states involved. Nonetheless, Adler does acknowledge that, liberal cognitive structure/ region is conducive to producing a pluralistic security community.[199] It, however, as he argues, remains as one of many cognitive structures that

---

[193] Ibid., 124–26.

[194] Ibid., 124–29.

[195] Adler, "Imagined (Security) Communities", pp. 250, 252–54.

[196] Ibid., p. 254.

[197] Ibid., pp. 253–54. Also see Adler and Barnett, "A Framework for the Study of Security Communities", pp. 40–41.

[198] Adler, "Imagined (Security) Communities", pp. 254–55.

[199] Ibid., pp. 250, 258.

could give rise to such a community.[200] Adler and Barnett make plain in their study, it is their aim to explain that liberalism is *not* a necessary condition for the development of a pluralistic security community; other cognitive structures, namely, states' common identities, also possess the capabilities of producing such a community.[201]

Nevertheless, Deutsch and Adler respectively observes, states' identities should endow with one basic character in order to breed a pluralistic security community. That is, such identities have to be peaceful in nature. Deutsch explains, as long as a state's identities are, in essence, militaristic, expansionist or ideological crusading, the establishment of a security community between it and other states would not be likely.[202] Since these values are violent in nature, the adoption of military means by a state, which possesses such values, to settle its interstate disputes remains possible. Adler explains further, even though states share common identities, these shared identities will not produce a pluralistic security community if they are fundamentally brutal.[203] He points out, the emergences of security communities are most unlikely among states bound by totalitarian ideologies, as such ideas permit all possible means to achieve state goals, including violent ways.[204]

Therefore, within the framework of a pluralistic security community, common identities of the states involved can be defined as those derived from their shared culture, common language, historical ties or shared political values and institutions; in which these identities are peaceful in nature. As such, liberal democracy is one of the above mentioned states' common identities. It represents a culture of peaceful settlement of conflicts, and a culture which encourages community bonds.[205] In short, liberal democracy is by nature peaceful.

---

[200] Ibid.
[201] Adler and Barnett, "A Framework for the Study of Security Communities", pp. 40–41. Also see Barnett and Adler, "Studying Security Communities in Theory, Comparison, and History", p. 425.
[202] Deutsch et al., *Political Community and the North Atlantic Area*, pp. 124–26.
[203] Adler, "Imagined (Security) Communities", pp. 257–59.
[204] Ibid., pp. 9–10, 126.
[205] Ibid., pp. 250, 258–60.

A Special Relationship Leads to a Pluralistic Security Community

While a special relationship and a pluralistic security community are basically different from each other, they are yet interlinked. Both concepts represent a relationship of common identities as well as power between two sovereign states. Several bilateral relationships function as a special relationship-cum-security community. For instance, the relationship between the United States and Britain, and between the United States and Canada.

As presented in Chapter 1, the peaceful traits of a special relationship imply the qualities of a pluralistic security community which is by essence peaceful. The aspiration for peace recurrently appears in a special relationship. For example, amid the emergence of the Anglo-American special relationship in the 1890s, a steadily growing number of elites from the United States and the United Kingdom had expressed their compelling conviction that war should be "unthinkable" between the two states.[206] Similar robust conviction could hardly be found in their other bilateral ties at the time, "certainly not with such regularity and vigor".[207] Likewise, Churchill's statement on Anglo-American relations in 1956 exhibited such aspiration for peace,

> It is our duty to remove misunderstandings...these are the things to which we should do well to devote constant attention and undiminishing enthusiasm. I earnestly hope that we have reached the end of misunderstanding and that we shall move forward steadily together...[208]

[206] Srdjan Vucetic, "The Anglosphere: A Genealogy of an Identity in International Relations", PhD dissertation, The Ohio State University, 2008, p. 92.

[207] Kenneth Bourne, *Britain and the Balance of Power in North America, 1815–1908* (Berkeley: University of California Press, 1967), pp. 320–21; Anne Orde, *The Eclipse of Great Britain: The United States and British Imperial Decline, 1895–1956* (New York: St. Martin's Press, 1996), p. 24; Stephen R. Rock, *Why Peace Breaks Out: Great Power Rapprochement in Historical Perspective* (Chapel Hill and London: University of North Carolina Press, 1989), pp. 29–62; Stephen R. Rocke, *Appeasement in International Politics* (Lexington: University Press of Kentucky, 2000), p. 29; Bruce M. Russett, *Community and Contention: Britain and America in the Twentieth Century* (Cambridge, MA: Cambridge University Press, 1963), pp. 4–39, quoted in Vucetic, "The Anglosphere", p. 92.

[208] Winston S. Churchill, "The Benjamin Franklin Medal", in *Winston S. Churchill: His Complete Speeches 1897–1963, Vol VIII*, edited by Robert Rhodes James (New York: Chelsea House, 1974*b*), p. 8671.

However, the exceptional wish for peace which regularly emanates from a special relationship, does not warrant the relation to have the capacity to maintain peace between the two states involved without them prepare or even consider to use violence as a means to resolve their disputes. Such a capability constitutes the defining characteristic of a pluralistic security community.

The emergence of the Anglo-American special relationship at the turn of the twentieth century did not immediately give birth to their capacity to settle their bilateral conflicts without contemplating or preparing to employ violent means. After 1905, the U.S. Navy Department regularly exercised its Red Plan, a war plan designed to deal with possible conflicts with the British fleet.[209] On the other hand, as late as 1926, Canada, where its defence was still closely intertwined with the responsibility of the Royal Navy, developed military plan aimed at preventing American invasion.[210] Such war planning indicate that, despite sharing special ties, the United States and Great Britain during this period still considered war between them as possible.

The United States and the United Kingdom, meanwhile, were suspicious of each other's naval power. Britain was alarmed by America's desire to expand its navy in the late 1910s.[211] With the absence of any other comparable navies, and the still limited strategic commitments of the United States, Britain feared that America's naval expansion was in fact directed at them whom at that time possessed the world's greatest navy.[212] The United States, on the other hand, was worried that Britain, with its supreme naval power — particularly with the existence of British alliance with another great naval power: Japan — could exert its will on America whenever it wished to do so.[213]

---

[209] Sean M. Shore, "No Fences Make Good Neighbors: The Development of the Canadian–US Security Community, 1871–1940", in *Security Communities,* p. 347. Also see Kissinger, "Reflections on a Partnership", pp. 575–76.

[210] Shore, "No Fences Make Good Neighbors", pp. 336, 347.

[211] Allen, *Great Britain and the United States*, pp. 704, 733. Also see Richard Lawrence Storatz, "Anglo-American Relations: A Theory and History of Political Integration", PhD dissertation, Columbia University, 1981, p. 403.

[212] Storatz, "Anglo-American Relations", pp. 403–4.

[213] Allen, *Great Britain and the United States*, pp. 703–5, 733–34.

These evidences reveal that both the military power of the United States and the United Kingdom remained in each other's mind as a plausible threat. Anglo-American relations, therefore, was not a pluralistic security community — where the states concerned would not even consider to use violence as a means to settle their disputes — even though the relations were clearly special, namely closer than the two states' other bilateral ties, since the 1910s.

It was not until 1937 when the United States decided to officially withdraw the Red Plan thus marks a permanent end to the two states' consideration or preparation to adopt military means in dealing with their bilateral disputes.[214] The decades taken by the Anglo-American special relationship to eventually equip the two states with the ability to completely abandon the thinking of engaging in or preparing for an armed conflict against each other, demonstrate that certain conditions need to be in place before a special relationship can be equated with a pluralistic security community.

---

[214] Shore, "No Fences Make Good Neighbors", p. 347. Also see Haglund, "The US–Canada Relationship", in *America's 'Special Relationships'*, p. 64; and Kissinger, "Reflections on a Partnership", p. 576.

3

THE CONCEPTUAL FOUNDATIONS FOR A SPECIAL RELATIONSHIP

A theory needs concepts to formulate its explanations. To develop a theoretical framework of a special relationship, this chapter seeks to outline the definitional concepts that constitute such relationships. Based on the review of literature in Chapter 2, this study defines a special relationship as follows:

> A special relationship exists between two states when two sources of closeness, that of the two states' common identities and shared strategic interests, coexist in their relations.
>
> Common identities of two states are derived from their shared culture, common language, historical ties or shared political values and institutions. Common strategic interests of two states, on the other hand, mean the two states rely on each other's material presence for survival.
>
> Common identities of two states sharing a special relationship spawn their mutual sentimental expressions of closeness. The sentimental associations, combine with the two states' mutual sense of closeness engendered by their common strategic interests, result in the two states sharing an understanding that their relationship is *closer* than their other bilateral ties. The shared understanding, in turn, stirs up the two states'

respective *expectation* that their relationship *should be* closer than their bilateral ties with others. Such an expectation leads to a higher intensity of interactions between the two states as compared with that of their other bilateral relations.

The above definition brings to light the key conceptual components that constitute a special relationship: the concepts of power, identity and expectation. This chapter hence begins with the explanations of the three concepts.

As this study looks at how a special relationship could evolve into a pluralistic security community, the defining feature of such a community, namely, dependable expectations of peaceful change, therefore also stands as one of the key conceptual components of a special relationship.

The most obvious characteristic of a pluralistic security community is the absence of war among the states involved. As such, such a community is founded on the war avoidance norms shared by the states involved. States have to learn to avoid war between them before being able to renounce their defense gesture against each other. Viewed in this light, the concept of norms has to be among the key conceptual components of a special relationship.

Norms and dependable expectations of peaceful change are the other two conceptual components that will be explained in this chapter.

The understandings of the five conceptual components put forward by this chapter form the foundation for the explanation of the dynamics of a special relationship and its transformation into a pluralistic security community, which will be established in the following chapter.

POWER

Survival is the fundamental need of every state. Anything will be meaningless for a state if it could not survive in the first place. Hence, regardless of how a state might evolve, one principle remains unchanged — its will to exist. This tenet underscores the essentiality of power for a state. Power is commonly understood as the best means to ensure the survival of a state.

This section first defines what is power. It then addresses the question of why a state pursues power. This section subsequently moves to explain the meanings of power balance and power imbalance between states. It argues that power balance between states is a cause for power competition and a basis of order between them; power imbalance between states, meanwhile, is an accelerator of war or a basis of peace between them. Finally, this section explains the reason behind the strategic cooperation between two states, and the dynamics of such cooperation.

The Definition of Power

This study defines power as the material capacity of a state. The elements of a state's material capacity include the size of population of the state and its territory, its natural resources, economic strength and military force.

The wealth of a state reflected its economic strength.[1] A state's wealth can be measured in terms of its GDP per capita.[2] For example, India — a developing state — is less wealthy than Switzerland – a developed state.[3] In 2010, India's GDP per capita was US$1,265, which was lower than Switzerland's at US$67,246.[4]

States Pursue Power for Survival

Power has crucial meaning for a state. It indicates a state's ability to create or destroy. In an anarchical international system where there is no central authority above all the sovereign states, a state needs power to realize its goal as no authority could restrict its aspiration and ensure its security. While power undoubtedly is indispensable for a state, one question remains debatable — whether power serves as a means or an end for a state? This question can be fundamentally addressed by answering the question — why states pursue power?

---

[1] "The World's Richest Countries", *Forbes*, 22 February 2012.
[2] Ibid.
[3] World Economic Forum, *The Global Competitiveness Report 2011–2012*, available at <http://reports.weforum.org/global-competitiveness-2011-2012/> (accessed 22 September 2011).
[4] Ibid.

The arguments of realism have been centred around explaining why states pursue power. Classical realism argues that it is the human natural will to power that account for a state's need for power.[5] Because human by nature are power hungry, a state which is formed by human beings thus always has "a limitless lust for power".[6] Such a tendency denotes that a state will not stop looking for power and invariably seek to expand its power when opportunities arise. As Frederick the Great had put it, "the permanent principle of rulers": "to extend as far as their power permits".[7] Structural realism, on the other hand, argues that it is the anarchical structure of international system that forces states to compete for power so as to maximize their security.[8] As there is no overarching authority above all sovereign states, no one can guarantee the security and well-being of a state but a state itself. A state therefore needs power to ensure its survival. Hence, in structural realists' perspective, it is the human natural will to survive, not the will to power, that explains why states need to pursue power.

Despite classical and structural realists holding different understanding of human nature, such a difference, however, is built on an irrefutable truth — human after all needs to first secure its survival. Dunne and Schmidt have explained, "Survival is held to be a precondition for attaining all other goals, whether these involve conquest or merely independence."[9] Classical realists' attempt to explain international politics by linking it to the cornerstone character of human nature, in fact, does not seize the fundamental essence of human nature. Beneath human's innate propensity for power, lies a deeper root of human nature — its raw desire to survive. How could a human be power hungry if it could not exist in the first

---

[5]   John J. Mearsheimer, *The Tragedy of Great Power Politics* (U.S.: W.W. Norton & Company, Inc., 2001), p. 19.

[6]   Hans J. Morgenthau, *Scientific Man vs. Power Politics* (Chicago & London: University of Chicago Press, 1967), p. 194.

[7]   Felix Gilbert, *To the Farewell Address: Ideas of Early American Foreign Policy* (Princeton and New Jersey: Princeton University Press, 1961), pp. 89–90.

[8]   Mearsheimer, *The Tragedy of Great Power Politics*, p. 19. Also see Tim Dunne and Brian C. Schmidt, "Realism", in *The Globalization of World Politics*, edited by John Baylis and Steve Smith (New York: Oxford University Press, 2005), p. 166.

[9]   Dunne and Schmidt, "Realism", p. 174.

place? That being so, human inherent aspiration for power is always founded on the assumption that its very survival is not fundamentally at stake. As Waltz writes, "in crucial situations...the ultimate concern of states is not for power but for security".[10] A state's desire for power is founded on, and preceded by, its concern for security.

Classical realism's challenge to defensive realism (structural realism) has been on defensive realism's view of how a state would pursue power, not on the fundamental principle that shores up defensive realism, namely, human inherent will to survive. From classical realists' perspective, it is always problematic for defensive realists to assume that all states learn the same lessons from the past — expansion always leads to failure — which consequently results in states aiming at maximizing their security by pursuing a limited amount of power sufficient to preserve, not upset, the balance of power among the states.[11] Classical realists argue, states operate according to human nature — power hungry, not in conformity with lessons that they should learn from history.[12] They maintain, history has shown that most great powers are expansionist, and states rarely derive any lesson from the past which points out that expansion is bound to be futile.[13]

Moreover, classical realists contend that, one can never be certain of a state's real intention to pursue power; whether it is power or security-maximizer. History has shown that states often concealed their desire for hegemony with the name of preserving national security.[14] As Zakaria writes, "It is difficult to think of Napoleon's expansion as motivated by insecurity, yet he claimed it was just that."[15] Hence, classical realists believe that a state will seek for more power whenever it has the capability to do so, and will not satisfy with the amount of power which it deems

---

[10] Kenneth N. Waltz, "The Origins of War in Neorealist Theory", in *The Origin and Prevention of Major Wars,* edited by Robert I. Rotberg and Theodore K. Rabb (Cambridge: Cambridge University Press, 1989), p. 40.

[11] Dunne and Schmidt, "Realism", p. 170. Also see Mearsheimer, *The Tragedy of Great Power Politics*, p. 20; and Fareed Zakaria, *From Wealth to Power: The Unusual Origins of America's World Role* (Princeton: Princeton University Press, 1998), p. 28.

[12] Zakaria, *From Wealth to Power*, pp. 10, 31.

[13] Ibid.

[14] Ibid., p. 26.

[15] Ibid.

necessary to preserve its security as defensive realists have maintained.[16] In other words, classical realism's criticism on defensive realism has been to justify that states' appetite for power is not restricted by their sense of security. Yet, for such an argument to be valid, it must share the same principle in which defensive realism has embraced — human aims to survive — as without survival, it is impossible for a state to start longing for power beyond the amount which it deems needed for its security.

However, there is no one conclusive explanation on a state's appetite for power. Both classical and structural realisms find evidences in the real world that match with their respective arguments. Some states seek for expansion because they can, and some will not even if they can.[17] This difference is largely attributed to the international environment that a state is embedded in. Zakaria has pointed out, "the situation in which states find themselves vis-à-vis their fellows is the most powerful force shaping international outcomes."[18] Whether a state becomes an expansionist or remains at status quo is, to a large extent, shaped by its external conditions apart from its own preferences.

Moreover, one could not be certain of what precisely the word "survival" means for a state. The meaning of survival is not mutually exclusive with the meaning of well-being. A state usually equates its very survival not just with the state's basic security, but also with the state's well-being. The fierce competition among states in the global economy indicates that the well-being of a state has crucial meaning in policymakers' understanding of "state's survival". As David Cameron, former British Prime Minister, said, "There is no national security, unless you have economic security."[19] That said, the power-maximalist

---

[16] Ibid., pp. 21, 28.
[17] As Zakaria observes, "…most great power have been expansionist"; on the other hand, "history furnishes many examples of rising states that did not correspondingly extend their political interests overseas". See Zakaria, *From Wealth to Power*, pp. 10, 32.
[18] Ibid., p. 34.
[19] The U.S. President Barack Obama and British Prime Minister David Cameron, Press Conference at Lancaster House, London, UK, 25 May 2011, available at <http://www.whitehouse.gov/photos-and-video/video/2011/05/25/president-obama-prime-minister-cameron-joint-press-availability>.

behaviour of states is not just simply for the sake of wanting power, but also there is a basis of wanting to survive.

In short, classical and structural realisms contradict each other in terms of the explanation of the strategy that a state would adopt in its pursuit of power — whether it seeks for a limited or limitless amount of power, not in terms of the principle that underpins a state's power-seeking behaviour. Both types of realisms are built on the tenet that human has a raw will to survive. Therefore, a state pursues power fundamentally for survival.

Survival is Essentially Linked to the Existence of Self

Survival essentially concerns the existence of self. Hence, one's will to survive is rooted in its awareness of "self". The desire of oneself to exist generates its natural tendency to be self-interested. An actor is self-interested inherently means it has an ultimate goal of wanting to survive. In this sense, for every state, its national interest is fundamentally about its aim to survive.[20]

An actor's understanding of self is founded on two identities, namely, corporate identity and self-identity.[21] The corporate identity, which is essentially about the intrinsic consciousness of individual security and well being, furnishes the actor motivational energy to engage in action, which means it is prior to interaction.[22] By participating in social interactions, actor forms its self-identity in which such an identity is based on the relationship of self to the others.[23] As such, the concept of self-identity entails the dynamics of identification with other. According to Wendt, "identification is a continuum from negative to positive — from conceiving the other as anathema to the self to conceiving it as an extension of the self."[24] The nature of identification determines the

---

[20] As Dunne and Schmidt write, "the core national interest of all states must be survival". See Dunne and Schmidt, "Realism", p. 164.

[21] Alexander Wendt, "Collective Identity Formation and the International State", *The American Political Science Review* 88, no. 2 (1994): 385.

[22] Ibid.

[23] Ibid., pp. 385–86.

[24] Ibid., p. 386.

extent to which the boundaries of the self are drawn.[25] Yet, because of the differentiating dynamics that derive from actors' corporate identities, positive identification among actors will rarely lead to the perfect match between their respective conceptions of self.[26]

Owing to the fact that this research is essentially the study of bilateral relations between two states, the corporate identity of an actor hence refers to the individualistic character of a state, and an actor's self-identity, on the other hand, means a state's appreciation of self in relations to other states.

Actors acquire their self-identities through the mutually constitutive dynamics of their conceptions of self and their intersubjective understandings, namely, the normative structure, in which such understandings shape and are shaped by the dynamics of identification between actors.[27] As discussed in earlier chapter, intersubjective understandings denote a stable set of identities and interests which emerge out of mutually constitutive interactions among actors and their shared intersubjective understandings.[28] Such understandings are expressed in terms of norms and practice.[29] Although intersubjective understandings are essentially the cognitive collective knowledge of actors, they are experienced as if they exist independent of the actors.[30] Hence, intersubjective understandings define actors' social reality.[31] The fact that intersubjective understandings

---

[25] Ibid.

[26] Ibid.

[27] Alexander Wendt, "Anarchy is What States Make of It: The Social Construction of Power Politics", *International Organization* 46, no. 2 (1992): 397–99. Also see Michael Barnett, "Social Constructivism", in *The Globalization of World Politics*, p. 267.

[28] Wendt notes that constructivists "share a cognitive, intersubjective conception of process in which identities and interests are endogenous to interaction". See Wendt, "Anarchy is What States Make of It", pp. 394, 399, 403. Also see Jeffrey T. Checkel, "The Constructivist Turn in International Relations Theory", *World Politics* 50, no. 2 (1998): 326.

[29] Ted Hopf, "The Promise of Constructivism in International Relations Theory", *International Security* 23, no. 1 (1998): 173. Also see Wendt, "Anarchy is What States Make of It", p. 399; and Emanuel Adler, "Seizing the Middle Ground: Constructivism in World Politics", *European Journal of International Relations* 3, no. 3 (1997*b*): 327.

[30] Wendt, "Anarchy is What States Make of It", p. 327.

[31] Ibid.

emerge out of the process of social interactions does not mean that such understandings are in a state of flux. Once a set of intersubjective understandings have been institutionalized — which means the internalization of new identities and interests by the actors involved — such understandings would stand as a social fact which resists change, and often persists beyond the lives of the actors as they are constantly reproduced through norms and practices.[32]

The identifications among actors amid the mutually constitutive dynamics between actors and their intersubjective understandings indicate that, under the material structure of anarchy and the distribution of power, social interactions could generate cooperative or conflictual intersubjective understandings founded on actors' respective appreciations of self.[33] The conceptions of self hence understandably impose meanings on the objective presence of anarchy and the distribution of power, in turn, the material existence shapes and is shaped by the understandings of self.[34] For example, Britain owning 500 nuclear weapons is less threatening to the United States than five North Korean nuclear weapons, because Britain is a friend of the U.S. (an extension of the U.S.'s self) and North Korea an enemy to the U.S. (an anathema to the U.S.'s self).[35] Two states identify with each other negatively when they are embedded in conflictual intersubjective understandings in which each view the other's power as a threat and a source of conflict/ competition. On the other hand, two states identify positively with one another when they share cooperative intersubjective understandings in which each perceive the other's power as an opportunity and a source of cooperation.

---

[32] Ibid., pp. 399, 407. Also see Adler, "Seizing the Middle Ground", p. 327; and Wendt, "Collective Identity Formation and the International State", p. 388.

[33] Wendt, "Anarchy is What States Make of It", p. 399.

[34] Ibid., pp. 399–400. Also see "Constructivism is the view that the manner in which the material world shapes and is shaped by human action and interaction depends on dynamic normative and epistemic interpretations of the material world." Adler, "Seizing the Middle Ground", p. 322.

[35] Alexander Wendt, "Constructing International Politics", *International Security* 20, no. 1 (1995): 73.

In short, a state after all is self-interested owing to its instinctive will to survive, namely, the existence of self. Yet, the dynamics of identification lead to different understandings of self, hence different meanings of one's power has for a particular self. A state will pursue power with its friend (an extension of the self) to achieve their collective-self interests, and will compete for power with its foe (an anathema to the self) to secure their respective self interests, all of which, to achieve one ultimate goal — striving for survival.

Balance of Power — A Cause for Power Competition and a Basis of Order

The presence of power balance between states is a cause for power competition among them. When power balance exists between states, no one is in a dominant position.[36] Hence, the states concerned compete with each other for dominance, prevent the counterparts from becoming a dominant power, and aim to secure their respective survival.[37]

The tendency to compete spawns negative identifications between the states involved, as power competition denotes "more for one actor means less for another".[38] As Wendt writes, "conceptions of self and interest tend to 'mirror' the practices of significant others over time".[39] When a party acts in ways that the receiving party perceives as threatening, driven by its intrinsic consciousness of survival which stems from its corporate identity, the receiving party will react in a similar way so as to protect itself from being threatened.[40] As Waltz observes, "competition produces a tendency toward the sameness of the competitiors" as failure to imitate would jeopardize its very survival.[41] This dynamics of

---

[36] Hans J. Morgenthau, *Politics Among Nations: The Struggle for Power and Peace* (New York: Alfred A. Knopf, 1978), pp. 173, 215. Also see Mearsheimer, *The Tragedy of Great Power Politics*, p. 21.

[37] Ibid.

[38] Dunne and Schmidt, "Realism", p. 172.

[39] Wendt, "Anarchy is What States Make of It", p. 404.

[40] Wendt, "Collective Identity Formation and the International State", p. 385. Also see ibid., pp. 404–7.

[41] Kenneth N. Waltz, *Theory of International Politics* (Canada: Addison-Wesley Publishing Company, 1979), pp. 127–28.

"competition breeds competition" reflects the mutually reinforcing effect of the negative identifications between competing states, which motivates them to understand each other in egoistic terms.

Power balance between states, meanwhile, serves as a basis of order among them. Order is "peaceful coexistence under conditions of scarcity".[42] By peaceful coexistence, it means states coexist without a war in a significant period of time.

Because of the presence of power balance between the states concerned, no one among them has the military capacity to prevail over the others, yet each of them is able to defend itself against the attack of the counterparts. As a result, the states concerned would find it very costly to turn their conflicts into a war between them.[43] The power balance, therefore, furnishes a basis of order between the states concerned. It hinders them from launching a war against each other, and in consequence, they coexist peacefully.

The following examples demonstrate that power balance between states is a cause for their power competition as well as a basis of order between them:

Power Competition between India and China and a Basis of Order between them

The relationship between India and China has been defined by their deep and enduring competition.[44]

---

[42] I. William Zartman, "The Quest for Order in World Politics", in *Imbalance of Power: US Hegemony and International Order,* edited by I. William Zartman (U.S.: Lynne Rienner Publishers, 2009), p. 3.

[43] Robert Jervis, "Security Regimes", *International Organization* 36, no. 2 (1982): 361–62. Also see Volker Rittberger, Manfred Efinger and Martin Mendler, "Toward an East–West Security Regime: The Case of Confidence- and Security-Building Measures", *Journal of Peace Research* 27, no. 1 (1990): 63–64; and Amitav Acharya, "A Regional Security Community in Southeast Asia?" in *The Transformation of Security in the Asia Pacific Region,* edited by Desmond Ball (London: Frank Cass, 1996), p. 180.

[44] John W. Garver, *Protracted Contest: Sino–Indian Rivalry in the Twentieth Century* (U.S.: University of Washington Press, 2001), pp. 4–5.

Power balance exists between the two states.[45] Both India and China are one of the largest and most populous states in the world. Each of them is also one of the most powerful military power in the world.[46] Both, in the meantime, are nuclear powers.

As neither China nor India is in a dominant position vis-à-vis the other, the two neighbouring states compete with each other to become the dominant power in their region, with the goal of securing their respective survival.[47]

India seeks to exclude China from South Asia and Indian Ocean in order to establish its dominant position in the region.[48] India believes that its existence can be best protected by acquiring such dominance.[49] It sees itself as the guarantor of peace and stability of the entire South Asian region.[50] The security of India's South Asian neighbours is perceived by India as its own security.[51] India has been trying to restrict ties between its South Asian neighbours and China.[52] It, meanwhile, forges a set of close relations with states in the Himalayan region — Nepal and Bhutan — aiming to deny China access to the region.[53] Nepal and Bhutan both are economically and militarily dependent on India.[54] In 1998, India had succeeded in becoming a nuclear power. India needs such a status to deter China's expansion into South Asia.[55]

China, on the other hand, seeks to prevent India from becoming the dominant power in South Asia, which is part of its efforts in striving to become the prominent power in Asia.[56] China wants to establish its

---

[45] Ibid., p. 11.
[46] "The 'Power Index' Measures the 10 Most Powerful Militaries in the World", *Business Insider Australia*, 13 June 2013, available at <http://www.businessinsider.com.au/10-most-powerful-militaries-in-the-world-2013-6?op=1#3-china-8> (accessed 9 July 2014).
[47] Garver, *Protracted Contest*, pp. 11, 14, 16, 29–30.
[48] Ibid., pp. 16–18, 21.
[49] Ibid.
[50] Ibid.
[51] Ibid.
[52] Ibid., p. 31.
[53] Ibid., p. 5.
[54] Ibid., p. 30.
[55] Ibid., pp. 8, 14, 30–31.
[56] Ibid., pp. 14–15, 29–30.

dominance in Asia so as to ensure that its survival would not be threatened by other powers.[57] China believes that an Indian-dominated South Asia would become a threat to its southwestern territories.[58] It maintains a strategic partnership with Pakistan, aiming to weaken India's standing in South Asia.[59] Pakistan has been receiving crucial military assistance from China.[60] Also China makes use of the smaller South Asian states' resistance to India's domination to undermine India's influence in the region.[61] It develops close military ties with these smaller South Asian states, providing them with military technology.[62]

The prolonged rivalries between India and China had led to a war between them in 1962 and a series of their militarized confrontations and intense political conflicts.[63]

The presence of power balance between India and China, however, functions as a basis of order between them. The two states have not plunged into a war between them since their war in 1962. Both parties have been struggling to preserve their peaceful coexistence as war between them is very costly.[64]

Franco–German Competition and a Basis of Order between them

A unified German state was established in January 1871 after Prussia defeated France in the Franco–Prussian War in 1870. Prussia annexed the French provinces of Alsace and Lorraine at the end of the war, making them part of the new Germany. The southern German states, in the meantime, had decided to join the newly unified German state. From 1870 onwards, Germany emerged as a powerful state on the European continent.[65]

---

[57] Ibid.
[58] Ibid.
[59] Ibid., p. 5.
[60] Ibid.
[61] Ibid., pp. 17, 19, 30.
[62] Ibid., pp. 21, 30.
[63] Ibid., pp. 3–5.
[64] Ibid., pp. 3, 9.
[65] Mearsheimer, *The Tragedy of Great Power Politics*, pp. 183–86.

Power balance existed between Germany and France after 1870 even though Germany had become a powerful state. While Germany possessed the strongest army in Europe, the French army, however, was not substantially weaker than the German army.[66]

As no one was in a dominant position in Europe, France and Germany competed with one another to become the dominant power in the region.[67] Germany was consistent in striving to expand its industrial might and military capacity.[68] It established an alliance with Russia and Austria in 1873, aiming to permanently prevent France from becoming the dominant power in Europe.[69] The triple alliance collapsed in 1875. In that same year, Germany threatened to go to war with France when France was moving towards expanding its armed forces.[70] France sought for Britain's and Russia's assistance to deter Germany's aggression.[71]

France embarked on an aggressive military expansion since 1886, talking about its revenge against Germany.[72] Germany in response openly warned of a war with France and strengthened the momentum of its military expansion.[73] It signed a treaty with Russia in 1887, aiming to forestall a military alliance between France and Russia.[74] Years later, France and Russia had moved to form an alliance against Germany.

Despite the intense competition between Germany and France following the unification of Germany, there was no war between the two states in the four decades since 1871. The power balance between them furnished a basis of order in their relations.

---

[66] Ibid.
[67] Paul R. Hensel, "The Evolution of the Franco–German Rivalry", in *Great Power Rivalries,* edited by William R. Thompson (U.S.: University of South Carolina Press, 1999), p. 101. Also see Thomas G. Otte, "From 'War-in-Sight' to Nearly War: Anglo–French Relations in the Age of High Imperialism, 1875–1898", *Diplomacy & Statecraft* 17, no. 4 (2006): 701–3.
[68] Mearsheimer, *The Tragedy of Great Power Politics*, p. 188.
[69] Otte, "From 'War-in-Sight' to Nearly War", pp. 695–96.
[70] Ibid.
[71] Ibid. Also see Mearsheimer, *The Tragedy of Great Power Politics*, p. 184.
[72] Otte, "From 'War-in-Sight' to Nearly War", pp. 701–3. Also see Hensel, "The Evolution of the Franco–German Rivalry", p. 101.
[73] Ibid.
[74] Ibid. Also see Mearsheimer, *The Tragedy of Great Power Politics*, pp. 184–86.

Germany's desire to invade France had been deterred by the military power of France alone as well as that of Russia and Britain.[75] Germany understood that it had yet to be powerful enough to secure a victory in its annexation of French territories, even if the territories were defended by French alone.[76] Germany was also aware that Britain and Russia would come to France's assistance if it invaded France.[77] Britain and Russia would not accept Germany's emergence as the dominant power in Europe.[78]

France's intention to attack Germany, on the other hand, had been effectively hampered by the fact that Germany's military power was relatively stronger than that of France.[79]

The presence of power balance between Germany and France generated great cost for them if they were to engage in a war with each other. The two states, as a consequence, coexisted peacefully from 1871 to 1914.

Started from early 1900s, the balance of power between Germany and France began to tilt towards Germany.[80] The German army was the world's most powerful one by the early 1900s.[81] Germany became the strongest industrial power in Europe during the same period.[82] Germans were increasingly convinced that their nation-state would become the dominant power in Europe. Since then Germany began to pursue an aggressive and expansionist policy.[83] It decided to build a formidable navy that would challenge Britain's naval supremacy.[84] Germany's expansionism persisted until the outbreak of the First World War in 1914.[85]

---

[75] Mearsheimer, *The Tragedy of Great Power Politics*, pp. 183–88.

[76] Ibid.

[77] Ibid.

[78] Otte, "From 'War-in-Sight' to Nearly War", p. 696.

[79] Mearsheimer, *The Tragedy of Great Power Politics*, p. 186.

[80] Ibid., p. 188.

[81] Ibid.

[82] Ibid.

[83] Ibid. Also see Hensel, "The Evolution of the Franco–German Rivalry", p. 101.

[84] Ibid.

[85] Ibid.

Imbalance of Power — An Accelerator of War or a Basis of Peace

The presence of power imbalance between states will lead to two different outcomes. Either power imbalance will become an accelerator of war between the states concerned or it will serve as a basis of peace between them.

Power Imbalance — An Accelerator of War

When power imbalance exists between states, the weaker ones view the immense power of their overwhelmingly powerful counterpart as a threat to their survival. They therefore intensify their defense against their mighty counterpart with the goal of securing their existence. In the face of its weaker counterparts' resistance to its expression of dominance over them, the overwhelmingly powerful state — among the states concerned — in consequence will turn the dominant behaviours into confrontational ones.

The weaker states' determination to confront the dominance of their overwhelmingly powerful counterpart and the subsequent response of the powerful one to turn the dominant behaviours into its confrontations against its weaker counterparts intensify the hostilities between the two parties. The intensification of hostilities often leads to a war between the strong and the weak. In other words, the power imbalance between the states concerned is an accelerator of war between them.

Power Imbalance — A Basis of Peace

When power imbalance exists between states, the weaker ones funda-mentally rely upon the immense power of their overwhelmingly powerful counterpart to safeguard their survival. In the meantime, the overwhelmingly powerful one — among the states concerned — is strategically dependent on its weaker counterparts to form its international strategic preponderance, which ultimately protects its very existence.

Because the weaker states — among the states concerned — need their overwhelmingly powerful counterpart to protect their survival, they therefore have to accept the dominance of their mighty counterpart and cease their confrontational behaviours against the counterpart. In other words, the overwhelmingly powerful state — among the states concerned

— is able to express its dominance over its weaker counterparts. Such dominant behaviours, in the meantime, have been partially defused by the overwhelmingly powerful state's strategic reliance on its weaker counterparts. Consequently, the overwhelmingly powerful state's dominant behaviours towards its weaker counterparts will not become confrontational ones.

In short, the power imbalance between the states concerned ensures the absence of confrontation among them. It serves as a basis of peace between these states.

The following examples show the two different outcomes of the presence of power imbalance between states:

Power Imbalance between China and Vietnam — An Accelerator of War

China had always been unequally stronger than Vietnam.[86] Historically, China had shown a tendency to dominate Vietnam.[87] The resistance to China's dominance has been a key feature of Vietnamese national consciousness.[88]

Because of China's immense power vis-à-vis Vietnam, Vietnam is always fearful and suspicious of China — its northern neighbour.[89] It perceives China as its principal rival and a threat to its survival.[90] Vietnam was always determined to confront China's dominance, aiming to safeguard Vietnam's existence.[91] As China was facing resistance from Vietnam amidst its expression of dominance over Vietnam, such dominant behaviours turned into confrontational ones. Vietnam's

---

[86] Brantly Womack, *China and Vietnam: The Politics of Asymmetry* (New York: Cambridge University Press, 2006), p. 1.

[87] Ibid., pp. 2, 9–10, 191, 193, 209.

[88] Ibid., pp. 24, 191. Also see Nguyen Nam Duong, "Vietnamese Foreign Policy Since *Doi Moi*: The Dialectic of Power and Identity", PhD dissertation, The University of New South Wales, 2010, p. 61.

[89] Womack, *China and Vietnam*, p. 9.

[90] Ibid., p. 10. Also see William R. Thompson, "Why Rivalries Matter and What Great Power Rivalries Can Tell Us About World Politics", in *Great Power Rivalries*, p. 12.

[91] Womack, *China and Vietnam*, pp. 2, 9–10, 209.

refusal to become a deferential client to China after the end of the Vietnam War had contributed to China's decision to invade Vietnam in 1979.[92]

Vietnam's determination to confront China's dominance and China's subsequent response to turn the dominant behaviours into confrontational ones intensified the two states' hostilities towards each other, which often led to a war between them.[93] In other words, the power imbalance between China and Vietnam was an accelerator of war between them.

In January 1974, China's navy attacked the South Vietnamese troops stationed on the Paracels Islands and took control of the islands since then. In February 1979, China invaded Vietnam and captured five capitals of Vietnam's provinces bordering China. China announced its withdrawal from Vietnam shortly after it had succeeded in occupying all of the five capitals. The withdrawal was completed by 16 March 1979. In early 1988, a fierce battle broke out between China's and Vietnam's navies in area around the Spratly Islands. The two states each had claimed sovereignty over these islands. Vietnam's navy was quickly defeated by China's in the battle. Seventy Vietnamese sailors had been killed in the battle.

Power Imbalance between Russia and Finland — An Accelerator of War

For centuries, Finland was under the domination of Russia.[94] It was part of Russia since the early eighteenth century. Finland declared its independence on 6 December 1917 shortly after the revolution of Russia, which took place in March that year. Getting rid of the Russian troops on Finland's soils was the prime goal of the Finnish government during the first years of Finland's independence.[95]

Russia was overwhelmingly stronger than Finland.[96] In the eyes of Finland, Russia was its traditional enemy and the prime threat to

---

[92] Ibid., pp. 187–88, 192–94, 209.

[93] Ibid., pp. 26–27, 191–94, 209.

[94] Eloise Engle and Lauri Paananen, *The Winter War: The Soviet Attack on Finland 1939–1940* (U.S.: Stackpole Books, 1992), pp. xiii–xiv.

[95] Ibid.

[96] D.G. Kirby, *Finland in the Twentieth Century* (U.S.: University of Minnesota Press, 1979), p. 122.

its survival.[97] Since its independence, Finland had been finding ways to confront Russia's dominance with the goal of protecting Finland's existence. It proposed the formation of some kind of alliance between Finland, Sweden and the three Baltic states within the framework of the League of Nations to confront the perceived threat posed by the Soviet Union.[98] Finland associated with the Western powers — Britain and France — and Germany, hoping that they would protect the existence of Finland.[99] Finland also sought to establish a defensive alliance with Sweden.[100] In the early 1930s, the Soviet proposed the formation of an eastern security system. It tried to include Finland in this architecture.[101] Finland was hostile to the Soviet proposal.[102] It responded by declaring its solidarity with the Nordic neutrals.[103]

Russia was facing Finland's resistance in its move to dominate Finland. Finland's attempt to form an alliance within the League of Nations against the Soviet prompted the Soviet hostilities towards Finland.[104] Confronted with Finland's resistance, Russia's expression of dominance over Finland began to turn into confrontational ones. In 1935, Russia informed Finland that it might have to occupy parts of Finland to fortify the security of Russia should war break out between the Soviet and Germany.[105]

The Soviet continued to sought ways to incorporate Finland into its sphere of influence to safeguard its own survival. In the face of an increasingly aggressive Nazi Germany, Russia began to demand territorial concessions from Finland since 1938.[106] Russia wanted to set up its military bases in these territories, aiming to prevent Germany from invading Russia through Finland.[107] Russia's demand for territorial

---

[97] Ibid., pp. 106–8, 115.
[98] Ibid., pp. 112–13.
[99] Ibid., pp. 107, 110–11, 115–16.
[100] Ibid., pp. 112–13, 116.
[101] Ibid., pp. 115–16.
[102] Ibid.
[103] Ibid.
[104] Ibid., p. 115.
[105] Ibid., p. 117.
[106] Ibid., pp. 117–21.
[107] Ibid., pp. 109–10, 117–21.

concessions was accompanied by its offer of economic and military assistance to Finland.

Finland adamantly rejected Russia's demand.[108] It perceived such demand as Russia's attempt to dominate Finland.[109] Finland was fully aware of the risk of a war with Russia — its giant neighbour — which would be brought about by its decision to deny Russia access to its territories.[110] It moved to mobilize its army to prepare for a possible war with Russia.[111]

Finland's determination to resist Russia's dominance led to Russia's decision to confront Finland.[112] The two states' hostilities towards each other had been intensified as a result.[113] Russia invaded Finland in November 1939. The power imbalance between the two states had been an accelerator of war between them. The world's largest military power — Russia — had invaded one of the world's smallest states — Finland.[114] Finland capitulated in March 1940. Russia in the end had acquired more territories from Finland than it previously demanded.[115]

Power Imbalance between the United States and Western Europe — A Basis of Peace

The states in Western Europe relied on the overwhelmingly powerful America — a superpower — for their basic security in the face of the threat from the Soviet Union — the other superpower.[116] Meanwhile, America was strategically dependent on its weaker counterparts in Western Europe to constitute its strategic preponderance in the region in

---

[108] Ibid., pp. 121–22.

[109] Ibid., p. 118.

[110] Ibid., pp. 121–22.

[111] Ibid.

[112] Ibid., pp. 119–22.

[113] Ibid.

[114] William R. Trotter, *A Frozen Hell: The Russo–Finnish Winter War of 1939–1940* (U.S.: Algonquin Books of Chapel Hill, 1991), p. 3.

[115] Kirby, *Finland in the Twentieth Century*, pp. 128–29.

[116] Josef Joffe, "Europe's American Pacifier", *Foreign Policy*, no. 54 (1984): 67–69, 72, 74, 81–82.

order to contain the Soviet aggression.[117] Such strategic preponderance ultimately served to secure America's very survival.[118]

As the Western European states needed America to protect their survival, they therefore had to accept America's dominance and cease their confrontational behaviours against America. In other words, America was able to express its dominance over the Western European states. Such dominant behaviours, meanwhile, had been partially defused by America's strategic reliance on these states. Consequently, America's dominant behaviours towards the Western European states did not turn into confrontational ones.

The Western European states allowed America to dictate their defence policy.[119] They hosted American troops and allowed America to locate its strategic weapons on their soils.[120] Because of America's dominance, violent conflicts among the Western European states had been prevented.[121]

In other words, the power imbalance between America and Western Europe ensured the absence of confrontation between them as well as within Western Europe. The power imbalance, therefore, functioned as a basis of peace between America and Western Europe.

Peace prevailed in Western Europe since the end of the Second World War. There was no war in Western Europe and no border in the region had been changed by force.

Strategic Cooperation

Two states will cooperate with each other when they share common strategic interests.[122] As Walt writes, states will align with each other for survival when they face common external threats.[123] Both states need each

---

[117] Ibid., pp. 67, 81–82.
[118] Ibid.
[119] Ibid., pp. 68, 72.
[120] Ibid., pp. 78, 82.
[121] Ibid., pp. 66, 73–74.
[122] As defined in this study, common strategic interests of two states mean the two states rely on each other's material presence for survival. A state's strategic interest means a material presence which is fundamental to its survival.
[123] Stephen M. Walt, *The Origins of Alliances* (Ithaca and London: Cornell University Press, 1987), pp. 17–33, 147–48, 262–63.

other for survival, hence both see its counterpart's interest as its own interest, when their survival are being threatened. For example, driven by their shared perceptions of the threats posed by India, China and Pakistan each sees threat exerted by India on its counterpart as its own threat.[124] China assisted Pakistan in its development of nuclear weapons when Pakistan was threatened by India's emergence as a nuclear power.[125]

The mutual positive identifications between two states, which derive from them sharing common strategic interests, lead to the two states' shared understanding that their ties is closer than their other bilateral relations. For example, the strategic cooperation between China and Pakistan had led the former Prime Minister of Pakistan, Shaukat Aziz, to assert that the two states "enjoy all weather friendship based on complete trust and confidence".[126] Similarly, China's policymakers view Pakistan as their traditional old friend.[127] Such an understanding — that their ties is closer — generates aspiration for peace between the two states concerned while stirring up their mutual expectation that their relationship should be more intimate than their other bilateral ties owing to their shared strategic interest. The desire for peace between two states bound by strategic ties can be observed from a remark made by a Chinese top military officer on China's relations with Pakistan, "…no matter what changes may take place in international situation and in each other's country, the two peoples always support each other, sympathize with each other and help each other."[128] On the other hand, the expectation

---

[124] Swaran Singh, "Introduction", in *China–Pakistan Strategic Cooperation: Indian Perspectives,* edited by Swaran Singh (New Delhi: Manohar Publishers, 2007), p. 17.

[125] Satyabrat Sinha, "China in Pakistan's Security Perceptions", in *China–Pakistan Strategic Cooperation*, p. 93.

[126] Singh, "Introduction", pp. 17–18. Also see Former Prime Minister of Pakistan Shaukat Aziz's Inaugural Speech to the International Conference on "China and the Emerging Asian Century" at the Institute of Strategic Studies, Islamabad, 27 September 2005, quoted in Singh, "Introduction", p. 22.

[127] Anindyo J. Majumdar, "The Changing Imperatives", in *China–Pakistan Strategic Cooperation*, p. 40.

[128] "Pakistan President Meets Chinese Military Delegation", *Xinhua*, 6 May 1997, quoted in Srikanth Kondapalli, "Pakistan in China's Security Perceptions", in *China–Pakistan Strategic Cooperation*, p. 53.

dynamics between two states with strategic cooperation are illustrated by the expectation of Pakistani policymakers and experts that their state remains central to China's strategic vision of South Asia.[129]

The strategic cooperation-induced positive identifications between the two states involved may eventually result in the extension of their respective conceptions of self to each other in which both view the counterpart as part of self, namely, as a friend, hence sharing cooperative intersubjective understandings. For example, despite experiencing significant changes in the environment of world politics such as China's new rapprochement with India and improving India–Pakistan relations, China–Pakistan strategic cooperation remains astonishingly durable and comprehensive which continues to underwrite the politico-strategic dynamics in South Asia.[130] As Garver writes, "China's cooperative relation with Pakistan is arguably the most stable and durable element of China's foreign relations."[131] The enduring character of strategic ties between China and Pakistan indicates that such cooperation has been spawned and sustained by their shared cooperative intersubjective understandings.

However, two states' shared cooperative intersubjective understandings that are produced by their strategic cooperation alone are not fundamentally long-lasting. As strategic interest is a state's material interest, there is always a possibility that two states' common strategic interest will no longer exist due to the disappearance of a material presence. Once the common strategic interest vanishes, the strategic cooperation-induced positive identifications between the two states involved will come to a halt, their egoistic tendency driven by their respective corporate nature will emerge, and ultimately, weaken if not eliminate their shared cooperative intersubjective understandings.[132] For example, the intimate friendship between China and Vietnam since the 1950s had turned into implacable hostility in the mid-1970s when their common threat — the United

---

[129] Singh, "Introduction", p. 21.
[130] Singh, "Introduction", pp. 17–18. Also see Majumdar, "The Changing Imperatives", pp. 35, 39–40.
[131] Garver, *Protracted Contest*, p. 187.
[132] Wendt, "Collective Identity Formation and the International State", pp. 385, 387.

States — had ended its war in Vietnam, which subsequently gave rise to their strategic competition, namely, the two states' respective desire to dominate Indochina.[133]

IDENTITY

This section first explains the basic dynamics of identity. It spells out that a state's understanding of self is constituted by its corporate and self identities, in which an actor's sense of self underpins and spawns its will to survive. As such, an actor constantly seeks to protect and enhance its identity so as to secure a stable sense of self, which also means securing its survival. This section then reveals that national identity, founded on a nation's pre-existing ethnic community, consists of civic and ethnic elements. It explains that national identity needs to be unique, so as to mark a nation's existence vis-à-vis the world of nations. National identity, therefore, denotes a state's intrinsic consciousness to exist. It generates a state's tendency to appreciate self in egoistic terms. This section then moves to explain the double-edged effects of two states' common identities which derive from their shared ethnic pasts. While generating a shared perception among the two states concerned that they share a closer relation than their other bilateral ties, the two states' common identities, on the one hand, serve as a source of conflicts between them, hence breeds their mutual negative identifications; on the other hand, as a source of cooperation, which is interweaved with positive identifications between the two states.

The Basic Dynamics of Self

As mentioned in the previous section, corporate identity and self-identity constitute an actor's understanding of self. Driven by its corporate nature, which is its intrinsic consciousness of individual security and well-being, a state has a natural tendency of "in-group favoritism and

---

[133] Womack, *China and Vietnam*, pp. 1–2, 25–27. Also see Steven J. Hood, *Dragons Entangled: Indochina and the China–Vietnam War* (U.S.: An East Gate Book, 1992), pp. xv–xvi, 29–31.

out-group discrimination", hence is "cognitively predisposed to be self-interested" when it comes into interaction with other states.[134] Viewed in this light, the corporate nature of a state generates its tendency to understand self in egoistic terms. Yet, such a tendency does not render immutable group egoism of a state, as self-identity entails identifications with others, therefore "the boundaries of the self are not inherently limited to corporate identity".[135]

An actor's sense of self serves as the foundation of its natural will to survive. By referring identity as "ego identity", Erikson observed that, "…in the social jungle of human existence, there is no feeling of being alive without a sense of ego identity."[136] An actor will read its survival as under threat when its sense of self is in jeopardy. As a consequence, an actor constantly seeks to protect and enhance its identity, so as to acquire a stable sense of self which equally means securing its very survival.[137] Such dynamics can be observed from the fact that millions of people in the past two centuries were willing to die for their "nation", an identity which is founded on the fraternal association of a particular population.[138] In sum, the in-group or inter-groups identification of a state essentially concerns its sense of self which underpins and spawns its will to survive.

National Identity

According to Smith, a nation is a "named human population sharing an historic territory, common myths and historical memories, a mass, public culture, a common economy and common legal rights and duties for all

---

[134] Jonathon Mercer, "Anarchy, Self-Help, and Relative Gains", Stanford University, Typescript (1993), quoted in Wendt, "Collective Identity Formation and the International State", p. 387.

[135] Wendt, "Collective Identity Formation and the International State", p. 387.

[136] Erik H. Erikson, *Identity and the Life Cycle: Volume I* (U.S.: Indiana University Press, 1959), p. 89.

[137] William Bloom, *Personal Identity, National Identity and International Relations* (Cambridge: Cambridge University Press, 1990), pp. 37–40.

[138] Benedict Anderson, *Imagined Communities: Reflections on the Origin and Spread of Nationalism* (London, New York: Verso, 1991), p. 7.

members."[139] Such a definition reflects the dualistic nature of national identity in which every nation is constituted by civic and ethnic elements in "varying degrees and different forms".[140] A nation is civic in the sense that it is a political–legal community with well-defined territories, a mass public culture and a common economy.[141] It has its ethnic basis because pre-existing ethnic community forms the grounds for a claim to nationhood, in which such community provides the answer to the question of "who is the nation".[142] The culture of an ethnic community which forms a nation is usually being inculcated into its national culture through the nation's public education system, where such a public culture is ethnic as well as civic.[143]

Smith defines an ethnic community as a population with cultural collectivity that emphasizes the myths of common ancestry and shared historical memories, consists of one or more elements of shared culture, with a mythical association to specific territories and a sense of solidarity among the population.[144] Such a definition reveals the subjective nature of an *ethnie* in which it is the myths, not the facts, of common ancestry that underpin the foundation of an *ethnie*.[145] The mythical tie of an *ethnie* is essential for its survival as it is its fictive descent that generates the sense of ethnic identification.[146]

Smith observes that many modern nations have been formed around pre-existing dominant *ethnies*, for such communities, like nations, are founded on common myths and memories, and are closely associated with specific territories.[147] The boundaries and identities of a nation hence are often determined by the myths and memories of its pre-existing dominant *ethnies*.

---

[139] Anthony D. Smith, *National Identity* (London: Penguin Books, 1991), p. 14.

[140] Ibid., p. 13.

[141] Ibid., pp. 12–15, 40.

[142] Anthony D. Smith, "Theories of Nationalism: Alternative Models of Nation Formation", in *Asian Nationalism,* edited by Michael Leifer (London and New York: Routledge, 2000), p. 7.

[143] Ibid. Also see Smith, *National Identity*, pp. 13, 40, 61.

[144] Smith, *National Identity*, pp. 20–23.

[145] Ibid., p. 22.

[146] Ibid.

[147] Ibid., pp. 38–40. Also see Smith, "Theories of Nationalism", pp. 12–13.

National identity is vital for every individual. It allows people to define and locate individual self in a world of nations.[148] This explains the necessity of every nation's identity to be distinctive. As Anderson writes, "no nation imagines itself coterminous with mankind".[149] A nation needs its own character so as to ensure its existence against other nations. Such a requirement underpins the importance of a community's ethnic past, as it furnishes the reservoir of historical culture for the population to rediscover their collective identity that is unique and authentic, thereby marks their existence as a nation in the modern world.[150]

The essentiality of cultural uniqueness for a claim to nationhood underscores the indispensability of fictive common ancestry of a nation's pre-existing ethnic community. Such mythical descents allow nationalists to return, rediscover and reinterpret the *ethnie*'s glorious and moral pasts which, in turn, furnish the present generations with cognitive maps of the community's history, place and destiny that inspire and mobilize them into forming a nation based on their ethnic ties.[151]

The transformation of a pre-existing ethnic community into a modern nation takes place in the form of nationalism. Nationalism is a political ideology centred on cultural doctrine that preaches the cultural distinctiveness of an actual or potential nation.[152] Such an ideology, by reinventing an *ethnie*'s pasts into irreplaceable national identity, evokes the fraternal association of its people, summons and elevates them to the centre political stage to quest for a nation, and legitimizes the continued existence of such a nation.[153] As Smith defines, nationalism is "an ideological movement for attaining and maintaining autonomy, unity and identity on behalf of a population deemed by some of its members to constitute an actual or potential 'nation'."[154] This understanding reveals that, by pursuing autonomy, unity and identity

---

[148] Smith, *National Identity*, p. 17. Also see Anthony D. Smith, *Nations and Nationalism in a Global Era* (Cambridge: Polity Press, 1995), p. 154.

[149] Anderson, *Imagined Communities*, p. 7.

[150] Smith, *National Identity*, pp. 64, 70, 75.

[151] Ibid., pp. 64–69.

[152] Ibid., pp. 73, 74, 84.

[153] Ibid., pp. 78, 84. Also see Smith, "Theories of Nationalism", p. 1.

[154] Smith, *National Identity*, p. 73.

which are essentially founded on cultural differentiation, nationalism not only mobilizes people towards forming a nation, it also ensures people's sustained efforts in perpetuating the existence of the nation. In other words, nationalism, which realizes and legitimizes a nation, also serves as a principle that informs the nation-state's foreign policy. Through the fraternal identification, the people of a nation will preserve, defend and enhance their distinctive national identity such that the nation will not become invisible vis-à-vis the world of nations.[155] This being said, national identity constitutes the corporate identity of a state as, founded on distinctive qualities of a nation, national identity denotes a state's intrinsic consciousness to exist. The dynamics of national identity generate a state's tendency to appreciate self in egoistic terms.

The Double-edged Effects of Common Identity

The nature of a pre-modern ethnic community has crucial impacts on relations between states which originated from the same *ethnie*. An *ethnie* emphasizes on its myths of common ancestry and historical memories which form its mythical attachments to specific stretches of territory. Yet, instead of its actual residence on a land, it is the community's fictive associations with the land that contribute to ethnic identification.[156] A nation, on the other hand, is founded on myths of common descent and memories of its pre-existing *ethnie*, and possesses physical control of the territories which it considers as homeland.[157] The close relationship between a nation and an *ethnie* reveals a phenomena in which a pre-modern ethnic community continues to spawn bonds between nation-states who are founded on the *ethnie*, and possess the actual territorial control of lands within the *ethnie*'s associating sacred territories. As Huntington had pointed out, a civilization usually stretches across several nation-states as in the case of Latin American and Arab civilizations.[158]

---

[155] Ibid., p. 70. Also see Bloom, *Personal Identity, National Identity and International Relations*, pp. 26, 79.

[156] Smith, *National Identity*, p. 23.

[157] Ibid., p. 40.

[158] Samuel P. Huntington, "The Clash of Civilizations?" *Foreign Affairs* 72, no. 3 (1993): 24.

Because of their mutual positive identifications that stem from their common ethnic ties, two nation-states who originate from the same *ethnie* share an understanding that their relationship is closer than their other bilateral relationships. For example, states that associate with each other based on cultural affinities such as Pan-Arabism, Pan-Africanism and Pan-Latin-Americanism, where through such associations advocate their cultural closeness, and in turn, set them apart from the culturally different others.[159] Such an understanding — that their relationship is closer — generates aspiration for peace between the two nation-states who share common ethnic pasts while stirring up their mutual expectation that their relationship should be more intimate than their relations with culturally different others. For example, at the peak of Pan-Arabism between 1940s and late 1960s, such cultural closeness evoked the desire for peace among Arab states where they advocated Arab unity as their transcendent goal.[160] On the other hand, the expectation dynamics between nation-states with cultural affinity are exemplified by the breaking-off of relations between Saudi Arabia and Egypt shortly after Egypt had reached a peace agreement with Israel in 1979. Saudi felt betrayed and was infuriated by Egypt as it did not match with Saudi's expectation that, as a member of the Arab World, Egypt should stand together with its culturally affiliated Arabian states in their struggle against Israeli, their common enemy with different culture, instead of having a separate peace with Israel.[161]

However, although two nation-states originating from the same *ethnie* share the perception of having a close relationship, their common identity spawns paradoxical impacts on their bilateral relations.

---

[159] Smith, *Nations and Nationalism in a Global Era*, pp. 119–20.

[160] Fouad Ajami, "The End of Pan-Arabism", in *Pan-Arabism and Arab Nationalism: The Continuing Debate,* edited by Tawfic E. Farah (Boulder and London: Westview Press, 1987), p. 96. Also see Elie Chalala, "Arab Nationalism: A Bibliographic Essay", in *Pan-Arabism and Arab Nationalism*, p. 18.

[161] Bassam Tibi, *Conflict and War in the Middle East: From Interstate War to New Security* (New York: St. Martion's Press, 1998), pp. 139–41. Also see Ajami, "The End of Pan-Arabism", p. 108; and Abdul-Monem Al-Mashat, "Stress and Disintegration in the Arab World", in *Pan-Arabism and Arab Nationalism*, pp. 170–73.

Such common identity, which rests on their common ethnic pasts, is a source of conflicts as well as a source of cooperation for the two states involved.

As every national identity needs to be unique for the sake of a nation-state's existence vis-à-vis other nations, nation-states, even though founded on the same *ethnie*, have to explain their respective cultural distinctiveness based on their common mythical ethnic pasts. As a consequence, the inevitable similarities in their national identities due to their common origins strengthen the need of the nation-states involved to emphasize their respective distinctive qualities. In other words, because they are similar hence they, in fact, need to enhance their differences. Such necessities of differentiating self from the sameness spur conflicts between the nation-states involved.

This phenomenon can be observed from the relationships between the United States and Canada and the relations among the Arab states. Underpinned by their common identity which derives from their shared Anglo-Saxon heritage, and facilitated by their geographical proximity, the United States and Canada have experienced "unparalleled cultural and commercial integration of two national societies".[162] The high degree of integration and similarities between the two states pose great concerns among Canadians on their existence vis-à-vis the ubiquitous presence of predominantly powerful Americans.[163] Such worries are exemplified by a Canadian who wrote about Australia with envy: "They (Australians)

---

[162] Sean M. Shore, "No Fences Make Good Neighbors: The Development of the Canadian–US Security Community, 1871–1940", in *Security Communities,* edited by Emanuel Adler and Michael Barnett (Cambridge: Cambridge University Press, 1998), p. 335. Also see Albert K. Weinberg, *Manifest Destiny: A Study of Nationalist Expansionism in American History* (Chicago: Quadrangle Books, 1963), p. 363; Srdjan Vucetic, "The Anglosphere: A Genealogy of an Identity in International Relations", PhD dissertation, The Ohio State University, 2008, p. ii; Stephane Roussel, *The North American Democratic Peace: Absence of War and Security Institution-Building in Canada–US Relations, 1867–1958* (Montreal and Kingston, London, Ithaca: McGill-Queen's University Press, 2004), p. 78; and John Sloan Dickey, *Canada and the American Presence: The United States Interest in an independent Canada* (New York: New York University Press, 1975), p. 180.

[163] Dickey, *Canada and the American Presence*, p. 80.

worry not at all about the preservation of their national identity. Who could ever mistake an Australian?", in which the underlying meaning of the writing is: who could not mistake a Canadian as an American?[164] As a consequence, anti-Americanism becomes the premise of Canadian nationalism.[165] Canada seeks for its uniqueness by emphasizing its difference with its culturally similar neighbour. Bothwell has described the Canadians' sentiments about the United States in the 1960s, "For Canadians, relations between the two countries were not a means of expressing similarities but of defining and even amplifying differences."[166] Such conscious efforts to draw distinctions culminate in Canada and the United States to routinely embroil in myriad of policy disputes such as Canadian government's insistence to maintain its peacekeeping role in Vietnam instead of joining the war with the United States in Vietnam during the 1960s, and its criticisms on the U.S.'s efforts to escalate this war; Canadian government's decision not to participate in the U.S.-led invasion of Iraq in 2003 on the basis that such a military intervention should not be implemented without a UN mandate, and the criticisms by the majority members of the then ruling Liberal Party that such an invasion was unnecessary.[167]

For the Arab states, on the other hand, the dynamics of common identity in the name of Pan-Arabism or Pan-Islamism have prompted some of them to emphasize on their unique national identities so as to assert their respective existence amid the cultural similarities in the Arab World.[168] Consequently, the differentiating dynamics between

---

[164] Speech to Hamilton Canadian Club, 29 April 1964. In Arnold D.P. Heeney Papers, MG 30 E144, Vol. 10, NAC, quoted in Vucetic, "The Anglosphere", p. 183.

[165] Dickey, *Canada and the American Presence*, p. 72. Also see Vucetic, "The Anglosphere", p. 182.

[166] Robert Bothwell, *Alliance and Illusion: Canada and The World, 1945–1984* (Vancouver and Toronto: UBC Press, 2007), p. 215.

[167] David G. Haglund, "The US–Canada Relationship: How 'Special' is America's Oldest Unbroken Alliance?" in *America's 'Special Relationships': Foreign and Domestic Aspects of the Politics of Alliance,* edited by John Dumbrell and Axel R. Schafer (London and New York: Routledge, 2009), p. 68. Also see Vucetic, "The Anglosphere", pp. 207–10, 220, 229–30, 279.

[168] Al-Mashat, "Stress and Disintegration in the Arab World", pp. 171–73. Also see Ajami, "The End of Pan-Arabism", p. 98.

nationalisms and Pan-Arab or Pan-Islamic identity have become the sources of tensions among the Arab states.[169] For example, Iraq's accentuation on its sovereignty rather than embracing Arab unity in the late 1950s had resulted in the escalation of its tensions with Egypt.[170] Similarly, Egypt's advocation of "Egyptianism" against Pan-Islamism in the late 1970s had led to its serious conflicts with Saudi Arabia.[171]

In sum, because of a nation-state's basic needs to be unique, nation-states' common identities which derive from their shared ethnic pasts become a source of conflicts between them. The nation-states concerned consciously seek to enhance their differences out of their sameness in the form of national identities, consequently, breed negative identifications between them, strengthening their respective tendency to understand each other in egoistic terms.

Paradoxically, such common identities, on the other hand, spawn positive identifications between the nation-states involved. As Huntington has observed, groups or states which come from the same civilization naturally associate positively with each other, in which civilization commonality underpins cooperation between them particularly amid the coexistence with other civilizations.[172] The cultural affinity-induced positive identifications may eventually result in the extension of the appreciations of self of the two states involved to each other, which ultimately lead them to understand the counterpart as part of self, hence sharing cooperative intersubjective understandings. For example, because of their shared identity founded on common Anglo-Saxon heritage, the United States, United Kingdom, Canada, Australia and New Zealand view each other as collective-self, in which violent conflict between them is unthinkable, namely, they constitute a security community, and cooperation among them are deep, which entail the "most sensitive areas of state sovereignty".[173]

---

[169] Al-Mashat , "Stress and Disintegration in the Arab World", pp. 167, 171–73.
[170] Walt, *The Origins of Alliances*, pp. 74–75.
[171] Al-Mashat, "Stress and Disintegration in the Arab World", pp. 171–73. Also see Tibi, *Conflict and War in the Middle East*, pp. 139–41.
[172] Huntington, "The Clash of Civilizations?", p. 35.
[173] Vucetic, "The Anglosphere", pp. 2, 22.

The cultural affinity-induced positive identifications between the states involved will intensify when they coexist with other states founded on different *ethnies*, especially when these culturally different states pose threats to them. As Huntington has pointed out, the increasing interactions between different civilizations intensify civilization consciousness and awareness of commonalities within a civilization and differences between civilizations.[174] Such intensification of positive identifications between the states which share common identities enhances the saliency of their common strategic outlook, hence results in the deepening of their cooperation when confronted with perceived threats posed by culturally different others. For example, during the Cold War, the United States and Canada, bound by their common Anglo-Saxon identity, had forged between them one of the closest military alliance in the world to resist their perceived common external threat exerted by the culturally different Soviet Unions.[175]

EXPECTATION

As mentioned in previous sections, when two states perceive that they share a closer relation than their other bilateral ties, it consequently stirs up their mutual expectation that both should be more intimate than their relationships with others. Such an expectation often produces paradoxical effects on the relations between the two states involved.

An expectation is an assumed result.[176] Because of them sharing a perception of having closer relations than their other bilateral ties, the two states concerned logically assume that the counterpart should act in ways which are consistent with such a perception. For example, in the early 1940s, because of their common culture and historical ties, Britian perceived its relations with the United States as a relationship of family ties.[177] Such view produced Britain's tendency to expect that the

---

[174] Huntington, "The Clash of Civilizations?", p. 25.
[175] Haglund, "The US–Canada Relationship", pp. 61, 64–65. Also see Dickey, *Canada and the American Presence*, p. 77.
[176] James P. Leahy, *Bridging the Expectation Gap: The Key to Happiness* (U.S.: AuthorHouse, 2006), p. xi.
[177] David Reynolds, *The Creation of the Anglo-American Alliance 1937–41: A Study in Competitive Co-operation* (London: Europa Publications Limited, 1981), pp. 287, 293.

United States should help them in facing the threat from Nazi Germany, and would eventually join Britain in its war against Nazi Germany.[178] The expectation held by Britain on the United States was illustrated by Churchill's firm determination to fight on against Nazi Germany amid the pressure that called for a compromise peace as he assumed that the U.S., because of their intimate ties, would eventually join them to fight the Nazi Germany.[179]

Owing to the fact that expectation is an assumed but not an actual result, it hence leads to one outcome or another, namely, match or mismatch of expectation. Such different outcomes produce virtually opposite effects. As Leahy has observed, when expectation is met, a person will experience happiness, and when expectation is not met, a person will experience disappointment.[180] Fairlie, on the other hand, discerns that in the atmosphere of high expectation, people's unmet expectation would turn into forces rife with frustration.[181] As relations among states are essentially operated by humans, such expectation dynamics apply to the relationships between two states.

For two states sharing a perception of having closer relations than their other bilateral ties, when either of the states' expectation on its counterpart has been matched by the counterpart's intention, substantial cooperation between them will be produced and the positive identifications among them will be reinforced. For example, between 1950s and 1975, because of their close ties that derives from revolutionary comradeship of communist parties, Vietnam expected lavish aid and advice from China in its struggle against France and later the United States for independence.[182] Such an expectation was matched by China's intention to provide unrestricted support to Vietnam owing to their communist fraternal ties, China's desire to export its model of successful revolution

---

[178] Ibid., pp. 10, 287, 293.
[179] Ibid.
[180] Leahy, *Bridging the Expectation Gap*, p. x.
[181] Henry Fairlie, *The Kennedy Promise: The Politics of Expectation* (London: Eyre Methuen, 1973), pp. 13–15.
[182] Womack, *China and Vietnam*, pp. 162–63.

and to extend its influence abroad.[183] As a consequence, the cooperation between the two states in these years was intense and intimate, where their relationship was often being described — "as close as lips and teeth", and Vietnam expressed its gratitude for China's friendship and wholehearted support.[184]

On the other hand, when either of the states' expectation on its counterpart does not match with the counterpart's intention, the positive identifications that come with the expectation quickly turn into acute negative identifications between them and substantial conflicts among them ensued. For example, after Vietnam's victory in the Vietnam War and the subsequent reunification of the state, China expected Vietnam to be a grateful and deferential client, willing to forswear its ties with China's rival — the Soviet Union, and request less aid from China.[185] Such an expectation did not match with Vietnam's intention. Vietnam intended to be an independent power and had the desire to consolidate its sphere of influence in Indochina. Thus, it declined to join China in its struggle against the Soviet Union and instead, forged closer ties with the Soviet.[186] As a consequence, the unfulfilled expectation led China to interpret Vietnam's uncooperative behaviour as a sign of hostility, consequently, it refused to provide new aid to Vietnam in response to such perceived hostility.[187] Vietnam subsequently moved toward an alliance with the Soviet Union which culminated in China's invasion of Vietnam in February 1979.[188]

In sum, the dynamics of expectation generates double-edged effects on relations between the two states involved. The matching of expectation results in substantial cooperation between them. The mismatch of expectation, on the other hand, leads to substantial conflicts between them.

---

[183] Ibid.

[184] Ibid., pp. 162–63, 187.

[185] Ibid., pp. 186, 188.

[186] Ibid., pp. 188, 192–93. Also see Hood, *Dragons Entangled*, pp. 34–35.

[187] Ibid., pp. 190–92. Also see Hood, *Dragons Entangled*, p. 34.

[188] Ibid., pp. 190–92. Also see Hood, *Dragons Entangled*, pp. 34–35, 50–51.

NORMS

Norms are "collective expectations for the proper behaviour of actors with a given identity".[189] Norms hence understandably are derived from an actor's identity. For example, as Berger has observed, antimilitarism, which constitutes the integral part of Germany's and Japan's national identities after their disastrous defeat in the Second World War, has rendered the two states very reluctant in resorting to the use of military force in pursuing national objectives.[190] They have adhered to such norms despite experiencing tremendous changes in post-1945 international environment and the augmentation of their respective power, which periodically required the two states to reconsider their antimilitary stands.[191]

Once established, Acharya writes, "norms have a life of their own".[192] They produce independent effects that shape an actor's behaviour, and redefine its identity and interest.[193] In other words, established norms become the intersubjective understandings shared by the actors involved, in which norms shape, and are shaped by, their conception of self.[194] For example, in the mid-1980s, rooted in new collective understandings about international politics and their evolving identities, the reformers in the Soviet Union, under the leadership of Mikhail Gorbachev, had ushered in new political order to the Soviet that envisioned the USSR as a democratic and peaceable state which believed in values

---

[189] Peter J. Katzenstein, "Introduction: Alternative Perspectives on National Security", in *The Culture of National Security: Norms and Identity in World Politics*, edited by Peter J. Katzenstein (New York: Columbia University Press, 1996*b*), p. 5. Also see Ronald L. Jepperson, Alexander Wendt, and Peter J. Katzenstein, "Norms, Identity, and Culture in National Security", in *The Culture of National Security*, p. 54.

[190] Thomas U. Berger, "Norms, Identity, and National Security in Germany and Japan", in *The Culture of National Security*, pp. 317–18, 330–33.

[191] Ibid., pp. 317–18, 332, 355.

[192] Amitav Acharya, *Constructing a Security Community in Southeast Asia: ASEAN and the Problems of Regional Order* (London and New York: Routledge, 2001), p. 24.

[193] Ibid.

[194] Wendt, "Anarchy is What States Make of It", 397–99. Also see Checkel, "The Constructivist Turn in International Relations Theory", pp. 327–28.

common to all mankind.[195] Such norms, encapsulated in the term — "New Thinking", generated independent effects once they were incorporated in the reformative policy prescriptions introduced by the Soviet leaders. The implementation of the "New Thinking" norms precipitated more radical reforms in the Soviet, and later resulted in the collapse of the Warsaw Pact regimes, where such norms triggered the popular uprisings in the Soviet's Eastern European allies, and rendered Moscow to adhere to the new norm of not imposing its will — especially by using force — on its Warsaw Pact allies to crush these uprisings.[196] The dramatic events that ensued after the introduction of the "New Thinking" norms demonstrated that, even though it was the Soviet leaders that initiated the forming of the new norms, once established, such norms by themselves were able to engender effects which were independent of, and well beyond the control of, the Soviet leaders.

Norms generate either regulative or both regulative and constitutive effects on actors. Norms, on the one hand, regulate the behaviours of an actor by prescribing standards of proper behaviours of a defined identity.[197] The regulatory effects of norms can be discerned from relations among states which constitute a security regime. The behaviours of states in a security regime are restricted by discernable war avoidance norms, in which each member state expects others to reciprocate.[198] However, such norms in a security regime are yet to constitute the collective-self identity among its member states, which would ensure the total absence of possible violent conflict among them as each views others as part of self. In a security regime, despite the presence of war avoidance norms, member states are still engaged in competitive military build-up.[199] On the other hand, norms define an actor's identity by specifying actions which

---

[195] Robert G. Herman, "Identity, Norms, and National Security: The Soviet Foreign Policy Revolution and the End of the Cold War", in *The Culture of National Security*, pp. 271–75, 311.

[196] Ibid., 305–7.

[197] Katzenstein, "Introduction: Alternative Perspectives on National Security", p. 5. Also see Jepperson, Wendt and Katzenstein, "Norms, Identity, and Culture in National Security", p. 54.

[198] Acharya, "A Regional Security Community in Southeast Asia?", pp. 180, 191.

[199] Ibid.

reflect that particular identity.[200] For example, in a security community, the practice of peaceful change by the member states constitutes their extension of self-conception to each other, thereby, reinforces the mutually identifying "we-feeling" among them.[201]

Norms can be categorized into social and legal norms. Social norms spawn informal social controls.[202] While legal norms, which are the formal laws, "become most effective when informal social controls break down".[203] As Acharya has pointed out, a security community is essentially founded on social norms instead of the legal ones.[204] Deutsch has described the presence of peaceful change among states in a security community as rooted in them sharing a sense of community where each views others as part of self.[205] This points to the fact that the norm of peaceful change that constitutes a security community is by nature social, as the norm is fundamentally upheld and sustained by the social bonds shared among the member states.

As mentioned in previous sections, when two states share a perception where their relationship is closer than their other bilateral ties, such a perception spawns aspiration for peace between them. The aspiration for peace indicates their tendency to eschew from possible violent conflict between them, hence serves as the foundation for the emergence of war avoidance norms shared by the two states. For example, since the late 1970s, the desire for peace between Argentina and Brazil, which stems

---

[200] Katzenstein, "Introduction: Alternative Perspectives on National Security", p. 5. Also see Jepperson, Wendt and Katzenstein, "Norms, Identity, and Culture in National Security", p. 54.

[201] Karl W. Deutsch, Sidney A. Burrell, Robert A. Kann, Maurice Lee, Jr., Martin Lichterman, Raymond E. Lindgren, Francis L. Loewenheim, and Richard W. Van Wagenen, *Political Community and the North Atlantic Area: International Organization in the Light of Historical Experience* (Princeton, NJ: Princeton University Press, 1957), pp. 5, 129. Also see Checkel, "The Constructivist Turn in International Relations Theory", pp. 327–28; Wendt, "Anarchy is What States Make of It", pp. 400–1; Wendt, "Collective Identity Formation and the International State", p. 386.

[202] Acharya, *Constructing a Security Community in Southeast Asia*, p. 25.

[203] Peter J. Katzenstein, *Cultural Norms and National Security: Police and Military in Postwar Japan* (Ithaca and London: Cornell University Press, 1996a), p. 43.

[204] Acharya, *Constructing a Security Community in Southeast Asia*, p. 25.

[205] Deutsch et al., *Political Community and the North Atlantic Area*, pp. 5, 129.

from their similar Latin American culture, has contributed to them sharing war avoidance practices such as confidence building measures, arms control agreements, defensive military posture and reduction in military spending.[206] However, the war prevention norms spawned by the aspiration for peace between two states do not mean the permanent elimination of possible armed conflict between them, namely, the existence of a security community. States might still engage in competitive military practices while adhering to war avoidance norms. For example, despite sharing war prevention practices, Brazil's and Argentina's military practices are still essentially competitive, as exemplified by Brazil's rejection to Argentina's idea of early notification to each other their respective new arms purchases and military exercises. As such, although the presence of war avoidance norms founded on the aspiration for peace between two states is essential for them to become a security community, the existence of such norms, however, does not indicate their status as a security community.

DEPENDABLE EXPECTATIONS OF PEACEFUL CHANGE

Dependable expectations of peaceful change forms the key distinguishing feature of a security community.[207] It is stable expectations among member states in a security community where neither side would prepare or even consider to use organized violence as a means to settle interstate disputes.[208] As such, the presence of an understanding of collective-self among the states involved is necessary in order for them to entertain dependable expectations of peaceful change.[209] This is because armed conflict is unthinkable among states which view each other as part of self.

---

[206] Andrew Hurrell, "An Emerging Security Community in South America?" in *Security Communities*, pp. 228–61.

[207] Emaduel Adler and Michael Barnett, "A Framework for the Study of Security Community", in *Security Communities*, p. 34.

[208] Ibid.

[209] Ibid., pp. 38–39, 45.

The requirement of the existence of a collective-self understanding for the practice of dependable expectations of peaceful change indicates that such peaceful change functions between states which share cooperative intersubjective understandings. Cooperative intersubjective understandings are founded on the states involved sharing the conception of collective-self.[210] States embedded in such understandings view their respective interests in collective-self terms, hence pursue among them altruistic security practices, which means they do not defend themselves against each other.[211]

States practising dependable expectations of peaceful change entail three distinctive features. Among the states involved, there is the absence of war, absence of the preparation for war against each other, and absence of the consideration of waging a war against one another.[212] Viewed in this light, war avoidance norms are the foundation for the presence of dependable expectations of peaceful change among states.[213] States involved need to at least be able to avoid war between them, before they could learn to forswear competitive security measures directed at each other. In this sense, dependable expectations of peaceful change are built on norms and they, in fact, by themselves are norms. As Wendt has pointed out, intersubjective understandings are usually expressed in terms of shared norms.[214] The emergence of dependable expectations of peaceful change between states denotes the consolidation of the war avoidance norms shared by the states into their shared norms where they would not even consider using force against each other.

---

[210] Wendt, "Anarchy is What States Make of It", pp. 400–1.

[211] Ibid.

[212] Acharya, *Constructing a Security Community in Southeast Asia*, p. 16.

[213] Christopher B. Roberts, "ASEAN's Security Community Project: Challenges and Opportunities in the Pursuit of Comprehensive Integration", PhD dissertation, The University of New South Wales, 2008, pp. 73–74, 76.

[214] Wendt, "Anarchy is What States Make of It", pp. 399–401.

4

THE EVOLUTION OF A
SPECIAL RELATIONSHIP INTO
A PLURALISTIC SECURITY
COMMUNITY

This chapter explains the dynamics of a special relationship and its transformation into a pluralistic security community. The first section of this chapter reveals the double-edged effects of a special relationship. A special relationship produces substantial cooperation and substantial conflicts between the two states involved. This section explains that the intertwined three sources of conflict in a special relationship — power competition between the two states involved; their drives to assert the superiority of their respective national identity over that of their culturally similar counterpart; and the mismatch of expectation between them — breed and enhance the negative identifications between the two states involved, which lead them to understand each other in egoistic terms. In other words, the two states share conflictual intersubjective understandings, despite having special ties with each other.

The second section of this chapter explains that a special relationship constitutes a security regime. A security regime refers to the war avoidance norms around which expectations of the states involved converge. Each of the states observes the norms in the belief that others will reciprocate. This section reveals that the war avoidance norms in a special relationship that come with the emergence of the relationship are produced by the two sources of closeness of the two states involved — common identities and shared strategic interests. As both states in a special relationship observe their shared war avoidance norms, the substantial conflicts between them, therefore, will not easily turn into violent ones. Finally, this section points out that a special relationship — as a security regime — serves as the foundation for the two states to transform into a pluralistic security community. Yet, one element needs to be in place, without which the transformation could not take place.

The chapter's final section reveals that the presence of power imbalance in a special relationship is necessary if it is to transform into a pluralistic security community. It points out that two states in a special relationship start to share an understanding of collective-self, namely, they constitute a pluralistic security community, when one of them has become overwhelmingly powerful.

THE DOUBLE-EDGED EFFECTS OF A
SPECIAL RELATIONSHIP

As explained in Chapter 2, two states' common identities give birth to their similar strategic understandings. Yet, both the states respectively need to own a certain amount of power in order to shape their similar strategic understandings into their common strategic interests. Once each of the two states starts to own the necessary amount of power, they would be able to forge between themselves a special relationship. That said, a special relationship is produced, when, at the very least, power balance exists between the two states involved.

The presence of power balance and the twin sources of closeness — common identities and shared strategic interests — in a special relationship, give birth to the relationship's double-edged effects. A special relationship produces substantial cooperation and substantial conflicts between the two states involved.

By substantial cooperation, it means, cooperation between two states that are deeper than those forged in their other bilateral relations. Whereas by substantial conflicts, it means, conflicts between two states that are more intense than those happen in their other bilateral ties, which are characterized as friendly or normal relations. In other words, while a special relationship engenders cooperation and conflicts between the two states concerned, it is fundamentally not a hostile bilateral relation.

Substantial Cooperation

This section outlines the dynamics of the substantial cooperation in a special relationship. Such dynamics would be demonstrated in the subsequent two sections.

The substantial cooperation in a special relationship are strategic partnerships between the two states involved. Such cooperation are the outcomes of the combination of the three sources of cooperation in the relationship, that of the two states' common identities, shared strategic interests, and the matching of their mutual expectation with their respective intention. As explained in Chapter 2, two states bound by a special relationship share an expectation that their relationship should be closer than their other bilateral ties.

When the presence of common identities and shared strategic interests between the two states concerned gives rise to their mutual need for strategic cooperation, both expect the other's move for such cooperation. The expectation is matched by the counterpart's intention to collaborate, hence substantial cooperation between the two states takes place. The strategic partnerships reinforce the two states' mutual positive identifications which stem from their common identities and shared strategic interests.

The U.S.–Canada and U.S.–UK special relationships respectively demonstrates the presence of substantial cooperation in a special relationship.

Cooperation in the U.S.–Canada Special Relationship

The presence of common identities and common strategic interests

In the mid-1930s, both the United States and Canada shared similar strategic apprehension of ways to improve international difficulties amidst the Great Depression. Founded on their common identities which are rooted in the principles of liberty, both democracies intersubjectively viewed freer trade relations as the means to set forth an era of economic recovery, hence the preservation of world peace.[1] The necessary amount of power that each possessed, allowed the United States and Canada to rely on each other in forging a freer trade regime. The United States was Canada's largest trading partner. Canada, on the other hand, was an economic power that America had to cooperate with, in its efforts to establish a U.S.-dominated North America economy. Both needed each other to forge freer trade in North America, so as to preserve the prosperity and peace in the region.[2]

Canada's expectation was matched by the United States' intention

The combination and interactions of common identities and shared strategic interests with the United States ushered in Canadians' goodwill towards it and the solidarity spirit between the two states. Canada argued for a united front with the United States, politically and economically, for the well-being of both states, and to showcase to the world, amid the rise of militarism in Europe and in the Far East, how the two North American democracies would stand together and resolved their differences peacefully.[3] The need for strategic cooperation strengthened the expectation among Canadians of a close relation with the United States. They were optimistic about the two states towards establishing a cooperative relation, and believed that Canada and the United States were bound by fundamental unity.[4]

---

[1]　Jack L. Granatstein and Norman Hillmer, *For Better Or For Worse: Canada and the United States to the 1990s* (Toronto: Copp Clark Pitman Ltd., 1991), pp. 104–6, 110–11, 115.

[2]　Ibid., pp. 108–9.

[3]　Ibid., pp. 105–11.

[4]　Ibid., pp. 110–11.

The expectation for cooperation was expressed by then Canadian Prime Minister, Mackenzie King, in his proposal to lower the trade barriers between the United States and Canada. Such expectation was matched by the United States' intention of wanting reciprocal tariff cuts. As a result, the two states signed a trade agreement on 15 November 1935, their first commercial accord in over seventy years, which ended the unofficial trade war between them.[5] The collaboration reinforced the mutual positive identifications between Canada and the United States. Then United States President, Franklin Roosevelt, commented on the trade agreement: "The power of good example surpasses preachments; it excels good resolutions; it is far better than agreements unfulfilled."[6] King, on the other hand, said, "What possible tribute to the date could be greater than the cause…[of] international good-will, as against international hate, should receive an enduring monument."[7] Canadian major newspapers, meanwhile, reacted favourably with the trade agreement.

Substantial cooperation

The trade pact was substantial cooperation between the United States and Canada. It was an agreement that embraced a freer trade regime, at a time when protectionism and economic nationalism were rampant in the world. It addressed the two states' fundamental security concern of an increasingly chaotic world, in which the agreement solidified the U.S.–Canada solidarity to weather such international uncertainties, and served as a force to reorient the world towards freer trade and peace.[8] Most importantly, the trade pact facilitated the emergence of the close political and security cooperation between the United States and Canada in the subsequent years.[9]

---

[5]   Ibid., p. 108. Also see Richard N. Kottman, "The Canadian–American Trade Agreement of 1935", *The Journal of American History* 52, no. 2 (1965): 275.

[6]   Granatstein and Hillmer, *For Better Or For Worse*, p. 107.

[7]   Ibid.

[8]   Ibid., p. 109. Also see Kottman, "The Canadian–American Trade Agreement of 1935", pp. 275, 296.

[9]   Kottman, "The Canadian–American Trade Agreement of 1935", p. 275.

The United States' expectation was matched by Canada's intention

The steady rise of fascism and militarism in Japan, Italy and Germany precipitated the United States to move closer to Canada.[10] The U.S.–Canada relations had become essential for the United States in protecting North America from the aggression of these European or Asian powers.[11] The U.S.–Canada common strategic threat posed by the fascist powers led Roosevelt to expect closer security cooperation with Canada. Leveraged on their recent economic collaboration, in 1936, he started to discuss defense matters with his Canadian counterpart.[12] On several occasions, Roosevelt called for the U.S.–Canada solidarity to safeguard their mutual freedom from foreign threats. While speaking at Quebec in 1936, Roosevelt asserted, "Americans and Canadians are not foreigners to one another, and amid the grave problems that face the world today, it is time to tighten the close bonds which already unite our two peoples."[13] In August 1938, at Queen's University in Kingston, Ontario, he pledged, "The Dominion of Canada is part of the sisterhood of the British Empire. I give to you the assurance that the people of the United States will not stand idly by if domination of Canadian soil is threatened by any other Empire."[14] Such appeal for cooperation was matched by Canada's equivalent desire to deter foreign invasion. King made a reciprocal pledge: Canada would ensure its soil "as a homeland for free men in the western hemisphere", and prevent enemies from invading the United States through Canadian territory.[15]

Substantial cooperation

The demonstration of the U.S.–Canada solidarity was substantial cooperation between them. The commitment of these two powerful North American democracies to each other's security, served to deter

---

[10] John Herd Thompson and Stephen J. Randall, *Canada and the United States: Ambivalent Allies* (Athens and London: The University of Georgia Press, 1994), p. 145.

[11] Ibid.

[12] Ibid.

[13] Ibid.

[14] Granatstein and Hillmer, *For Better Or For Worse*, pp. 103–4.

[15] Ibid.

the threats exerted by the fascist powers.[16] The goodwill which stemmed from this mutual security commitment, smoothed the way for the signing of the U.S.–Canada trade agreement in November 1938. The trade accord further reduced the trade barriers between the two states, while reinforced their unity aimed at curbing the aggressive Nazi Germany.[17] Both states were aware that "they were in a grand enterprise together".[18]

Cooperation in the Anglo-American Special Relationship

The presence of common identities and common strategic interests

The strategic environment in the late 1920s was uncertain for the two English-speaking world powers — Great Britain and the United States. The rivalries between France and Italy, the two relatively weak naval powers, threatened British security in the Mediterranean; and Japan's ambition to gain naval parity with Britain and the United States jeopardized the two states' interests in the Far East. Chief among these challenges was the Japanese attempt to upset the naval balance in the Western Pacific.[19] The two English-speaking powers were determined to prevent this from happening.[20]

The Anglo-American common identities led to their similar understanding of interests abroad. Both needed each other's capacity to ensure an international order that preserved such interests, especially at a time when a culturally different power sought to challenge that order. The comment made by the U.S. Ambassador to Great Britain in the late 1920s, Alanson Bigelow Houghton, reflected the dynamics of mutual strategic dependence of the two powers, which had its roots in their common identities:

---

[16] Ibid., pp. 104, 120. Also see Thompson and Randall, *Canada and the United States*, p. 147.

[17] Granatstein and Hillmer, *For Better Or For Worse*, pp. 116–18. Also see Thompson and Randall, *Canada and the United States*, pp. 146–47.

[18] Granatstein and Hillmer, *For Better Or For Worse*, pp. 117–18.

[19] Phillips Payson O'brien, *British and American Naval Power: Politics and Policy, 1900–1936* (London: Praeger Publishers, 1998), pp. 213, 245. Also see Brian J.C. McKercher, *Transition of Power: Britain's Loss of Global Pre-Eminence to the United States, 1930–1945* (Cambridge: Cambridge University Press, 1999), p. 43.

[20] McKercher, *Transition of Power*, p. 60. Also see O'brien, *British and American Naval Power*, pp. 213, 245.

...being what we are, it is inevitable that we should look out on the world and its affairs from much the same point of view...We certainly think in much the same terms. We have much the same scale of values. We want the same kind of world. Consciously or unconsciously, we are seeking the same kind of future.[21]

Great Britain's expectation was matched by the United States' intention

Presented with the common need to contain Japan's naval expansion, coupled with the need for the United States to reduce its arms spending, and Great Britain's desire to be more focused on its other international threats, the two English-speaking powers had come to a conclusion: they should end their naval rivalries and shifted their attention towards consolidating their shared interests abroad.[22] Both powers expected each other's move for such cooperation.

In July 1929, then British Prime Minister, Ramsay MacDonald, demonstrated his desire for Anglo-American cooperation by cancelling the building of three small auxiliary vessels and slowing down construction of two cruisers, expecting that the United States would reciprocate.[23] The expectation coincided with America's intention to cooperate. Before long, then U.S. President, Herbert Hoover, responded. He decided to suspend three vessels authorized by the fifteen cruiser bill.[24] These goodwill gestures paved the way for the consensus reached between the two states, in which they would end their naval rivalries by accepting parity between their fleets.

Substantial cooperation

The consensus reached was substantial cooperation between the United States and Great Britain. It practically ended the naval competition

---

[21] Harry C. Allen, *Great Britain and the United States: A History of Anglo-American Relations (1783–1952)* (New York: St. Martin's Press Inc., 1955), p. 732.
[22] McKercher, *Transition of Power*, pp. 50, 58–59, 61–62.
[23] Ibid., p. 37.
[24] Ibid.

between the two powers since the Great War; it became the foundation for Britain to call for a naval conference in London in January 1930, and the conference would serve as a platform for the two English-speaking powers to curb Japan's naval ambition.[25] Meanwhile, the fact that other naval powers were suspicious of the Anglo-American understanding reached prior to the conference, demonstrates the close cooperation between the two states.[26] The French argued, instead of making preparations for the convening of the London Naval Conference, which aimed to limit naval armament, what the preliminary Anglo-American discussions had really achieved was the acceptance of parity between the two navies.[27]

While moving towards the start of the London Naval Conference, the United States and the United Kingdom worked closely to deal with Japan's determination to increase the navy ratio from 100:60 to roughly around 100:70, each for the Royal Navy and United States Navy vis-à-vis Imperial Japanese Navy. Both the Western powers consulted with each other closely on their respective naval discussions with Japan prior to the conference, so as to ensure the effectiveness of their joint efforts to contain Japan.[28] On the eve of the naval conference, the two English-speaking powers had colluded to confront Japan. They wanted to force Japan to relinquish its original plan for naval expansion.[29] As then U.S. Secretary of State, Henry Stimson, told British Prime Minister, MacDonald, of how they should respond, if Japan refused to budge and withdrew from the conference:

> We might make a treaty without them and they know that in that case they ran a great danger of having two cruisers laid down to their one by both the United States and Great Britain and that if it was done under those circumstances those four cruisers would be more likely than not to be used against their one in case of trouble.[30]

---

[25] Ibid., pp. 39, 42, 51, 60, 62.

[26] Allen, *Great Britain and the United States*, p. 749.

[27] Ibid. Also see McKercher, *Transition of Power*, p. 43.

[28] McKercher, *Transition of Power*, pp. 43, 46–47.

[29] Ibid., pp. 51–52.

[30] Ibid., p. 52.

Presented with such a prospect, Japan eventually capitulated. It accepted the terms proposed by Britain and America — "an overall fleet ratio of 100 for the United States, 102.4 for Britain (owing to weaker gun power in her smaller vessels), and 63.6 for Japan".[31]

The Anglo-American joint effort to contain Japan was substantial cooperation between them. Both powers confronted a culturally different power with the complementary effects of their navies; the Anglo-American naval supremacy in the Far East had been preserved as a consequence.

The strategic cooperation between the United States and Great Britain since 1929, which was produced after the matching of their mutual expectation for collaboration, reinforced the positive identifications between them. The partnership ushered in sustained cooperation between the two English-speaking powers that lasted until 1933.[32]

Substantial Conflicts

This section outlines the dynamics of the three sources of conflict in a special relationship. Such dynamics would be demonstrated in the following two sections.

There are three sources of conflict in a special relationship: power competition between the two states involved; their drives to assert the superiority of their respective national identity over that of their culturally similar counterpart; and the mismatch of expectation between them. These three sources of conflict, through their mutual reinforcements, produce substantial conflicts between two states which share a special relationship.

Balance of power — a cause for power competition

Power competition in a special relationship is essentially caused by the presence of power balance between the two states involved. When power balance exists in a special relationship, no one in the relationship is in a dominant position. Hence, the two states concerned compete with each other for dominance, prevent its counterpart from becoming a dominant power, so as to ensure their respective survival.

---

[31] Allen, *Great Britain and the United States*, pp. 749–50.
[32] McKercher, *Transition of Power*, pp. 38, 59–60.

Power competition and the assertion of the superiority of national identity

The respective national identity of two states bound by a special relationship is founded on their pre-modern common identities. As a consequence, there are inevitable similarities in the national identities of the two states concerned. Both the states, therefore, need to emphasize their difference based on their common identities, so as to ensure their respective distinctive existence in the world of nations. The differentiation is expressed in superiority sense.

The power politics between two states which share a special relationship, combined with the sense of distinctiveness of their respective national identity as opposed to the counterpart, create the two states' sense of superiority of their respective national identity over that of their culturally similar counterpart. The superiority complex has the element of power politics because it is founded on the power politics-induced mindset of comparison.

When two states bound by a special relationship compete with one another for power, their drives to assert the superiority of their respective national identity over that of their culturally similar counterpart will be strengthened. At the same instant, these superiority sentiments toughen the two states' respective will to compete against each another.

Power competition and the mismatch of expectation

Power competition between two states with special relations leads to the mismatch of expectation between them. When one of the states in a special relationship demonstrates competitive behaviours against the counterpart, they run counter to the counterpart's expectation where it should not receive such treatments, since they share a relationship which is closer than their other bilateral ties. The mismatch of expectation produces resentments on the side of the state, which is being treated competitively, towards its counterpart, and its retaliative measures to strengthen its power ensued.

The intertwined three sources of conflict that are embedded in a special relationship, breed and enhance the negative identifications between the two states involved. Consequently, both states understand each other in egoistic terms, hence, sharing conflictual intersubjective understandings.

Conflict in the U.S.–Canada Special Relationship

This section demonstrates the dynamics of the three sources of conflict in the U.S.–Canada special relationship and shows that the three sources of conflict, through their mutual reinforcements, produced substantial conflicts between the two states. Also this section illustrates that the negative identifications between the United States and Canada, which were bred and enhanced by the intertwined three sources of conflict in their special ties, resulted in them sharing conflictual intersubjective understandings.

America to expand its economic power

In 1910, then U.S. President, William Taft, proposed to have a reciprocal trade agreement with Canada, which was to forge closer economic ties between the two states through tariff reductions. The U.S. proposal for reciprocity was largely part of its contemplation for economic power expansion, reinforced by its belief in the ideas of liberty. The presence of power balance between America and the British Empire, prompted the two parties to vie for economic supremacy, so as to ensure their respective survival.[33] Both powers sought ways to dominate the world economy. The British Empire maintained its economic preponderance through a system of imperial trade preferences.[34] The United States, on the other hand, strived to expand its economic dominance worldwide by adopting the open door policy which emphasized equal access to markets and investments.[35] The concept of open door stemmed from the central idea of America's national identity — the principles of liberty.

Within the context of rivalries between America and the British Empire, by means of reciprocal trade, the United States aimed to detach Canada from the empire, and integrate Canadian market into a unified

---

[33] Granatstein and Hillmer, *For Better Or For Worse*, pp. 4, 22. Also see Kathleen Burk, *Old World, New World: The Story of Britain and America* (Great Britain: Abacus, 2009), p. 461; and Frank C. Costigliola, "Anglo-American Financial Rivalry in the 1920s", *The Journal of Economic History* 37, no. 4 (December 1977): 914.

[34] Granatstein and Hillmer, *For Better Or For Worse*, pp. 47–48.

[35] Ibid., p. 47. Also see Costigliola, "Anglo-American Financial Rivalry in the 1920s", p. 916.

North America economy.[36] Reciprocity, as the U.S. policymakers saw it, served the broader goal of America to become the world's dominant economic power.[37] The remarks made by President Taft on reciprocity reveal the dynamics of competition between British Imperialism and American Continentalism. In his letter to Theodore Roosevelt, Taft confided,

> The agreement would produce a current of business between Canada and the United States that would make Canada only an adjunct of the United States. It would transfer all their important business to Chicago and New York, with their bank credits and everything else, and it would increase greatly the demand of Canada for our manufactures. I see this is an argument made against reciprocity in Canada, and I think it is a good one.[38]

In another occasion, Taft said, Canada was at the "parting of the ways", "they must soon choose whether or not to be a member of a developing and necessarily exclusive British Empire economic club or to continue and deepen their commercial friendship with the United States. They could not do both."[39]

<u>America's desire to expand and its sense of superiority of its liberty</u>
America's desire to triumph over Imperialism boosted, and was boosted by, its drive to differentiate itself, in superiority sense, from the culturally similar Canada. The power politics between the United States and Canada, combined with Americans' sense of uniqueness of their national identity vis-à-vis Canada, give birth to Americans' sense of superiority of their identity over that of Canada, in which such superiority complex is founded on the power politics-induced mindset of comparison.

The English concepts of liberty, which constitute the core ideas of the United States' and Canada's respective nationhood, give rise to the

---

[36] Granatstein and Hillmer, *For Better Or For Worse*, p. 47.
[37] Thompson and Randall, *Canada and the United States*, p. 88.
[38] Ibid., p. 90.
[39] Granatstein and Hillmer, *For Better Or For Worse*, p. 48.

similarities between the two states' national identities.[40] The United States
hence needs to distinguish itself out of the sameness with Canada, so as
to ensure the uniqueness and authenticity of America's existence. Such
differentiation is expressed in terms of the superiority of American liberty
over that of Canadian.

In America's understanding, liberty is achieved through revolution.[41]
Canadians' experience of attaining liberty through evolution in self-
government within the British Empire, for Americans, is at odds with
the sacred character of liberty; hence the moral significance of Canadian
nationhood is not comparable with that of America.[42] The United States'
sense of superiority of their liberty was expressed, when they rejected
Canadian experience as real liberty. They thought, Canadian politics were
dominated by a small group of pro-British elites, that was deceptive and
suppressive, which prevented Canada from reaching its true destiny —
to forge a union with the United States.[43] These superiority sentiments
motivated, and were motivated by, America's leading politicians' support
for reciprocity with Canada. In 1911, then Speaker of the House of
Representatives, Champ Clark, said:

> I am for it [reciprocity] because I hope to see the day when the American
> flag will float over every square foot of the British North American
> possessions, clear to the North Pole...I do not have any doubt whatever
> that the day is not far distant when Great Britain will see all her North
> American possessions become a part of this Republic.[44]

Canada to assert its power

Canada's connection with the British Empire provided them with a sense
where power balance existed between Canada and the United States.[45]

---

[40] Samuel P. Huntington, *Who Are We? America's Great Debate* (Great Britain: The Free
    Press, 2005), p. 47. For more discussion see Chapter 2, pp. 38–39.
[41] William L. Morton, *The Canadian Identity* (Toronto and Buffalo: University of
    Toronto Press, 1961), pp. 58–59.
[42] Ibid., pp. 58–59, 84.
[43] Ibid., pp. 58–59.
[44] Granatstein and Hillmer, *For Better Or For Worse*, pp. 52–53. Also see Thompson and
    Randall, *Canada and the United States*, pp. 88–90.
[45] Granatstein and Hillmer, *For Better Or For Worse*, p. 80.

Such an understanding allowed Canadians to always embrace British Imperialism, when they were to remain powerful, and to check America's power, thereby ensured Canada's survival.

The Canadian government's announcement of a reciprocal trade agreement with the United States in 1911 sparked widespread resistance among Canadians to America's economic power, triggered their desire to assert Canada's power by riding on the mighty British Empire, with the aim to secure Canada's existence. Reciprocity was rejected by prominent politicians and businessmen in Canada. They were convinced, Canada would become a powerful state, due to its position in the British Empire, that being so, did not have to become an economic and political dependant of the United States, an outcome which they believed reciprocity was bound to produce.[46] The Conservative party of Canada argued,

> We must decide whether the spirit of Canadianism or Continentalism shall prevail on the northern half of the continent...With Canada's youthful vitality, her rapidly increasing population, her marvellous natural resources, her spirit of hopefulness and energy, she can place herself within a comparatively brief period in the highest position within this mighty Empire. The future lies in a strong Canada within a revitalized British Empire, not in a reciprocity agreement that is bound to lead to political union, whatever its economic consequences.[47]

Canada's will to be powerful and its sense of superiority of its culture

Canada's will to consolidate its power in response to America's tendency to expand its economic clout, mutually reinforced with its impulse to affirm the superiority of Canadian culture over that of America.

The English culture which forms the foundation of the United States' and Canada's respective national identity, results in close similarities between them.[48] Canadians and Americans share virtually identical

---

[46] Ibid., pp. 49–52. Also see Thompson and Randall, *Canada and the United States*, pp. 89–90.

[47] Granatstein and Hillmer, *For Better Or For Worse*, p. 52.

[48] Huntington, *Who Are We? America's Great Debate*, p. 47.

ideas, habits and lifestyle.[49] Moffett, a social scientist, described, "The Americans and the English Canadians have been welded into one people. Canadians...are already Americans without knowing it."[50] The close similarities of Canadian national identity with America's, oblige Canada to stress its difference vis-à-vis the United States, by that, to make certain the distinctive existence of Canada in the world.

The differentiation is expressed in superiority sense. Canada's sense of superiority of its identity over America's, illustrates the combination of its power politics with the United States, and the politics of its national identity in relation to the United States. The ubiquitous influence of the giant neighbour — the United States — in Canadians' daily life, triggers Canada's determination to employ its version of English values and ideals as a shield against America's influence.[51] To prevail over America's influence, Canada emphasizes the superiority of its culture when compared to that of America. Canadians hold a conviction: they possess authentic English values and ideals, which make them morally superior to, and politically more civilized than, the United States.[52] For them, American culture is superficial and corrupted; it has to be rejected.[53]

Canada's sense of superiority of its culture over that of America, strengthened its resolve to check America's power. It benchmarked itself against the achievement of the relatively stronger America, with the aim

---

[49] Granatstein and Hillmer, *For Better Or For Worse*, pp. 54–55. Also see Thompson and Randall, *Canada and the United States*, p. 85.

[50] Thompson and Randall, *Canada and the United States*, p. 85.

[51] Granatstein and Hillmer, *For Better Or For Worse*, pp. 27, 53–54. Also see Thompson and Randall, *Canada and the United States*, p. 85; James Sturgis, "Learning About Oneself: The Making of Canadian Nationalism, 1867–1914", in *Kith and Kin: Canada, Britain and the United States from the Revolution to the Cold War*, edited by C.C. Eldridge (Cardiff: University of Wales Press, 1997), p. 97; and Robert Bothwell, *Canada and the United States: The Politics of Partnership* (Canada: University of Toronto Press, 1992), p. 13.

[52] Granatstein and Hillmer, *For Better Or For Worse*, pp. 27, 53, 85, 91. Also see Thompson and Randall, *Canada and the United States*, pp. 125, 196.

[53] Granatstein and Hillmer, *For Better Or For Worse*, pp. 53–55, 89–91. Also see Thompson and Randall, *Canada and the United States*, p. 85; and Sturgis, "Learning About Oneself", p. 99.

to surpass America, and rejected closer economic ties between them. Such resolve simultaneously toughened Canadians' sense of superiority of their English culture over America's, which was derived from Canada's emphasis of its British connection.[54] Canadians asserted, "Canada, with its superior political inheritance from Britain, would catch up, and Canadians would build a country materially equal to America and morally superior to it."[55] Canadian Prime Minister, John Macdonald, who won the election of 1891, while criticizing his opponents' proposition of reciprocity with the United States during the campaign, vowed: "A British subject I was born — a British subject I will die. With my utmost effort, with my last breath will I oppose the 'veiled treason' which attempts by sordid means and mercenary proffer to lure our people from our allegiance."[56]

The mutually reinforcing dynamics of Canada's superiority sentiments and its resolution to consolidate its power, prompted the defeat of the Liberal government, who embraced the platform of reciprocity with America, in Canada's general election of 1911. The election was essentially a referendum on reciprocity, in which Canadians clearly rejected it.[57] Canadian commentators noted the sheer scale of Canadians "swept by a wave of emotion and sentiment" during the election, owing to the implications of America's annexation through reciprocity.[58] "In all sincerity many good and loyal souls were seized by a genuine alarm that their nationality was in danger", they observed.[59] Canadians' firm resistance to possible America's economic expansion in Canada, triggered their strong sense of Canadians' superiority over Americans. The newly elected Prime Minister, Robert Borden, declared, "In rejecting reciprocity, Canada has simply affirmed her adherence to a policy of national development which she has pursued for many years."[60] Borden's

---

[54] Granatstein and Hillmer, *For Better Or For Worse*, pp. 27, 53.
[55] Thompson and Randall, *Canada and the United States*, p. 69.
[56] Granatstein and Hillmer, *For Better Or For Worse*, pp. 24–27.
[57] Thompson and Randall, *Canada and the United States*, p. 91.
[58] Ibid. Also see Granatstein and Hillmer, *For Better Or For Worse*, p. 53.
[59] Granatstein and Hillmer, *For Better Or For Worse*, p. 53.
[60] Thompson and Randall, *Canada and the United States*, p. 91.

remark demonstrated Canada's determination to prevent America's economic expansion in its soil, which strengthened, and was strengthened by, its affirmation of Canada's existence vis-à-vis America in superiority sense.

Power competition and the mismatch of expectation

Canadians' negative identifications with the United States, which were caused by their determination to prevent Canada from becoming a satellite of America, and their assertion of the superiority of Canadian culture, had been escalated by their rejection of reciprocity with America.[61] The negative identifications contributed to the United States' negative understanding of Canada. The negative sentiment towards Canada, coupled with America's desire to expand its economic power, induced America's propensity to adopt protective economic policies directed at Canada during the 1920s and early 1930s.[62]

Throughout the 1920s, America started to raise its tariffs, year by year, against Canadian exports. In 1930, America denied Canada of its preferential immigration treatments, subjecting it to the same immigration requirements as those imposed on migrants from outside the Western Hemisphere. These protective economic policies ran counter to Canada's expectation that it should be treated more friendly by the United States, when compared to other states, since Canada and the United States share a special relationship.[63] The mismatch of expectation bred resentments among Canadians towards the United States. Canadian journalist, Roberts, noticed a prevalent sense of anti-Americanism in Canadian society, "caused by the thoughtlessness and intolerance of the United States toward its northern neighbor".[64] In response to America's new immigration restrictions, a Canadian MP lamented, "our boasts of friendship [with

---

[61] Ibid.

[62] Granatstein and Hillmer, *For Better Or For Worse*, pp. 93–94.

[63] Ibid., p. 54. Also see Sean M. Shore, "No Fences Make Good Neighbors: The Development of the Canadian–US Security Community, 1871–1940", in *Security Communities,* edited by Emanuel Adler and Michael Barnett (Cambridge: Cambridge University Press, 1998), p. 348.

[64] Thompson and Randall, *Canada and the United States*, p. 128.

the United States] are very extravagant, in fact, our friendship is not as deep as we...are inclined to suggest".[65]

The introduction of Smoot-Hawley Tariff Act of 1930, which would raise U.S. tariffs to record levels, exacerbated Canadians' discontent at the United States. Canadians' reactions to the Act before its passage, illustrated the expectation dynamics in the U.S.–Canada special relationship.

The Canadian media highlighted to American public that the new tariffs should not be imposed on Canada, as the two-way trade between Canada and the United States "was the largest between any two nations in the world".[66] Then Canadian Prime Minister, Mackenzie King, reminded the United States that Canada "would nudge closer to Britain" if the United States insisted on implementing the new tariffs.[67] From King's perspective, the U.S.–Canada relations were close and should remain close; he expected no drifting apart from each other by means of raising the tariffs.

The eventual passage of the Smoot-Hawley Tariff Act into law contradicted with Canadians' expectation. As a consequence, Canada's resentments towards the United States intensified; its tit-for-tat measures to fortify its power ensued. Canada retaliated with successive countervailing tariffs. The steady increase of Canada's tariffs in the subsequent years set off the United States anger towards Canada, which once again displayed the expectation dynamics in the U.S.–Canada relations. Then U.S. Secretary of State, Cordell Hull, described the preferential tariff agreements reached between Canada and other members of the British Empire at the 1932 Ottawa Conference as "the greatest injury, in a commercial sense, that has been inflicted on this country [America] since I have been in public life".[68] America perceived Canada as its special partner; it expected Canada to stay close with America.

---

[65] Ibid., p. 129.
[66] Ibid., p. 130. Also see Granatstein and Hillmer, *For Better Or For Worse*, pp. 56–57, 92.
[67] Granatstein and Hillmer, *For Better Or For Worse*, p. 96.
[68] Bothwell, *Canada and the United States*, pp. 14–15.

Conflictual intersubjective understandings

The Canadians' rejection of reciprocity with the United States, and the trade disputes between them in the following decades, were substantial conflicts between the two states. The issue of reciprocity was caused by the combination of power competition between the United States and Canada, and their drives to assert the superiority of their respective national identity over that of their culturally similar counterpart. Whereas the trade clashes were the results of the combination of power competition, and the dynamics of mismatch of expectation between the two states. The three sources of conflict that were embedded in the reciprocity and trade disputes — power competition, the assertion of the superiority of national identity, and the mismatch of expectation — through their mutual reinforcements, deepened the anti-American sentiments that were at the core of Canadian national psyche.[69] A Canadian newspaper concluded, "Continentalism always and ever must be the enemy and assassin of Canadianism."[70]

The intertwined three sources of conflict bred and enhanced the negative identifications between the United States and Canada. They shaped the two states' understanding of each other in egoistic terms, hence, resulted in them sharing conflictual intersubjective understandings. In almost the first four decades of the twentieth century, the relationship between the United States and Canada was fundamentally competitive. War plannings of the two states directed at each other were still in place well into the late 1930s.[71]

Conflict in the Anglo-American Special Relationship

This section demonstrates the dynamics of the three sources of conflict in the Anglo-American special relationship, and shows that the three sources of conflict, through their mutual reinforcements, produced

---

[69] Sturgis, "Learning About Oneself", p. 98. Also see Granatstein and Hillmer, *For Better Or For Worse*, pp. 54–55; and Thompson and Randall, *Canada and the United States*, pp. 128–31.

[70] Sturgis, "Learning About Oneself", p. 99.

[71] For more discussion see Chapter 2, pp. 55–56. Also see Granatstein and Hillmer, *For Better Or For Worse*, pp. 71–72, 127.

substantial conflicts between the two states. Also this section illustrates that the negative identifications between the United States and Britain, which were bred and enhanced by the intertwined three sources of conflict in their special ties, resulted in them sharing conflictual intersubjective understandings. The discussion begins as follows:

There was turbulence in the relationship between the United States and Great Britain since the end of the First World War. The presence of power balance between the two states led them to compete with each other for economic and naval supremacy, so as to ensure their respective survival.[72]

In the early 1920s, the United States championed the principles of free competition and equal access to markets and investments, opposed the policies of regulation and special privileges, in its attempt to dominate the world economy.[73] Britain, meanwhile, strived to counter America's economic expansion by aiming to integrate Europe and Russia into a closed door economic system, founded on preferential treatments in trade, and linked to sterling.[74]

America's desire to compete and its sense of superiority of its liberty

The United States' motivation to compete with Britain for economic dominance strengthened, and was strengthened by, its drive to assert the superiority of its liberty over that of Britain.

The sense of superiority is an outcome of the combination of the power politics between America and Britain, and the politics of America's national identity in relation to Britain. While the United

---

[72] Granatstein and Hillmer, *For Better Or For Worse*, pp. 4, 22. Also see McKercher, *Transition of Power*, pp. 172, 202; and Burk, *Old World, New World*, p. 461; and Costigliola, "Anglo-American Financial Rivalry in the 1920s", p. 914.

[73] Costigliola, "Anglo-American Financial Rivalry in the 1920s", pp. 915–16. Also see Alan P. Dobson, *Anglo-American Relations in the Twentieth Century: Of Friendship, Conflict and the Rise and Decline of Superpowers* (London and New York: Routledge, 1995), pp. 44–45, 48.

[74] Costigliola, "Anglo-American Financial Rivalry in the 1920s", p. 917. Also see Dobson, *Anglo-American Relations in the Twentieth Century*, p. 49.

States had achieved its independence from Great Britain through revolution, Americans and British were essentially one people.[75] They share the same race, ethnicity, culture and language.[76] America hence needed to reinterpret its identity founded on its common identities with Britain, so as to consolidate the existence of this newborn nation, in the midst of an international environment that had the strong presence of the culturally similar British Empire. Americans believed that they inherited the sacred and authentic English concepts of liberty which Britain itself had deviated from.[77] They were endowed with the responsibility to defend "these traditional English values against the efforts of the British government to subvert them".[78] One of the founding fathers of the United States, Benjamin Franklin, said: "It was a resistance in favor of a British constitution, which every Englishman might share...a resistance in favor of the liberties of England."[79]

In the early decades of the twentieth century, America's will to prevail over British imperialism energized Americans' sense of superiority of their liberty over that of British.[80] They consistently criticized British imperialism and showed deep anti-colonialism sentiments. Even when the two states were allies during the Second World War, America emphasized its dislike of the British Empire that was at odds with Americans' ideas of liberty, and made clear that it did not join the war to preserve the Empire.[81] "I can't believe that we can fight a war against fascist slavery, and at the same time not work to free people all over the world from a backward colonial policy", Roosevelt once told Churchill.[82] Americans disregarded the British concept of freedom of the seas as "not freedom at all", as it preserved Britain's arbitrary power

---

[75] Huntington, *Who Are We? America's Great Debate*, p. 47.
[76] Ibid.
[77] Ibid. Also see Morton, *The Canadian Identity*, p. 59.
[78] Ibid.
[79] Ibid.
[80] David Reynolds, "Rethinking Anglo-American Relations", *International Affairs* 65, no. 1 (1989): 102.
[81] Allen, *Great Britain and the United States*, pp. 825–26.
[82] Ibid., p. 825.

of imposing a blockade.[83] In their views, the British "were incapable of grasping the magnanimity" of American idea of freedom of the seas.[84]

The United States' sense of superiority of its liberty over that of Britain simultaneously bolstered its determination to compete with Great Britain. America continuously campaigned for breaking up the British Empire's network of imperial preferences. It exerted pressure on Britain to renounce these preferences when opportunity arose.[85]

As part of its contemplation to triumph over Britain's economic power, the United States demanded the Allied powers of the First World War, especially Britain, to pay their debts to America, made during the war, in full.[86] Throughout the war, the United States had lent approximately $10,000 million to others. Britain, on the other hand, had lent approximately $8,000 million to others, and borrowed approximately $4,000 million from the United States. In short, by the end of the war, Britain was being owed more than it owed to America.[87]

Britain's consideration on its war debts was dominated by its attempt to regain leadership in the world economy.[88] It sought to consolidate its economic clout by extending its sterling-based network of imperial preferences to Europe and Russia, so as to strengthen its bargaining position against the United States on the debt issue.[89] It wanted to prevent default on its debts to America, so as to preserve its reputation as a trustworthy debtor — a necessary condition for Britain to acquire leadership role in the world economy.[90]

As Britain's war debts payment would weaken its economy dearly, it thus strived to nullify the debts through an all-round cancellation of inter-Allied indebtedness, or to reduce them by paying the debts only

---

[83] O'brien, *British and American Naval Power,* p. 136. Also see ibid., p. 702.
[84] O'brien, *British and American Naval Power,* p. 136.
[85] Allen, *Great Britain and the United States,* p. 827.
[86] Dobson, *Anglo-American Relations in the Twentieth Century,* pp. 47–48.
[87] Allen, *Great Britain and the United States,* p. 752. Also see Dobson, *Anglo-American Relations in the Twentieth Century,* p. 47.
[88] Dobson, *Anglo-American Relations in the Twentieth Century,* p. 52.
[89] Ibid.
[90] Ibid., p. 47. Also see Allen, *Great Britain and the United States,* p. 757.

with the reparations that it would receive from Germany.[91] The United States rejected all such proposals and insisted full payment of the war debts.

America's determination to collect the war debts in full hardened, and was hardened by, its disdain for the imperialistic attitudes of the Allies, which attempted to expand their respective empire through their peace treaty with Germany.[92] Then U.S. Treasury Secretary, David Houston, in his explanation to Austen Chamberlain, then Chancellor of the Exchequer, about America's insistence on the full repayment of debts, wrote,

> This nation has neither sought nor received substantial benefit from war. On the other hand Allies, although having suffered greatly in loss of life and property, have, under terms of treaty of peace and otherwise, acquired very considerable accessions of territories, populations, economic and other advantages. It would therefore seem that if a full account were taken of these and of whole situation there would be no desire or reason to call upon Government of this country for further contributions.[93]

Power competition and the mismatch of expectation

Upon America's resolute rejection of any cancellation or reduction of war debts, Britain acceded to make full payment of its debts in 1923. The United States' policy on Britain's war debts contradicted Britain's expectation that it should be treated more friendly by the United States, when compared to other states, owing to their special relationship. While Britain had to unconditionally honour its debts to the United States, the other European powers were able to make such payments with more generous terms. These terms included interest rates lower than that imposed on Britain, and some escape or postponement provisions of which Britain did not enjoy. Whereas these European powers were allowed to finance most of their debts to America with German reparations and their other debts, Britain's debt payments to

---

[91] Allen, *Great Britain and the United States*, pp. 752–53, 756–57. Also see Dobson, *Anglo-American Relations in the Twentieth Century*, pp. 47, 53.

[92] Dobson, *Anglo-American Relations in the Twentieth Century*, p. 48.

[93] Ibid.

the United States far exceeded its receipts from German reparations and from its debtors. In a nutshell, Britain accounted for 41 per cent of the total war debts to America, yet it had contributed 74 per cent of all the war debt payments received by the United States.[94]

The mismatch of expectation produced resentments among the British towards the United States.[95] Despite being a special partner of America, Britain would have to meet its war debt payments to the United States at a cost higher than that subjected to the other powers, let alone receive preferential treatments from the United States. Then Chancellor of the Exchequer, Winston Churchill, denounced America's policy as selfish, extortionate, and that it was the outcome of avarice.[96] Americans were "sunk in selfishness", he lamented.[97] Such resentments stirred up Britain determination to compete with the United States. Churchill asserted, Britain needed "to have the power to resist American dictation".[98]

As a result, Britain decided to reaffirm its naval supremacy.[99] In the 1927 Geneva Naval Conference, Britain rejected America's demand for naval parity. Churchill, who dominated the naval policy of the British government, wrote in his memo,

> There can really be no parity between a Power whose navy is its life and a Power whose navy is only for prestige…It always seems to be assumed that it is our duty to humour the United States and minister to their vanity. They do nothing for us in return, but exact their last pound of flesh.[100]

Britain deemed that it was time to stand up against the United States.[101] Its refusal to accept naval parity resulted in the collapse of the conference.[102]

---

[94] Allen, *Great Britain and the United States*, p. 758.

[95] Ibid., pp. 757, 760.

[96] O'brien, *British and American Naval Power*, p. 196.

[97] Ibid.

[98] Ibid.

[99] Ibid., pp. 188, 192–94.

[100] Ibid., pp. 184, 188, 192–93, 195.

[101] Ibid., p. 193.

[102] Ibid., pp. 193–94.

Conflictual intersubjective understandings

The economic and naval rivalries between the United States and
Great Britain throughout the 1920s constituted substantial conflicts
between them. America's demand for Britain to honour its war debts
to America in full, was part of its efforts to prevail over Britain's
economic power. Such an attempt to compete, mutually bolstered by
Americans' drive to affirm the superiority of their liberty over that of
British. Britain's subsequent decision to reassert its naval supremacy,
was the result of the combination of its antipathy towards the United
States — due to the unmet expectation by the U.S. — and its will to
compete with the U.S.

The underlying three sources of conflict, which gave rise to the
rivalries between the two states — power competition, the assertion of
the superiority of national identity, and the mismatch of expectation —
reinforced one another, and prompted the exacerbation of Anglo-American
relations in the late 1920s.

In July 1927, amid the disputes over the issue of naval parity,
Churchill assessed, "No doubt it is quite right in the interests of peace
to go on talking about war with the United States being 'unthinkable'.
Everyone knows that this is not true."[103] Then head of the American
Department of the British Foreign Office, Robert Craigie, in his analysis
of Anglo-American relations, concluded that, "Except as a figure of
speech, war is *not* unthinkable between the two countries. On the
contrary, there are present all the factors which in the past have made
for wars between states."[104] Meanwhile, comparisons were drawn
between Anglo-American relations of this period, and Britain–Germany
relations in the run-up to the First World War. In the United States,
enraged by Britain's refusal to accept naval parity in the Geneva
Conference, Americans became deeply suspicious of Britain.[105] They were
more determined than before to press for America's naval supremacy.[106]

---

[103] Ibid., p. 179.
[104] Dobson, *Anglo-American Relations in the Twentieth Century*, p. 62.
[105] O'brien, *British and American Naval Power*, pp. 195, 198–200.
[106] Ibid.

The intertwined three sources of conflict bred and enhanced the negative identifications between America and Great Britain. Both states, as a consequence, were entrenched in egoistic understanding of self, when they interact with each other. In other words, they shared conflictual intersubjective understandings. Not until the late 1930s, Anglo-American relations remained fundamentally competitive. For the whole of the 1920s, Great Britain was the most formidable potential foe for Americans.[107] War plannings of the two states directed at each other endured up to the late 1930s.[108]

A SPECIAL RELATIONSHIP AS A SECURITY REGIME

Security Regime

A security regime refers to the war avoidance norms around which expectations of the states involved converge.[109] Each of the states observes the norms in the belief that others will reciprocate.[110]

Aspiration for Peace

The establishment of a security regime is spawned by the aspiration for peace of the states concerned against one another. States which form a security regime share the belief that security can be maintained through restraining themselves from resorting to violence, when they are to settle their disagreements.[111] The aspiration for peace was discernible in

---

[107] Ibid., pp. 181–82.

[108] Ibid. For more discussion see Chapter 2, pp. 55–56.

[109] Janice Gross Stein, "Detection and Defection: Security 'Regimes' and the Management of International Conflict", *International Journal* 40, no. 4 (1985): 603. Also see Robert Jervis, "Security Regimes", *International Organization* 36, no. 2 (1982): 357; Stephan Haggard and Beth A. Simmons, "Theories of International Regimes", *International Organization* 41, no. 3 (1987): 493; Volker Rittberger, Manfred Efinger and Martin Mendler, "Toward an East–West Security Regime: The Case of Confidence- and Security-Building Measures", *Journal of Peace Research* 27, no. 1 (1990): 56; Acharya, "A Regional Security Community in Southeast Asia?", pp. 180, 191; and Joseph S. Nye Jr., "Nuclear Learning and U.S.–Soviet Security Regimes", *International Organization* 41, no. 3 (1987): 399.

[110] Jervis, "Security Regimes", p. 357.

[111] Ibid., pp. 360–61.

the Concert of Europe — a security regime from 1815 to 1823.[112] Then British Foreign Secretary, Castlereagh, when advising his officials about the diplomacy in the Concert, wrote,

> His [Royal Highness'] only desire is, and must be, to employ all His influence to preserve the peace, which in concert with His Allies he has won.
>
> To this great end you may declare that all His Royal Highness' efforts will be directed; to this purpose all minor considerations will be made subordinate; wherever His voice can be heard, it will be raised to discourage the pursuit of secondary and separate interests at the hazard of that general peace and goodwill, which, after so long a period of suffering it should be the object of all the Sovereigns of Europe to preserve to their people.[113]

The presence of aspiration for peace in a security regime indicates that the member states identify with each other positively. A security regime is essentially the member states' normative consensus of refraining from using force against each other.[114] It thus reveals the positive identifications between the states involved, as the consensus is their shared intersubjective understanding interweaves with the wish for peace. In other words, a security regime is a form of cooperation, in which the states involved do not understand each other in pure egoistic terms.[115]

Jervis has pointed out, the restraints observed by the United States and Soviet Union, which prevented them from launching a war against one another, is a form of cooperation, but not a security regime.[116] Such restraints mostly stemmed from their fear of retaliation, as both sides possessed the ability to punish the other.[117] Therefore, the U.S.–

---

[112] Ibid., pp. 362–63.

[113] Charles Webster, *The Foreign Policy of Castlereagh, 1812–1822* (London: G. Bell, 1963), 2: 510–11, quoted in Jervis, "Security Regimes", pp. 363–64.

[114] Rittberger, Efinger and Mendler, "Toward an East–West Security Regime", p. 57.

[115] Jervis, "Security Regimes", pp. 357, 364.

[116] Ibid., p. 357.

[117] Ibid., p. 372.

Soviet security cooperation did not entail positive identifications; it was rooted in their respective pure egoistic understanding of self vis-à-vis the other.[118]

While states in a security regime identify with each other positively, their understandings of one another, however, are basically egoistic. The member states view each other as partners as well as rivals.[119] It is in their shared interest to adhere to the war avoidance norms, hardly because they are concerned about the counterparts' security, but essentially because such adherence ensures their respective security.[120] A state in a security regime might still resort to the use of force, if it deems its key interests are threatened by the counterparts.[121] That said, a security regime mostly restricts the behaviours of the states involved, it does not alter the fundamentally competitive relations between them.[122] Nevertheless, states in such a regime at least intersubjectively recognize that their security relations are closer, when compared to their security ties with states which are not in the regime.[123]

More than a Basis of Order

The emergence of a security regime is built on the existence of power balance between the states involved. As explained in Chapter 3, while power balance between states is a cause for their competition, it also serves as a basis of order between them. Order is "peaceful coexistence under conditions of scarcity". By peaceful coexistence, it means states coexist without a war in a significant period of time.

Because of the presence of power balance between them, states in a security regime find it very costly to turn their conflicts into violent

---

[118] Ibid., pp. 357, 371–72. Also see Nye Jr., "Nuclear Learning and U.S.–Soviet Security Regimes", p. 375.

[119] Jervis, "Security Regimes", p. 364.

[120] Ibid., pp. 364–65.

[121] Ibid., pp. 362–64.

[122] Nye Jr., "Nuclear Learning and U.S.–Soviet Security Regimes", p. 399. Also see Rittberger, Efinger and Mendler, "Toward an East–West Security Regime", p. 70.

[123] Jervis, "Security Regimes", pp. 366–67. Also see Rittberger, Efinger and Mendler, "Toward an East–West Security Regime", pp. 55–56, 67.

ones.[124] Each of them does not possess the capacity to prevail over the others, yet each has the capacity to defend itself against the attack of the counterparts. The power balance, therefore, furnishes a basis of order between the states in the regime. It hinders them from plunging into a war against one another, hence allows them to coexist peacefully.[125]

Yet, a security regime is more than a basis of order. The order engendered by a balance of power entails no positive identifications between the states involved. The power balance simply generates great cost for the states to be involved in an armed conflict between them. In other words, in a balance of power international system, it is the member states' respective plain egoistic-self consideration that leads to the absence of war between them. On the other hand, Nye points out, if the U.S.–Soviet peaceful coexistence can already be explained on the basis of pure self-interest, in which such coexistence is obviously caused by the power balance between them, regime then becomes a redundant explanation.[126] His observation indicates, a security regime can explain a power balance-induced cooperation, yet a balance of power is insufficient to explain a regime-based cooperation. That said, a security regime is more than a balance of power. States in a security regime, based upon their peaceful coexistence, observe war avoidance norms that are interweaved with positive identifications between them.

Convergence of Expectations — Reasonable Expectations of Peaceful Change

A security regime demonstrates the expectation dynamics in the security relationship of the states involved. As each of them intersubjectively acknowledges that they share a closer security relation than their other security ties, each expects that the counterparts would commit to

---

[124] Jervis, "Security Regimes", pp. 361–62. Also see Rittberger, Efinger and Mendler, "Toward an East–West Security Regime", pp. 63–64; and Acharya, "A Regional Security Community in Southeast Asia?", p. 180.

[125] Jervis, "Security Regimes", pp. 361–62. Also see Nye Jr., "Nuclear Learning and U.S.–Soviet Security Regimes", p. 375.

[126] Nye Jr., "Nuclear Learning and U.S.–Soviet Security Regimes", p. 375.

preserving their peaceful relations, as an expression of the closeness of their security ties. The states' shared war avoidance norms provide a point for each of them to live up to the expectation, while expecting others to reciprocate; consequently, engendering the convergence of their mutual expectations around the war avoidance norms.[127]

The convergence of expectations means that states in a security regime share reasonable expectations of peaceful change. It is reasonable as the regime introduces a measure of certainty to the member states, of which war is unlikely between them; nevertheless, war remains possible between them.[128] It is reasonable as the regime renders the member states' behaviours against one another fairly predictable; still, they do not possess the ability to predict each other's action.[129] The prospect of a surprise attack in a security regime has been reduced, not eliminated.[130]

A Special Relationship Constitutes a Security Regime

A special relationship constitutes a security regime. It demonstrates the dynamics of a security regime. A special relationship is built on the existence of power balance between the two states involved. The relationship is produced only when the two states respectively starts to own a certain amount of power. A special relationship is intertwined with the aspiration for peace of the two states involved against each other. They identify with each other positively, and intersubjectively recognize that their relations, especially their security ties, are closer than their other bilateral relationships. Also, a special relationship contains war avoidance norms that are observed by the two states involved. The undefended border between the United States and Canada exemplified the presence of such norms in a special relationship.[131]

---

[127] Jervis, "Security Regimes", pp. 364–67. Also see Nye Jr., "Nuclear Learning and U.S.–Soviet Security Regimes", p. 399.

[128] Jervis, "Security Regimes", pp. 362–64. Also see Acharya, "A Regional Security Community in Southeast Asia?", pp. 180, 191.

[129] Rittberger, Efinger and Mendler, "Toward an East–West Security Regime", p. 66.

[130] Ibid.

[131] Shore, "No Fences Make Good Neighbors", pp. 341–47.

The war avoidance norms in a special relationship are produced by the two sources of closeness of the two states involved — their common identities and shared strategic interests. Before the coexistence of these two sources of closeness starts to emerge, war avoidance norms do not exist between the two states concerned. Anglo-American relations from the 1850s demonstrated the absence of war avoidance norms between them; and the subsequent establishment of such norms, when the coexistence of their common identities and shared strategic interests started to emerge.

No War Avoidance Norms with the Absence of the Two Sources of Closeness

In 1850, the Clayton-Bulwer Treaty had been signed by America and Great Britain, in which both parties agreed not to gain any exclusive control over the possible canal route in Central America that would connect the Atlantic and the Pacific. This treaty did not represent the war avoidance norms between the two states; it was an outcome of expediency. Both parties needed this treaty to defuse their competition in Central America, as they had other more urgent matters to deal with.[132] The United States was plagued by the increasingly bitter internal cleavage between North and South, whereas Britain's attention was absorbed by its possible war in Crimea.

Both states therefore compromised to make the treaty.[133] It temporarily shelved their conflicts in Central America; it entailed no aspiration for peace between them.[134] Then U.S. Secretary of States, John Clayton, when pondered upon the reasons for a settlement of disputes over a canal in Central America, wrote, "We are deeply anxious to avoid any collision with the British Government in relation to this matter; but that collision will become inevitable if great prudence be not exercised on both sides."[135] Clayton's thought was dominated by his apprehension of

---

[132] Allen, *Great Britain and the United States*, pp. 424–25.
[133] Ibid., p. 429.
[134] Ibid., pp. 429, 431.
[135] Ibid., pp. 427–28.

the imminent arm clashes between America and Great Britain, not by his goodwill towards Britain.

The difficulties arose between the United States and Britain on issues surrounding Central America, in the subsequent years of the signing of the Clayton-Bulwer Treaty, vindicated the absence of war avoidance norms between them. The two states held fundamentally different interpretations on the treaty. The United States judged that the treaty obliged Britain to withdraw entirely from Central America.[136] Britain, on the other hand, affirmed that the treaty did not apply to its existing possessions in Central America.[137] America's suspicion towards Britain intensified, when Britain included several islands located around the Bay Islands as its colony in Central America in 1852.[138] These disputes were culminated in the U.S. navy's bombardment of a British protectorate in Central America — Greytown — in July 1854, after the broke out of violent conflicts between American citizens and the local authorities.[139]

Until the 1850s, war avoidance norms did not exist in Anglo-American relations. Throughout the decade, the power owned by the United States, and the power projection of Great Britain in the Western Hemisphere, had yet to engender a basis of order between them. America had shown no restrain to attack a British dominion in Central America. Britain, at the same time, was determined to curb the United States' expansion in North and South America, which involved military means.[140] Then British Prime Minister, Viscount Palmerston, wrote in July 1857 that the United States would undoubtedly expand in South America, "but it is for our interest that this should not happen until the Swarms are prepared to separate from the Parent Hive".[141] The absence of a basis of order between the United States and Great Britain indicates that the two states still lack the foundation upon which their

---

[136] Ibid., pp. 431–34.
[137] Ibid.
[138] Ibid., p. 433.
[139] Ibid., pp. 434–35.
[140] Ibid., pp. 423, 437.
[141] Ibid., p. 437.

shared war avoidance norms could emerge. Both states' attacks on each other had not been halted.

Meanwhile, while Britain was already a world power, the amount of power owned by the United States had not reached to a level that, matched with Britain's existing power, would kick-start the emergence of their common strategic interests; in which such interests are rooted in their common identities-induced similar strategic understandings. Anglo-American relations until the 1850s were characterized by their explicit strategic competition, rather than mutual strategic dependence. Both states sought to assert their respective strategic preponderance in Central America. In the mid-1850s, Britain strengthened its military presence in the Caribbean; America, in turn, increased its naval forces in the Gulf of Mexico.[142] American filibusterers established a new government in Nicaragua to advance America's interests; Britain, in turn, helped arm Costa Rica to confront this newly formed government.[143]

The absence of the emergence of common strategic interests between the United States and Great Britain meant their two sources of closeness — common identities and shared strategic interests — had yet to coexist between them. As a consequence, the two states' aspiration for peace directed at each other, were not sufficiently strong to produce their shared war avoidance norms, namely, a security regime between them.

A Basis of Order Was In Place

The consistent growth of America's power since the 1850s, coupled with the British Empire's consolidation of power in North America during the 1860s, ushered in a basis of order between them since the 1860s.

In the first years of the 1860s, it was clear for Britain that the United States was bound to become a great power.[144] The power possessed by the United States since the 1860s was great enough to halt Britain's tendency to confront America militarily.[145] As a consequence,

---

[142] Ibid., pp. 436–37.
[143] Ibid.
[144] Ibid., p. 441.
[145] Ibid.

Britain decided to remove its clashes with the United States in Central America. In 1860, it relinquished its control over Mosquito Coast and Bay Islands in Caribbean, and accepted the United States' forthcoming expansion in Central America.[146]

In the meantime, America's impulse to expand in North America had been effectively thwarted by Britain. Shortly after the Civil War, America's desire to annex Canada had intensified.[147] It decided to purchase Alaska from Russia in March 1867, as a step towards incorporating Canada into the United States.[148] The prospect of being annexed by the United States, coupled with Britain's impending decision to withdraw its army from North America, alarmed the colonies of British North America.[149] As a consequence, they formed between them a confederation — the Dominion of Canada — in July 1867, so as to defence themselves against America's annexation.[150]

The power of Canada had been consolidated through the political integration, and cemented by Britain being its ultimate security guarantor. As a result, the British Empire was able to project an amount of power in North America that could terminate America's challenge to Canada's territories.[151] Henceforth, a basis of order between the United States and Great Britain had surfaced. Both states respectively possessed the capability to deter each other's attack, hence they started to coexist peacefully.

More than a Basis of Order — The Coexistence of the Two Sources of Closeness Started to Emerge

While the presence of power balance between America and Great Britain since the 1860s furnished a basis of order between them, it also triggered

---

[146] Ibid., pp. 438–42.

[147] Ibid., p. 503.

[148] Ibid. Also see George C. Herring, *From Colony to Superpower: U.S. Foreign Relations Since 1776* (New York: Oxford University Press, 2008), p. 257.

[149] Allen, *Great Britain and the United States*, pp. 503–5. Also see Shore, "No Fences Make Good Neighbors", pp. 341–42.

[150] Ibid.

[151] Thompson and Randall, *Canada and the United States*, p. 40. Also see Shore, "No Fences Make Good Neighbors", pp. 342–44; and Granatstein and Hillmer, *For Better Or For Worse*, p. 4.

the emergence of their common strategic interests. In the course of the 1860s, the power owned by the United States, and Britain's projection of power in North America, had respectively increased to a level which started to shape their similar strategic understandings into their common strategic interests. Both were already the great powers in North America. Each, at the same time, preferred a peaceful North America that reflected its way of life, while serving as a shield for its internal development, and as a footing for it to engage in overseas activities.[152]

During the 1860s, America had to implement reconstruction in its southern states following the end of the Civil War. The 1860s also marked the beginning of America's expansion abroad.[153] It ousted the French-installed Emperor of Mexico after the Civil War. In Central America, America sought to acquire Virgin Islands, to establish a naval base at Samana Bay, and to build a canal in the area.[154] It extended its economic clout to Cuba. At the Pacific, America acquired Midway Island, and established its control on Hawaii and Samoa. As for Britain, it needed to shift its focus to Europe, Africa and Asia during the same period, to confront Germany, which had emerged as a new imperial power.[155] Canada, on the other hand, was preoccupied with its internal integration and expansion.[156]

Since they were compelled to coexist peacefully due to the presence of power balance between them, coupled with the fact that both share similar way of life, the United States and Britain therefore wanted their friendly coexistence in North America. Such coexistence would ease their defense against one another, in the context of a peaceful North

---

[152] Allen, *Great Britain and the United States*, pp. 510–12. Also see Shore, "No Fences Make Good Neighbors", pp. 341–42; and Thompson and Randall, *Canada and the United States*, p. 39; and Granatstein and Hillmer, *For Better Or For Worse*, pp. 11–12.

[153] Allen, *Great Britain and the United States*, p. 442. Also see Herring, *From Colony to Superpower*, pp. 255, 259, 263.

[154] Herring, *From Colony to Superpower*, pp. 256–57, 259–60.

[155] Thompson and Randall, *Canada and the United States*, pp. 39, 41. Also see Shore, "No Fences Make Good Neighbors", pp. 341–42.

[156] Shore, "No Fences Make Good Neighbors", pp. 342–43. Also see Allen, *Great Britain and the United States*, p. 505; and Thompson and Randall, *Canada and the United States*, pp. 38–39.

America, which largely reflected their respective way of life rooted in their common democratic values and English culture.[157]

The two parties' desire for friendly coexistence was expressed in their aspiration for peace directed at each other. In 1868, America's Minister to the United Kingdom, Reverdy Johnson, wrote to then U.S. Secretary of State, William Seward, that he observed "the strongest evidence" of friendly feelings expressed by the British government and British people towards the United States.[158] Around 1869, the impressive goodwill gestures demonstrated by J.L. Motley, then America's Ambassador to the United Kingdom, towards Britain, prompted British Foreign Secretary, George Clarendon, to declare that "he could contemplate the possibility of war between Great Britain and any other foreign power, but war with America inspired him with abhorrence."[159] The existence of power balance between the United States and Great Britain since the 1860s, therefore, was more than a basis of order between them. It engendered their mutual positive identifications.

It should be noted that America's and Great Britain's desire for friendly coexistence directed at each other, did not constitute their common strategic interest. Such a desire at most indicated the emergence, not the presence, of their common strategic interests. The sense of mutual strategic dependence between them with regard to North America's security order was not yet discernible. Their desire for friendly coexistence merely accounted for their respective need for a peaceful North America, which guaranteed their separate way of life, and where each could immerse in its internal matters and external engagements. It would take several decades for the emergence of Anglo-American common strategic interests to complete.

By the 1910s, it was clear for America and the British Empire that they were strategically dependent on each other.[160] Americans and

---

[157] Shore, "No Fences Make Good Neighbors", pp. 335, 338, 348–49, 354.

[158] Allen, *Great Britain and the United States*, p. 506.

[159] Ibid., p. 507.

[160] For more discussion see Chapter 2, pp. 14–24. Also see Granatstein and Hillmer, *For Better Or For Worse*, p. 54; and Shore, "No Fences Make Good Neighbors", p. 348.

Canadians, by then, view North America as their common region that was distinct from war-ridden Europe.[161] A region that was permanently peaceful, breed by their common democratic values and English culture.[162] Both parties had come to view their pacific politics as "North American values".[163]

War Avoidance Norms Surfaced

Nevertheless, the emergence of Anglo-American common strategic interests, combined with the presence of their common identities, produced aspiration for peace between them, which were suffice to give rise to their shared war avoidance norms.[164] The 1871 Treaty of Washington marked the surface of Anglo-American shared war avoidance norms.

Both parties signed the treaty to ensure their friendly coexistence.[165] They resolved their differences once and for all through the treaty.[166] They settled their tensions accumulated since the American Civil War.[167] They reached agreements on their disputes over U.S.–Canada boundaries and the access to fisheries in North America. Those were the differences that might lead them to war, of which if remained unresolved, they would be preoccupied with the tasks of defending themselves against one another.[168]

The 1871 Treaty of Washington reflected the basis of order between America and Great Britain. It confirmed America's acceptance of Canada's borders, which essentially meant the U.S.–Canada peaceful coexistence in

---

[161] Shore, "No Fences Make Good Neighbors", pp. 335, 348, 354.

[162] Ibid., pp. 335, 338, 348, 354.

[163] Ibid., p. 335.

[164] Allen, *Great Britain and the United States*, pp. 506–7, 515, 517.

[165] Thompson and Randall, *Canada and the United States*, p. 39. Also see Allen, *Great Britain and the United States*, pp. 510–15; and Granatstein and Hillmer, *For Better Or For Worse*, pp. 11–12.

[166] Granatstein and Hillmer, *For Better Or For Worse*, p. 10.

[167] Allen, *Great Britain and the United States*, pp. 510–17. Also see Shore, "No Fences Make Good Neighbors", p. 342; ibid., pp. 10–13; and Herring, *From Colony to Superpower*, p. 255.

[168] Allen, *Great Britain and the United States*, pp. 509–17.

North America.[169] The treaty also represented the beginning of America's and Great Britain's commitment to avoid war between them.[170] The 1871 Treaty of Washington, therefore, marked the establishment of a security regime between the United States and Britain/Canada. Henceforth, war avoidance norms began to characterize the U.S.–Britain/Canada relations.

Shortly after the signing of the Treaty of Washington, the United States and Canada decided to demilitarize their border.[171] Such demilitarization, which produced the undefended U.S.–Canada border, was an outcome of their shared war avoidance norms. The undefended border demonstrated the two parties' gestures to defuse their defense against each other, hence reduced — not eliminated — the possibility of war between them. Both sides' war planning against each other remained active, while they rendered their border to be undefended.[172]

In the early twentieth century, the U.S.–Canada war avoidance norms gave birth to their bilateral bureaucratic institutions, charged to resolve the two states' disputes over boundaries. These mechanisms included the International Boundary Commission and International Joint Commission.[173] The bilateral bureaucratic institutions depoliticized the two states' border conflicts by concentrating their minds upon hammering out technical solutions for these complicated differences via negotiation.[174] As a result, these mechanisms encouraged the non-confrontational character of the U.S.–Canada relations, thereby hindered them from turning their sovereignty disputes into violent disagreements.[175]

---

[169] Thompson and Randall, *Canada and the United States*, p. 40. Also see Herring, *From Colony to Superpower*, p. 255.

[170] Allen, *Great Britain and the United States*, p. 517. Also see Granatstein and Hillmer, *For Better Or For Worse*, p. 13; Shore, "No Fences Make Good Neighbors", p. 359; and Herring, *From Colony to Superpower*, p. 255.

[171] Shore, "No Fences Make Good Neighbors", pp. 333, 341–43, 349. Also see Granatstein and Hillmer, *For Better Or For Worse*, p. 13.

[172] Shore, "No Fences Make Good Neighbors", p. 347.

[173] Thompson and Randall, *Canada and the United States*, pp. 72–76.

[174] Ibid.

[175] Ibid.

*Convergence of Expectations — Reasonable
Expectations of Peaceful Change*

A special relationship, as a security regime, engenders the convergence
of expectations of the two states involved, around their shared war
avoidance norms. As each observes the norms in the belief that the
counterpart will reciprocate, the war avoidance norms hence ensure
the two states' mutual expectations — that the counterpart would commit
to maintaining their peaceful ties — to be persistently matched by their
respective intention to preserve a peaceful relation between them. While
a special relationship produces substantial conflicts between the two
states concerned, the convergence of their expectations around their
shared war avoidance norms, serves to prevent the conflicts from easily
turning into violent ones. In other words, two states bound by a special
relationship share reasonable expectations of peaceful change. War
between them is unlikely, not unthinkable. Each of them is convinced
that the counterpart will not use force to settle their disputes, yet no
one is certain about it.

The Anglo-American and U.S.–Canada special relationships demonstrate the dynamics of the convergence of actors' expectations around
their shared war avoidance norms. Shortly after both states demilitarized
their border, the U.S.–Canada war avoidance norms — in the form of
their undefended border — became a point around which their mutual
expectations for friendly coexistence converged. Both sides began to view
that peace prevailed in their relationship.[176] In 1880, Canadian Prime
Minister, John Macdonald, revealed his evaluation: "My opinion is, that
from the present aspect of affairs, and from a gradual improvement in
the feeling between the people of the United States and the people of
Canada, that the danger of war is annually decreasing…"[177] Macdonald's
assessment was based upon the fact that the U.S.–Canada border had
been demilitarized for years.[178]

---

[176] Shore, "No Fences Make Good Neighbors", p. 344.
[177] Ibid., p. 346.
[178] Ibid., pp. 342–46.

The strength of their shared war avoidance norms, which warrant the convergence of their expectations, became evident, when the two parties — U.S.–Britain/Canada — were confronted with a crisis between them. In December 1895, then U.S. President, Grover Cleveland, issued a message to Congress stating that Great Britain would have to accept arbitration on the border dispute between British Guiana and Venezuela.[179] He threatened to use force, should Britain refused to accept the outcome of the arbitration.[180] Both Houses provided their unanimous support to the President. While America contemplated using force against Britain, the fact that America embraced arbitration as the basis of its actions, demonstrated its tendency to avoid war with Britain. The arbitration was the expression of war avoidance norms observed by the United States and Great Britain.[181]

British leaders' responses to the United States' threat of war clustered around the Anglo-American war avoidance norms. They exhibited their commitment to preserving a peaceful relation with the United States, in the belief that the U.S. would also assume the same obligation. The Prince of Wales, in response to the event, broke the convention of royal silence: "I earnestly trust, and cannot but believe, that the present crisis will be arranged in a manner satisfactory to both countries, and will be succeeded by the same warm feeling of friendship which has existed between them for so many years."[182]

Canadians, on the other hand, remained convinced that the United States' threat of war should not be taken seriously.[183] They dismissed Cleveland's message as a political gesture meant for domestic consumption amid America's election season.[184]

Restrained by their shared war avoidance norms, America and Britain decided to jointly conduct the arbitration on the British Guiana–Venezuela border dispute, so as to ensure an outcome that could prevent a war

---

[179] Allen, *Great Britain and the United States*, pp. 532–37.
[180] Ibid., p. 537.
[181] Ibid., p. 540.
[182] Ibid., p. 539.
[183] Shore, "No Fences Make Good Neighbors", p. 346.
[184] Ibid.

between America and Britain.[185] Both parties compromised through the process. Britain in the end was able to secure most of its preferred boundary with Venezuela. America, meanwhile, compelled Venezuela to accept the result of the arbitration.[186] A war therefore had been averted through the two parties simultaneously adhered to their shared war avoidance norms.

By the 1920s, the strength of the Anglo-American war avoidance norms was unmistakable. While Anglo-American rivalries during the 1920s prompted some British ministers and advisors to conclude that war had become likely between the two states, such a conclusion had been effectively curbed by the firmly established war avoidance norms of the two states.[187] British policy remained anchor around the norms.[188] The British government reiterated publicly its unwavering commitment to preserving peaceful ties with America. In February 1928, British Foreign Secretary, Austen Chamberlain, announced in the House of Commons: "preparation for a war with the United States has never been and never will be the basis of our policy in anything".[189]

Reasonable Expectations of Peaceful Change — The Foundation for a Pluralistic Security Community

A special relationship, as a security regime, where the two states involved share reasonable expectations of peaceful change, reveals its quality of constituting the foundation for a pluralistic security community. A pluralistic security community comprises of sovereign states which maintain dependable expectations of peaceful change among them, namely, their capacity to know that neither of them would prepare or even consider to use violence as a means to resolve their disputes. The most obvious characteristic of such a community, therefore, is the absence of war among the states involved. As such, war avoidance norms — a

---

[185] Allen, *Great Britain and the United States*, pp. 539–40.
[186] Ibid.
[187] Dobson, *Anglo-American Relations in the Twentieth Century*, pp. 62–63. Also see ibid., p. 748.
[188] Dobson, *Anglo-American Relations in the Twentieth Century*, p. 63.
[189] Ibid.

security regime — are the foundation for the presence of a pluralistic security community. States involved choose to avoid war, before they could learn to forswear competitive security measures directed at each other.

War avoidance norms, as established norms in a special relationship, while mostly regulating the behaviours of the two states concerned, generate constitutive effects on their respective understanding of self vis-à-vis the counterpart. Such norms engender reasonable expectations of peaceful change between the two states and are interwoven with the two states' mutual positive identifications. The war avoidance norms thus mark the beginning of the consolidation of peaceful change between the two states into dependable expectations of peaceful change between them. States involved maintain among them dependable expectations of peaceful change, when they share a collective-self understanding, which emerges through their positive identifications. That said, a special relationship, which forms a security regime, serves as the basis for the two states involved to transform into a pluralistic security community. States in a pluralistic security community are bound by their collective understanding of self in relation to one another.

In 1914, Theodore Roosevelt wrote in his private letter,

> I cannot help hoping and believing that in the end nations will gradually get to the point that, for instance, Canada and the United States have now attained, where each nation, as a matter of course, treats the other with reasonable justice and friendliness and where war is unthinkable between them.[190]

The United States and Canada, bound by their special relationship, discerned the prevalent peaceful character in their relations, and began to view them sharing North American identity.[191] They had arrived at a position, which looked set to establish their shared collective-self understanding, in the form of North American identity — that of

---

[190] Shore, "No Fences Make Good Neighbors", p. 354.
[191] Ibid., pp. 335, 348, 354. Also see Granatstein and Hillmer, *For Better Or For Worse*, p. 54.

the U.S.–Canada Security Community. However, one element remained absent, without which they could not transform into a security community.

A SPECIAL RELATIONSHIP TRANSFORMS INTO A PLURALISTIC SECURITY COMMUNITY

The Anglo-American and U.S.–Canada special relationships evolved into security communities around the late 1930s and early 1940s. It was at a time when America had emerged as a dominant power among them, and that obvious power imbalance between them came into existence. The presence of power imbalance in a special relationship is necessary, if it is to transform into a pluralistic security community.

The Overwhelmingly Powerful Counterpart — The Guarantor of Survival

Britain's Survival Suddenly Rested Upon America's Immense Power

The Anglo-American special relationship epitomizes the mutual strategic dependence between the two states. Both rely on each other to preserve their similar vision of international order, which is rooted in the English concepts of liberty, hence ultimately safeguard their similar way of life. However, from March 1939 onwards, Britain found itself increasingly reliant on the United States to ensure its very survival.

The balance of power in Europe started to tilt towards Nazi Germany — a totalitarian power — after it annexed Prague in March 1939.[192] Britain, as a consequence, began to realize its reliance on America's immense latent power, in the face of existential threat posed by German expansion.[193] Nazi Germany, with its totalitarian nature, also threatened America's strategic interests.[194] Thereafter, Britain intentionally sought for

---

[192] McKercher, *Transition of Power*, pp. 267–69, 271, 277.
[193] Ibid., pp. 267–68, 270–71. Also see Allen, *Great Britain and the United States*, p. 743.
[194] For more discussion see Chapter 2, pp. 38–39. Also see Allen, *Great Britain and the United States*, p. 797.

Anglo-American cooperation to guarantee its survival.[195] Britain's growing dependence on the United States was conspicuous, when Roosevelt responded to British urge for help by saying: as long as Britain "took that attitude of complete despair, the British would not be worth saving anyway".[196]

The surrender of France to Nazi Germany on 22 June 1940 marked the emergence of power imbalance between the United States and Great Britain.[197] After the collapse of France, Nazi Germany suddenly commanded the preponderant position in Europe. Britain, on the other hand, unexpectedly had to fight for its survival all alone, against the onslaught of Germany.[198] Along the course of defending its survival, Britain quickly lost its global pre-eminence.

Britain was essentially bankrupted in its efforts to withstand German invasion.[199] It had to rely on external assistance, without which it could not weather the war. At that juncture, Britain looked to its brother across the ocean — America — for help. Britain realized that the rapid shrinking of its power meant that its survival would be inevitably rested upon America's power.[200] It needed America's power to uphold its existence, even though it consequently had to accept America's dominance.[201] For Britain, rallied around the powerful America amid the Nazi threat, meant safeguarding the American way of life, which also largely entailed British way of life, as both are founded on the English concepts of liberty.[202]

After the fall of France, the United States was determined to confront Nazi Germany.[203] With such determination, America converted its immense potential strength into real economic and military power, which dwarfed

---

[195] McKercher, *Transition of Power*, pp. 267–68, 271.
[196] Ibid., p. 274.
[197] Ibid., pp. 280–81, 288–89, 296.
[198] Ibid., pp. 288–89, 296, 299, 302.
[199] Ibid., p. 300.
[200] Ibid., pp. 289, 291, 300, 302, 342–43.
[201] Ibid., pp. 289, 291, 300, 301–2, 308–11, 343.
[202] Allen, *Great Britain and the United States*, pp. 784, 797, 826. Also see ibid., p. 281.
[203] McKercher, *Transition of Power*, pp. 281, 296.

that possessed by Britain.[204] Meanwhile, Britain's power continued to shrink in favour of the United States, when it adamantly tied its fundamental security around America's immense power.

Britain had to transfer its political, economic and strategic capital to America's hands, in order to secure America's assistance in its fight against the Axis powers.[205] Britain's gold and dollar reserves depleted massively due to its purchase of goods from the United States to support its war effort. It had to allow the United States to build eight military bases in British possessions in Newfoundland and the Caribbean under the ninety-nine year leases, in exchange for fifty outdated U.S. destroyers. Britain had to renounce substantial economic interests at America's advantage during their negotiation for the lend-lease agreement, so as to secure America's supply of war materials.[206] It had to pass its interests in East Asia to the United States because of the need to fight for its survival in Europe.[207]

The power imbalance between the United States and Great Britain became indisputable after June 1940. Britain right away accepted this fact. Shortly after becoming the British Foreign Secretary in December 1940, Anthony Eden concluded: "I accepted the fact that the United States must in time become the dominant partner in Anglo-American councils."[208] Henceforth, Britain irrevocably relies upon America for its basic security. Britain, which has declined into a second rank power, needs America's immense power to preserve an international order which ultimately secures their similar way of life. Such an order continues to be challenged by culturally different powers, which seek to impose their own values in international politics.

Britain fundamentally relied upon the United States to confront the totalitarian superpower — Russia — soon after the end of the Second World War. It allowed the United States nuclear bombers to be based in the United Kingdom to deter the Soviet Union. It accepted America's

---

[204] Ibid., pp. 281, 296, 335–36, 339, 343.

[205] Ibid., p. 302.

[206] Ibid., pp. 300–1.

[207] Ibid., p. 306.

[208] Ibid., p. 311.

supreme command role in the NATO naval forces of the Atlantic, which was also responsible for the security around Britain's coastline. The U.S. navy was by then the largest navy in history, as large as all the other navies combined.[209]

Britain's fundamental reliance on America for security renders it to understand America as part of self. Because America's immense power constitutes the guarantor of British way of life, America's power hence becomes a magnet for Britain. It intensifies Britain's positive identifications with the United States. Britain rallies around the overwhelmingly powerful America to ensure its very survival.

America's Immense Power Halts Britain's Confrontational Behaviours Against America

As Britain — a second rank power — needs the superpower America to secure its basic survival, it thus has to accept America's dominance, and cease its confrontational behaviours against America.

America demanded Britain's concessions, of which would strengthen America's strategic preponderance, while it was providing material support for Britain's war effort against Nazi Germany.[210] These demands sparked widespread discontent among British elites towards the United States.[211] Britain nevertheless complied with America's terms. It understood that it needed to do so, since its survival was rested upon America's power.[212]

Britain accepted with equanimity America's leadership in NATO naval forces, despite it being the world's strongest naval power for three centuries.[213] It was obliged to forswear its sense of supremacy and follow America's lead, as the overwhelmingly powerful United States guaranteed its security against the existential threat posed by the Soviet Union.

---

[209] Allen, *Great Britain and the United States*, pp. 750, 901.
[210] McKercher, *Transition of Power*, pp. 301–2, 309–10.
[211] Ibid., pp. 301–2.
[212] Ibid.
[213] Allen, *Great Britain and the United States*, pp. 743, 750, 901.

Canada's Security Guarantor — From Great Britain to the United States

Britain's preoccupation in facing German invasion after the collapse of France in June 1940, and its subsequent swift decline in power, presented a basic problem for Canada: it could no longer count on Great Britain as its ultimate security guarantor.[214]

Canada — an enormously smaller power relative to America — in consequence looked to its southern giant neighbour for protection against the possible invasion of Nazi Germany.[215] Shortly after the fall of France, then U.S. Minister to Canada, Pierrepont Moffat, observed,

> there has been a growing public demand throughout Canada for the conclusion of some form of defence understanding with the United States...the old fear that co-operation with the United States would tend to weaken Canada's ties with Great Britain has almost entirely disappeared.[216]

Canada needed the United States to replace Britain as its security guarantor, precisely for the same reason of which its mother country had decided to rely upon the U.S. for survival: America's immense power protects American way of life — which largely entails Canadian way of life — from the challenge of culturally different powers. While Canadians had been emphasizing their British connection so as to distance themselves from Americans, the threat exerted by Nazi Germany and the reality of Britain's sharp decline, compelled Canada to embrace the mighty America for protection.[217] Like its mother country, Canada needed to secure its way of life by rallying around America, which was determined to use its overwhelming power to preserve the American way of life against German aggression.[218] Canadian

---

[214] Shore, "No Fences Make Good Neighbors", pp. 336, 344. Also see Thompson and Randall, *Canada and the United States*, p. 184.

[215] Granatstein and Hillmer, *For Better Or For Worse*, pp. xvi, 133–34. Also see Thompson and Randall, *Canada and the United States*, pp. 69, 152–55.

[216] Granatstein and Hillmer, *For Better Or For Worse*, p. 133.

[217] Ibid., pp. 27, 53, 133–34, 143. Also see Thompson and Randall, *Canada and the United States*, pp. 152–55.

[218] Granatstein and Hillmer, *For Better Or For Worse*, pp. 133–34.

way of life, like those of America and Britain, is founded on the English concepts of liberty.

Facing the Nazi threat, Canada decidedly placed its fundamental security under the protection of the overwhelmingly powerful United States.[219] It agreed to transfer the strategic control of Canadian forces to the United States, if North America was under attack. The drastic decline of Britain and the emergence of America as a superpower — the U.S.–UK power imbalance — prompted Canada to irrevocably rest upon America for its basic security.[220] For the same reason that it had previously clung to Great Britain, Canada relies on America's immense power as the shelter for its way of life, amidst the presence of culturally different powers, which seek to fashion an international order that reflects their own values.

Canada further consolidated its dependence on America for basic security, when they were confronted with the Soviet threat. Canada's armed forces had been placed under America's command through NATO and NORAD (North American Air Defense Agreement), as Canada needed America's protection against possible Soviet attack. Canada's armed forces were equipped with American weapons, and its air defense system was largely provided by the United States.

The United States being the guarantor of Canada's basic survival, results in Canadians to understand the U.S. as part of self. Because the United States' immense power constitutes the shelter for Canadian way of life, the U.S.'s power hence becomes a magnet for Canada. It intensifies Canada's positive identifications with the United States. Canada rallies around the mighty America to secure its very existence.

America's Immense Power Halts Canada's Confrontational Behaviours Against America

Like its mother country, Canada accepts America's dominance and halts its confrontational behaviours against America, owing to the fact that it counts on the superpower America for basic security.

---

[219] Ibid., pp. 140–41. Also see Thompson and Randall, *Canada and the United States*, pp. 152–53.

[220] Thompson and Randall, *Canada and the United States*, p. 184.

Former Canadian Prime Minister, Mackenzie King, once admitted, "if the Americans felt security required it, they would take peaceful possession of part of Canada."[221] King's remark reflected Canadians' understanding. They would accept America's possession of Canada, if America deems it necessary, and do not see it as an act of invasion. They understand that Canada's security is founded upon America's power. If America is to acquire part of Canada, Canadians know that such acquisitions are essential for preserving Canada's existence.

During the Cold War, Canada did not resist America's dominance in deciding Canada's defense gesture against external threats.[222] It understood that "defense cooperation with the United States was desirable and inevitable".[223] Without America, Canada alone was unable to secure itself against the Soviet threat.

The Strategic Importance of the Weaker Counterpart

The emergence of power imbalance between Britain and Canada versus America, necessitates the two states to irreversibly count on America's immense power for basic security. America's rise as a superpower, however, makes explicit the strategic importance of Britain and Canada to America.

The American way of life was confronted with the prospect of a world dominated by totalitarian powers, after Nazi Germany annexed France in June 1940. The United States was determined to prevent this from happening. It exercised its immense power to achieve strategic preponderance worldwide, so as to defeat Nazi Germany, hence secure the American way of life.[224] Thereafter, America attained its global predominance. It needs this status to preserve its preferred international order, which ultimately safeguards its survival — its way of life, in the face of culturally different powers, which seek to challenge that order.[225]

---

[221] Ibid., p. 166.
[222] Thompson and Randall, *Canada and the United States*, p. 197.
[223] Ibid.
[224] McKercher, *Transition of Power*, pp. 281, 309, 343. For more discussion see Chapter 2, pp. 38–39.
[225] McKercher, *Transition of Power*, pp. 280–81, 309, 337, 339, 343. For more discussion see Chapter 2, pp. 38–39.

America's move towards acquiring its global preponderance crystallized its need for partners in international affairs. It needs the power of these partners to constitute its global preponderance. With the partners' cooperation, the United States will then be able to project and impose American values worldwide.

It will be remembered that a special relationship is produced after the two states involved start to share common strategic interests. The two states' common strategic interests are founded on their similar strategic understandings rooted in common identities, and created by their necessary amount of power.

While Britain's and Canada's survival is rested upon America's overwhelming power, each of them continues to possess the necessary amount of power which produces their strategic standing in U.S. foreign policy. America's survival is not fundamentally dependent on Britain and Canada, yet, it remains necessary for America to forge strategic partnerships with them, in order to preserve its strategic preponderance worldwide, which ultimately secures its very survival. In other words, despite being the junior partner in the Anglo-American and U.S.–Canada special relationships, the power owned by Britain and Canada sustains their respective ability to project an amount of cost that would cripple America's status as a global superpower, if America does not seek strategic cooperation with them. Without Britain's and Canada's cooperation, an American-defined world order, which is founded on the English concepts of liberty, would be in peril.

America's own assessment makes plain its strategic dependence on its special junior partners. The policy analysis of the U.S. State Department in June 1948 concluded that "the partnership with Britain was a requirement of American national interest".[226] It explained, because of the power that Britain possessed, "British friendship and cooperation is not only desirable in the United Nations and in dealing with the Soviets; it is necessary for American defence."[227] America

---

[226] John Baylis, ed., "The Search for a New Relationship, 1945–50", in *Anglo-American Relations since 1939: The Enduring Alliance* (Manchester and New York: Manchester University Press, 1997), p. 49.
[227] Ibid.

needed British democracy, the analysis revealed, to become a leading force in the unification of a democratic Western Europe, amidst the aggressiveness of Soviet totalitarianism.[228] In other words, America relies on Britain to preserve a Europe that it preferred — a Europe that reflects the principles of liberty.

Britain Projects an Unbearable Amount of Cost

Upon Britain's request, America provided its firm material support to Britain's fight against Nazi Germany in Europe. America understood, the lack of strategic cooperation with Britain would cost America dearly. It would mean the likely defeat of Britain, hence a Europe controlled by totalitarian powers. Such an outcome meant America lost its strategic buffer against totalitarianism, thus had to defend its democracy by itself.

America unmistakably foresaw the cost of not cooperating with Britain, when it was confronted with the decision of whether to deepen its nuclear partnership with Britain in the 1960s.

The United States' decision to cancel the development of its air-launched missile — Skybolt — in 1962 essentially deprived Britain of its nuclear deterrent.[229] Skybolt was a nuclear delivery vehicle of which America had agreed to supply to Britain. It would be the only delivery vehicle for Britain's nuclear weapons. Britain subsequently requested the supply of Polaris — America's nuclear-armed submarine-launched ballistic missile — from the United States, to replace Skybolt. America was reluctant to consider the request, as the non-proliferation of nuclear weapons in Europe seemed best serve its interest.[230]

Faced with the prospect of losing its nuclear deterrent, Britain presented America with the cost that America would have to bear, if it chose to end its nuclear partnership with Britain. When meeting with President Kennedy in December 1962, British Prime Minister, Harold Macmillan, made clear that Britain would only accept an agreement that guaranteed

---

[228] Ibid., pp. 49–50.
[229] John Baylis, ed., "Challenges to the Nuclear Partnership, 1960–63", in *Anglo-American Relations since 1939*, p. 118.
[230] Ibid.

America's supply of Polaris to Britain, or there would be no agreement at all.[231] He told the President, "Let us part as friends…if there is to be a parting, let it be done with honour and dignity."[232] Macmillan went further. He warned Kennedy that the failure to reach an agreement on Polaris could give birth to an anti-American government in the United Kingdom, which would mean "the end of the close and harmonious relationship between the two countries".[233]

Kennedy gave in having confronted with such a prospect. The United States at last agreed to provide Britain with its most advanced nuclear weapon system of the time — the Polaris. Kennedy's capitulation is understandable. The United States could not afford to lose Britain as its special junior partner, which is obviously much weaker than the U.S., yet retains the power that has decisive impacts on America's global preponderant standing.[234]

Britain is all too aware that it has to be powerful enough, if it is to preserve its strategic value to the United States. A major review conducted by the British Foreign Office in March 1949 concluded, while close partnership with the United States was essential for Britain's security, Britain should "remain a major European and world power" and "sustain its own independent military capacity", so that it is "independent enough to influence U.S. policy".[235] "Britain must be the partner, not a poor relation, of the United States", the review asserted.[236]

Canada Projects an Unbearable Amount of Cost

America yielded to Canada's resistance, when Canada firmly stood by its judgement on the security arrangements in Canada. The U.S.–Canada Permanent Joint Board on Defence (PJBD) produced their second joint defence plan in 1941, which proposed the transfer of Canadian forces' strategic control to the United States, once the U.S. had joined the Allies' fight against the Axis powers. Canada vehemently refused to accept the

---

[231] Ibid., pp. 118–19.
[232] Ibid., p. 119.
[233] Ibid.
[234] Baylis, ed., "The Search for a New Relationship, 1945–50", p. 39.
[235] Ibid., pp. 38–39.
[236] Ibid.

proposal.[237] America, in consequence, retracted its demand to control Canadian forces. Canada's refusal, however, did not account for its confrontation against the United States. Such response was not essentially linked to the use of force against the United States. Both states at last agreed to coordinate their military efforts through mutual consultations.[238] Each would retain full control of their own armed forces.[239]

America was obliged to give way to Canada's adamant resistance. It recognized the consequences of having an uncooperative Canada as its neighbour. While being the very junior special partner of the United States, Canada remains sufficiently strong to exert its influences towards realizing a North America that reflects its democratic values and English culture.[240] Put simply, Canada persists as a power that has regional impact. Without Canada's cooperation, America's strategic preponderance in North America would be at stake.[241] America needs to secure cooperation with Canada, if it is to preserve an American-defined regional order of North America, which is founded on the English concepts of liberty.

Canada is well aware that it needs to be powerful enough, so as to ensure America's strategic reliance on Canada, amidst America's effort to preserve its dominance in North America. In response to the United States' declaration of its commitment to protect Canada against foreign aggression in 1938, Canada reaffirmed its determination to defend itself, which would therefore prevent an invasion on the U.S. soil through Canadian territory.[242] Then Canadian Prime Minister, Mackenzie King, put forward a question to Members of Parliament, "Is it likely that Canada would be able to maintain friendly relations with the United States if we do nothing to defend our own coasts but simply take the attitude that we shall look to them for our defence?"[243] King understood, Canada needed

---

[237] Granatstein and Hillmer, *For Better Or For Worse*, pp. 140–43.
[238] Ibid.
[239] Ibid.
[240] Ibid., pp. 112, 119–20.
[241] Ibid., pp. 46–47, 108–9, 119–20.
[242] Ibid., pp. 103–4, 126.
[243] Ibid., pp. 126–27.

to remain sufficiently strong, without which the U.S.–Canada relations would be defined by the United States' outright dominance over Canada, rather than its strategic reliance on Canada.

America Views Its Special Junior Partners as Part of Self

America identifies positively with Britain and Canada owing to its strategic reliance on the two weaker counterparts to constitute its global preponderance — an American-defined world order founded on the English concepts of liberty — of which would ultimately secures its very survival. America, meanwhile, is able to express its dominance in its relations with Britain and Canada, owing to its role as their security guarantor; hence, prevents such dominant behaviours from turning into confrontational ones. In other words, the United States' negative associations with Britain and Canada have been prevented.

Because America is able to express its dominance over Britain and Canada, coupled with the fact that it is strategically dependent on the two weaker partners, America — the overwhelmingly powerful counterpart — in consequence views Britain and Canada as part of self.

Power Imbalance — A Necessary Condition

Britain and Canada — the two weaker counterparts — view America as part of self, as they fundamentally rely upon the overwhelmingly powerful America in securing their basic survival, namely, their ways of life. America's immense power protects the American way of life, which covers that of Britain and Canada, as they are all founded on the English concepts of liberty. The similar way of life shared by America, Britain and Canada continues to be challenged by culturally different powers, which seek to impose their own values in international politics.

On the other hand, America — the overwhelmingly powerful counterpart — views Britain and Canada as part of self, for two reasons. First, America is able to express its dominance over Britain and Canada, owing to its role as their security guarantor; in consequence, such dominant behaviours will not become confrontational ones. Second, America is strategically dependent on Britain and Canada to constitute an American-dominated world order, which is rooted in the English concepts of liberty. Such world order would ultimately safeguard America's survival, and it continues to be challenged by culturally different powers.

In short, the presence of power imbalance in the Anglo-American and U.S.–Canada special relationships produces the collective-self understanding in each of the bilateral ties; namely, the Anglo-American and U.S.–Canada security communities. As such, the presence of power imbalance in a special relationship is necessary, if it is to transform into a pluralistic security community. The power imbalance is necessary, as the power of the stronger state in the relationship has to be immense in degree, so as to render the weaker one in the relationship to fundamentally rely on its overwhelmingly powerful counterpart for survival — for protecting its way of life, which continues to be challenged by culturally different powers. The power imbalance is necessary, as the power of the stronger one in the relationship needs to be massive enough, so that its expressions of dominance would be accepted by the weaker counterpart, hence prevents such dominant behaviours from turning into confrontational ones. It is necessary to have power imbalance, as the overwhelming power of the stronger one gives birth to its international strategic preponderance, of which would make explicit its strategic reliance on its weaker counterpart, to preserve such preponderance. All these effects of the power imbalance combined, enables the two states concerned to apprehend one another in collective terms.

In essence, power imbalance in a special relationship furnishes a basis of peace between the two states involved. The weaker state in the relationship ceases its confrontational behaviours against its over-whelmingly powerful counterpart, as it counts on the counterpart's immense power for basic security. Meanwhile, the dominant behaviours of the powerful one in the relationship have been mostly accepted by its weaker counterpart, and partially defused by its strategic reliance on the weaker counterpart; hence, its confrontational behaviours against its weaker counterpart have been neutralized. The power imbalance in a special relationship, therefore, ensures the absence of confrontation between the two states involved.

From "Reasonable" to "Dependable" Expectations of Peaceful Change

The power imbalance in a special relationship guarantees the absence of confrontation between the two states involved. It also results in the two states sharing a collective-self understanding. Founded on a special relationship's existing function as a security regime, the effects of power imbalance in the relationship enable its transformation into a pluralistic security community.

With them viewing each other as part of self, shielded by the absence of confrontation between them, the reasonable expectations of peaceful change shared by the two states in a special relationship consolidate into their mutual dependable expectations of peaceful change. The two states by then no longer view armed conflicts between them as unlikely; for them, such conflicts have become impossible, for an attack on the counterpart means an attack on itself. In other words, the power imbalance in a special relationship transforms the shared war avoidance norms of the two states involved into their shared intersubjective appreciation, that war between them is unthinkable. The two states' mutual aspiration for peace, produced by their special ties, have been translated into their capacity to maintain peace between them — that of their ability to know that neither side would even consider using force against one another. In short, with the presence of power imbalance in a special relationship, the two states involved begin to share cooperative intersubjective understandings, namely, they constitute a security community.

The Anglo-American and U.S.–Canada Security Communities

Since the late 1930s, Anglo-American and U.S.–Canada relations are each bound by the two states sharing an understanding of collective-self. The United States and Canada, in particular, apprehend each other as part of self, in the form of North American identity.[244]

For the two states in each of the bilateral relations, the absence of the thought of waging a war against each other, has been intersubjectively recognized as a given fact. Most notably, the undefended U.S.–Canada

---

[244] Shore, "No Fences Make Good Neighbors", pp. 333, 335, 355.

border, which was previously an outcome of the two states' shared war avoidance norms, is now an expression of the U.S.–Canada security community. The undefended border has become a given fact for Americans and Canadians.[245]

While conflicts persist in Anglo-American and U.S.–Canada relations, the presence of dependable expectations of peaceful change in each of the relations ensures each of the two parties' ability to manage their conflicts without the contemplation to use force.

Throughout the Suez crisis in 1956, the conflict between the United States and Britain did not lead to their consideration to turn the conflict into a violent one. Britain and France decided to invade Egypt, after the President of Egypt, Abdul Nasser, nationalized the Suez Canal in July 1956. The canal was jointly owned by Britain and France. America imposed strong economic pressure on Britain, aiming to stop its invasion on Egypt.[246] As a consequence, Britain accepted America's demand for a ceasefire and the withdrawal of British troops from Egypt.[247]

While America exerted pressure on Britain to halt its military operation in Egypt, the thought of pressing Britain with America's military might, however, did not emerge throughout America's dealing with Britain during the crisis.[248] On the other hand, Britain's anger and sense of betrayal towards the United States, borne out of the U.S.'s pressure, did not give rise to its consideration to confront the U.S. with force.[249]

As for U.S.–Canada relations, anti-Americanism endures as the premise of Canadian nationalism. Canada continues to emphasize the superiority of its national identity over that of America. Nevertheless, Canada's anti-American sentiments fall within the understanding of collective-self shared by the United States and Canada. They do not

---

[245] Ibid., p. 360.

[246] Dobson, *Anglo-American Relations in the Twentieth Century*, pp. 117–18. Also see John Dumbrell, *A Special Relationship: Anglo-American Relations from the Cold War to Iraq* (New York: Palgrave, 2006), pp. 53–54.

[247] Ibid.

[248] Raymond Dawson and Richard Rosecrance, "Theory and Reality in the Anglo-American Alliance", *World Politics* 19, no. 1 (1966): 40.

[249] Dobson, *Anglo-American Relations in the Twentieth Century*, pp. 117–19. Also see Dumbrell, *A Special Relationship*, pp. 53–54.

transform into fundamental differences between the two states, which would entail their consideration of using force against each other.

The American Ambassador to Canada in the 1960s, W.W. Butterworth, noticed Canadians' sense of superiority vis-à-vis the United States.[250] He explained to the U.S. State Department that Canadian nationalism was rooted in "a desire to prove they are not what they suspect, a second-class American".[251] Butterworth later criticized Canadian government for what he observed as promoting anti-Americanism in Canada, through a series of TV programmes that "carry slanted and venomous attacks on US policy and US society", and that portrayed "American society as welter of fear, hate, depravity, rot, and disintegration".[252] Butterworth's observation reflected Canada's tendency to express the superiority of its culture over that of America, by viewing Americans as having a culture that was corrupted.

Despite the discernible anti-American sentiments in Canada during the 1960s, Canada, however, remained fundamentally aligned with the United States.[253] The close integration of the U.S.'s and Canada's defence measures persists unscathed.

TABLE 4.1
Chronological Transformation of the U.S.–UK and U.S.–Canada Relations

Since the 1860s	Since the 1910s	Since the late 1930s
• The emergence of a special relationship between the United States and Britain/ Canada.	• The presence of a special relationship between the United States and Britain.	• The Anglo-American special relationship evolved into a pluralistic security community.
• The establishment of a security regime — war avoidance norms — between the United States and Britain/ Canada.	• The presence of a special relationship between the United States and Canada.	• The U.S.–Canada special relationship evolved into a pluralistic security community.

---

[250] Robert Bothwell, *Alliance and Illusion: Canada and the World, 1945–1984* (Vancouver and Toronto: UBC Press, 2007), p. 215.

[251] Ibid.

[252] Ibid., pp. 233–34.

[253] Thompson and Randall, *Canada and the United States*, p. 187.

Part II

History of Indonesia–Malaysia Relations, 1957–2017

5

NOT YET SPECIAL: INDONESIA–MALAYA/MALAYSIA RELATIONS, 1957–65

This chapter explains that a special relationship did not exist between the Sukarno-led Indonesia and Malaya/Malaysia. Indonesia and Malaya/Malaysia were bound by their common identities rooted in the Malay way of life. Because of them sharing common identities, both states shared similar strategic understanding of the regional order of archipelagic Southeast Asia. However, Malaya did not possess the necessary amount of power that would engender Indonesia's recognition of its strategic reliance on Malaya; whereas the amount of power owned by Indonesia had surpassed a level that produced Malaya's strategic dependence on Indonesia. Besides, Indonesia did not immediately realize its mutual strategic dependence with Malaysia, during the period when Malaya had expanded into Malaysia. In short, the similar strategic understanding of Indonesia and Malaya/Malaysia had not been shaped into their common strategic interests by the power owned by Indonesia and Malaya/Malaysia. Indonesia aimed for its strategic preponderance over Malaya/Malaysia; whereas Malaya/Malaysia desired for its mutual strategic dependence with Indonesia.

Two sources of closeness — common identities and common strategic interests — did not coexist in the relationship between Malaya/Malaysia and the Sukarno-led Indonesia. In other words, there was no special relationship between the two states.

The three sources of conflict that were embedded in the ties between Malaya/Malaysia and the Sukarno-led Indonesia — Indonesia's assertion of its dominance over Malaya/Malaysia and Malaya/Malaysia's attempt to balance against Indonesia's aim for regional dominance; the two states' drive to emphasize the superiority of their respective nationhood over that of their culturally similar counterpart; the mismatch of expectation between them — were mutually reinforcing one another. The two states plunged into armed conflicts as a result.

INDONESIA–MALAYSIA COMMON IDENTITIES — THE MALAY WAY OF LIFE

The pre-existing dominant ethnic community in archipelagic Southeast Asia forms the basis for the establishments of Indonesia and Malaysia as two sovereign nation-states. The culture of the ethnic community, namely, the Malay way of life, constitutes the central character of the two states' respective national identity.[1] As such, Indonesia and Malaysia are bound by their common identities rooted in the Malay way of life. The Malay way of life is constituted by the combination of three essential elements — the notion of kingdom, the Malay language and Islam. Within the mindset of kingdom, the people of the dominant ethnic community in archipelagic Southeast Asia speak the Malay language and adhere to Islam.[2]

---

[1]   Anthony Reid, "Understanding *Melayu* (Malay) as a Source of Diverse Modern Identities", in *Contesting Malayness: Malay Identity Across Boundaries,* edited by Timothy P. Barnard (Singapore: Singapore University Press, 2004), pp. 2–3.

[2]   Anthony Milner, *The Malays* (United Kingdom: Wiley-Blackwell, 2008), pp. 74, 76, 81, 85, 99, 101. Also see Joseph Chinyong Liow, *The Politics of Indonesia–Malaysia Relations: One Kin, Two Nations* (London and New York: Routledge, 2005), pp. 31–36. Also see Reid, "Understanding *Melayu* (Malay) as a Source of Diverse Modern Identities", in *Contesting Malayness,* pp. 1–24.

Several sources show that scholars and policymakers of Indonesia and Malaysia believe that the notion of kingdom, the Malay language or Islam is the basic similarity between the two states. In Article 160 of the Malaysian Constitution, Malay is being defined as "a person who professes the religion of Islam, habitually speaks the Malay language" and "conforms to Malay custom".[3] Ahmad Nizar Yaakub in his study "Malaysia and Indonesia: A Study of Foreign Policies with Special Reference to Bilateral Relations" maintains that there are basic similarities in culture, language (the Malay language), and religion (Islam) between Indonesia and Malaysia.[4] Joseph Liow in his study *The Politics of Indonesia–Malaysia Relations: One Kin, Two Nations* notes that the history of interactions among kingdoms in the Indo-Malay world, the Malay language and Islam are pillars for the social-cultural construction of relatedness between Indonesia and Malaysia.[5] Similarly, Anthony Milner in his study "The Malays" observes that "there was a degree of civilizational homogeneity" across much of the archipelagic Southeast Asia, namely, "Islamic, Malay-speaking and structured around *kerajaan* [Kingdom] polities".[6]

The Malay way of life lies within the notion of kingdom — *kerajaan* or *Negara* — in which *Sultan* or *Raja* is the pre-eminent ruler of a *kerajaan* or *Negara*.[7] Such an understanding of kingdom underpins the presence of the Malay civilization that stretches across archipelagic Southeast Asia.[8] Consequently, the region is being perceived as *Nusantara*, which means the Malay world or Malay archipelago. As Milner has pointed out, the Malay civilization has its roots in the *kerajaan* system.[9] J.A.C Mackie's study "Konfrontasi: The Indonesia–Malaysia Dispute

---

3   *Federal Constitution* (Petaling Jaya: ILBS, 2006), p. 198.
4   Ahmad Nizar Yaakub, "Malaysia and Indonesia: A Study of Foreign Policies with Special Reference to Bilateral Relations", PhD dissertation, The University of Western Australia, 2009, pp. 13, 102.
5   Liow, *The Politics of Indonesia–Malaysia Relations*, pp. 29–34.
6   Milner, *The Malays*, pp. 3, 85.
7   Ibid., pp. 60, 66, 81, 84–85. Also see Liow, *The Politics of Indonesia–Malaysia Relations*, pp. 31–32.
8   Milner, *The Malays*, pp. 74, 76, 85, 99.
9   Ibid.

1963–1966", meanwhile, demonstrates that policymakers of Indonesia and Malaysia view the ancient kingdoms in the Malay world as the two states' commonalities. Mackie observes:

> Pride in the greatness of the ancient Malay–Indonesian kingdoms is taught in the schoolrooms of both nations without much concern about the boundaries created by the colonial powers — pride in Srivijaya and Majapahit, in the Sultanates of Malacca, Brunei, Atjeh and Mataram, to mention only the most eminent.[10]

Three most prominent ancient kingdoms in archipelagic Southeast Asia — Srivijaya (AD 683–1377), Majapahit (AD 1293–1525) and Malacca (AD 1402–1511) — crystallize the understanding of this region as the Malay world.[11] These three ancient Kingdoms are believed to have exerted their authority and influence throughout the archipelago.[12] Yaakub explains that the ancient empires of Srivijaya, Majapahit and Malacca are being recognized by Indonesians and Malaysians as "the greatest achievements of their common ancestors".[13] The mythical glorious pasts of their common ancestors, demonstrated by the reach of the three ancient Kingdoms, render the dominant ethnic community in archipelagic Southeast Asia to view this region as one entity.[14] The understanding of "one entity" forms the geographical basis of Indonesians' and Malaysians' perception that archipelagic Southeast Asia is the Malay world — within which the Malay way of life flourishes.

Indonesian and Malaysian nationalists as well as scholars share the view that the supposed reach of the ancient empires of their common ancestors is the territorial basis of the Malay world. Indonesia's prominent ideologue, Mohammad Yamin, believed that an independent Indonesia

---

[10] J.A.C. Mackie, *Konfrontasi: The Indonesia–Malaysia Dispute 1963–1966* (London: Oxford University Press, 1974), p. 15.

[11] Liow, *The Politics of Indonesia–Malaysia Relations*, pp. 30–31. Also see Yaakub, "Malaysia and Indonesia", pp. 95–97.

[12] Liow, *The Politics of Indonesia–Malaysia Relations*, pp. 30–31. Also see Milner, *The Malays*, p. 49; and Yaakub, "Malaysia and Indonesia", pp. 95–96.

[13] Yaakub, "Malaysia and Indonesia", p. 97.

[14] Ibid., pp. 94–97.

known as *Indonesia Raya* should be a modern territorial expression of the Malay world, which was derived from the kingdom of Majapahit.[15] Ibrahim Yaacob, a prominent Malay nationalist, once described: "The aim of *Melayu Raya* is the same as *Indonesia Raya* which is the aspiration of the Malay nationalist movement, that is to revive again the heritage of Srivijaya..."[16] Yaakub's study, on the other hand, maintains that under the Srivijaya and Majapahit empires, the Malay world was united as one political entity.[17] Somewhat differently, Lily Zubaidah Rahim in her study *Singapore in the Malay World: Building and Breaching Regional Bridges* argues that "Singapore was integral to kingdoms within the Malay world such as Srivijaya, Majapahit..."[18]

Indonesian and Malaysian policymakers speak about the idea of the Malay world. An Indonesian minister once said: "after all, Indonesia and Malaysia are part of the Malay Archipelago [Malay World] and are one big family."[19] Malaysian Foreign Minister, Ghazali Shafie, said in his speech at the Third Malaysia–Indonesia Colloquium held in Bali in December 1992: "What I am driving at is that the relationship between the peoples of Indonesia and Malaysia goes back to the age of *Rumpun Melayu*. It was colonialism of the West which divided the Malay World and now perforce we are discussing in Bali about the relationship between two people, the people of which belong to the same cluster..."[20]

The notion of Kingdom — *kerajaan* or *Negara* — is inextricably linked to the Malay language.[21] Through the *kerajaan* or *Negara*

---

[15] Liow, *The Politics of Indonesia–Malaysia Relations*, p. 45. Also see Frederik Holst, *(Dis-) Connected History: The Indonesia–Malaysia Relationship* (Germany: Regiospectra, 2007), p. 329.

[16] Liow, *The Politics of Indonesia–Malaysia Relations*, p. 56.

[17] Yaakub, "Malaysia and Indonesia", pp. 95–96.

[18] Lily Zubaidah Rahim, *Singapore in the Malay World: Building and Breaching Regional Bridges* (Oxon: Routledge, 2009), p. 150.

[19] Liow, *The Politics of Indonesia–Malaysia Relations*, p. 25.

[20] Ghazali Shafie, *Malaysia, ASEAN and the New World Order* (Bangi: Universiti Kebangsaan Malaysia Press, 2000), p. 382.

[21] Milner, *The Malays*, p. 81.

polities that were scattered across archipelagic Southeast Asia, and facilitated by trade among them, the Malay language had become the lingua franca of the region.[22] With this common language as the medium of communication, Islam had spread throughout archipelagic Southeast Asia since it had been introduced to this region around the thirteenth century.[23] Thereafter, Islam emerged as the dominant religion in the archipelago.[24]

Just like the notion of kingdom, the Malay language and Islam are being regarded as the basic similarities between Indonesia and Malaysia. Anthony Reid in his study "Understanding *Melayu* (Malay) as a Source of Diverse Modern Identities" argues that Malaysia, Indonesia and Brunei each has a "core culture", which is "a cultural complex centred in the language called Melayu".[25] Melayu — the Malay language — is the national language of the three states. Meanwhile, Liow's study also notes that the Malay language emerged as the national language of both Malaysia and Indonesia.[26] The Malay language, according to Liow, is a bonding agent and an avenue of affiliation for the two states.[27] He maintains that "the Malay language provided a channel through which the sense of kinship affinity could be better communicated throughout the Malay-speaking Indo-Malay World".[28]

As for Islam, Marshall Clark's and Juliet Pietsch's study *Indonesia–Malaysia Relations: Cultural Heritage, Politics and Labour Migration* points out that "Islam has long been promoted as a pillar of cultural connection between Indonesia and Malaysia."[29] They maintain that "Islam

[22] Ibid., pp. 3, 76, 81, 85, 99. Also see Liow, *The Politics of Indonesia–Malaysia Relations*, p. 33.

[23] Liow, *The Politics of Indonesia–Malaysia Relations*, p. 34.

[24] Ibid.

[25] Reid, "Understanding *Melayu* (Malay) as a Source of Diverse Modern Identities", in *Contesting Malayness*, pp. 2–3.

[26] Liow, *The Politics of Indonesia–Malaysia Relations*, p. 34.

[27] Ibid.

[28] Ibid.

[29] Marshall Clark and Juliet Pietsch, *Indonesia–Malaysia Relations: Cultural Heritage, Politics and Labour Migration* (London and New York: Routledge, 2014), p. 117.

has played a cohesive role" between the two states.[30] Likewise, Liow argues that "Islam provided a cultural avenue through which affiliation could be built, whereby the Indo-Malay Archipelago can be broadly viewed as a single religious entity."[31]

Indonesian and Malaysian policymakers speak about their basic similarities. When discussing about Indonesian President Sukarno's decision to launch his policy of confrontation against Malaysia, Malaysian Prime Minister Tunku Abdul Rahman confided: "We in Malaysia, especially those of his own blood and religion, would have been happy to have worked together with him for peace and economic well-being throughout Southeast Asia, our regional homelands."[32] In February 1966, eight high-ranking Indonesian army officers led by Ali Murtopo paid a goodwill visit to Malaysia in an effort to end the confrontation between the two states.[33] When meeting with Malaysian Prime Minister, the Indonesian army officers said: "We pray that friendship and brotherhood in the true spirit of Islam will return to our two countries."[34] When Indonesia and Malaysia had succeeded in reaching a peace accord in August 1966 to end their confrontation, Indonesia's Foreign Minister Adam Malik asserted: "No victor and no vanquished. This is a great victory for the Malay race."[35] In 2002, Amien Rais, the chairman of Indonesian People's Consultative Assembly (MPR), expressed his disappointment towards Malaysia's decision to cane Indonesian illegals in Malaysia: "Frankly, I feel disappointed, angry, and unable to accept the fact that Malaysia, a modern country which belongs to the same Malay ethnic group (as Indonesia), has resorted to punishing Indonesian illegal workers in a way that is really inhuman."[36]

---

[30]　Ibid.

[31]　Liow, *The Politics of Indonesia–Malaysia Relations*, p. 34.

[32]　Tunku Abdul Rahman, *Looking Back: Monday Musings and Memories* (Malaysia: MPH Group Publishing, 2011), p. 152.

[33]　Ibid., pp. 156–57. Also see Michael Leifer, *Indonesia's Foreign Policy* (London: George Allen & Unwin, 1983), pp. 108–9.

[34]　Ibid.

[35]　Ibid., pp. 156–58. Also see Leifer, *Indonesia's Foreign Policy*, pp. 108–9.

[36]　"Amien Warns KL Not to Play with Fire", *The Jakarta Post*, 19 August 2002.

INDONESIA–MALAYA SIMILAR STRATEGIC UNDERSTANDING

On 31 August 1957, Malaya won its independence from Britain. Because of the sense of closeness which stemmed from their common identities, Malaya's nearest and largest neighbour — Indonesia — had shown clear enthusiasm for the achievement of Malaya.[37]

Leaders of the two newly independent states shared similar strategic apprehensions of the regional order of archipelagic Southeast Asia. They viewed the region as one entity which reflected the Malay way of life — that of the Malay archipelago or Malay world. For Indonesian and Malayan leaders, the Malay world served as a shield which safeguarded the survival of their respective state, where each was built around the Malay way of life.

In June 1945, Sukarno outlined the principles of *Pancasila* — his philosophical basis for Indonesia's nationalist movement. Amid explaining these principles, Sukarno proclaimed that the unity of Indonesia was rested upon the glory of Srivijaya and Majapahit Kingdoms.[38] In other words, the geographical expression of Indonesia's survival should reflect the territories of these ancient kingdoms, which means the entire Malay archipelago. Indonesia's prominent ideologue, Mohammad Yamin, perceived the entire archipelago as the home of Malay civilization, hence the Motherland for the dominant ethnic community in this region.[39] He demanded "the Motherland of the people be transformed into the territory of a state".[40] For Yamin, the Malay archipelago — in the form of a state — should be the land for the existence of those of Malay stock, named as Indonesians.[41]

Malaya's main foreign policymaker, Ghazali Shafie, used the word "*serumpun*" to describe the meaning of the Malay archipelago. For

---

[37] Yaakub, "Malaysia and Indonesia", p. 104.

[38] John D. Legge, *Sukarno: A Political Biography* (Great Britain: Allen Lane The Penguin Press, 1972), pp. 184–85.

[39] Ibid., p. 190.

[40] Ibid.

[41] Ibid.

him, the *serumpun* concept belongs exclusively to the dominant ethnic community in the Malay archipelago.[42] *Serumpun* refers to living in togetherness like what the bamboos do.[43] Bamboos grow from the same root.[44] While each of the bamboos grows autonomously, they, however, live in togetherness.[45] Bamboos survive the strong force of turbulent winds because they live in togetherness.[46] Shafie deemed that Malay civilization was founded on the bamboo's way of survival — *serumpun*.[47] He maintained, the people of Malay stock — in the form of states — should live in togetherness in the Malay archipelago, so that the Malay way of life would not vanish.[48]

For the Malays in Malaya and the indigenous people of Indonesia, the Malay world's function as a shield was made evident by the presence of culturally different others in the region. The dominant ethnic community in archipelagic Southeast Asia feared the political and economic primacy of the Europeans and Chinese in this area.[49] Such concerns strengthened the positive identifications between the indigenous people of Malaya and Indonesia, based upon the mindset of the Malay world.[50] In an attempt to address the perceived Chinese challenge to the Malays in Malaysia, Malay political elite, Abdullah Ahmad, asserted that, "The States that go to make up Malaysia are, in fact, only part of a larger Malayo-Indonesian World..."[51] For Abdullah, the sheer size of the Malay world, overwhelmingly populated by the people of Malay

---

[42] Ghazali Shafie, *Malay Rumpun and Malaysia Bangsa towards 2020* (Bangi: Universiti Kebangsaan Malaysia Press, 2009), pp. 25–26.

[43] Ibid., pp. 11–12.

[44] Ismail Hussein, "Malay Studies in the Malay World", *Malay Literature* 6, no. 1 (1993): 12.

[45] Ibid. Also see Shafie, *Malay Rumpun and Malaysia Bangsa towards 2020*, pp. 11–12, 27–28; and Shafie, *Malaysia, ASEAN and the New World Order*, p. 187.

[46] Ibid. Also see Shafie, *Malaysia, ASEAN and the New World Order*, p. 195.

[47] Shafie, *Malay Rumpun and Malaysia Bangsa towards 2020*, pp. 11–12, 25–27.

[48] Ibid.

[49] Liow, *The Politics of Indonesia–Malaysia Relations*, p. 48. Also see Lily Zubaidah Rahim, *Singapore in the Malay World*, p. 149.

[50] Liow, *The Politics of Indonesia–Malaysia Relations*, p. 48.

[51] Abdullah Ahmad, *Tengku Abdul Rahman and Malaysia's Foreign Policy 1963–1970* (Kuala Lumpur: Berita Publishing, 1985), pp. 7–8.

stock, could effectively curb the Chinese influence in Malaysia, hence, ensure Malaysia's existence as a Malay nation-state.

INDONESIA TO ASSERT ITS STRATEGIC PREPONDERANCE OVER MALAYA

While Indonesian and Malayan leaders shared similar strategic understanding, the two states were not bound by common strategic interests. Both parties' understandings of each other were based on different footings.

The Indonesian elites did not see Malaya as of the same rank with Indonesia. For the great majority of Indonesian leaders, Indonesia was a major power on the world stage.[52] A combination of factors gave rise to such an understanding: Indonesia had succeeded in its revolutionary struggle against a major European power — the Netherlands; it was the largest state in Southeast Asia; it was the fifth most populous state in the world.[53]

Indonesia's sense of being a major power was consolidated by the success of the Asian-African Conference held in Bandung in April 1955. This conference had brought together the leaders of twenty-nine independent Asian and African states, most notably, India and China. These states shared a common experience — the struggle against colonialism and imperialism. The Bandung Conference cemented the concept of the "Third World", which refers to "former colonial or semicolonial countries in Africa, Asia, and Latin America that were subject to European (or rather pan-European, including American and Russian) economic or political domination".[54]

Since the conference, two central ideas had emerged to be associated with the Third World concept. First, the Third World states would support

---

[52] Leifer, *Indonesia's Foreign Policy*, pp. xiv, 56. Also see Franklin B. Weinstein, *Indonesian Foreign Policy and the Dilemma of Dependence: From Sukarno to Soeharto* (Ithaca and London: Cornell University Press, 1976), pp. 189–190, 203–5.

[53] Ibid.

[54] Odd Arne Westad, *The Global Cold War: Third World Interventions and the Making of Our Times* (Cambridge: Cambridge University Press, 2005), pp. 2–3.

each other against imperialist interventions, and assist in liberating those which were still being colonized.[55] Second, the Third World states embraced the principles of non-alignment, which meant they would not choose side in the Cold War.[56] As such, the Third World states represented a force of its own in international politics.

The Bandung Conference symbolized the emergence of this new force — the Third World; a stand-alone force that worried both the United States and the Soviet.[57] It also marked Indonesia's rise as a leader of the Third World.[58] Together with India, Egypt and Yugoslavia, Indonesia had since been recognized as one of the leaders of the Third World.[59] President Sukarno's speech at the Bandung Conference exemplified Indonesia's acknowledgement of such a leadership role:

> we can mobilize all the spiritual, all the moral, all the political strength of Asia and Africa on the side of peace. Yes we! We the people of Asia and Africa...far more than half the human population of the world, we can mobilize what I have called the Moral Violence of Nations in favour of peace.[60]

Thereafter, the Sukarno regime perceived Indonesia to be a state of consequence in world affairs, representing the force of the Third World. Indonesia's sense as a major power — a leader of the Third World — provided the basis for its determination to assert its strategic preponderance in archipelagic Southeast Asia. The assertion was aimed at addressing a fundamental security issue of Indonesia — its disintegration as a state.

Since the end of 1956, Indonesia had been plagued by a series of regional coups in Sumatra and Sulawesi. These regional discontents were prompted by the regions' demand for greater autonomy and

---

[55] Ibid., pp. 104–5.
[56] Ibid., pp. 98–99, 101.
[57] Ibid., pp. 103, 105–7.
[58] Ibid., pp. 99, 107. Also see Donald E. Weatherbee, *International Relations in Southeast Asia: The Struggle for Autonomy* (Singapore: Institute of Southeast Asian Studies, 2010), p. 67.
[59] Westad, *The Global Cold War*, pp. 103–4, 107.
[60] Legge, *Sukarno*, p. 265.

greater share of national wealth; precipitated by the evident decline of Indonesia's economy.[61] By the mid-1950s, corruptions were rampant in Indonesia, its inflation was mounting, poverty remained obvious, living standards and export continued to fall.

The rebellions in Sumatra and Sulawesi had been receiving military and logistical supports from the United States and Australia.[62] A widespread support for the Communist Party of Indonesia (PKI) had emerged in Indonesia's society after its independence. The PKI had been positioning itself as a party that was defending the interests of the poor.[63] The rise of communism in Indonesia coupled with Indonesia's status as a Third World leader alarmed the Western powers — the United States and Australia.[64] The West worried that Indonesia by pursuing its own paths of economic and social development might result in other undeveloped states following Indonesia's example hence creating a spread of communism and non-alignism in Southeast Asia as well as the world at large.[65] Such an outcome posed a direct threat to the U.S. dominance in Southeast Asia.[66] Consequently, the United States and Australia had made a decision that they would strive to break up Indonesia by supporting the rebel movements both in Sumatra and Sulawesi.[67]

President Sukarno and the central command of Indonesian army quickly allied with each other to halt the disintegration of Indonesia.[68] Indonesia expressed its strategic preponderance in archipelagic Southeast Asia, so as to ensure its integrity. For Sukarno and the army leaders, by maximizing Indonesia's sphere of influence in the region, they could then minimize the prospect of Indonesia falling apart.[69] The Sukarno

---

[61] Ibid., pp. 272–73. Also see Leifer, *Indonesia's Foreign Policy*, pp. 38, 42, 46.
[62] Clinton Fernandes, *Reluctant Indonesians: Australia, Indonesia, and the Future of West Papua* (Australia: Scribe Publications, 2006), p. 23.
[63] Ibid., pp. 22–23.
[64] Ibid.
[65] Ibid.
[66] Ibid. Also see Weatherbee, *International Relations in Southeast Asia*, pp. 70–71.
[67] Fernandes, *Reluctant Indonesians*, pp. 22–23.
[68] Legge, *Sukarno*, pp. 286–87. Also see Leifer, *Indonesia's Foreign Policy*, pp. 46–47.
[69] Leifer, *Indonesia's Foreign Policy*, pp. xiv–xv.

regime took two actions to establish the preponderant gesture of Indonesia. In March 1957, it declared a nationwide State of War and Siege to curb the regional coups. Such a declaration centralized the power in Indonesia at the hands of its army with President Sukarno — the Commander-in-Chief — possessing the ultimate authority. The centralization of power would allow the regime to effectively execute its will of preserving the unity of Indonesia.

In December 1957, the regime declared its Archipelago Doctrine, known as the Djuanda Declaration:

> The government declares that all waters surrounding, between and connecting the islands constituting the Indonesian state, regardless of their extension or breadth, are integral parts of the territory of the Indonesian state and therefore, parts of the internal or national waters which are under the exclusive sovereignty of the Indonesian state.... The delimitation of the territorial sea (the breadth of which is 12 miles) is measured from baselines connecting the outermost points of the islands of Indonesia.[70]

The doctrine revealed Indonesia's will to maximize its territory through legal means, based upon its existing structure as an archipelagic state. Most notably, it extended the customary 3 miles breadth of territorial sea to 12 miles.

In a nutshell, the Sukarno regime centralized the power in Indonesia, which subsequently served as the foundation for it to begin asserting Indonesia's strategic preponderance in archipelagic Southeast Asia by declaring its Archipelago Doctrine. These two moves constituted the regime's strategy for preserving Indonesia's integrity.

Indonesia's Archipelago Doctrine reflected its strategic understanding of viewing the Malay world/Malay archipelago as a shield that protected its survival. The doctrine raised concerns among Indonesia's neighbours. They feared if Indonesia was intended to restore the "golden age" boundaries of ancient Majapahit Empire.[71]

---

[70] Dino Patti Djalal, *The Geopolitics of Indonesia's Maritime Territorial Policy* (Jakarta: Centre for Strategic and International Studies, 1996), p. 29.

[71] Weatherbee, *International Relations in Southeast Asia*, p. 14.

Indonesia's desire to assert its strategic preponderance mutually reinforced with the strong nationalist sentiments in Indonesian society. Because of the fragmented character of Indonesian state and society, a strong sense of nationhood was needed so as to ensure the unity of its people; in other words, to safeguard the existence of Indonesia.[72] The common anti-colonial revolutionary struggle against the Dutch for the independence of Indonesia formed the central content of Indonesia's nationalism that fostered the unity of the state.[73] In an effort to sustain Indonesia's unity, President Sukarno persistently instigated a sense of continuous revolutions against colonialism-imperialism among Indonesian people.[74] Such instigations also meant to ensure his own political survival.

Sukarno was a force of his own in Indonesia's politics. He was the embodiment of the Republic's unity, hence the source of legitimacy in Indonesia's politics.[75] Yet, Sukarno got no organized power base.[76] He depended on public recognition of him as the symbol of national unity to preserve his authority in Indonesia, which was independent of the army and parties in the state.[77] Consequently, Sukarno had to constantly instill a strong sense of nationhood among the Indonesian mass public by using his charismatic personality and great oratory skills.[78] He needed to do so in order to rally the people around him, embrace him as the symbol of Indonesia, thus sustaining his authority in the state. In other words, Sukarno relied on nationalism to perpetuate his political existence in Indonesia. He used it to maintain his power base. Put simply, the nature of Indonesia's politics guaranteed strong nationalism in its society.

---

[72] Legge, *Sukarno*, pp. 90, 272, 332. Also see Leifer, *Indonesia's Foreign Policy*, pp. xiv, 45, 55–56.

[73] Legge, *Sukarno*, pp. 80–81, 86, 90, 104–5. Also see Max Lane, *Unfinished Nation: Indonesia Before and After Suharto* (London & New York: Verso, 2008), pp. 7, 21, 26–27.

[74] Legge, *Sukarno*, pp. 291, 315, 332. Also see Leifer, *Indonesia's Foreign Policy*, pp. 45, 56–57.

[75] Legge, *Sukarno*, pp. 225, 231, 308. Also see Leifer, *Indonesia's Foreign Policy*, p. 54.

[76] Legge, *Sukarno*, p. 297. Also see Leifer, *Indonesia's Foreign Policy*, pp. 54–55.

[77] Legge, *Sukarno*, pp. 270, 275, 297, 307–8.

[78] Ibid., pp. 235, 307–8, 332. Also see Leifer, *Indonesia's Foreign Policy*, pp. 45, 55–56.

With a combination of the aims of ensuring personal survival and promoting national unity, President Sukarno stirred up Indonesians' national pride by inspiring them with a belief that Indonesia was a leader of the Third World, charged to champion the revolutionary struggles against colonialism-imperialism worldwide.[79] Such nationalistic aspirations boosted, and were boosted by, Indonesia's resolve to assert its strategic preponderance in archipelagic Southeast Asia. The immediate manifestation of these mutually reinforcing dynamics was Indonesia's claim of sovereignty over West Irian — a territory where Indonesia had yet to inherit from the former Netherlands East Indies.

Sukarno described West Irian as "a colonial sword poised over Indonesia".[80] He evoked intense nationalist sentiments in Indonesian society on the issue of West Irian.[81] For Indonesians, the claim of West Irian became a fundamental expression of their struggle against Dutch colonial rule.[82] The Indonesian mass public had been mobilized to "perfecting their revolution" through incorporating West Irian — the Dutch last possession of the former Netherlands East Indies — into Indonesia.[83]

It was against this background — Indonesia's perception of itself as a world's major power, charged to lead the Third World, readied to assert its strategic preponderance in archipelagic Southeast Asia, which were mutually reinforced with Indonesians' strong nationalist sentiments — that the Sukarno regime came to deal with the existence of Malaya.

Buttressed by its sense where Malaya was only a little state relative to Indonesia, the Sukarno regime aimed to exercise its dominance over Malaya, as part of its efforts to establish Indonesia's regional preponderance.[84]

---

[79] Leifer, *Indonesia's Foreign Policy*, pp. 55–56. Also see Weinstein, *Indonesian Foreign Policy and the Dilemma of Dependence*, p. 163.

[80] Leifer, *Indonesia's Foreign Policy*, p. 61.

[81] Ibid., p. 47.

[82] Ibid., pp. 47–48, 61.

[83] Ibid., p. 61. Also see Legge, *Sukarno*, pp. 291, 315.

[84] Mackie, *Konfrontasi*, p. 168. Also see Liow, *The Politics of Indonesia–Malaysia Relations*, p. 81.

The regime had shown active interest in shaping the affairs of Malaya.[85] Such dominant behaviours were fortified by Malaya's weak military capacity and Indonesia's evident influence in Malaya.

Malaya had virtually no armed forces immediately after its independence. It had no air force and navy. It possessed only several battalions of the Malay Royal Regiment as opposed to Indonesia's half a million army. Malaya's security was almost entirely dependent on the 1957 Anglo-Malayan Defence Agreement (AMDA).[86] Under this treaty, Britain would protect Malaya from any external attack and develop Malaya's armed forces; in return, Malaya would allow the stationing of British, Australian and New Zealand's armed forces at its bases to defend the Commonwealth and preserve the peace in Southeast Asia; Malaya would also assist Britain if its colonial territories — Hong Kong, Singapore, North Borneo, Sarawak and Brunei — were under attack.[87]

As for Indonesia's influence, the pro-Indonesian forces in Malaya were powerful enough to exert pressure on Malaya's government. These forces were generally represented by the opposition parties in Malaya's parliament, Malay nationalists within UMNO — the ruling party, and the Indonesian-trained journalists who controlled most of the Malay press in Malaya.[88] Further, many of the Malays in Malaya were sympathizers of Indonesia's aspirations.[89] It was estimated that around one third of the Malay population in Malaya were of Indonesian origin.[90]

---

[85] Liow, *The Politics of Indonesia–Malaysia Relations*, pp. 79–81.

[86] Johan Saravanamuttu, *Malaysia's Foreign Policy, the First Fifty Years: Alignment, Neutralism, Islamism* (Singapore: Institute of Southeast Asian Studies, 2010), p. 48.

[87] Abdullah Ahmad, *Tengku Abdul Rahman and Malaysia's Foreign Policy 1963–1970* (Kuala Lumpur: Berita Publishing, 1985), pp. 8–9, 26.

[88] Liow, *The Politics of Indonesia–Malaysia Relations*, pp. 82–85, 105. Also see Chandran Jeshurun, *Malaysia: Fifty Years of Diplomacy 1957–2007* (Singapore: Talisman Publishing, 2007), pp. 19, 37–38.

[89] Liow, *The Politics of Indonesia–Malaysia Relations*, p. 83. Also see Federation of Malaya, *Parliamentary Debates, 6th December 1960* (Kuala Lumpur: House of Representatives, 1960), pp. 3413–14.

[90] Liow, *The Politics of Indonesia–Malaysia Relations*, p. 42.

The Malayan Prime Minister, Tunku Abdul Rahman, had to withstand strong opposition from these pro-Indonesian forces to the signing of AMDA.[91] They accused Tunku of being pro-West and wanted Malaya to embrace the Bandung model, namely, the Third World.[92] The Tunku's leadership was at risk when he had to make AMDA an issue of confidence at an emergency UMNO Executive Committee meeting in the face of the forceful attacks on this treaty mounted by the Malay nationalists in the party.[93] He nevertheless succeeded in securing a unanimous vote from the Committee which endorsed the defence treaty.

On the other hand, even though Malaya's basic security was inextricably linked to the West, the Malayan government refused to join the Southeast Asia Treaty Organization (SEATO), in view of the anticipated staunch opposition at home, especially from the pro-Indonesian forces in Malaya's parliament.[94] SEATO was a collective defence organization constituted by the United States, Britain, Australia, New Zealand, France, Pakistan, the Philippines and Thailand, which aimed at curbing the communist presence in Southeast Asia.[95] Indonesia criticized SEATO as America's imperialist design in Southeast Asia.[96]

Indonesia's desire to express its dominance over Malaya bolstered, and was bolstered by, its drive to differentiate itself, in superiority sense, from the culturally similar Malaya. The Malay way of life, which constituted the central character of Indonesia's and Malaya's respective national identity, resulted in inevitable similarities between the two states. Indonesia hence needed to enhance its difference as opposed to

---

[91] Saravanamuttu, *Malaysia's Foreign Policy, the First Fifty Years*, pp. 50–51. Also see Jeshurun, *Malaysia*, pp. 19, 37–38; and Liow, *The Politics of Indonesia–Malaysia Relations*, pp. 82–83.

[92] Ibid.

[93] Ibid.

[94] Liow, *The Politics of Indonesia–Malaysia Relations*, pp. 82–83. Also see Abdullah Ahmad, *Tengku Abdul Rahman and Malaysia's Foreign Policy 1963–1970*, pp. 26–27, 62–63; and Jeshurun, *Malaysia*, pp. 37–38.

[95] Weatherbee, *International Relations in Southeast Asia*, pp. 65–66.

[96] Abdullah Ahmad, *Tengku Abdul Rahman and Malaysia's Foreign Policy 1963–1970*, pp. 26–27, 33, 62–63.

Malaya, so as to emphasize its distinctive existence in the world. Such differentiation was expressed in superiority sense.

The power politics between Indonesia and Malaya, combined with Indonesians' sense of uniqueness of their national identity vis-à-vis Malaya, gave birth to Indonesians' sense of superiority of their identity over that of Malaya. The superiority complex was founded on the power politics-induced mindset of comparison.

The similarities between Indonesians and Malayans were demonstrated by the closeness between them, which stemmed from their common identities.[97] Because of their close identifications with Indonesians, the people of Malaya had provided material and moral support to Indonesians' fight against the Netherlands for independence.[98] Hundreds of Malayans went to Indonesia to join the fight, and many had sacrificed their lives.[99] Meanwhile, Indonesians gave their strong moral support to the subsequent independence movement in Malaya.[100]

Despite the solidarity among the people of Indonesia and Malaya in the course of their respective struggle for independence, Indonesians insisted on their disdain for Malaya's way of achieving its independence. For most of the Indonesian political and military elites, independence had to be achieved through revolution; in order for their independence to be authentic, people had to fight for it through armed struggle.[101] Malaya's independence, from Indonesians' perspective, was given by the imperialist — Britain; Malayans did not fight for it; hence, Malaya's independence was an inferior one, when compared to that of Indonesia, which was achieved through a bloody revolution.[102]

---

[97] Government of Malaysia, *Malaya–Indonesia Relations 31st August 1957 to 15th September 1963* (Kuala Lumpur: Jabatan Chetak Kerajaan, 1963), p. 1.

[98] Ibid.

[99] Ibid.

[100] Ibid.

[101] Liow, *The Politics of Indonesia–Malaysia Relations*, p. 80. Also see Jeshurun, *Malaysia*, pp. 39–40.

[102] Ibid. Also see Radio Address by Sukarno, December 1962, quoted in Peter Carey, "Introduction", in *Born in Fire: The Indonesian Struggle for Independence: An Anthology*, edited by Colin Wild and Peter Carey (Athens: Ohio University Press, 1988), p. xix. Also see Legge, *Sukarno*, p. 363.

In short, Indonesia emphasized the superiority of their nationhood over Malaya's, which was expressed in the language of Indonesians' revolutionary fighting spirit.

Such disdain for Malaya was further reinforced by the fact that Malaya was fundamentally reliant on Britain — whom Indonesia regarded as a colonial-imperial power — for its security.[103] And Malaya upheld the Sultanates as its prime symbol. For Indonesians, the Sultanates, which represented the feudalistic elements in society, were antithetical to Indonesia's revolutionary spirit that embraced egalitarianism, hence they should be demolished.[104] The sultans and traditional elites in Sumatra had been decimated, shortly after Indonesians embarked on their revolution in August 1945.

Indonesia's sense of superiority of its nationhood over that of Malaya strengthened, and was strengthened by, its impulse to dominate Malaya. Among its neighbouring states, the Indonesian elites had "singled out" Malaya as "a state requiring revolutionizing" due to Malaya's "fake independence".[105] Such predisposition to dominate Malaya prompted President Sukarno to express his superiority sentiments towards the Tunku — then Chief Minister of British Malaya — during a public rally in Jakarta in 1955. Looking and pointing at the Tunku, Sukarno pronounced: "Here is a man I am trying to persuade to fight."[106] The Tunku was at the rally. He was there for his official goodwill visit to Indonesia.

Essentially, in the eyes of the Sukarno regime, there was no common strategic interest between Indonesia and Malaya. Malaya had yet to possess the necessary amount of power that would secure Indonesia's

---

[103] Legge, *Sukarno*, pp. 363–64. Also see Mackie, *Konfrontasi*, pp. 32–33.

[104] Leifer, *Indonesia's Foreign Policy*, p. 76. Also see Liow, *The Politics of Indonesia–Malaysia Relations*, pp. 61–67, 74; and Abdullah Ahmad, *Tengku Abdul Rahman and Malaysia's Foreign Policy 1963–1970*, p. 32.

[105] Frederick P. Bunnell, "Guided Democracy Foreign Policy: 1960–1965 — President Sukarno Moves From Non-Alignment to Confrontation", *Indonesia* 2 (October 1966): 37–76. Also see Liow, *The Politics of Indonesia–Malaysia Relations*, pp. 79–80.

[106] Marvin C. Ott, "The Sources and Content of Malaysian Foreign Policy Toward Indonesia and the Philippines: 1957–1965", PhD dissertation, The Johns Hopkins University, 1971, p. 111.

recognition of its strategic reliance on Malaya. Instead of perceiving its mutual strategic dependence with Malaya, Indonesia desired for its strategic preponderance over Malaya. Such aspiration for dominance coincided with Indonesia's strategic understanding. With Malaya that lay within its sphere of influence, the Malay archipelago — mainly represented by Indonesia and Malaya — constituted a shield that ensured the survival of Indonesia.

MALAYA DESIRED FOR MUTUAL STRATEGIC DEPENDENCE WITH INDONESIA

The Malayan leaders, on the contrary, believed that Indonesia and Malaya needed each other for survival. In a 1963 government report titled "Malaya-Indonesia Relations 31st August 1957 to 15th September 1963", the Tunku administration expressed Malaya's desire to "forge the closest links with Indonesia".[107] Two sources of closeness — common identities and shared strategic interests — produced Malayan leaders' wish for intimate ties with Indonesia. From Malayans' perspective, not only did Indonesia share "sentimental and blood ties" with Malaya, but they were also each other's nearest neighbour.[108]

The understanding of geographical proximity with Indonesia indicated Malaya's realization of its mutual strategic dependence with Indonesia. The amount of power owned by Indonesia had surpassed a level that produced its strategic standing in Malaya's foreign policy. Based upon their common identities-induced similar strategic understandings — that of the Malay archipelago constituted a shield that protected their respective survival — the presence of Indonesia as the largest state in Southeast Asia, created Malaya's need for strategic partnership with Indonesia.

Malayan policymakers were all too aware, that Malaya was a small state in archipelagic Southeast Asia, with Indonesia as its largest and

---

[107] Government of Malaysia, *Malaya–Indonesia Relations 31st August 1957 to 15th September 1963*, p. 1.
[108] Ibid.

nearest neighbour.[109] Malaya therefore needed to secure Indonesia's strategic cooperation, so that their shared "regional homelands" — the Malay archipelago — could serve as a shield that safeguarded their respective survival as a state which was built around the Malay way of life.[110] Prime Minister Tunku Abdul Rahman confided: "We... especially those of his [President Sukarno] own blood and religion, would have been happy to have worked together with him for peace and economic well-being throughout Southeast Asia, our regional homelands."[111] Also he explained: "As we were too small to stand alone, our only hope for security was to live in close association with Indonesia in particular, and other countries in Southeast Asia in general."[112]

Malaya's intention towards Indonesia was unmistakable. It wanted to establish a special relationship with Indonesia — a closer relation between Malaya and Indonesia when compared to their other bilateral ties.[113] The desire for special associations reflected Malaya's realization of its blood ties with Indonesia, and that both states were strategically dependent on each other.

It should be noted that Malaya emphasized on its mutual strategic dependence with, not its outright reliance on, Indonesia. It wanted the relationship to be equal. In other words, both parties would have to rely on each other for survival. The Tunku revealed his conversation with Sukarno, "I made it quite clear that Malaya was only a small country. The Malay people looked to Indonesia for guidance and help, although we maintained that independence and sovereignty were our heritage."[114] While acknowledging that it was a small state as compared with Indonesia, Malaya considered itself as a power to be reckoned with in Southeast Asia.

---

[109] Abdul Rahman, *Looking Back*, p. 113.
[110] Ibid., pp. 113, 152.
[111] Ibid.
[112] Ibid.
[113] Jeshurun, *Malaysia*, p. 42.
[114] Abdul Rahman, *Looking Back*, p. 113.

A combination of factors — the size and the geographical location of Malaya; the resources that it possessed; its greater prosperity against other states in the region; and its military alliance with Britain — rendered the belief among Malayans that Malaya was a consequential power in Southeast Asia.[115] These elements, especially the Anglo-Malayan military alliance and Malaya's greater wealth as opposed to Indonesia's, prompted Malayans to perceive that power balance existed between Malaya and Indonesia.[116] Throughout the early 1960s, the GDP per capita of Malaya (later Malaysia) was evidently higher than that of Indonesia (see Table 5.1).

TABLE 5.1
GDP per capita and Total Population of Malaya and Indonesia in the Early 1960s

Year	Malaya GDP per capita (constant 2005 US$)	Indonesia GDP per capita (constant 2005 US$)	Malaya Total Population	Indonesia Total Population
1960	815	286	8,160,975	88,692,697
1961	849	296	8,429,369	90,860,197
1962	875	295	8,710,678	93,101,152
1963	909	281	8,999,247	95,420,835
1964	928	284	9,287,442	97,828,538
1965	970	279	9,569,784	100,329,810

Source: World Development Indicators.

With its solid material capacity, Malaya was ready to take the lead in fashioning its preferred order in Southeast Asia, with the aim of securing Indonesia's cooperation; it was also ready to compete with Indonesia.[117]

---

[115] Abdullah Ahmad, *Tengku Abdul Rahman and Malaysia's Foreign Policy 1963–1970*, pp. 9, 24, 26, 33. Also see Liow, *The Politics of Indonesia–Malaysia Relations*, p. 97.
[116] Ibid.
[117] Government of Malaysia, *Malaya–Indonesia Relations 31st August 1957 to 15th September 1963*, p. 4. Also see Jeshurun, *Malaysia*, pp. 25–26; and Abdullah Ahmad, *Tengku Abdul Rahman and Malaysia's Foreign Policy 1963–1970*, pp. 20–21, 33, 64.

These attempts were aimed at securing Malaya's survival. In the minds of the Malayan leaders, there was no Indonesia's supremacy in Southeast Asia; there would be only Indo-Malay mutual reliance, which represented the presence of the Malay archipelago.[118]

THE FIRST ENCOUNTER

Indonesia–Malaya relations were put to test in the first days of Malaya's independence. In September 1957, Malaya abstained from voting to include the issue of West Irian on the agenda of the Twelfth Session of the UN General Assembly. The decision was at odds with Indonesia's expectation. Indonesia expected to receive "absolute support" from Malaya, owing to their close bonds originated from their common roots, and such support would reflect Indonesia's dominance over Malaya.[119]

The mismatch of expectation produced Indonesia's resentment towards Malaya; and its assertion of dominance over Malaya ensued.[120] Indonesia demanded an explanation from Malaya for not supporting its cause at the UN.[121] Malaya explained that it was too preoccupied with its domestic affairs, and would only vote for issues that were directly related to Malaya.[122] Still, Indonesia's show of dominance was real in Malaya.

The Malaya's pro-Indonesian forces put up their criticisms on the Malayan government for not siding with Indonesia at the UN.[123] Besides, the Malay public in Malaya had also voiced their support for

---

[118] Mubin Sheppard, *Tunku: His Life and Times* (Malaysia: Pelanduk Publications, 1995), p. 116. Also see Abdullah Ahmad, *Tengku Abdul Rahman and Malaysia's Foreign Policy 1963–1970*, pp. 33–34.

[119] Leifer, *Indonesia's Foreign Policy*, p. 65.

[120] Ibid. Also see Liow, *The Politics of Indonesia–Malaysia Relations*, pp. 91–92.

[121] Tun Dr Ismail A. Rahman Papers, Drifting into Politics, Unpublished Memoirs Folio 12 (2), p. 50. Courtesy of ISEAS Library, ISEAS – Yusof Ishak Institute, Singapore.

[122] Mackie, *Konfrontasi*, p. 31.

[123] Liow, *The Politics of Indonesia–Malaysia Relations*, pp. 91–92.

Indonesia's struggle for West Irian.[124] Because of the palpable support of the Malay public, together with the pressure exerted by Indonesia and the Malaya's pro-Indonesian forces, the Tunku administration came to realize the fundamental importance of West Irian to Indonesia.[125] The Malays in Malaya and the overwhelming majority of Indonesians wanted West Irian to be part of Indonesia; in other words, they viewed the territory as belonged to the Malay world.[126] The Malayan government thus needed to support Indonesia's claim on West Irian, considering that the territory was inextricably linked to the understanding of the Malay world or Malay archipelago held by the Malaya's Malays and Indonesians. The presence of the Malay world was crucial to Malaya's security. Malaya saw it as a shield that protected Malaya's existence as a Malay nation-state.

The Tunku administration promptly adjusted its policy. In November 1957, Malaya's Permanent Representative to the UN, Dr Ismail, set forth Malaya's support for Indonesia's struggle for West Irian, when he spoke before the UN Political Committee. According to Dr Ismail, his speech was "impassioned" and "emotionally in favour of Indonesia".[127] The Indonesian delegates who heard the speech "cried with emotion".[128]

Malaya threw its support behind the Indonesia's cause since then.[129] Malaya voted for Indonesia when the issue of West Irian was raised again at the UN in November 1957. It publicly backed Indonesia's claim on the territory. It continued to stand behind Indonesia whenever there was a vote for the issue at the UN. Most notably, Malaya consistently denied the Dutch access to the transit facilities in Malaya, amidst Indonesia's

---

[124] Ibid., p. 95. Also see Federation of Malaya, *Parliamentary Debates, 6th December 1960* (Kuala Lumpur: House of Representatives, 1960), pp. 3413–14.

[125] Ibid. Also see Greg Poulgrain, *The Genesis of Konfrontasi: Malaysia Brunei Indonesia 1945–1965* (Australia: Crawford House Publishing, 1998), p. 183.

[126] Leifer, *Indonesia's Foreign Policy*, pp. 30, 48, 61.

[127] Ooi Kee Beng, *The Reluctant Politician: Tun Dr. Ismail and His Time* (Singapore: Institute of Southeast Asian Studies, 2006), p. 90. Also see Jeshurun, *Malaysia*, p. 41; and Mackie, *Konfrontasi*, p. 31.

[128] Ibid.

[129] Mackie, *Konfrontasi*, p. 31.

fight against the Netherlands for West Irian.[130] This policy remained in place even when the issue of West Irian had already been resolved.[131] Malaya too exerted pressure on the British government to prevent the Dutch troops from transiting through the British-rule Singapore en route from West Irian to Europe.[132] The Dutch army decided not to dock their ships at Singapore partly due to the pressure brought to bear by Malaya.[133]

The Malayan government, therefore, saw its policy on West Irian as its strategic cooperation with Indonesia.[134] Prime Minister Tunku Abdul Rahman made plain to his British counterpart: should clashes break out between Indonesia and the Netherlands, "Malaya...because of her affinity with Indonesia, might have to declare openly her support of Indonesia".[135] For the Malayan government, assisting Indonesia to take over West Irian from the Dutch meant consolidating the presence of the Malay world. The support of Malaya — as Malayans saw it — was crucial to the success of Indonesia's claim on West Irian, because Malaya was a power of consequence in Southeast Asia.

Meanwhile, the emotional reaction of the Indonesian UN delegates, who burst into tears after listening to Dr Ismail's defend of Indonesia's case for West Irian, did not indicate Indonesia's acknowledgment of sharing strategic partnerships with Malaya. The reaction was merely the delegates' sentimental expression which stemmed from their sense of sharing common identities with Malaya. For Indonesia, its fight for West Irian was in fact a Third World leader's struggle against colonialism-imperialism. Such a fight was accompanied by the support from the Soviet Union and the Third World states. In other words, Indonesia perceived itself as a major power

---

[130] Ibid. Also see Government of Malaysia, *Malaya–Indonesia Relations 31st August 1957 to 15th September 1963*, p. 11.

[131] Ibid.

[132] Ibid.

[133] Ibid.

[134] Abdullah Ahmad, *Tengku Abdul Rahman and Malaysia's Foreign Policy 1963–1970*, p. 37.

[135] Abdul Rahman to Macmillan, 19 October 1960, quoted in Liow, *The Politics of Indonesia–Malaysia Relations*, pp. 95–96.

shaping the events on the world stage. Indonesia's demand for Malaya's backing on its pursuit of West Irian, therefore, was not prompted by its realization of being strategically dependent on Malaya. The demand was rather an outcome of Indonesia's aim for strategic preponderance over Malaya, based upon its sense as a major power. The demand was too triggered by Indonesia's close identification with Malaya, owing to their shared cultural ties. In the eyes of Indonesia, Malaya should support its quest for West Irian, because both states shared intimate ties; also because Indonesia demanded so.

THE REBELLIONS

The West was increasingly unnerved by the radicalization of the Indonesian public and their growing support for the PKI.[136] It was largely an outcome of President Sukarno's actions.[137] Since the mid-1950s, President Sukarno began to embrace leftist policies. Sukarno had been contemplating establishing leftist authoritarian rule in Indonesia.[138] He also wanted to consolidate Indonesia's ties with the Soviet Union and China.[139]

By December 1957, the U.S. Secretary of State, Dulles, had informed his deputy that he would like to "see things to a point where we could plausibly withdraw our recognition of the Sukarno government and give it to the dissident on Sumatra".[140] Dulles' message was subsequently being conveyed to the rebels in Sumatra.[141] Knowing that they could count on America's support, the rebels announced on 15 February 1958 the formation of a rebel government in Sumatra named "Pemerintah

---

[136] Fernandes, *Reluctant Indonesians*, pp. 25–26.
[137] Ibid.
[138] Westad, *The Global Cold War*, pp. 129–31. Also see Liow, *The Politics of Indonesia–Malaysia Relations*, pp. 87–89.
[139] Ibid.
[140] Audrey R. Kahin and George McT. Kahin, *Subversion as Foreign Policy: The Secret Eisenhower and Dulles Debacle in Indonesia* (Seattle and London: University of Washington Press, 1997), p. 132. Also see Fernandes, *Reluctant Indonesians*, pp. 26–27; and Westad, *The Global Cold War*, pp. 129–30.
[141] Fernandes, *Reluctant Indonesians*, pp. 26–27.

Revolusioner Republik Indonesia (PRRI) — Revolutionary Government of the Republic of Indonesia".[142] The PRRI government was constituted by a group of dissident politicians and military officers in Sumatra. They proclaimed PRRI to be the alternative government of Indonesia, which sought to represent all Indonesians.[143] The PRRI rebels were predominantly Sumatran.

The rebel movement in Sulawasi, named Piagam Perjuangan Semesta Alam (Permesta), provided its support to the PRRI.[144] The two rebel movements were all backed by the United States in its efforts to break up Indonesia to prevent the rise of communism and non-alignism in the state.[145] The rebels were anti-Communist.[146] They were receiving political and military supports from the United States and its allies — Britain, Australia, the Philippines and Taiwan — in the region.[147]

Malaya announced a policy of non-involvement in the wake of the establishment of PRRI.[148] Yet, Malaya was sympathized with the Sumatran rebellion. The PRRI members were allowed to regularly visit Malaya to promote their cause.[149] The Sumatran rebels — who had escaped to Malaya — were granted asylum in Malaya, when the Indonesian army had successfully dismantled the rebel movements in Sumatra and Sulawesi by the end of 1958.[150]

Malaya's covert support for the Sumatran rebellion was motivated by its identity as well as power politics with Indonesia. While the Malays in Malaya and the indigenous people in Indonesia were bound

---

[142] Ibid. Also see Leifer, *Indonesia's Foreign Policy*, pp. 47–49; Legge, *Sukarno*, pp. 293–95; and Liow, *The Politics of Indonesia–Malaysia Relations*, pp. 87–89.

[143] Ibid.

[144] Yaakub, "Malaysia and Indonesia", p. 105.

[145] Fernandes, *Reluctant Indonesians*, pp. 22–29. Also see Westad, *The Global Cold War*, pp. 129–31.

[146] Leifer, *Indonesia's Foreign Policy*, pp. 49–51. Also see Westad, *The Global Cold War*, pp. 129–30.

[147] Fernandes, *Reluctant Indonesians*, pp. 22–29. Also see Westad, *The Global Cold War*, pp. 49–51.

[148] Government of Malaysia, *Malaya–Indonesia Relations 31st August 1957 to 15th September 1963*, pp. 4–5.

[149] Ibid. Also see Liow, *The Politics of Indonesia–Malaysia Relations*, p. 89.

[150] Ibid. Also see Legge, *Sukarno*, pp. 294–96.

by their Malay way of life, the Malays and the Sumatrans, however, perceived themselves of sharing greater ties, when compared to the links between the Malaya's Malays and other indigenous people of Indonesia.[151] Facilitated by the geographical proximity between the Malay Peninsula and the island of Sumatra, most of the Malays in Malaya had their origins in Sumatra.[152] The similarities between the Malays and the Sumatrans were so close that Sumatra was being viewed as the "cradle of the Malay race" by the Malaya's Malays.[153]

Meanwhile, for the great majority of Indonesians, the cultural traits shared by the Malays in Malaya and the Sumatrans were essentially tied to certain geographical areas.[154] Indonesians perceived people with such cultural characters as *"Suku Melayu"*, who resided across the coastal areas of Sumatra, the Riau islands and Kalimantan.[155] In the eyes of Indonesians, *"Suku Melayu"* was a minority in the Republic, which made up only a small proportion of Indonesia's population.[156] The sense of being *"Suku Melayu"* in the midst of Indonesia's vast population cemented Sumatrans' leaning towards the Malays in Malaya.[157]

The emphasis on the Malay primacy in Malaya's national identity further consolidated the Malay–Sumatran intimacy. The Malays in Malaya were faced with a sizeable presence of ethnic minorities. In 1957, the Malays accounted for almost 50 per cent of the total population in Malaya; followed by the Chinese — 37 per cent; and Indians — 12 per cent.[158] More importantly, the economic wealth of the Malayan Chinese was disproportionately greater than that owned by their Malay

---

[151] Liow, *The Politics of Indonesia–Malaysia Relations*, pp. 40–42, 87.
[152] Ibid.
[153] Ibid., p. 90.
[154] Ibid., pp. 48–49.
[155] Ibid. Also see Milner, *The Malays*, p. 1.
[156] Ibid.
[157] Liow, *The Politics of Indonesia–Malaysia Relations*, pp. 40–42, 88–89. Also see Dewi Fortuna Anwar, *Indonesia in ASEAN: Foreign Policy and Regionalism* (Singapore: Institute of Southeast Asian Studies, 1994), p. 25.
[158] Cheah Boon Keng, *Malaysia: The Making of a Nation* (Singapore: Institute of Southeast Asian Studies, 2002), pp. 79–80.

counterparts.[159] As a result, the Malays in Malaya were plagued with a strong sense of insecurity and disadvantage.[160] They constantly feared of their "disappearance from the world".[161] The Malays, therefore, strived to preserve their political supremacy in Malaya — that of a Malay-Malaya — so as to safeguard their survival.[162] The roar: "Hidup Melayu!" — Long Live the Malays — had rarely failed to galvanize the Malayan Malays.[163]

Such a powerful sense of ensuring the Malays' existence resulted in the Malayan government's commitment to passively assisting and protecting the Sumatran rebels. For the Tunku administration, looking after the Sumatrans meant preserving the existence of the Malays.[164] The Malay elites in the administration apprehended the Sumatrans through the lens of their national identity, namely, the Malays that were at the core of Malaya.[165]

Malaya apprehended the unique existence of the Malays in relation to Indonesia by affirming the superiority of Malaya's national identity over Indonesia's. The inevitable similarities of Malayan and Indonesian national identities, which were founded on the Malay way of life, obliged Malaya to stress its difference vis-à-vis Indonesia, in order to ensure the distinctive existence of Malaya/Malay-Malaya in the world of nations. Because of its sense of uniqueness of its national identity against Indonesia, coupled with its power politics with Indonesia — which were based on comparison, Malaya emphasized the superiority of its nationhood over Indonesia's. The superiority, according to Malayans, was proven by the wisdom of Malaya.

Malayans demonstrated their indifference to Indonesians' disparagement where Malaya possessed a fake independence. They were dismissive of

---

[159] Ibid., pp. 85–86. Also see Milner, *The Malays*, p. 202; and Abdullah Ahmad, *Tengku Abdul Rahman and Malaysia's Foreign Policy 1963–1970*, pp. 5–7.

[160] Ibid.

[161] Milner, *The Malays*, pp. 16, 202, 237–38.

[162] Cheah, *Malaysia*, pp. 17, 72.

[163] Ibid.

[164] Liow, *The Politics of Indonesia–Malaysia Relations*, pp. 87–90.

[165] Ibid. Also see Cheah, *Malaysia*, pp. 5–6, 72.

the anti-colonial revolutionary fighting spirit vigorously advocated by Indonesians. The Tunku wrote, "...there were people who were mocking Malaya's 'pseudo-independence'... the newly independent countries found it expedient to blow hot air and played up their newly-won independence, unsettling the minds of the people of the country and their neighbours...Malaya went on smoothly and quietly about her business...."[166] Also he wrote, "Some found it fashionable to find fault with everything associated with imperialism and colonial rule, whereas we were quietly pursuing our course for peace and goodwill..."[167] The Tunku was most probably expressing his disregard for Indonesians' contempt for Malaya. Indonesia under the Sukarno regime positioned itself to be the champion of the revolutions against colonialism-imperialism worldwide. The regime persistently inculcated in Indonesian people a strong sense of revolutionary spirit.

Malayans argued that, contrary to Indonesians, who attained their independence through a cruel, bloody and destructive fight, Malayans, however, achieved theirs "without a drop of blood".[168] It did not cost people's lives because — as being argued — Malayans fight for their independence with "tact and diplomacy", and "without making much noise".[169] Further, Malayans underlined their success in engendering stability and progress in Malaya, as opposed to Indonesia, which was stuck in the middle of social, economic and political disorder.[170]

In short, Malayans differentiated themselves from Indonesia by accentuating their professed wisdom which was perceived as central to the accomplishments of Malaya. Malayans believed that the Malayan wisdom was demonstrated by their ability to achieve independence with no loss of life, even though — Malayans emphasized — they did in fact fight for their nationhood.[171] Malayans too perceived that

---

[166] Tunku Abdul Rahman, *Lest We Forget: Further Candid Reminiscences* (Malaysia: Eastern Universities Press, 1983), pp. 123–24.

[167] Ibid., p. 114.

[168] Ibid., pp. 33, 36.

[169] Ibid., pp. 36–37, 115, 124.

[170] Ibid., pp. 33, 105, 116–17, 185. Also see Abdul Rahman, *Looking Back*, pp. 89, 99; and Cheah, *Malaysia*, p. 83.

[171] Abdul Rahman, *Lest We Forget*, pp. 36–37.

the self-proclaimed wisdom was exhibited through their competency in ensuring the stability and progress of Malaya. In the eyes of Malayans, Indonesians lacked such wisdom.

Indonesians were enraged by Malayans' justification that Malaya was "a model for all newly independent nations".[172] Malaya's sense of superiority of its nationhood — as represented by the Malayan wisdom — over that of Indonesia, strengthened its resolve to check Indonesia's power. Prime Minister Tunku Abdul Rahman expressed his sense of wisdom, when he wrote about Indonesia in his letter to Dr Ismail dated 24 November 1958:[173] "Conditions in Indonesia are not too good and...becoming worse and worse every day. How they expect to recover God alone knows..."

Subsequently, the Tunku administration firmly adhered to a series of measures that had the effects of curbing the Sukarno regime's attempt to establish Indonesia's regional preponderance. Malaya refused to crush or expel the Sumatran rebels who had already settled in Malaya, despite constant pressure from Jakarta requesting Malaya to do so.[174] In October 1960, Malaya once again granted asylum to a group of Indonesian rebels; this time, a group of Indonesian diplomats based in Europe, who had defected to the Sumatran rebel movement.[175] Meanwhile, Malaya began to seriously ponder upon the idea of integrating Sumatra into the Federation of Malaya.[176]

The measures and the contemplation indicated Malaya's resolve to quell the Indonesian central government's aspiration for dominance in archipelagic Southeast Asia.[177] Specifically, Malaya wanted to prevent the rise of communism in Indonesia.

---

[172] Liow, *The Politics of Indonesia–Malaysia Relations*, p. 97.

[173] Tunku Abdul Rahman to Tun Dr Ismail, 24 November 1958, IAR/3/2/66, quoted in Jeshurun, *Malaysia*, pp. 41–42.

[174] Ooi, *The Reluctant Politician*, pp. 122–23. Also see Tun Dr Ismail A. Rahman Papers, Drifting into Politics, Unpublished Memoirs Folio 12 (2), p. 52. Courtesy of ISEAS Library, ISEAS – Yusof Ishak Institute, Singapore. Also see Mackie, *Konfrontasi*, p. 29.

[175] Government of Malaysia, *Malaya–Indonesia Relations 31st August 1957 to 15th September 1963*, pp. 4–6.

[176] Poulgrain, *The Genesis of Konfrontasi*, pp. 174–75.

[177] Liow, *The Politics of Indonesia–Malaysia Relations*, pp. 68, 90.

The Tunku administration was staunchly anti-communist. Malaya's internal security had been threatened by the Chinese-led Communist insurgency. The Tunku explained the foreign policy of his administration: "Malaya's independent foreign policy was not neutral, the country's fundamental security concerns made it undoubtedly anti-Communist... It was simply to protect our independence."[178] He declared in December 1958: "...let me tell you that there are no such things as local Communists. Communism is an international organization which aims for world domination..."[179] In order to protect Malaya's very survival, the Tunku administration "instinctively" supported any state that faced Communist threats.[180] It drew on the regional political forces in Sumatra — which were also anti-communist — to contain the central government in Jakarta, which was increasingly pro-Communist.[181]

Malaya's reactions to the Sumatran rebellion, in the meantime, reflected its intention to perpetuate the existence of the Malays — that was to solidify the existence of Malaya — by looking after the Sumatrans, who, in the eyes of Malayans, were also Malays.

Malaya's will to balance against Indonesia simultaneously boosted Malayans' sense of superiority of their nationhood over Indonesia's, which was characterized by Malayans' self-acknowledged wisdom. The government of Malaya explained, it offered asylum to the defected Indonesian diplomats considering the "pathetic plight" of these defectors.[182] For Malayans, the Indonesian rebels were pathetic because they had to run away from Indonesia due to its instability and bloodshed, and seek shelter in Malaya, which was stable and free from violence.

Malaya's responses to the Sumatran rebellion did not match with the Indonesian central government's expectation. The Indonesian authority

---

[178] Interview with Tunku Abdul Rahman, 28 December 1982, quoted in Abdullah Ahmad, *Tengku Abdul Rahman and Malaysia's Foreign Policy 1963–1970*, p. 26.

[179] *The Straits Times*, 7 December 1958, quoted in Saravanamuttu, *Malaysia's Foreign Policy, the First Fifty Years*, p. 52.

[180] Jeshurun, *Malaysia*, p. 22.

[181] Liow, *The Politics of Indonesia–Malaysia Relations*, pp. 68, 90.

[182] Government of Malaysia, *Malaya–Indonesia Relations 31st August 1957 to 15th September 1963*, p. 6.

expected the Malayan government to take extraordinary measures to help suppress the Sumatran rebels.[183] It believed Malaya should provide such level of support, as the two states were intimately associated with one another, owing to their blood ties; and it strived for its dominance over Malaya. For the Sukarno regime, Malaya's active support in crushing the rebels would represent its deference to Indonesia's wishes.[184]

The mismatch of expectation resulted in the Indonesian central government's anger towards Malaya.[185] However, the anger did not immediately engender the government's retaliative measures aimed at preventing Malaya's attempt to curb the power of Indonesia.[186] The central tasks of the Indonesian authority at that period were to eliminate the rebellions at the outer islands and consolidate its internal control, so as to prevent Indonesia from falling apart. These tasks would absorb most of the energy of the Sukarno regime until it had succeeded in dismantling the existing liberal parliamentary democracy in Indonesia, and replaced it with a presidential system on 5 July 1959.[187] President Sukarno and the Indonesian army had forged between themselves an effective partnership to form this new political system termed as Guided Democracy.[188] The President was the centre of this system, possessing strong executive power with no constitutional limit on the President's exercise of arbitrary power.[189]

Still, the Indonesian authority's resentment towards Malaya persisted, while being preoccupied with its domestic affairs.[190] The anger would contribute to its intense conflict with Malaya some years later.[191]

---

[183] Ibid., p. 4.

[184] Liow, *The Politics of Indonesia–Malaysia Relations*, p. 90.

[185] Poulgrain, *The Genesis of Konfrontasi*, pp. 174–75. Also see Liow, *The Politics of Indonesia–Malaysia Relations*, p. 89.

[186] Ibid.

[187] Leifer, *Indonesia's Foreign Policy*, pp. 53–54, 61. Also see Legge, *Sukarno: A Political Biography*, pp. 272, 297–306.

[188] Ibid.

[189] Legge, *Sukarno: A Political Biography*, pp. 301, 314–17.

[190] Poulgrain, *The Genesis of Konfrontasi*, pp. 174–75. Also see Leifer, *Indonesia's Foreign Policy*, p. 51; and Liow, *The Politics of Indonesia–Malaysia Relations*, pp. 89–90.

[191] Ibid.

THE FRIENDSHIP TREATY

It was obvious that the Indonesia–Malaya relations were strained by their respective reactions to the Sumatran rebellion. Nevertheless, despite the tense encounter, the two states continued to discern a measure of goodwill from their counterpart, which was essentially stemmed from their awareness of sharing common identities. The mutual positive associations were expressed in the form of Indonesia–Malaya Treaty of Friendship signed by the two states on 17 April 1959.[192] It was Malaya's first friendship treaty with another state.

The signing of the friendship treaty indicated precisely the absence of a special relationship between Indonesia and Malaya. The central focus of the treaty was on cooperation in the realm of culture such as the standardization of the use of the Malay language — the common language of the two states; and the cultural and educational exchanges between the two states.[193] The treaty did not entail any strategic cooperation between Indonesia and Malaya.[194] It basically reflected the two states' desire to highlight their close historical, racial and cultural bonds.[195] In other words, the treaty was not a manifestation of the special ties — the coexistence of common identities and shared strategic interests — between Indonesia and Malaya. It was the one source of closeness in Indonesia–Malaya relations — the two states' common identities that bred and sustained their mutual sense of closeness — that led to their signing of the friendship treaty.

The result of the implementation of the friendship treaty further corroborated the fact that this treaty was not an expression of the strategic partnership between Indonesia and Malaya. Within the framework of the treaty, Indonesia and Malaya had tried but failed to agree on a standardized Malay language system.[196] They were unable to succeed in cultural cooperation, let alone strategic collaboration. Indonesia preferred

---

[192] Liow, *The Politics of Indonesia–Malaysia Relations*, pp. 84–86.
[193] Government of Malaysia, *Malaya–Indonesia Relations 31st August 1957 to 15th September 1963*, p. 3, Appendix II.
[194] Ibid.
[195] Ibid.
[196] Ibid., pp. 3–4.

strategic preponderance over Malaya, whereas Malaya wanted mutual strategic dependence with Indonesia. The two states, consequently, did not share common strategic interests, despite sharing a friendship treaty.

THE REGIONAL PRESCRIPTIONS

"...nation-building cannot be confined to home affairs alone; the country must play a role in international affairs", the Tunku wrote.[197] Malaya with its sound material basis strived to ensure its international presence by strongly committed to the United Nations; and aimed to consolidate its existence by advancing regional cooperation in Southeast Asia.

Malaya needed to secure cooperation with other Southeast Asian states, as it was not large enough to shape a regional order all by itself. The shaping of regional order was meant to safeguard Malaya's survival. In terms of regional environment, Malaya wanted a peaceful external climate so that it could immerse in its internal social and economic developments.[198] It, meanwhile, perceived the preferred peaceful Southeast Asia as fundamentally reflecting the Malay way of life, constituting a protection for Malaya's existence as a Malay nation-state.[199]

Malaya, therefore, made plain that considering the limit of its size, the security of Malaya was depended upon its cooperation with Indonesia — the largest state in Southeast Asia — in particular, and with other Southeast Asian states in general.[200] Indonesia and Malaya together represented the presence of the Malay world in Southeast Asia. Dr Ismail described his task after being appointed as the Foreign Minister of Malaya in February 1959: "The foreign issue that occupied my attention as Minister of External Affairs was to see that our relations with Indonesia remained on the best of terms."[201]

---

[197] Abdul Rahman, *Looking Back,* p. 84.
[198] Abdul Rahman, *Lest We Forget*, pp. 116–17. Also see Abdul Rahman, *Looking Back*, p. 152; and Jeshurun, *Malaysia*, pp. 44–45.
[199] Abdul Rahman, *Looking Back*, p. 152.
[200] Ibid., p. 113.
[201] Tun Dr Ismail A. Rahman Papers, Drifting into Politics, Unpublished Memoirs Folio 12 (2), p. 52. Courtesy of ISEAS Library, ISEAS – Yusof Ishak Institute, Singapore.

With this strategic equation in mind — cooperating with the states in Southeast Asia, primarily with Indonesia — Malaya embarked on its initiative in establishing a friendly regional environment of Southeast Asia that was rooted in the cultural similarities among the states in the region.[202] The preferred regional climate would allow Malaya to ease its defense against other states in Southeast Asia.

In his first visit to the Philippines in January 1959, Prime Minister Tunku Abdul Rahman revealed Malaya's proposal of establishing SEAFET — the Southeast Asia Friendship and Economic Treaty.[203] SEAFET was to be an organization aimed at promoting Southeast Asia's economic, social and cultural developments through regional cooperation.[204] The proposed regional body was officially made known to the public in the joint communiqué of the Tunku and Garcia, the Philippines' President. Malaya subsequently drafted the treaty and invited Indonesia, Thailand, Cambodia, Laos, South Vietnam and Burma to participate in the creation of SEAFET. Only Thailand and South Vietnam responded constructively.[205] Indonesia rejected and was infuriated by Malaya's proposal.[206]

Malaya's embrace of leadership role in the creation of a friendly regional order of Southeast Asia stood against Indonesia's preference for regional preponderance. Malaya's proposal of regional cooperation, as a result, triggered Indonesia's assertion of its regional preponderant standing, which mutually reinforced with Indonesians' sense of superiority of their nationhood over Malaya's. The Indonesian press called for its government to "nip in the bud the puerile, vain and flamboyant hopes" of setting up SEAFET, and claimed that such an undertaking would be "a charitable act" of the Indonesian government.[207] The Indonesian

---

[202] Saravanamuttu, *Malaysia's Foreign Policy, the First Fifty Years*, p. 78.

[203] Ibid., p. 65. Also see Abdul Rahman, *Looking Back*, pp. 86, 179.

[204] Ibid. Also see Government of Malaysia, *Malaya–Indonesia Relations 31st August 1957 to 15th September 1963*, p. 4; and Jeshurun, *Malaysia*, pp. 25–26, 88.

[205] Saravanamuttu, *Malaysia's Foreign Policy, the First Fifty Years*, pp. 65–66.

[206] Ibid.

[207] Niranjan Kumar Hazra, "Malaya's Foreign Relations 1957–1963", M.A. dissertation, University of Singapore, 1965, p. 129, quoted in Saravanamuttu, *Malaysia's Foreign Policy, the First Fifty Years*, p. 66.

consul general in Singapore maintained that as long as SEAFET was represented by member states which were "not really independent", there were bound to be splits in the organization.[208] Indonesians reminded Malaya of Indonesia's dominant status by demonstrating their confidence in Indonesia, which — in their view — was mighty and able to comfortably dissolve any possible attempt to form SEAFET. The rejection of SEAFET crystallized Indonesians' sense of possessing a real independence vis-à-vis that of Malaya. In the eyes of Indonesians, the idea of SEAFET should be crushed, owing to its "puerility" considering that the idea was a design of Malayans, who administered a fake independence. Unlike Malaya — Indonesians maintained — Indonesians' independence was truly authentic, because they had fought for it through a bloody revolution.

Malaya understood its mutual strategic dependence with Indonesia. It continued to seek for Indonesia's participation in the creation of a friendly climate of Southeast Asia, despite Indonesia's hostile rejection to Malaya's proposal of regional cooperation. In October 1959, Malayan Prime Minister Tunku Abdul Rahman once again took the lead in fostering regional cooperation in Southeast Asia. This time, Malaya proposed the formation of ASA (Association of Southeast Asia) — a regional body which was built on the idea of SEAFET.[209] The Tunku wrote to President Sukarno and leaders of other Southeast Asian states explaining the idea of ASA, and invited their participation in the establishment of this body.[210]

The purpose of ASA was to encourage the states of Southeast Asia to live in togetherness in the region, especially through their economic, social and cultural cooperation.[211] Malaya believed that through living in togetherness in the form of ASA, the Southeast Asian states would be able to stand on their own feet, decide their own destiny, and prevent

---

[208] Saravanamuttu, *Malaysia's Foreign Policy, the First Fifty Years*, p. 66.
[209] Government of Malaysia, *Malaya–Indonesia Relations 31st August 1957 to 15th September 1963*, p. 4, Appendix III. Also see Liow, *The Politics of Indonesia–Malaysia Relations*, pp. 83–84; and Jeshurun, *Malaysia*, pp. 25–26.
[210] Ibid.
[211] Ibid.

them from being exploited by powers outside the region.[212] In other words, Malaya strived for an independent Southeast Asia through its friendly coexistence with other states in the region — a regional climate that constituted a shield for Malaya's existence.[213]

The idea of ASA reflected Malaya's strategic thinking of *serumpun*: the states of Southeast Asia should live in togetherness in the region like the way bamboos live, so that their respective survival could always be guaranteed. The *serumpun* concept — the bamboo's way of survival, as Malaya saw it, belonged exclusively to the Malay civilization.

Indonesia rejected Malaya's proposal to create ASA stating that cooperation among states could instead be implemented through Asian-African solidarity.[214] Just like SEAFET, Malaya's decision to champion the formation of ASA was perceived by Indonesia as a challenge to its desired primacy in archipelagic Southeast Asia.[215] Meanwhile, in the eyes of Indonesians, Malaya's proposal of ASA — which amounted to its prescription for the regional order of Southeast Asia — constituted an affront to Indonesia's prestige as a world leader based in Southeast Asia.[216] Indonesia perceived itself as a leader of the Third World leading the worldwide revolutionary fights against colonialism-imperialism. In short, it was the intertwining of Indonesia's aim for regional supremacy and its national pride vis-à-vis Malaya that prompted the rejection of Indonesia to the idea of ASA.

Indonesia's repeated rejection to Malaya's ideas of regional coopera-tion resulted in Malaya's disgruntlement towards Indonesia. The disgruntlement was owing to the mismatch of Malaya's expectation with Indonesia's intention. Malaya considered its relations with Indonesia as closer than their other bilateral ties in Southeast Asia, not only because the two states were bound by their blood ties, but also because Malaya acknowledged that both parties were strategically dependent

---

[212] Ibid. Also see Abdul Rahman, *Looking Back*, pp. 179–80.
[213] Weatherbee, *International Relations in Southeast Asia*, pp. 22–23.
[214] Government of Malaysia, *Malaya–Indonesia Relations 31st August 1957 to 15th September 1963*, p. 4, Appendix IV.
[215] Liow, *The Politics of Indonesia–Malaysia Relations*, pp. 83–84, 102–3.
[216] Ibid.

on each other. Malaya expected Indonesia to be supportive of the creation of SEAFET and ASA, since — as Malaya saw it — the proposed regional bodies were the embodiment of Indonesia–Malaya strategic partnership. In the eyes of Malaya, Indonesia should support Malaya's proposals of regional cooperation, simply because these propositions were the consequences of Malaya's mutual strategic dependence with Indonesia. Yet, Indonesia intended to establish its strategic preponderance in archipelagic Southeast Asia, not seek strategic cooperation with Malaya.

The Tunku later revealed his discontent at Indonesia's repudiation of SEAFET and ASA. He pointed out that Indonesians tended to think that they "should not play or even appear to play second fiddle".[217] The bad feelings towards Indonesia strengthened Malaya's determination to press ahead with the formation of ASA.[218] Together with Thailand and the Philippines, Malaya co-founded the ASA in July 1961.

Malaya's resolve to institute regional cooperation in the form of ASA bolstered, and was bolstered by, its drive to assert the superiority of its nationhood over Indonesia's, which was expressed in the language of Malayan wisdom. The Malayan press compared ASA with Bandung — that was the occasion that cemented the concept of the "Third World" and marked the rise of Indonesia as a Third World's leader — commenting that: "the one remains what it was at Bandung, the expression of nationalist fervour among ex-colonial territories; the other is an association looking to economic, social and cultural advance."[219] Malaya's intention to weaken the Bandung spirit which signified Indonesia's influence in Southeast Asia, mutually reinforced with Malaya's underlining of ASA's ability in delivering stability and progress, that was the substance of Malaya's professed wisdom. Unlike ASA — Malaya maintained — the Bandung spirit was no more than

---

[217] Interview with Tunku Abdul Rahman, 28 December 1982, quoted in Abdullah Ahmad, *Tengku Abdul Rahman and Malaysia's Foreign Policy 1963–1970*, p. 33.

[218] Government of Malaysia, *Malaya–Indonesia Relations 31st August 1957 to 15th September 1963*, p. 4.

[219] "Beginning at Bangkok", *Straits Times*, 4 August 1961, quoted in Liow, *The Politics of Indonesia–Malaysia Relations*, p. 86.

spirited anti-colonial sentiments, implying that Indonesia was devoid of the ability to produce stability and progress.

THE FIGHT FOR WEST IRIAN

The establishment of Guided Democracy on 5 July 1959 marked the rise of Sukarno as the central figure of Indonesia's political system. Sukarno, as the President of Indonesia, became the source of authority in the system of Guided Democracy — a presidential system that was created by the joint efforts of Sukarno and the Indonesian army.[220] Sukarno too remained as the source of legitimacy in Indonesia's politics.[221]

However, the new political system was essentially built on a balance of power between the competing political forces in Indonesia.[222] Sukarno, as a result, had to balance these political forces against one another, so as to preserve his supreme status in the system.[223]

One party that had survived through the demise of the parliamentary democracy in Indonesia was the Communist Party of Indonesia, PKI (Partai Komunis Indonesia). Sukarno made use of the forces of PKI to curb the power of the Indonesian army.[224] It had then become clear that the power structure of the presidential system of Guided Democracy was a triangular relationship between President Sukarno, the Indonesian army and the PKI, with the President settled at the top of the triangular structure.[225]

While occupying the central position in Indonesia's politics, Sukarno understood that he was a force of his own with no organizational power base vis-à-vis the army and the PKI, which were the organized political forces in Indonesia.[226] Sukarno knew that, just like the years before the creation of Guided Democracy, his stature as the pre-eminent

---

[220] Legge, *Sukarno*, pp. 309, 311–17.

[221] Ibid., pp. 307–8. Also see Leifer, *Indonesia's Foreign Policy*, pp. 54–55.

[222] Legge, *Sukarno*, pp. 311, 317–18.

[223] Ibid., pp. 317–24. Also see Leifer, *Indonesia's Foreign Policy*, pp. 54–55.

[224] Legge, *Sukarno*, pp. 318–24. Also see Leifer, *Indonesia's Foreign Policy*, pp. 54–55.

[225] Ibid.

[226] Leifer, *Indonesia's Foreign Policy*, pp. 52–55. Also see Weinstein, *Indonesian Foreign Policy and the Dilemma of Dependence*, pp. 302–3.

figure of Indonesia would serve as the basis for the existence of his power base.[227]

Shortly after the creation of Guided Democracy, President Sukarno, who was the commander-in-chief of the new regime, put the task of recovering West Irian from the colonial control of the Dutch as the prime and central task of Indonesia.[228] The decision was a result of Sukarno's aim to ensure his political survival and to consolidate the integrity of Indonesia.

The forming of Guided Democracy was essentially a response to the regional rebellions in Indonesia.[229] The new regime's raison d'être therefore was its ability to impose unity in Indonesia. With the power of the Indonesian state centralized at the hands of its President as never before, Sukarno executed the ongoing strategy of keeping Indonesia intact with greater determination and effectiveness. Indonesia under the strong leadership of Sukarno decided to utterly assert its regional preponderance by struggling to restore West Irian.[230] The Indonesian government wanted to make use of the struggle to establish its solid internal control throughout Indonesia.[231] The struggle was also meant to minimize the prospect of Indonesia falling apart by maximizing its sphere of influence.[232]

Meanwhile, Sukarno intended to use the issue of West Irian to promote the national unity of Indonesia.[233] He had transformed the claim on West Irian into Indonesia's fundamental national demand — a struggle to perfecting the revolution of Indonesia. The struggle for West Irian had evoked a strong sense of nationhood among the people of Indonesia. They rallied around President Sukarno — the pre-eminent leader of Indonesia — aiming to take possession of West Irian by expelling the Dutch from the territory.[234]

---

[227] Ibid. Also see Legge, *Sukarno*, pp. 307–8.
[228] Leifer, *Indonesia's Foreign Policy*, p. 52.
[229] Legge, *Sukarno*, pp. 282, 287, 297–305.
[230] Leifer, *Indonesia's Foreign Policy*, pp. 48, 52, 61–63.
[231] Ibid.
[232] Ibid., p. 61.
[233] Ibid., pp. 52, 55–56, 61.
[234] Ibid., pp. 61–62, 73.

Also, Sukarno needed the West Irian issue to safeguard his political survival having operated in the triangular power structure of Guided Democracy. By transforming the claim on West Irian into a fundamental national goal of Indonesia, the two competing political forces — the Indonesian army and the PKI — were obliged to uphold Sukarno who symbolized Indonesia, and abide by his call to fight for the territory.[235] They needed to do so to sustain their respective legitimate existence in Indonesia. In other words, Sukarno's plan to recover West Irian would entail a combination of Indonesia's outright assertion of regional preponderance and a strong expression of Indonesian nationalist sentiments.

The Foreign Minister of Indonesia, Dr Subandrio, spelled out Indonesia's policy on its claim on West Irian at the very beginning of the operating of Guided Democracy. Dr Subandrio termed the policy as "Confrontation". He explained, Indonesia would confront the Dutch in all fields, including the military field if necessary, along its struggle to acquire West Irian from the Dutch.[236]

In August 1960, Indonesia demonstrated its resolve to confront the Netherlands by breaking its diplomatic ties with the Netherlands. The military capacity of Indonesia continued to expand signalling the Republic's intention to capture West Irian by force.[237] Indonesia had been able to secure a steady supply of heavy weapons from the Soviet Bloc shortly after its leaning towards the Communist Camp in the mid-1950s. The government of Indonesia purchased these weapons with a series of loans provided by the Soviet Union since 1957. From the late 1950s, the military balance between Indonesia and the Dutch in West Irian had started to tilt towards Indonesia.[238] It would appear that the new Sukarno regime of Guided Democracy had redefined the central tenet of Indonesian foreign policy — independent and active. Independent, for the new regime, referred to the stand-alone global force of the Third World that represented the international front

---

[235] Ibid., pp. 52, 55–56, 61–62, 73.

[236] Ibid., pp. 63, 65.

[237] Ibid., pp. 62–65.

[238] Ibid.

of anti-colonialism-imperialism.[239] Whereas active meant Indonesia would take the lead in organizing the Third World to fight against colonialism-imperialism worldwide.[240]

It had become increasingly obvious for the Tunku administration that the West Irian dispute might lead to military clashes between Indonesia and the Dutch.[241] Malaya felt obliged to help Indonesia to obtain West Irian peacefully, which was meant to strengthen the existence of the Malay world while preserving a peaceful external climate for Malaya.[242] Malaya's Ambassador to Indonesia, Senu Abdul Rahman, time and again wrote to his Foreign Minister — Dr Ismail, urging Malaya to intervene in the dispute of West Irian.[243] Senu was known to have close feelings towards Indonesia.[244] His request reflected the view of the Malay public in Malaya, that Malaya should assist Indonesia in obtaining West Irian, as the territory belonged to the Malay world, also because Malaya, as a power of consequence in Southeast Asia, was capable of providing consequential support to Indonesia. From Malaya's perspective, if it was to intervene in the West Irian dispute, the objective of the intervention was to provide its strategic backing for Indonesia.

On 20 September 1960, Prime Minister Tunku Abdul Rahman wrote to President Sukarno, offering to mediate on the issue of West Irian, with the purpose of assisting Indonesia to secure the territory from the Dutch.[245] The Tunku had made plain in the letter that Malaya wanted West Irian to become part of Indonesia.[246] He confided to the President, in view of the complexity of the dispute, the two states — Indonesia and Malaya — should move in unison, one step after another, towards

---

[239] Weinstein, *Indonesian Foreign Policy and the Dilemma of Dependence*, pp. 165–67.

[240] Ibid.

[241] Liow, *The Politics of Indonesia–Malaysia Relations*, p. 91.

[242] Ibid. Also see Government of Malaysia, *Malaya–Indonesia Relations 31st August 1957 to 15th September 1963*, p. 8, Appendix VII.

[243] Ooi, *The Reluctant Politician*, pp. 123–24. Also see Jeshurun, *Malaysia*, p. 32.

[244] Jeshurun, *Malaysia*, p. 64.

[245] Government of Malaysia, *Malaya–Indonesia Relations 31st August 1957 to 15th September 1963*, p. 8, Appendix VII.

[246] Ibid.

achieving the goal of incorporating West Irian into Indonesia.[247] Obviously, the Tunku saw his participation in the settlement of the West Irian dispute as practically Malaya's strategic collaboration with Indonesia.

The Tunku outlined in the letter his strategy of securing West Irian from the Dutch. He proposed that West Irian to be first transferred to the United Nations as a trust territory, after which the territory had to be transferred to Indonesia in the shortest time possible.[248] On behalf of President Sukarno, Indonesian Prime Minister, Djuanda, accepted Tunku's offer to assist Indonesia in acquiring West Irian by acting as a mediator in the territorial dispute.[249]

In November 1960, the Tunku with his role as a mediator met with the Dutch Prime Minister, Jan de Quay, in the Netherlands to discuss the issue of West Irian. Both Prime Ministers signed a joint communiqué at the end of the meeting stating that "the Netherlands Government was willing to subject their policies in Netherlands New Guinea to the scrutiny and judgment of the United Nations".[250]

Despite the signing, both parties hold different interpretations on the joint communiqué. The Tunku spelt out his understanding of the communiqué in the press conference that followed: the Netherlands was willing to subject West Irian to the investigation of the UN and would abide by the subsequent judgment of the UN.[251] The Dutch government disagreed with Tunku's interpretation. They later clarified that the joint communiqué did not entail the Dutch sovereignty over Netherlands New Guinea whatsoever, and that the Netherlands would only subject its policies in Netherlands New Guinea to the scrutiny and judgment of the United Nations.[252]

The Netherlands in effect reiterated its sovereignty over West Irian through the joint communiqué. The Dutch assertion of sovereignty struck at the core of Indonesia's concern for survival. It challenged Indonesia's

---

[247] Ibid.

[248] Ibid.

[249] Ibid., p. 8, Appendix VIII.

[250] Ibid., p. 9. Also see Liow, *The Politics of Indonesia–Malaysia Relations*, p. 92.

[251] Government of Malaysia, *Malaya–Indonesia Relations 31st August 1957 to 15th September 1963*, Appendix IX.

[252] Ibid., Appendix IX, Appendix X.

aim to establish its regional preponderance — the Sukarno regime's remedy for Indonesia's survival. It also challenged Indonesians' sense of existence, as Indonesia's possession of West Irian would symbolize the completion of Indonesians' fight against colonialism-imperialism for independence. Crucially, the Dutch assertion posed a direct challenge to Sukarno's political survival, which needed West Irian to preserve his supremacy in Indonesia.

Very quickly, the communiqué was openly rejected by the Foreign Minister of Indonesia, Dr Subandrio — the closest confidant of Sukarno. He declared: "We cannot accept anything less than a complete transfer of sovereignty from the Netherlands to Indonesia."[253] He dismissed the idea of introducing the UN into the West Irian dispute.[254] Dr Subandrio, in the meantime, publicly criticized the Tunku for not consulting with Jakarta before acting.[255]

As Indonesians saw it, Malaya's issuing of the joint communiqué with the Netherlands was an affront to the authority of Indonesia. Malaya did not at least inform Indonesia of the communiqué before issuing it, particularly when it concerned the sovereignty of Indonesia. The signing of the joint communiqué was out of Indonesia's anticipation and Indonesia only get to know it through the media.[256] Indonesia expected Malaya's "unwavering support" for its claim on West Irian, rather than issuing a communiqué that led to the Dutch reiteration of their sovereignty over the territory.[257] The expectation was the result of Indonesia's aim for dominance over Malaya as well as Indonesia's close association with Malaya, which stemmed from their sense of sharing common roots.

The contradiction of Malaya's action with Indonesia's expectation prompted the launching of a furious attack on Malaya by Indonesia

---

[253] Leifer, *Indonesia's Foreign Policy*, p. 65.
[254] Government of Malaysia, *Malaya–Indonesia Relations 31st August 1957 to 15th September 1963*, p. 9.
[255] Liow, *The Politics of Indonesia–Malaysia Relations*, pp. 92–93.
[256] Ibid., pp. 92–94. Also see Government of Malaysia, *Malaya–Indonesia Relations 31st August 1957 to 15th September 1963*, Appendix X.
[257] Liow, *The Politics of Indonesia–Malaysia Relations*, p. 95.

through its media.[258] The bitter attack was permeated with Indonesians' assertion of their primacy over Malaya, which enhanced, and was enhanced by, their affirmation of the superiority of Indonesia over Malaya.

The Indonesian people came to perceive Malaya as "a colonial stooge", whose independence was given by the imperialist — Britain.[259] Unlike Malaya — as Indonesians saw it — Indonesians possessed a real independence, which was achieved through their violent struggle against Dutch colonial rule.

The Indonesian press asserted that the Tunku was "an agent of the British and of SEATO and only the Indonesian people and the Indonesian armed forces could solve the problem".[260] Indonesia sought to impress Malaya of its supreme standing by underlining its people's and its army's ability in shaping the outcomes of events. It was understood that Indonesia had a huge population. Indonesia considered Malaya's attempt to mediate in the West Irian issue as constituting a challenge to Indonesia's sovereignty and Indonesia's regional supremacy.[261] It deemed that the mediation was an insolent act, as Malaya had never struggled for its independence.[262] Indonesians maintained, the Tunku should not be trusted because he had not led a revolution to achieve national independence.[263]

The Malayan government was confronted with the real effects of Indonesia's expression of dominance over Malaya. The Malayan pro-Indonesian forces exerted pressure on the Tunku administration in Malaya's parliament. The members of parliament of the Malayan opposition parties criticized the Tunku for not consulting with Indonesia before issuing a joint statement with the Netherlands on the issue of West Irian.[264] They maintained that Malaya was siding with the Dutch in

---

[258] Government of Malaysia, *Malaya–Indonesia Relations 31st August 1957 to 15th September 1963*, pp. 9–10.

[259] Liow, *The Politics of Indonesia–Malaysia Relations*, p. 94.

[260] Government of Malaysia, *Malaya–Indonesia Relations 31st August 1957 to 15th September 1963*, p. 10.

[261] Liow, *The Politics of Indonesia–Malaysia Relations*, pp. 95–97.

[262] Ibid.

[263] Leifer, *Indonesia's Foreign Policy*, p. 65.

[264] Federation of Malaya, *Parliamentary Debates, 6th December 1960*, pp. 3412–14.

the territorial dispute, since — according to them — Malaya belonged to the Western Bloc.[265] They expressed their sympathy for the Indonesian media's vicious attack on the Tunku with regard to his mediation in the West Irian dispute, because — they alleged — the Tunku was obviously biased towards the Dutch.[266]

Malaya did not expect Indonesians' hostile response to its signing of the joint communiqué with the Netherlands. In the eyes of the Tunku, the communiqué represented his efforts in helping Indonesia to acquire West Irian — that was an expression of Malaya's strategic collaboration with Indonesia.[267] The Tunku expected Indonesia to capitalize on the Dutch acceptance of the UN involvement in the settlement of the West Irian dispute — as indicated in the communiqué — treating it as a step towards the eventual transfer of the territory to Indonesia.[268] Such a move — as Malaya saw it — would reflect Indonesia's close strategic coordination with Malaya.

The hostile reaction of Indonesia was exactly the opposite of the Tunku's expectation. The Tunku was incensed as a result. The Tunku's remark in the Malayan Parliament reflected his anger towards Indonesia:[269]

> ...why should I side, for instance, with the Dutch? ...it would not be in keeping with my own nationality to side with somebody who has got no blood connection whatsoever with us, whereas, on the other hand, the Malayans and Indonesians are, what we might call, "blood-brothers".

Malaya promptly launched its tit-for-tat measures against Indonesia's condemnation. It protested against Dr Subandrio's criticism of the Tunku and the Indonesian press's attacks on Malaya.[270] The Malayan government threatened to reveal the letter from Djuanda — who wrote this letter on behalf of President Sukarno — which indicated

---

[265] Ibid.

[266] Ibid.

[267] Government of Malaysia, *Malaya–Indonesia Relations 31st August 1957 to 15th September 1963*, p. 9, Appendix VII, Appendix VIII.

[268] Ibid.

[269] Federation of Malaya, *Parliamentary Debates, 6th December 1960*, pp. 3412–14.

[270] Government of Malaysia, *Malaya–Indonesia Relations 31st August 1957 to 15th September 1963*, p. 10.

Indonesia's approval of Malaya's offer to mediate in the dispute of West Irian, and also Indonesia's acceptance of the UN involvement in the dispute.[271]

Indonesia was well aware that revealing the letter of Djuanda would significantly undermine its credibility in the world. Indonesia was in need of the Third World states' support for its struggle for West Irian. It could not afford a loss of its credibility which might lead to the weakening of the support of these states. Dr Subandrio sought to prevent Malaya's disclosure of Djuanda's letter by sending a letter to the Tunku expressing Indonesia's gratitude for his previous efforts to mediate in the West Irian dispute.[272] With Indonesia's formal expression of gratitude, Malaya decided not to disclose the letter of Djuanda in consideration of its close ties with Indonesia.[273]

It would seem that the tensions between Indonesia and Malaya had been removed fairly quickly. The reality, however, indicated otherwise.

Indonesia was in the thick of its struggle to obtain West Irian. It had pulled all its energies and resources together to implement its confrontation against the Netherlands.[274] It needed to single-mindedly focus on its struggle for the territory — not engage in a conflict with Malaya — as the success of the fight was essential for Indonesia. Without the success, the existence of Indonesia as a state and the political survival of Sukarno — that was the viability of the regime of Guided Democracy — would be in jeopardy. Indonesia had to temporarily succumb to Malaya's challenge, for the sake of preserving the backing of the Third World states for its claim on West Irian. Indonesia's resentments towards Malaya, which had been accumulated throughout Malaya's intervention in the West Irian issue, would resurface several years later, but not at a time when it was confronting the Dutch.[275]

---

[271] Ibid., pp. 9–10, Appendix VIII. Also see Liow, *The Politics of Indonesia–Malaysia Relations*, p. 93.

[272] Ibid.

[273] Ibid.

[274] Liow, *The Politics of Indonesia–Malaysia Relations*, p. 91. Also see Leifer, *Indonesia's Foreign Policy*, pp. 75–77; and Mackie, *Konfrontasi*, pp. 79–80.

[275] Liow, *The Politics of Indonesia–Malaysia Relations*, pp. 102–3. Also see Leifer, *Indonesia's Foreign Policy*, p. 65.

Dr Ismail later recalled: Malaya's mediation in the West Irian dispute was "the foundation of our [Malaya's] strained relationship with Indonesia".[276]

The Tunku wrote a letter to President Sukarno in early December 1960 to detail his efforts at mediating in the West Irian dispute and to officially withdraw himself from being the mediator for the dispute.[277] Sukarno replied by the middle of December 1960, expressing Indonesia's appreciation for the Tunku's initiatives.[278] He too stated in the letter:[279]

> As Your Excellency knows,...the people of Indonesia regard West Irian as an Indonesian territory and do not accept the view that the Netherlands possesses the sovereignty over the territory...the Indonesian people regard the additional statements on the Joint-Communiqué as an attempt to force Indonesia to acknowledge the Dutch sovereignty over West Irian.

Indonesia was determined to incorporate West Irian into part of its territories. In September 1961, the Non-Aligned Movement (NAM) was founded in Belgrade. Indonesia was a key founding member of this movement. NAM was built on the force of the Third World established during the 1955 Bandung Conference. The movement emphasized the Third World solidarity and warned the superpowers not to spread the Cold War into the Third World.[280] Sukarno introduced his new idea of the Third World during the NAM meeting.

In his speech at the meeting, Sukarno declared:[281]

> There is a conflict which cuts deeper into the flesh of man and that is the conflict between the new emergent forces for freedom and justice and the old forces of domination, the one pushing its head relentlessly through the crust of the earth which has given it its lifeblood, the other striving desperately to retain all it can trying to hold back the course of history.

---

[276] Tun Dr Ismail A. Rahman Papers, Drifting into Politics, Chapter 14, Unpublished Memoirs, quoted in Ooi, *The Reluctant Politician*, p. 124.

[277] Government of Malaysia, *Malaya–Indonesia Relations 31st August 1957 to 15th September 1963*, Appendix IX.

[278] Ibid., Appendix X.

[279] Ibid.

[280] Westad, *The Global Cold War*, pp. 97–101, 107.

[281] Djakarta: Department of Information, 1967, p. 7, quoted in Leifer, *Indonesia's Foreign Policy*, p. 58.

Sukarno argued that the key division in the world was that between the New Emerging Forces and the Old Established Forces.[282] The Third World states represented the New Emerging Forces whereas the old forces were constituted by imperialists and colonialists.[283] "The safety of the world is always threatened by the Old Established Order", asserted Sukarno.[284] Being a leader of the Third World had a new meaning for Indonesia. Indonesia began to designate itself as the leader of the New Emerging Forces.[285] It saw itself leading the world's progressive forces to confront the reactionary forces of imperialism and colonialism.[286] Confronting the Dutch would demonstrate such leadership of Indonesia, in which the leadership was the national pride of Indonesia.

By December 1961, Indonesia began to threaten to capture West Irian by force. Because of the arms supplies from the Soviet Bloc, Indonesia had become a military power that could launch an attack on West Irian by the time it threatened to do so.[287] The Indonesian armed forces had started to infiltrate into West Irian indicating Indonesia's determination to use force.

Indonesia's threat of war posed a direct challenge to the American-dominated regional order of Southeast Asia. The United States as a result was obliged to intervene in the West Irian dispute.[288] The United States wanted to prevent another war in Southeast Asia while it was already facing one in Vietnam.[289] Meanwhile, it needed to contain the spread of the Soviet influence in the region. America did not want to see the Soviet flexing its military muscles in archipelagic Southeast

---

[282] Weinstein, *Indonesian Foreign Policy and the Dilemma of Dependence*, pp. 166–67. Also see Leifer, *Indonesia's Foreign Policy*, pp. 58–59; and Legge, *Sukarno*, pp. 343–44.

[283] Ibid.

[284] Ibid.

[285] Legge, *Sukarno*, p. 333. Also see Leifer, *Indonesia's Foreign Policy*, pp. 58–59.

[286] Ibid. Also see Weinstein, *Indonesian Foreign Policy and the Dilemma of Dependence*, pp. 166–67.

[287] Leifer, *Indonesia's Foreign Policy*, pp. 62–68.

[288] Ibid. Also see Weatherbee, *International Relations in Southeast Asia*, pp. 70–71.

[289] Ibid.

Asia through Indonesia launching a war against the Dutch to take possession of West Irian. With the mediation of the United States, a settlement had been reached in August 1962 ending the dispute between Indonesia and the Netherlands over West Irian. Indonesia had gotten what it wanted. West Irian would be transferred to Indonesia on 1 May 1963, after the initial transfer of the territory to a UN administration on 1 October 1962.

TIME TO CONFRONT MALAYSIA

Indonesia was at the peak of its sense of power.[290] It had succeeded in taking over West Irian. The victory represented the expansion of Indonesia's sphere of influence through the extension of its territories. For Indonesia, the success in acquiring West Irian signified the basic completion of the establishment of Indonesia's preponderant standing in archipelagic Southeast Asia. As Indonesia saw it, it had been able to create an external climate in which the alleged imperial powers — the Old Established Forces — had to give way to Indonesia's dominance in archipelagic Southeast Asia.[291] Besides, the successful execution of confrontation against the Dutch consolidated Indonesia's sense of being the leader of the New Emerging Forces.[292] It was the national pride of Indonesia. The nationalist sentiment motivated, and was motivated by, Indonesia's resolve to insist on its perceived regional preponderance.[293] In consequence — underpinned by its powerful military capacity which was recently in place — Indonesia came to perceive Malaya as not a power to be reckoned with.[294] Indonesia was a military giant when compared to Malaya during the 1960s (see Table 5.2).

---

[290] Mackie, *Konfrontasi*, p. 6.

[291] Leifer, *Indonesia's Foreign Policy*, p. 68.

[292] Ibid. Also see Mackie, *Konfrontasi*, p. 6.

[293] Ibid. Also see Abdullah Ahmad, *Tengku Abdul Rahman and Malaysia's Foreign Policy 1963–1970*, p. 37.

[294] Leifer, *Indonesia's Foreign Policy*, p. 82. Also see Mackie, *Konfrontasi*, p. 6; and Abdullah Ahmad, *Tengku Abdul Rahman and Malaysia's Foreign Policy 1963–1970*, p. 37.

TABLE 5.2
Comparison of Military Power of Indonesia and Malaya in the 1960s

Military Power	Indonesia	Malaya
Army	350,000 personnel	10,000 Regulars; 5,000 Reserves
Air Force	20,000 personnel Over 100 jet fighters: MiG-15s, 17s, 19s, 21s Bombers: TU-16s; about 50 IL-28s; B-26s Transports: Some IL-14s and C-130s	30 transport planes
Navy	26,000 personnel 1 Soviet-built heavy cruiser 5 destroyers 4 frigates 15 escort ships 27 light coastal craft 6 landing craft 20 submarines	10 vessels

Source: Compiled from *The Military Balance* 63, no. 1 (1963): 29–30 and Tunku Abdul Rahman, *Looking Back: Monday Musings and Memories* (Malaysia: MPH Group Publishing, 2011), pp. 123–24.

On 8 December 1962, an uprising broke out in the British Protectorate of Brunei. The revolt was mounted by members of the North Kalimantan National Army (TNKU), which was a military wing of the Brunei People's Party — Partai Rakyat Brunei (PRB). The PRB under the leadership of A.M. Azahari had been opposing Brunei's entry into the Federation of Malaysia.[295] It instead was avocating the formation of *Negara Kesatuan Kalimantan Utara* — Unitary State of North Kalimantan — which was a merger between Brunei, Sarawak and North Borneo.[296] A.M Azahari

---

[295] Mackie, *Konfrontasi*, pp. 113–16. Also see Leifer, *Indonesia's Foreign Policy*, p. 78.
[296] Ibid. Also see Anthony J. Stockwell, "Britain and Brunei, 1945–1963: Imperial Retreat and Royal Ascendancy", *Modern Asian Studies* 38, no. 4 (2004): 789, 793.

as the founder of PRB had close political ties with Indonesia. He had participated in Indonesia's struggle for independence before returning to Brunei in 1951.[297] Because of Azahari's contact with Indonesia, the PRB was seeking assistance from Indonesia in training its militia.[298]

The Federation of Malaysia was an idea of a federation that would merge the remaining colonies of Britain — Singapore, Sarawak, North Borneo and Brunei — with Malaya. The idea was publicly proposed by Malayan Prime Minister Tunku Abdul Rahman on 27 May 1961 at Singapore, when he met with the Foreign Correspondents of Southeast Asia at a luncheon. Indonesia did not oppose to the Tunku's proposal. In his letter to the *New York Times* on 13 November 1961, Dr Subandrio made known to the public Indonesia's position on the formation of Malaysia:[299]

> …we do not show any objection toward this Malayan Policy of merger. On the contrary, we wish the Malayan Government well if it can succeed with this plan.

The Tunku unveiled the plan of forming Malaysia at a time when Indonesia had to allocate most of its attention to the task of acquiring West Irian. Indonesia therefore was unlikely to oppose to the proposed federation since it was unable to be involved in another conflict while it was still confronting the Dutch.[300]

The Brunei revolt had been effectively crushed by the British authority within a week after the start of the revolt. The circumstances, however, were different by the time the uprising took place. Indonesia at that point in time was no longer occupied with any major conflict. Shortly after the crackdown on the Brunei revolt, Indonesia expressed its support for the rebel movement and declared its rejection for the formation of Malaysia. In January 1963, Indonesia decided to re-launch its policy of

---

[297] Poulgrain, *The Genesis of Konfrontasi*, p. 89.

[298] Ibid., pp. 256–71.

[299] Government of Malaysia, *Malaya–Indonesia Relations 31st August 1957 to 15th September 1963*, p. 11.

[300] Leifer, *Indonesia's Foreign Policy*, pp. 75–77. Also see Mackie, *Konfrontasi*, pp. 79–80.

confrontation. It would confront the creation of Malaysia to prevent the federation from coming into existence.

The Sukarno regime deemed that Indonesia's regional preponderance was basically in place after its success in incorporating West Irian into part of Indonesia. It wanted to fortify such preponderance of Indonesia so as to ensure Indonesia's integrity as a state.[301] The regime began to hold the view that Indonesia should get to decide the territorial changes that had taken place at its doorstep, especially when the Federation of Malaysia would share borders with Kalimantan of Indonesia.[302] Indonesia, consequently, sought to terminate the formation of Malaysia with the goal of consolidating its perceived preponderance in archipelagic Southeast Asia. For Indonesia, the preponderance was a shield that protected its existence as a state.

The Sukarno regime read the project of Malaysia as a British attempt to encircle Indonesia, in view of the fact that Malaysia's security would be guaranteed by Britain under AMDA.[303] It saw the British military bases in the proposed federation as real threats to Indonesia.[304] These bases had been used to support the rebel movements in Sumatra and Sulawesi in 1958.[305] Meanwhile, the regime feared that the establishment of Malaysia would eventually ignite Sumatrans' desire to join the federation, as Malaya was evidently wealthier than Indonesia.[306] On the other hand, the Indonesian army was worried that Malaysia might be dominated by the Chinese in Singapore and Malaya which would then encourage the Indonesian Chinese to undertake subversive

---

[301] Abdullah Ahmad, *Tengku Abdul Rahman and Malaysia's Foreign Policy 1963–1970*, pp. 37–39.
[302] Leifer, *Indonesia's Foreign Policy*, pp. 78–80. Also see Weinstein, *Indonesian Foreign Policy and the Dilemma of Dependence*, p. 168; and Liow, *The Politics of Indonesia–Malaysia Relations*, p. 98.
[303] Leifer, *Indonesia's Foreign Policy*, pp. 78–82. Also see Abdullah Ahmad, *Tengku Abdul Rahman and Malaysia's Foreign Policy 1963–1970*, p. 41.
[304] Ibid. Also see Weinstein, *Indonesian Foreign Policy and the Dilemma of Dependence*, p. 168.
[305] Ibid.
[306] Dewi Fortuna Anwar, *Indonesia in ASEAN*, p. 25. Also see Liow, *The Politics of Indonesia–Malaysia Relations*, p. 103.

activities in Indonesia.[307] In short, Indonesians perceived the existence of Malaysia as threatening Indonesia's survival, thus had to be crushed through the means of confrontation — the Indonesian way of claiming its desired regional preponderance.

Indonesia's aim to cement its perceived preponderance in archipelagic Southeast Asia mutually reinforced with its aspiration to become the leader of the New Emerging Forces — the basis for Indonesia's existence as a nation. The people of Indonesia had been united by their common belief that Indonesia was the champion of the revolutions against colonialism-imperialism happening around the globe.

The Brunei revolt was perceived by Indonesia as evidence of the Northern Borneo people's rejection to British colonial rule presented in the form of Malaysia — which Indonesia described as the Old Established Forces of neo-colonialism.[308] Having designated itself as the leader of the New Emerging Forces, Indonesia deemed necessary to fight against the alleged colonial presence at its immediate neighbourhood.[309] Because of the need to sustain the fragile national unity of Indonesia and to preserve his supremacy in the triangular power structure of Guided Democracy, President Sukarno was obliged to emphasize Indonesia's standing as the leader of the New Emerging Forces. Sukarno embraced such leadership role of Indonesia to inspire a sense of national pride among the Indonesian people and to ensure that the Indonesian people — including the PKI and the Indonesian army — continued to rally around him, who was the symbol of Indonesia.[310] As a result, the strength of Indonesia's leadership claim — that was to lead the New Emerging Forces — was always strong.

Sukarno's opposition to the idea of Malaysia demonstrated the mutually enhancing dynamics of Indonesia's assertion of regional

---

[307] Dewi Fortuna Anwar, *Indonesia in ASEAN*, pp. 25–26. Also see Weinstein, *Indonesian Foreign Policy and the Dilemma of Dependence*, p. 168; and Liow, *The Politics of Indonesia–Malaysia Relations*, p. 98.

[308] Liow, *The Politics of Indonesia–Malaysia Relations*, p. 98. Also see Leifer, *Indonesia's Foreign Policy*, pp. 78–79; and Dewi Fortuna Anwar, *Indonesia in ASEAN*, p. 25.

[309] Ibid. Also see Mackie, *Konfrontasi*, p. 1; and Poulgrain, *The Genesis of Konfrontasi*, p. 194.

[310] Leifer, *Indonesia's Foreign Policy*, pp. 56, 73, 79–81.

preponderance and its determination to confront the perceived colonial presence:[311]

> Why do we oppose it? Because Malaysia is a manifestation of neo-colonialism. We do not want to have neo-colonialism in our vicinity. We consider Malaysia an encirclement of the Indonesian Republic. Malaysia is the product of the brain and efforts of neo-colonialism...we are determinedly opposed, without any reservation, against Malaysia.

By April 1963, Indonesian guerrillas began to launch regular armed incursions into Sarawak. Indonesia's confrontation against Malaya was particularly intense.

President Sukarno stressed the superiority of Indonesian nationhood over that of Malaya, when he began to oppose the formation of Malaysia:[312]

> We were born in fire. We were not born in the rays of the full moon like other nations. There are other nations whose independence was presented to them. There are other nations who, without any effort on their part, were given independence by the imperialists as a present. Not us, we fought for our independence at the cost of great sacrifice. We gained our independence through a tremendous struggle which has no comparison in this world.

In the eyes of Sukarno, Malaya's independence — when compared to Indonesia's — was an inferior one, because it was a fake independence, as Malayans did not achieve their independence through armed struggle. Such superiority sentiment toughened Indonesia's resolve to confront Malaya in order to strengthen the supposed regional preponderance of Indonesia.

When announcing Indonesia's policy of confrontation against Malaysia on 20 January 1963, Dr Subandrio asserted that "Malaya had openly become a henchman of the imperialists and had acted with animosity towards Indonesia."[313] President Sukarno, meanwhile, stressed that "if

---

[311] George Modelski, ed., "We Are Being Encircled", in *The New Emerging Forces: Documents on the Ideology of Indonesian Foreign Policy* (Australia: The Australian National University, 1963), pp. 74–75.

[312] Radio Address by Sukarno, December 1962, quoted in Carey, "Introduction", p. xix.

[313] Leifer, *Indonesia's Foreign Policy*, pp. 78–79.

the Prime Minister, and the Federation leadership continued their present policy, Indonesia would have no choice but to face it with political and economic confrontation."[314] For the Indonesian authority, Malaya with its embrace of Malaysia had once again — this time unreservedly — vindicated itself to be a stooge of the imperial powers, underpinned by the fact that Malaya's independence was given by its colonial master. Indonesia therefore — as the authority saw it — was determined to confront Malaya, because Indonesia was the champion of the revolutions against colonialism-imperialism, owing to its successful armed struggle for independence.

Indonesia's assertion of strategic preponderance was unequivocal. Sukarno issued an order to the Indonesian army in February 1963. He emphasized: "...the enemy is besieging us. Therefore, keep on the alert and I order you to keep your weapons in your hands."[315] The Commander of the Indonesian navy at Sumatra ordered his troops to "burn on the spot any Malayan fishing boat caught in Indonesian waters".[316]

Indonesia's resolve to confront Malaya, in the meantime, boosted its sense of superiority of its nationhood over Malaya's. President Sukarno when expressing Indonesia's opposition to the creation of Malaysia made it crystal clear: "nations who will become strong and famous nations should be ready to face moments of danger...I have stated that we are standing on a principle of anti-colonialism and anti-imperialism."[317]

The determination of Indonesia to confront Malaya was further intensified by its resentments towards Malaya, which were resulted from Malaya's covert support for the Sumatran rebels and Malaya's intervention in the West Irian dispute.[318] Indonesia's justification for confronting Malaya reflected the effects of the resentments. The Indonesian government maintained that it needed to confront Malaya

---

[314] Government of Malaysia, *Malaya–Indonesia Relations 31st August 1957 to 15th September 1963*, p. 14.

[315] Ibid.

[316] Ibid.

[317] Ibid.

[318] Leifer, *Indonesia's Foreign Policy*, pp. 51, 65. Also see Liow, *The Politics of Indonesia–Malaysia Relations*, pp. 89–90, 102–3; and Poulgrain, *The Genesis of Konfrontasi*, pp. 174–75.

since Malaya had always been hostile to Indonesia and had sought to annex Sumatra during the PRRI revolt.[319]

While Indonesia's confrontation against Malaya had been fierce, it simply did not regard Malaya as a power to be reckoned with. Indonesia perceived itself as a major power on the world stage, which was on par with the status of Britain. It insisted that the only possible path to end its confrontation against Malaysia was through negotiations between Indonesia and Britain, without the involvement of Malaya.[320]

Malaya was infuriated with Indonesia. From Malaya's perspective, rather than implicating the need of launching a war against Malaya, Indonesia should instead forge friendly ties with Malaya, because they shared common origins and both were strategically dependent on each other. Indonesia's decision to confront Malaya contradicted with such expectation of Malaya.

The Tunku expressed his anger because of the mismatch of expectation. He responded to Dr Subandrio's declaration of Indonesia's confrontation against Malaya: "He had completely forgotten, or now preferred to overlook, that less than four years before, in April 1959, Indonesia and Malaya had signed a Treaty of Friendship in Kuala Lumpur."[321] The Tunku was angry that Indonesia treated Malaya with hostility despite sharing a friendship treaty with Malaya. For the Tunku, the treaty indicated the close ties between Indonesia and Malaya, which meant that their relationship should be friendly.

The comments made by the Tunku decades later still reflected the anger:[322]

> I wrote to Sukarno about the 'Malaysian Project' and he did not oppose it. Perhaps, it never crossed his mind it would materialize in the first place and hence he asked Subandrio to write that letter to the *New York Times* and make a speech at the UN. We were a sovereign nation and

---

[319] Government of Malaysia, *Malaya–Indonesia Relations 31st August 1957 to 15th September 1963*, p. 14.

[320] Liow, *The Politics of Indonesia–Malaysia Relations*, p. 100.

[321] Abdul Rahman, *Looking Back*, p. 106.

[322] Interview with Tunku Abdul Rahman, 28 December 1982, quoted in Abdullah Ahmad, *Tengku Abdul Rahman and Malaysia's Foreign Policy 1963–1970*, p. 37.

could not do more than that because it was essentially a matter between us, the British and the people of the territories concerned. I did not oppose his taking over West Irian, in fact I tried to help him to get it.

In the Tunku's understanding, Malaya's participation in the West Irian issue was Malaya's throwing of strategic support for Indonesia. It meant that Malaya — as the Tunku saw it — had always sought to maintain its strategic closeness with Indonesia. The Tunku was annoyed that Indonesia chose to confront Malaya in return.

Because of its resentments towards Indonesia — prompted by the mismatch of expectation — Malaya became more steadfast to press ahead with its plan to form Malaysia. The Tunku asserted: "Things were looking pretty grim for us, but in spite of all threats I was determined to go right ahead with Malaysia as planned..."[323]

Malaya's affirmation of the superiority of its nationhood — as represented by Malayans' self-acknowledged wisdom — over that of Indonesia bolstered, and was bolstered by, its resolve to fight against Indonesia's attempt to terminate the creation of Malaysia.

The Tunku emphasized the wisdom of Malaya in response to President Sukarno's efforts to confront Malaysia:[324]

I tried to appease his [Sukarno] wrath, if wrath it really was, but deep in my heart I knew it was pure jealousy, as all along he had viewed with envy Malaya's rise to prosperity since independence and the progress she had made, as compared with what was happening in his own country — political infighting, overspending, mismanagement and the rupiah sinking in value.

In the eyes of the Tunku, Malaya was better than Indonesia, which was evidenced by its ability in producing stability and progress — the substance of Malaya's professed wisdom.[325] Indonesia — the Tunku believed — lacked such wisdom, in view of its internal chaos and instability. The

---

[323] Abdul Rahman, *Looking Back*, p. 107.
[324] Ibid., p. 99.
[325] Interview with Tunku Abdul Rahman, 14 September 1983, quoted in Abdullah Ahmad, *Tengku Abdul Rahman and Malaysia's Foreign Policy 1963–1970*, p. 39.

Tunku deemed that Sukarno decided to confront Malaysia because he found hard to accept that Malaya was ahead of Indonesia.

The Tunku explained further:[326]

> ...it would have been a tremendous boost to have Sukarno's blessing for the birth of Malaysia...He chose to crush us once he could not get his way. We had to fight him, though reluctantly, to uphold our honour and sovereignty. We are Malays like him who value honour.

Malaya was determined to face up to the threats of Indonesia in order to uphold its national prestige vis-à-vis Indonesia, which was defined by the perceived wisdom of Malaya. Malaya stood firm to demonstrate itself to be a power that cannot be ignored. It would not agree to any talk between Britain and Indonesia on the issue of Malaysia.[327] Consequently, negotiation between Indonesia and Malaya appeared to be the only option for the settlement of the dispute over the Malaysia Project.[328]

The Philippines had taken the initiative to organize the three parties — Indonesia, Malaya and the Philippines — talks with the aim of easing their tensions arising from the issue of Malaysia. The Philippines was another party that opposed to the formation of Malaysia. It insisted that Sabah (North Borneo) was part of its territories.

A summit meeting of the three states was held in Manila in July 1963 as a result of the diplomatic efforts of the Philippines. It should be noted that by July 1963 Brunei had decided to withdraw itself from joining the proposed Federation of Malaysia. The tripartite summit meeting had given birth to the Manila Agreement. There were two central contents in the agreement. First, Indonesia and the Philippines would welcome the formation of Malaysia provided the Northern Borneo people's support for Malaysia was ascertained by the Secretary-General of the UN or his representative — through examining the results of the recent elections in Sabah and Sarawak — prior to the

---

[326] Interview with Tunku Abdul Rahman, 19 September 1983, quoted in Abdullah Ahmad, *Tengku Abdul Rahman and Malaysia's Foreign Policy 1963–1970*, p. 45.
[327] Liow, *The Politics of Indonesia–Malaysia Relations*, p. 100.
[328] Ibid.

establishment of the federation.[329] Second, the three states agreed to take initial steps towards the establishment of Maphilindo by setting up machinery for frequent and regular consultations among them.[330]

Maphilindo was the proposal of Macapagal, the President of the Philippines. It was meant to be a confederation of Indonesia, Malaya and the Philippines, which was predicated on their common Malay origins. President Macapagal hoped that such a confederation could be an alternative to the Federation of Malaysia. The consensus reached by the three states was that Maphilindo would be a grouping of the three states of Malay origins charged to advance their close cooperation without requiring them to surrender their respective sovereignty.[331]

Maphilindo as a prospective regional body reflected the similar strategic thinking of the three states concerned: the archipelagic Southeast Asia, overwhelmingly populated by the people of Malay blood, served as a shield that safeguard the respective survival of Indonesia, Malaya and the Philippines as a state which reflected the Malay way of life. Because of the sizeable presence of the Chinese in the region, the leaders of the three states became more aware of them sharing such alike strategic apprehension.[332] President Macapagal glorified: "…in Maphilindo and through Maphilindo, nourished constantly by their vision and enterprise, the Malay peoples shall be borne upon the true, the vast, the irresistible wave of the future."[333] The implications of Maphilindo alarmed the Prime Minister of Singapore, Lee Kuan Yew, a Singaporean Chinese.[334] Commentators argued that Maphilindo was bound to become the regional association of Southeast Asia aimed at curbing the influence of the Chinese in the region.[335]

---

[329] Abdullah Ahmad, *Tengku Abdul Rahman and Malaysia's Foreign Policy 1963–1970*, Appendix I – Manila Accord, Appendix II – Manila Agreement.

[330] Ibid.

[331] Ibid. Also see Liow, *The Politics of Indonesia–Malaysia Relations*, p. 100.

[332] Mackie, *Konfrontasi*, pp. 165–69.

[333] Ibid.

[334] Ibid.

[335] Ibid.

Yet — "similar strategic understanding" — that was all Maphilindo was about. The three states' different readings on what Maphilindo should be indicated the absence of "common strategic interests" between them.

Indonesia regarded Maphilindo as a vehicle for it to consolidate its dominance in archipelagic Southeast Asia.[336] It thought that Maphilindo could be used as a means to bring Malaya closer to the movement against the Old Established Forces led by Indonesia.[337] It also hoped to make use of Maphilindo to end the security links of Malaya and the Philippines with the Western powers thereby enhanced the regional supremacy of Indonesia.[338] Indonesian Army Chief of Staff, General Yani, envisioned that "within the framework of Maphilindo the primary responsibility for the security and stability of Southeast Asia now rested with Indonesia".[339]

Malaya, on the other hand, saw the creation of Maphilindo as a step towards the establishment of strategic cooperation between Indonesia and Malaya, having acknowledged the two states' mutual strategic dependence.[340]

As for the Philippines, its proposal of Maphilindo was mainly an act of expediency. The Philippines wanted to make use of Maphilindo to create its stronger presence in Asia thus demonstrating its independence from the United States.[341] The Philippines' sense of sharing common identities with Malaya and Indonesia was rather weak, in view of the fact that the Philippines was a predominantly Christian state while Islam was central to the Malay way of life. The Tunku raised his concern about the absence of a mosque in Manila when he attended the tripartite summit meeting of July 1963.[342] In his concluding address at the end of

---

[336] Ibid.

[337] Ibid.

[338] Ibid.

[339] Arnold C. Brackman, *Southeast Asia's Second Front: The Power Struggle in the Malay Archipelago* (London: Pall Mall Press, 1966), p. 187.

[340] Mackie, *Konfrontasi*, pp. 166–69.

[341] Ibid.

[342] Tunku Abdul Rahman, *Viewpoints* (Kuala Lumpur: Heinemann Educational Books, 1978), p. 136. Also see Abdul Rahman, *Looking Back*, p. 308.

the meeting, the Tunku said: "I came to this country not only to play, but to pray too. Unfortunately, however, there is no mosque in Manila where I can pray."[343] A stark sense of dissimilarity with the Philippines. In other words, the idea of viewing archipelagic Southeast Asia as the Malay world or Malay archipelago was essentially sustained by Indonesia and Malaya — not the Philippines. The Malay way of life formed the central character of Indonesia's and Malaya's national identity. Both states viewed the Malay world as a shield that protected their respective survival as a state built around the Malay way of life.

In short, the idea of Maphilindo — as a prospective regional body — was not an outcome of the mutual strategic dependence between Indonesia, Malaya and the Philippines; it was merely an expression of their similar strategic understanding. Indonesia did not see the need of forging strategic partnerships with Malaya and the Philippines, as both for Indonesia were just "little nations".[344] The amount of power owned by Malaya had not reached to a level that, matched with the power of Indonesia, would start to shape their similar strategic understanding into their common strategic interests.

In the eyes of Indonesia, the Manila Agreement basically attested to Indonesia's dominance in archipelagic Southeast Asia. Malaya had been obliged to negotiate with Indonesia and the Philippines with regard to the formation of Malaysia, instead of keeping it a matter solely between Malaya, Britain and the governments of the Borneo territories.[345] Through the negotiation, Malaya had been made to accept that the establishment of the new federation would be tied to the investigation of the UN. In Indonesia's understanding, Malaya would have to commit itself to the UN investigation in view of the pressure from Indonesia.[346] Upon returning to Jakarta, Sukarno announced that Confrontation would continue despite the conditional settlement reached at the tripartite summit meeting in Manila.[347]

---

[343] Ibid.
[344] Mackie, *Konfrontasi*, p. 168.
[345] Leifer, *Indonesia's Foreign Policy*, pp. 86–89.
[346] Ibid.
[347] Ibid.

On 29 August 1963, the Malayan government announced that irrespective of the UN mission's findings, the Federation of Malaysia would be established on 16 September 1963. On 13 September 1963, the UN Secretary-General, U Thant, published his report on the issue of Malaysia. U Thant found that "there is no doubt about the wishes of a sizeable majority of the peoples of these (Northern Borneo) territories to join in the Federation of Malaysia".[348]

Malaya's announcement on 29 August 1963 constituted a direct challenge to Indonesia's perceived regional preponderance. It had declared the date for the formation of Malaysia prior to the publishing of the UN mission's findings. It also stressed that the federation would be formed regardless of the findings. In Indonesia's understanding, such a move had violated the Manila Agreement, of which signified Indonesia's preponderant standing in archipelagic Southeast Asia.[349] Indonesia, in consequence, refused to accept the findings of the UN mission in response to Malaya's challenge to Indonesia's perceived regional dominance.

On 16 September 1963, the day when Malaysia was officially formed, Indonesia announced that the newly formed Malaysia would not enjoy diplomatic relations with Indonesia. Malaysia responded with the same decision. Before long, President Sukarno declared that Indonesia would "*Ganjang Malaysia*" — Crush Malaysia.[350] Indonesia stepped up its confrontation against Malaysia. The hope for the establishment of Maphilindo quickly faded away.

Indonesia intensified its military incursions into Sabah and Sarawak, which would be sustained throughout the following years.[351] These incursions had been effectively defeated by the British armed forces.[352] From August to October 1964, there had been sporadic landings of

---

[348] Ibid., pp. 90–91.
[349] Ibid., pp. 90–92. Also see Liow, *The Politics of Indonesia–Malaysia Relations*, pp. 100–1.
[350] Leifer, *Indonesia's Foreign Policy*, p. 92.
[351] Ibid., pp. 82, 93. Also see Abdullah Ahmad, *Tengku Abdul Rahman and Malaysia's Foreign Policy 1963–1970*, p. 57.
[352] Ibid.

Indonesian troops — by sea and by air — on the southern part of Peninsula Malaysia.[353] The Malaysian armed forces had successfully cracked down on these operations.[354] The meaning of Indonesia's military intrusions was clear: whether it was Malaya or Malaysia, the federation was not a power that Indonesia deemed should be taken note of. Indonesia's UN representative, Dr Sudjarwo, had made it clear in the UN Security Council:[355]

> I would not deny that our volunteers, our guerrillas with the militant youth of Sarawak and Sabah, some of whom have been trained in our territory, have entered so called 'Malaysian' territory in Sarawak and Sabah. They have been fighting there for some time. This is no secret...And now fighting has spread to other areas in 'Malaysia', such as Malaya.

Indonesia thought that it could launch military attacks on Malaysia whenever it wanted to. It believed that Malaysia was not strong enough to withstand such attacks.[356] Indonesia, meanwhile, strived to isolate Malaysia from the Third World. Because of its continuous armed incursions into Malaysia — a sovereign state, Indonesia had failed to secure international support — including the support of most of the Third World states — for its confrontation against Malaysia.[357] Indonesia had become internationally isolated.[358] It had decided to leave the UN in January 1965 in retaliation for Malaysia's admission to the UN Security Council.

---

[353] Government of Malaysia, *Indonesian Agression Against Malaysia, Volume I* (Kuala Lumpur: Government Press, 1965). Also see Abdullah Ahmad, *Tengku Abdul Rahman and Malaysia's Foreign Policy 1963–1970*, pp. 54–56; and Leifer, *Indonesia's Foreign Policy*, p. 100.

[354] Ibid.

[355] Government of Malaysia, *Malaysia's Case in the Security Council* (Kuala Lumpur: Ministry of Foreign Affairs, 1964), p. 15, quoted in Leifer, *Indonesia's Foreign Policy*, pp. 100–1.

[356] Abdullah Ahmad, *Tengku Abdul Rahman and Malaysia's Foreign Policy 1963–1970*, p. 54.

[357] Leifer, *Indonesia's Foreign Policy*, pp. 101–5.

[358] Ibid.

Crucially, the Soviet Union had lost its interest in backing Indonesia with its steady arms supplies.[359] The Soviet was worried about Indonesia's increasingly close alignment with China that had taken place since the early 1960s.[360] The Sino–Soviet split was official since 1960. By 1964, Indonesia would have to proceed with its confrontation against Malaysia without the Soviet's military support.[361] In other words, the United States would no longer had to be concerned much about its dominance in archipelagic Southeast Asia being challenged by the Soviet through Indonesia. In July 1964, the United States declared explicitly its support for Malaysia. The United States backed up the support with its offer of military assistance to Malaysia.

Indonesia's influence in Malaysia shrank sharply as a result of its confrontation against Malaysia.[362] The people of Malaysia were united behind the Tunku leadership in the face of Indonesia's confrontation, especially its military incursions into Malaysia. The Tunku-led ruling coalition had won a landslide victory in the general election held in April 1964. The need to protect Malaysia against the threats of Indonesia had been the main factor that led to the victory of the ruling coalition.[363] The fight against Confrontation was the ruling coalition's central platform for the general election.[364]

Indonesia had become isolated because of its confrontation against Malaysia. The Indonesian authority was increasingly impressed with Britain's military might, which was the bedrock of Malaysia's security under the AMDA.[365] The consistent failure of Indonesia's confrontation

---

[359] Ibid., pp. 98–99.

[360] Ibid., pp. 68–69. Also see Westad, *The Global Cold War*, p. 185.

[361] Leifer, *Indonesia's Foreign Policy*, pp. 98–99. Also see Abdullah Ahmad, *Tengku Abdul Rahman and Malaysia's Foreign Policy 1963–1970*, pp. 50–53.

[362] Liow, *The Politics of Indonesia–Malaysia Relations*, p. 107.

[363] Abdullah Ahmad, *Tengku Abdul Rahman and Malaysia's Foreign Policy 1963–1970*, p. 51. Also see Leifer, *Indonesia's Foreign Policy*, pp. 96–97; and Cheah, *Malaysia*, p. 100.

[364] Ibid.

[365] Weinstein, *Indonesian Foreign Policy and the Dilemma of Dependence*, p. 322. Also see Abdullah Ahmad, *Tengku Abdul Rahman and Malaysia's Foreign Policy 1963–1970*, pp. 41, 55–57.

against a united Malaysia pointed to one unmistakable reality: Malaysia was here to stay.

While executing the confrontation campaign against Malaysia, the politics in Indonesia had been in a fluid state. The PKI's ties with President Sukarno had become increasingly close amidst the Confrontation. Its membership, meanwhile, had surged dramatically. Consequently, the balance of power between the two competing political forces — the PKI and the Indonesian army — in the triangular power structure of Guided Democracy had become increasingly unstable. The anti-communist forces in Indonesia — which consisted of the army, the religious and nationalist groups — were consolidating their cooperation in response to the rise of the PKI.[366] To demonstrate its support for the confrontation campaign, the PKI had called for the establishment of a fifth force which would arm millions of workers and peasants to carry out Indonesia's military operations against Malaysia.[367] The Indonesian army viewed the proposal as a direct threat to its existence.[368] In early 1965, small-scale violent conflicts broke out between the PKI and Muslims in East Java and Aceh. The U.S. officers in Indonesia observed: "Although the tensions between the PKI and the Moslems remained in a low key for some months, they erupted again during the month of August in a manner which seemed to confirm the feeling of some Indonesians that a civil war between the two groups will eventually be fought."[369]

Before long, in the early hours of 1 October 1965, a mutiny in the Indonesian army took place in Jakarta.[370] Under the command of several junior officers, a group of armed soldiers abducted and killed six

---

[366] Douglas Kammen and Katharine McGregor, "Introduction: The Contours of Mass Violence in Indonesia, 1965–68", in *The Contours of Mass Violence in Indonesia, 1965–68,* edited by Douglas Kammen and Katharine McGregor (Singapore: NUS Press, 2012), pp. 14–16.

[367] Ibid. Also see Legge, *Sukarno*, pp. 379–80.

[368] Ibid.

[369] Airgram A-5, U.S. Consulate Surabaya to U.S. Embassy Jakarta, 16 September 1965, POL 18 INDON, NARA, quoted in Kammen and McGregor, "Introduction", p. 15.

[370] John Roosa, "The September 30th Movement: The Aporias of the Official Narratives", in *The Contours of Mass Violence in Indonesia, 1965–68*, pp. 27–28.

senior generals and a lieutenant. A few hours later, Indonesia's national radio station was forced to announce on air that a movement called "September 30th Movement" had been launched to protect President Sukarno from an impending coup organized by a group of CIA-backed generals. The movement later on announced the formation of a Revolutionary Council which would replace Sukarno's cabinet, and temporarily take control of all state power. A mutiny in the Indonesian army seemed to have transformed into a coup.[371]

The September 30th movement, however, began to loss its momentum since the morning of 1 October 1965. The movement was called off by its leaders in the morning of that day after President Sukarno had ordered them to do so.[372] Under the command of General Suharto, the Indonesian army managed to defeat the movement within a day. It was found out that a handful of PKI leaders were related to the launching of the September 30th Movement.[373] The failed movement prompted the Indonesian army — with the help of its domestic anti-communist alliance — to purge the PKI as an organization, the leftists and Sukarno's supporters in Indonesia through various forms of violence especially mass killings in order to take control of Indonesia.[374] The army-led mass violence campaign had been executed for almost three years, which lasted until 1968.[375] In mid-March 1966, President Sukarno was forced to transfer all his executive powers to General Suharto. By early March 1967, the Indonesian army had succeeded in defeating Sukarno. On 7 March 1967, the MPRS — Provisional People's Consultative Assembly of Indonesia — had banned Sukarno from participating in politics, and appointed Suharto as Acting-President. About a year later, Suharto was officially confirmed by the MPRS to be the second President of Indonesia. The bilateral relations of Indonesia and Malaysia would move into a new phase with the change of leadership in Indonesia.

---

[371] Ibid.

[372] Ibid., p. 39.

[373] Ibid., pp. 36–40.

[374] Kammen and McGregor, "Introduction", pp. 4–21.

[375] Ibid.

THE ABSENCE OF POWER BALANCE BETWEEN INDONESIA AND MALAYA/MALAYSIA

A basis of order did not exist between Indonesia and Malaya/Malaysia before the end of the Sukarno-regime. Indonesia had shown no restraint to launch military attacks on Malaysia. Malaysia, meanwhile, had contemplated launching an airstrike on Indonesia in retaliation against such attacks.[376] It had requested for a transfer of some sophisticated planes from Britain so that it could perform an attack on Indonesia.[377]

While Malaya had already expanded into Malaysia, Indonesia was not immediately impressed by the power owned by Malaysia. The material capacity of Malaysia had yet to put a stop to Indonesia's tendency to confront Malaysia militarily. Indonesia's sense of being a major power was at its peak after its success in taking over West Irian.

In other words, there was no foundation — that of the presence of power balance — in the relations between Malaysia and the Sukarno-led Indonesia upon which their shared war avoidance norms could emerge. The amount of power owned by Malaysia had yet to engender Indonesia's recognition of its strategic reliance on Malaysia. The similar strategic understanding of Indonesia and Malaysia had yet to be shaped into their common strategic interests. Two sources of closeness — common strategic interests and common identities — did not coexist in the relationship between Malaysia and the Sukarno-led Indonesia. Consequently, the two states' aspiration for peace directed at each other, were not sufficiently strong to produce their shared war avoidance norms — that was a security regime between them. The Indonesia–Malaya Treaty of Friendship, for example, was a product of the two states' mutual sense of closeness deriving from their one source of closeness — that of their appreciation of sharing common identities. The treaty contained no restraining effects. Indonesia did not seek to avoid having armed conflicts with Malaysia.

---

[376] Abdullah Ahmad, *Tengku Abdul Rahman and Malaysia's Foreign Policy 1963–1970*, pp. 56–57.
[377] Ibid.

In short, there was no special relationship between Malaya/Malaysia and the Sukarno-led Indonesia. Indonesia aimed for its strategic preponderance over Malaya/Malaysia. Malaya/Malaysia, meanwhile, desired for its mutual strategic dependence with Indonesia. The perceived preponderant standing of Indonesia in archipelagic Southeast Asia is being termed as the Malay archipelago complex, which is built on the conception of Indonesia as the dominent power in the region.[378]

The intertwined three sources of conflict in Indonesia–Malaya/Malaysia relations — Indonesia's assertion of its dominance over Malaya/Malaysia and Malaya/Malaysia's attempt to balance against Indonesia's aim for regional dominance; the two states' drive to emphasize the superiority of their respective nationhood over that of their culturally similar counterpart; the mismatch of expectation between them — bred and enhanced the negative identifications between the two states, which culminated in the armed conflicts between them. Indonesia's and Malaya/Malaysia's understanding of each other was well and truly entrenched in egoistic terms. In other words, they shared conflictual intersubjective understandings.

---

[378] N. Ganesan, "Rethinking ASEAN as a Security Community in Southeast Asia", *Asian Affairs* 21, no. 4 (1995): 217.

6

THE BEGINNING OF A SPECIAL RELATIONSHIP: INDONESIA– MALAYSIA RELATIONS, 1966–84

This chapter explains that a special relationship between Indonesia and Malaysia had emerged shortly after the fall of the Sukarno regime.

Indonesia's confrontation against Malaysia had been effectively defeated by Malaysia, in which the Anglo–Malaysian military alliance was the backbone of its security. The power owned by Malaysia had accordingly succeeded in halting Indonesia's tendency to launch military attacks on Malaysia. Indonesia began to share the same understanding held by Malaysia that power balance existed between the two states, which meant a basis of order had emerged between them. Indonesia and Malaysia began to coexist peacefully.

Meanwhile, the presence of power balance between Indonesia and Malaysia also meant that both states possessed the necessary amount of power that shaped their similar strategic understandings rooted in common identities into their common strategic interests. Since then, Indonesia and Malaysia needed each other to form the Malay world in archipelagic Southeast Asia — a shield that protected their existence as states built around the Malay way of life. Two sources of closeness — common identities and shared strategic interests — henceforth, coexisted in Indonesia–Malaysia relations. A special relationship, therefore, had emerged between Indonesia and Malaysia.

The two sources of closeness in Indonesia–Malaysia relations generated their mutual aspiration for peace, which were strong enough to give rise to the war avoidance norms shared by the two states. In other words, the Indonesia–Malaysia special relationship constituted a security regime between them.

Upon the establishment of their special relationship, Indonesia and Malaysia worked together to create a friendly regional climate of Southeast Asia, which essentially reflected the Malay way of life. Together they moved to establish ASEAN so as to forge a friendly order of Southeast Asia through regional cooperation. The creation of ASEAN was an expression of the Indonesia–Malaysia special relationship. ASEAN's essence as a security regime, in the meantime, was created and sustained by the special relationship.

While Indonesia and Malaysia identified intimately with each other because of their special ties, their egoistic understanding of one another, nonetheless, persisted. The reordering of the strategic landscape in Southeast Asia, which took place in the late 1960s, revealed such basic qualities of Indonesia–Malaysia relations. In order to respond to the changing strategic environment, Indonesia and Malaysia sought for each other's cooperation, aiming to create an autonomous Southeast Asia that ensured their basic security. In the meantime, they balanced against one another to safeguard their respective survival. The two states, as a consequence, were entangled in a situation of competitive cooperation.

INDONESIA'S UNDERSTANDING OF MALAYSIA SHAPED BY POWER

Indonesia's military campaign against Malaysia was repeatedly ended in failure. Underpinned by its military alliance with Britain, Malaysia was able to neutralize the military attacks from Indonesia. Owing to the confrontation campaign, 50,000 British troops had been brought to Malaysia under the Anglo-Malaysian Defence Agreement (AMDA). The mighty military presence was a powerful deterrent to Indonesia's aggressions. By 1964, it had become increasingly clear for the Indonesian army that Malaysia would not be defeated, rather it would endure as a state in Southeast Asia. The expansion of Malaya into Malaysia led to Indonesia's realization of its strategic reliance on Malaysia.

In April 1964, the Army Staff and Command College of Indonesia (Sekolah Staf Komando Angkatan Darat, SESKOAD) had produced an analysis on Indonesia's foreign policy titled "Indonesia's Free and Active Foreign Policy".[1] The SESKOAD study argued that Indonesia's threat from the north was not the presence of British neo-colonialism in the form of Malaysia; instead it was the communist states from the north, especially China, that were threatening the survival of Indonesia. The study concluded that Indonesia needed a strong Malaysia. A powerful Malaysia, the study explained, formed a buffer for Indonesia in the face of the communist threat from the north. Henceforth, the Indonesian army began to acknowledge Malaysia as vital to Indonesia's security.[2] It argued for the need for Indonesia to cultivate friendly relations with its neighbouring states in general, and with Malaysia in particular.[3] In other words, the Indonesian army wanted Indonesia to forge a special relationship with Malaysia.

The SESKOAD study stressed the importance of regional cooperation as a way for Indonesia to establish its friendly ties with neighbouring states.[4] It also emphasized the need for Indonesia to focus on internal stability and economic development.[5] It would appear that the SESKOAD study played a key role in bringing about Indonesia's decision to end its confrontation against Malaysia. The study, meanwhile, furnished a framework for the new Suharto regime's contemplation of Indonesia's foreign policy.

---

[1] Dewi Fortuna Anwar, *Indonesia in ASEAN: Foreign Policy and Regionalism* (Singapore: Institute of Southeast Asian Studies, 1994), pp. 29, 124.
[2] Ibid.
[3] Ibid.
[4] Ibid., pp. 29, 125–26.
[5] Ibid.

It was problematic that the Indonesian army attributed Indonesia's need for a strong Malaysia to the communist threat from the north. The Indonesian army's previous attempt to terminate the formation of Malaysia was genuine.[6] Indeed, it was General Nasution, Chief of Staff of the Indonesian armed forces, that called for Indonesians' vigilance against Malaysia, which — according to him — represented neo-colonialism aiming to encircle Indonesia.[7] In other words, the Indonesian army actually wanted to crush Malaysia, regardless of the communist threat from the north. Indonesia's inability to dismantle Malaysia, therefore the breakdown of Indonesia's attempt to establish its regional preponderance, prompted a change in the Indonesian army's understanding of Malaysia. It was in essence Malaysia's demonstration of its power — of which created through Malaya's expansion into Malaysia — that resulted in the Indonesian army's realization of Indonesia's strategic dependance on a strong Malaysia.

MORE THAN A BASIS OF ORDER — THE COEXISTANCE OF THE TWO SOURCES OF CLOSENESS

Based on the SESKOAD study — an analysis produced largely in response to the debacle of Indonesia's confrontation against Malaysia — the Indonesian army had come to the conclusion that the confrontation campaign should be ended.[8] Malaysia's power had succeeded in halting Indonesia's tendency to launch military attacks on it. Indonesia began to share the same understanding held by Malaysia that power balance existed between the two states. A basis of order had emerged between Indonesia and Malaysia. Both states respectively possessed the ability to deter the counterpart's armed attack. Both found it very costly to plunge into a violent conflict between them. Consequently, they had no alternative other than to coexist peacefully.

---

[6]   Michael Leifer, *Indonesia's Foreign Policy* (London: George Allen & Unwin, 1983), p. 107.

[7]   Ibid., pp. 78–79.

[8]   Anwar, *Indonesia in ASEAN*, pp. 28–29, 42–43.

An intelligence unit called "OPSUS" (*Operasi Khusus* — Special Operations) was formed by the head of the Indonesian army's Strategic Reserve Command, General Suharto, in late 1965. OPSUS in essence was an executive agency where "specific people and/or agencies were commissioned for specific intelligence operations, supported by a small permanent central staff".[9] Lieutenant General Ali Murtopo — a close confidant of Suharto — conducted special operations through OPSUS.[10] The initial task of OPSUS was to liaise secretly with Malaysia with the aim of ending Indonesia's confrontation against Malaysia.[11] OPSUS was answerable only to General Suharto. Permanent Secretary of Malaysia's Ministry of Foreign Affairs, Ghazali Shafie, was appointed by the Tunku administration to get in touch with the members of OPSUS. His mission was to seek ways to end Confrontation.

A series of secret meetings between OPSUS and Malaysia's officials were held in Bangkok and Hong Kong shortly after the abortive September 30th Movement in Indonesia. Ali Murtopo and Ghazali Shafie were engaged in in-depth discussions between them during the meetings.[12] Both acknowledged Indonesia's and Malaysia's mutual tendency of wanting to become close to each other whenever they felt a sense of insecurity.[13] The acknowledgement represented the matching of Indonesia's and Malaysia's expectation of a strategic partnership between them with their respective intention to cooperate with each other. Ali Murtopo and Ghazali Shafie used the Malay word "*Berkampung*" — to gather together — to express Indonesia's and Malaysia's recognition of their mutual strategic dependence.[14]

---

[9]   Clinton Fernandes, *The Independence of East Timor: Multi-Dimensional Perspectives – Occupation, Resistance, and International Political Activism* (Brighton, Portland and Toronto: Sussex Academic Press, 2011), p. 22.

[10] Ibid.

[11] Ibid. Also see Anwar, *Indonesia in ASEAN*, pp. 29–30, 42.

[12] Ghazali Shafie, *Malaysia, ASEAN and the New World Order* (Bangi: Universiti Kebangsaan Malaysia Press, 2000), pp. 149–52.

[13] Ibid.

[14] Ibid.

The presence of power balance between Indonesia and Malaysia, therefore, was more than a basis of order between them. While compelling Indonesia and Malaysia to coexist peacefully, the presence of power balance between them also resulted in them sharing common strategic interests.

Indonesia's power had created its strategic standing in Malaysia's security all along. Indonesia, on the other hand, acknowledged its strategic dependence on Malaysia ever since it was compelled to coexist peacefully with Malaysia. Because Malaysia possessed the ability to terminate Indonesia's challenge to its territories, and would remain as the state sharing the longest border with Indonesia in archipelagic Southeast Asia, Indonesia therefore understood: it was strategically dependent on Malaysia. The existence of Malaysia meant that it represented an integral part of the Malay world given the size of the new federation. Indonesia — like Malaysia — viewed archipelagic Southeast Asia as the Malay world. It had to secure Malaysia's strategic cooperation, so that the Malay world could function as a shield that safeguarded Indonesia's existence as a state which was built around the Malay way of life.

That said, by the time where power balance existed between Indonesia and Malaysia — that was the presence of a basis of order between them — the two states each possessed the necessary amount of power that produced their mutual need for strategic cooperation, and consequently, generated positive identifications between them. A basis of order — peaceful coexistence — alone entails no positive identification between the states concerned.

Ali Murtopo and Ghazali Shafie after the series of secret meetings had come to the conclusion: a special relationship should be established between Indonesia and Malaysia.[15] The special relationship — according to them — would be different from the normal diplomatic ties between modern states.[16] Both were of the view that "modern state/nation-state"

---

[15] Ghazali Shafie, *Malaysia, ASEAN and the New World Order*, pp. 149–50.

[16] Ibid., pp. 149–50, 190, 382.

was a Western concept.[17] In other words, Ali Murtopo and Ghazali Shafie — who represented their respective states — recognized that Indonesia and Malaysia shared a relation which was closer than their other bilateral ties.

Both of them stressed that streams, seas and straits were not borders that separated people, rather they were bridges that united people of a common region.[18] It was the understanding of the Malay world. Leaders of Indonesia and Malaysia regarded the lands and the waters in archipelagic Southeast Asia as a single undivided entity.[19] They were aware that only the people of Malay civilization incorporated the element of water in their understanding of homeland — a land for their existence.[20] The Malays in Malaysia and the indigenous people of Indonesia call their homeland *Tanah Air* — a place of land and water. They deem that they are the people of the lands and the seas; waters never separate them; waters always unite them; that is the Malay world.[21] The view of Ali Murtopo and Ghazali Shafie represented the consensus reached between Indonesia and Malaysia, that the two states should stand united; and together they formed the Malay world — a shield that protected their respective survival.

A special relationship between Indonesia and Malaysia had emerged. Two sources of closeness — common identities and shared strategic interests — coexisted in Indonesia–Malaysia relations. Both states were bound by their common Malay way of life. They too understood that both were strategically dependent on each other. The common strategic interests of Indonesia and Malaysia are founded on their similar strategic apprehensions rooted in common identities — that of the Malay world/Malay archipelago was a shield that safeguarded their respective survival — and created by their respective necessary amount of

---

[17] Ibid.
[18] Ibid., pp. 150, 190.
[19] Interview 925, Kuala Lumpur, 25 September 2012. Also see Dewi Fortuna Anwar, *Indonesia's Strategic Culture: Ketahanan Nasional, Wawasan Nusantara and Hankamrata* (Australia: Griffith University, 1996), p. 10.
[20] Ibid.
[21] Interview 925, Kuala Lumpur, 25 September 2012.

power. Both needed each other's power to ensure that archipelagic Southeast Asia was the Malay world, which ultimately protected Indonesia's and Malaysia's existence as states built around the Malay way of life.

The coexistence of common identities and shared strategic interests in Indonesia–Malaysia relations gave birth to their special ties. The two sources of closeness, meanwhile, generated the two states' mutual aspiration for peace that gave rise to the war avoidance norms shared by the two states.

Ali Murtopo and Ghazali Shafie aspired for "an enduring and durable entente" between Indonesia and Malaysia.[22] They proposed that "the principles of détente should be scrupulously observed" by Indonesia and Malaysia whenever a difficult situation arose between the two states.[23] They recommended ways to deal with border issues between Indonesia and Malaysia: border disputes should be sorted out at local level through bilateral mechanisms to prevent the disputes from becoming major conflicts between the two states; if there were shared borders fraught with uncertainties, the two sides should together survey and demarcate the shared borders or jointly develop areas around the borders for mutual benefit.[24] These recommendations indicated the beginning of Indonesia's and Malaysia's commitment to avoid war between them.

The secret meetings between OPSUS and Malaysia's officials took place at a time when Indonesia began to share the same longing of Malaysia for a peaceful external climate. By 1965, because of its obsession with revolutionary struggles and inattention to economic management, Indonesia was on the brink of economic collapse and in the midst of political chaos.[25] Restoring domestic stability and delivering economic progress became the central tasks of the emerging Suharto regime.[26] Without the desired outcomes, Indonesia was at risk of breaking apart. The new regime, in the meantime, wanted to make use of the two

---

[22] Ghazali Shafie, *Malaysia, ASEAN and the New World Order*, p. 158.

[23] Ibid.

[24] Ibid., pp. 150, 190.

[25] Anwar, *Indonesia in ASEAN*, pp. 37, 279.

[26] Ibid., pp. 35–38, 279.

central tasks to legitimize its rule in Indonesia.[27] As a consequence, a peaceful external environment became essential for Indonesia, for its government needed to concentrate on establishing domestic order and creating economic growth in Indonesia.[28]

Based on the realization of Indonesia's mutual strategic dependence with Malaysia, leaders of the emerging Suharto regime understood that a peaceful Southeast Asia that allowed it to immerse in domestic matters was to be created through regional cooperation.[29] The leaders — by embracing regional cooperation — wanted to cultivate Indonesia's friendly ties with other Southeast Asian states, aiming to create a shield of friendship around Indonesia.[30] Such a friendly regional environment — as the leaders saw it — would serve as a buffer for Indonesia, moving the threats to Indonesia away from its immediate vicinity.[31] The idea of a shield of friendship reflected Indonesia's strategic thinking of the Malay world. Indonesia aimed to establish friendly ties with Malaysia in particular, and with other Southeast Asian states in general. At the core of the shield of friendship lay the Indonesia–Malaysia special relationship. Indonesia together with Malaysia formed the Malay world — that was the shield that safeguarded Indonesia's existence.

Upon acknowledging the need for a special relationship between Indonesia and Malaysia, Ali Murtopo and Ghazali Shafie proposed that a regional organization of Southeast Asia to be established in order to create a friendly regional environment of Southeast Asia through regional cooperation.[32] The stability and peace of Southeast Asia, they argued, were dependent on Indonesia–Malaysia cordiality.[33] A consensus therefore had been reached: the proposed regional organization should be established only after the brotherly relationship between Indonesia and

---

[27] Ibid., pp. 40, 279.
[28] Ibid., pp. 46–47.
[29] Ibid., pp. 29, 46–47
[30] Ibid., pp. 29, 46–47, 297.
[31] Ibid.
[32] Ghazali Shafie, *Malaysia, ASEAN and the New World Order*, pp. 150–51, 158–59.
[33] Ibid.

Malaysia had been resumed, as the two states would be the mainstay of the organization.[34]

ENDING CONFRONTATION AND ESTABLISHING A SPECIAL RELATIONSHIP

Both OPSUS and its Malaysian counterparts presented their recommendations to their respective masters.[35] Talks about rapprochement between Indonesia and Malaysia based on their blood brotherhood began to prevail in both states.[36] Leaders of Indonesia and Malaysia were serious about the idea of Malay regionalism.[37] As in Indonesia, Suharto moved to consolidate his power.

The Indonesian army together with its domestic anti-communist alliance took a few months to completely wipe out the PKI through mass arrests and mass killings following the abortive September 30th Movement.[38] Suharto then — while removing Sukarno from power — went on to establish a regime with real power lying outside the representative institutions of Indonesia, and centralized at his hand as the President of Indonesia.[39] The Suharto regime — known as the New Order government — was dominated by the Indonesian army under the leadership of President Suharto. It emphasized political stability and economic development.[40] In March 1968, Suharto stressed that Indonesia's

---

[34] Ibid.

[35] Ibid., pp. 158, 190.

[36] Joseph Chinyong Liow, *The Politics of Indonesia–Malaysia Relations: One Kin, Two Nations* (London and New York: Routledge, 2005b), pp. 107–8.

[37] Ibid.

[38] Douglas Kammen and Katharine McGregor, "Introduction: The Contours of Mass Violence in Indonesia, 1965–68", in *The Contours of Mass Violence in Indonesia, 1965–68*, edited by Douglas Kammen and Katharine McGregor (Singapore: NUS Press, 2012), pp. 7–19. Also see Anwar, *Indonesia in ASEAN*, pp. 30–31; and John D. Legge, *Sukarno: A Political Biography* (Great Britain: Allen Lane The Penguin Press, 1972), pp. 398–400.

[39] Anwar, *Indonesia in ASEAN*, pp. 30–31. Also see Legge, *Sukarno*, pp. 398–400; and Robert E. Elson, *Suharto: A Political Biography* (Cambridge: Cambridge University Press, 2001), pp. 164–65, 182–83, 189, 202.

[40] Elson, *Suharto*, pp. 148, 175.

most important problem "in this period is development".[41] He — as President — named his first cabinet as "First Development Cabinet".[42] He made plain in his speech on 1 September 1968: "Successful development is premised on the prior securing of political stability."[43]

The New Order administration officially abandoned Sukarno's ideology of New Emerging Forces versus the Old Established Forces. It declared that Indonesia would no longer see itself as a leader of the Third World. In other words, the new regime had decided to remove the spirit of revolutionary struggle against colonialism-imperialism from serving as the basis of Indonesia's national identity.[44] The revolutionary rhetoric that was prevalent in Indonesia during the Sukarno-era had been replaced by *Pancasila* and the ideas of development and modernization.[45] The Suharto regime employed Sukarno's principles of *Pancasila* as the ideological basis for its establishment of political order in Indonesia.[46] The regime adopted an anti-democratic political ideology known as Organicism.[47] Organicism was associated with anti-Enlightenment Dutch orientalism, Japanese proto-fascism and elitist Javanese political thought.[48] It had been influential among Indonesian legal scholars who drafted Indonesia's constitution in 1945.[49] The central idea of Organicism was that the state and society form an organic unity hence there was no room for political competition or a democratic opposition.[50] To ensure the consolidation of Organicism in Indonesia's society, the Suharto regime implemented a political concept known as "floating mass", aiming to depoliticize the Indonesian mass

---

[41] *Kompas*, 21 March 1968, quoted in Elson, *Suharto*, p. 168.

[42] Elson, *Suharto*, pp. 167–68.

[43] Ibid., p. 175.

[44] Max Lane, *Unfinished Nation: Indonesia Before and After Suharto* (London & New York: Verso, 2008), pp. 38–39, 42–44, 50, 54.

[45] Elson, *Suharto*, pp. 159, 174–75.

[46] Ibid., pp. 160–61, 174–75. Also see Anwar, *Indonesia's Strategic Culture*, p. 21; and Liow, *The Politics of Indonesia–Malaysia Relations*, p. 109.

[47] Fernandes, *The Independence of East Timor*, p. 25.

[48] Ibid.

[49] Ibid.

[50] Ibid.

public.[51] "Floating mass" meant that the attention of the Indonesian public would be shifted away from political struggles and preoccupied them with the tasks of development.[52] In other words, the Indonesian people were a "floating mass", who were not tied to any political party.[53] "Heroes are needed not only at the time of the independence war, but also in the sphere of development. The struggle for development is a struggle to provide content to the independence that had been achieved so long ago", President Suharto asserted in his speech on the Heroes' Day of Indonesia in 1968.[54]

Based on the groundwork laid by the meetings between OPSUS and Malaysian officials, Malaysian Deputy Prime Minister, Tun Abdul Razak and Indonesian Foreign Minister, Adam Malik, began their negotiation in Bangkok in May 1966 to end Confrontation.[55] An agreement had been reached between Tun Razak and Adam Malik on 1 June 1966. Both parties would end Confrontation and diplomatic relations between Indonesia and Malaysia would be established. Malaysia, however, had made a symbolic concession that diplomatic relations of the two states would be established only after general elections had been held in Sabah and Sarawak.[56] It was to demonstrate that the people of Sabah and Sarawak would be given a chance to reaffirm their wish to join Malaysia.[57] Yet, the prospective elections were by no means a referendum on Malaysia.[58] The Suharto regime needed the concession

---

[51] Ibid. Also see Elson, *Suharto*, p. 190.

[52] Ibid.

[53] Ibid.

[54] Elson, *Suharto*, p. 175.

[55] Leifer, *Indonesia's Foreign Policy*, pp. 108–9. Also see Abdullah Ahmad, *Tengku Abdul Rahman and Malaysia's Foreign Policy 1963–1970* (Kuala Lumpur: Berita Publishing, 1985), p. 62.

[56] Leifer, *Indonesia's Foreign Policy*, pp. 108–9. Also see Abdullah Ahmad, *Tengku Abdul Rahman and Malaysia's Foreign Policy 1963–1970*, p. 62; and Franklin B. Weinstein, *Indonesian Foreign Policy and the Dilemma of Dependence: From Sukarno to Soeharto* (Ithaca and London: Cornell University Press, 1976), p. 340.

[57] Ibid.

[58] Ibid.

to prevent the Bangkok Agreement from being jeopardized by the residual political forces of Sukarno.[59]

Confronted with the residual influence of Sukarno in Indonesia, the Suharto regime announced in April 1966 that Indonesia intended to recognize Singapore as an independent state.[60] Such a move would demonstrate that Indonesia was not capitulating to Malaysia, while it was entering into peace talks with Malaysia.[61] Recognizing Singapore — which had recently separated from Malaysia — at the very least carried the meaning of weakening Malaysia, if not breaking up the newly formed federation. The move, therefore, would offset the political pressure exerted by Sukarno and his followers, who insisted on the continuation of the confrontation campaign.

The Malaysian government was enraged by Indonesia's announcement. It ran counter to Malaysia's expectation that Indonesia should first establish diplomatic relations with Malaysia instead of Singapore. Just a little while back, OPSUS and its Malaysian counterparts had been stressing the need for a special relationship between Indonesia and Malaysia.

In response to Malaysia's anger, Indonesia assured Malaysia that it would not accord official recognition to Singapore before a peace agreement had been reached between Indonesia and Malaysia.[62] Malaysia's anger had also been moderated by Indonesia's show of commitment to end Confrontation earlier on.[63] In February 1966, eight high-ranking Indonesian army officers led by Ali Murtopo paid a goodwill visit to

---

[59] Weinstein, *Indonesian Foreign Policy and the Dilemma of Dependence*, pp. 336–37. Leifer, *Indonesia's Foreign Policy*, pp. 108–9. Also see Anwar, *Indonesia in ASEAN*, pp. 30–31; and Elson, *Suharto*, pp. 139–41.

[60] Michael Antolik, *ASEAN and the Diplomacy of Accommodation* (New York: An East Gate Book, 1990), p. 20. Also see Chandran Jeshurun, *Malaysia: Fifty Years of Diplomacy 1957–2007* (Singapore: Talisman Publishing, 2007), pp. 94–96.

[61] Anwar, *Indonesia in ASEAN*, p. 41. Also see Weinstein, *Indonesian Foreign Policy and the Dilemma of Dependence*, pp. 336–39; and Abdullah Ahmad, *Tengku Abdul Rahman and Malaysia's Foreign Policy 1963–1970*, p. 62.

[62] Jeshurun, *Malaysia: Fifty Years of Diplomacy 1957–2007*, pp. 94–96. Also see Antolik, *ASEAN and the Diplomacy of Accommodation*, p. 20.

[63] Leifer, *Indonesia's Foreign Policy*, pp. 108–9.

Prime Minister Tunku Abdul Rahman in his hometown in Alor Star. The Tunku was moved by the visit.[64] The officers went all the way to meet him in his hometown. While meeting the Prime Minister, the officers expressed Indonesia's aspiration for peace with Malaysia: "We pray that friendship and brotherhood in the true spirit of Islam will return to our two countries."[65]

On 6 June 1966, Indonesia officially recognized Singapore as an independent state. On 11 August 1966, the Bangkok Agreement was signed by Tun Razak and Adam Malik in Jakarta. Confrontation had officially come to an end. The diplomatic ties between Indonesia and Malaysia was practically established. After the signing, Adam Malik asserted: "No victor and no vanquished. This is a great victory for the Malay race."[66]

The Bangkok Agreement marked the establishment of a special relationship between Indonesia and Malaysia, which was also a security regime between the two states. The agreement reflected the basis of order between Indonesia and Malaysia. It represented Indonesia's official acceptance of the existence of Malaysia, which meant its peaceful coexistence with Malaysia. Indonesia–Malaysia relations were characterized by their shared war avoidance norms after the singing of the Bangkok Agreement.

Almost immediately after the official ending of Confrontation, Indonesia and Malaysia went ahead to defuse their defence against each other.[67] It was an outcome of their shared war avoidance norms. Both demonstrated their respective commitment to avoid armed conflicts between them, in the belief that the counterpart would reciprocate. Upon Malaysia's request, Britain and its allies began to withdraw their armed forces from Sabah and Sarawak.[68] Malaysia's decision to defuse

---

[64] Ibid. Also see Tunku Abdul Rahman, *Looking Back: Monday Musings and Memories* (Malaysia: MPH Group Publishing, 2011), pp. 156–57.

[65] Ibid.

[66] Abdul Rahman, *Looking Back*, p. 158.

[67] Anwar, *Indonesia in ASEAN*, pp. 134–35. Also see Abdullah Ahmad, *Tengku Abdul Rahman and Malaysia's Foreign Policy 1963–1970*, pp. 128–31.

[68] Ibid.

its defence against Indonesia was also an expression of its special ties with Indonesia.

Ever since Singapore had separated from Malaysia, the relationship between Britain and Malaysia was declining.[69] Policymakers of Malaysia increasingly felt that Britain was pro-Singapore at the expense of Malaysia.[70] In the eyes of the Malaysian government, Britain was essentially pro-Chinese, since Singapore was ruled by its majority Chinese.[71] The Tunku was infuriated by Britain in June 1965, when Britain warned him not to launch a coup against Prime Minister Lee Kuan Yew of Singapore.[72] Malaysia was also irritated by Britain's attempt to pressure Malaysia to reach a defence agreement with Singapore.[73] Britain had informed Malaysia that its commitments to Malaysia's defence must be based on a defence treaty between Malaysia and Singapore.[74]

Confronted with the perceived alignment between Britain and Singapore — the two culturally different powers — Malaysia began to move away from Britain, and embrace its special ties with Indonesia.[75] Together with Indonesia, Malaysia could balance against Britain and Singapore by strengthening the presence of the Malay world in archipelagic Southeast Asia. UMNO — the Malay ruling party of Malaysia — had hinted earlier on: "If Malays were 'hard-pressed' and their interests unprotected they would be forced to merge their country with Indonesia."[76] The statement was made during the peak of tension between Malaysia and Singapore months before their separation.

---

[69] Abdullah Ahmad, *Tengku Abdul Rahman and Malaysia's Foreign Policy 1963–1970*, pp. 122–23.

[70] Ibid.

[71] Ibid.

[72] Ibid., pp. 119–23.

[73] Ibid., pp. 126–28.

[74] Ibid.

[75] Ibid., pp. 122–29.

[76] *Far Eastern Economic Review*, 20 May 1965, p. 344, quoted in Antolik, *ASEAN and the Diplomacy of Accommodation*, pp. 34–35.

In order to realize its rapprochement with Indonesia, Malaysia insisted that British troops in Sabah and Sarawak be withdrawn from the territories.[77] These troops were protecting Sabah and Sarawak under AMDA. Malaysian Deputy Prime Minister, Tun Razak, announced in June 1966: "Obviously with the end of Confrontation, British troops will have to leave Sarawak and Sabah."[78] The withdrawal of British troops meant not only to avoid wars with Indonesia, it was also Malaysia's gesture of moving closer to Indonesia. It demonstrated that Malaysia and Indonesia were able to take care of their own regional matters without foreign involvement. The British media expressed Britain's discontent. They stated that the British were being forced to leave Sabah and Sarawak.[79]

Very quickly, strategic cooperation between Indonesia and Malaysia ensued. In September 1966 — about a month after the signing of the Bangkok Agreement — an agreement for security cooperation had been reached between Indonesia and Malaysia. The two states agreed to undertake joint counter-insurgency operations aimed at eliminating communist insurgents operated along the border areas shared by the two states in Borneo.[80] In May 1967, a Border Crossing Agreement was signed by Indonesia and Malaysia in which they would together set up border checkposts along their common border in Borneo. The main function of these checkposts was to prevent the communist rebels on both sides of the border from joining forces with each other. Indonesia's and Malaysia's armed forces regularly shared intelligence

---

[77] Abdullah Ahmad, *Tengku Abdul Rahman and Malaysia's Foreign Policy 1963–1970*, pp. 128–31.

[78] *The Times*, 8 June 1966, quoted in Abdullah Ahmad, *Tengku Abdul Rahman and Malaysia's Foreign Policy 1963–1970*, p. 129.

[79] Abdullah Ahmad, *Tengku Abdul Rahman and Malaysia's Foreign Policy 1963–1970*, pp. 129–30.

[80] Anwar, *Indonesia in ASEAN*, p. 143. Also see Justus M. Van Der Kroef, "The Sarawak–Indonesian Border Insurgency", *Modern Asian Studies* 2, no. 3 (1968): 257; Government of Malaysia and Government of Indonesia, *GBC MALINDO Malaysia–Indonesia: 25th Anniversary General Border Committee Malaysia–Indonesia* (Kuala Lumpur: Jabatan Perdana Menteri Malaysia, 1997), p. 101; Leifer, *Indonesia's Foreign Policy*, pp. 122–23; and Liow, *The Politics of Indonesia–Malaysia Relations*, pp. 108–9.

and organized joint military operations during their fight against the communist insurgents. Meanwhile, Sarawak had been the principal supply base for Indonesian troops who were fighting the insurgents along the Sarawak–Indonesia border.[81] The strategic cooperation between Indonesia and Malaysia reinforced their mutual positive identifications. The two states had become a *de facto* alliance since the start of their security cooperation in Borneo.[82]

The border security cooperation of Indonesia and Malaysia entailed two central meanings. It was the military cooperation of the two states against communist insurgency that was threatening their respective survival. The security cooperation also served to shift the focus of Indonesia and Malaysia from defending their border against one another, to cooperating with each other to ensure the stability of their shared border. Essentially, Indonesia and Malaysia were committed to avoid wars between them by advancing border security cooperation.[83] An Indonesian army general revealed years later that such cooperation allowed Indonesia and Malaysia to overcome difficulties that arose between them.[84]

The Indonesia–Malaysia security cooperation enabled the two states to ease their defence against each other, in the context of a peaceful archipelagic Southeast Asia that reflected the Malay way of life. In other words, Indonesia and Malaysia had created their friendly coexistence that allowed them to immerse in their respective internal social and economic developments. However, the prospect of an armed conflict between Indonesia and Malaysia had been reduced, not eliminated. The Tunku had made plain in private that he did not fully trust the Indonesian government despite Indonesia's reconciliation with Malaysia.[85] While Indonesia and Malaysia identified positively with each other because

---

[81] Van Der Kroef, "The Sarawak–Indonesian Border Insurgency", pp. 245–46.
[82] Michael Leifer, *Conflict and Regional Order in Southeast Asia* (London: The International Institute for Strategic Studies, 1980), p. 8.
[83] Government of Malaysia and Government of Indonesia, *GBC MALINDO Malaysia–Indonesia*, pp. 14, 16, 101.
[84] Ibid., p. 17.
[85] Liow, *The Politics of Indonesia–Malaysia Relations*, p. 111.

of their special ties, their relationship remained fundamentally competitive. The two states continued to understand each other in egoistic terms.

On 16 August 1966 — five days after the signing of the Bangkok Agreement — then General Suharto issued a statement to the Indonesian parliament, Dewan Perwakilan Rakyat (DPR). The statement explained the terms of the Bangkok Agreement which ended Confrontation. It, meanwhile, revealed Indonesia's intention to create a regional body of Southeast Asia:[86]

> When this 'Malaysia' question has been settled we can step up activities in the field of foreign policy towards the establishment of close cooperation based on mutual benefit between the countries of Southeast Asia. We will then revive the idea of Maphilindo in a wider sphere, in order to achieve a Southeast Asia cooperating in different fields, especially in the economic, technical and cultural fields.

Indonesia was headed towards forging a friendly climate of Southeast Asia by advancing regional cooperation.

THE FORMING OF ASEAN — AN EXPRESSION OF THE INDONESIA–MALAYSIA SPECIAL RELATIONSHIP

The idea of regional cooperation had been a key agenda of Tun Razak–Adam Malik peace talks in Bangkok in May 1966.[87] Both parties agreed that closer regional cooperation was necessary to ensure the peace of Southeast Asia.[88] During the same period, the member states of ASA (Association of Southeast Asia) — Malaysia, Thailand and the Philippines — were on the path to revive the regional organization.

---

[86] Government of Indonesia, *Government Statement Before the Gotong-Royong House of Representatives on 16th August, 1966* (Djakarta: Department of Information, 1966), p. 48, quoted in Leifer, *Indonesia's Foreign Policy*, p. 119.

[87] Interview with Tun Abdul Razak, quoted in Abdullah Ahmad, *Tengku Abdul Rahman and Malaysia's Foreign Policy 1963–1970*, p. 63. Also see Liow, *The Politics of Indonesia–Malaysia Relations*, p. 110.

[88] Anwar, *Indonesia in ASEAN*, pp. 49–50.

ASA had been suspended since 1963 when the Philippines broke diplomatic ties with Malaysia because of its claim to Sabah. Adam Malik, nevertheless, proposed during the peace talks that a new regional association of Southeast Asia should be formed.

Indonesia was in need of a new regional association. It had previously accused ASA of threatening the Third World solidarity. Becoming a member of ASA would thus create an impression of Indonesia's capitulation.[89] Adam Malik therefore wrote a secret letter to Tun Razak in June 1967, proposing the forming of a bigger ASA.

Malaysia initially would prefer Indonesia to join ASA. Yet, it understood that it needed Indonesia's strategic cooperation in order to create a friendly regional climate of Southeast Asia, which essentially reflected the Malay way of life. Malaysia accepted Indonesia's proposal of establishing a new regional body. Both appreciated that they were central to the creation of a friendly order of Southeast Asia.[90] They knew that the desired regional environment would be basically in place, if they could demonstrate that both were able to sort out their conflict and cooperate with each other.[91] Other Southeast Asian states were bound to be influenced by the cooperation between Indonesia and Malaysia.[92] They would follow suit.[93]

On 8 August 1967, Indonesia, Malaysia, Thailand, Singapore and the Philippines co-founded the Association of Southeast Asian Nations (ASEAN) in Bangkok. The name ASEAN was coined by Indonesian Foreign Minister, Adam Malik. On 31 August 1967, diplomatic ties between Indonesia and Malaysia were officially established, which was after the general election had been held in Sabah. Sarawak's general election, however, was postponed.

---

[89] Liow, *The Politics of Indonesia–Malaysia Relations*, pp. 112–13.
[90] Johan Saravanamuttu, *Malaysia's Foreign Policy, the First Fifty Years: Alignment, Neutralism, Islamism* (Singapore: Institute of Southeast Asian Studies, 2010), p. 175. Also see Liow, *The Politics of Indonesia–Malaysia Relations*, pp. 112–13.
[91] Interview 917, Kuala Lumpur, 17 September 2012.
[92] Ibid.
[93] Ibid.

is the ASEAN Way, which the member states deem to be the distinctive character of interstate relations in ASEAN.[100] ASEAN Way denotes a decision-making process based upon consultation and consensus.[101] Such a process emphasizes on extensive informal negotiations with a shared commitment to moderation and accommodation, which inhibits the majority to prevail over the minority.[102] The establishment of ASEAN had led to the creation of a friendly atmosphere among the member states of this regional body.

It was the shared belief of Indonesia and Malaysia that they — the Malay world — were the dominant forces in the newly formed ASEAN.[103] The two states aimed for regional autonomy of Southeast Asia. Their strategic thinking of the Malay world, which apprehended archipelagic Southeast Asia as one entity, formed the basis for their longing for regional autonomy.[104] "When the chips are down", the Tunku argued, "the Americans and the British would not be able to defend the region effectively. The *Rumpun Melayu* of which is an integral part should defend themselves."[105]

Among the five member states of ASEAN, only Indonesia and Malaysia aimed for an autonomous regional security framework.[106] Singapore, Thailand and the Philippines, on the other hand, insisted that Western security guarantees were vital to their respective survival as well as the security of their region.[107] They host U.S. military facilities on their soil. The three are the allies of the United States.

During the negotiations leading up to the founding of ASEAN, Indonesia and Malaysia emphasized that foreign military bases should be removed from the member states of the prospective regional body.[108]

---

[100] Weatherbee, *International Relations in Southeast Asia*, pp. 107–8, 128–29, 304.

[101] Ibid. Also see Acharya, *Constructing a Security Community in Southeast Asia*, pp. 64–70.

[102] Ibid.

[103] Interview 917, Kuala Lumpur, 17 September 2012.

[104] Rahim, *Singapore in the Malay World*, pp. 98–99, 149. Also see Interview 1002, Singapore, 2 October 2012.

[105] Ghazali Shafie, *Malaysia, ASEAN and the New World Order*, p. 388.

[106] Acharya, *Constructing a Security Community in Southeast Asia*, pp. 54–56.

[107] Ibid.

[108] Liow, *The Politics of Indonesia–Malaysia Relations*, p. 113.

Singapore would not accept such a position.[109] A compromise, however, had been reached.[110] The 1967 Bangkok Declaration affirmed that all foreign bases in ASEAN member states were temporary in nature. Nevertheless, Major Benny Murdani of Indonesia later asserted that, "it seemed inevitable...that one day Malaysia and Indonesia would come together and Singapore would need to adjust its relations with Malaysia and Indonesia in order to fit in with the circumstances of the region".[111]

The essence of ASEAN as a security regime was created and sustained by the special relationship of Indonesia and Malaysia. Within ASEAN, only Indonesia and Malaysia defused their defence against each other. The security posture of ASEAN member states vis-à-vis their counterparts — apart from that between Indonesia and Malaysia — were undoubtedly competitive.

The Chinese-dominated Singapore had striven to maintain its strong military deterrence against Indonesia and Malaysia since the first years of its independence.[112] Singapore was alarmed by its exclusion from the peace talks between Indonesia and Malaysia in ending Confrontation.[113] It was troubled by the pace of the rapprochement of the two Malay states, and their stressing of their Malay blood-brotherhood following the end of Confrontation.[114] The Indonesia–Malaysia rapprochement prompted a Malaysian Minister to claim that Singapore "was now a nut in a nutcracker".[115]

Confronted with such a prospect, Prime Minister Lee Kuan Yew of Singapore announced, "Our long-term survival demands that there is no government in Malaysia that goes with Indonesia. Life would be

---

[109] Ibid.

[110] Ibid.

[111] Ibid., p. 115.

[112] Andrew Tan, *Intra-ASEAN Tensions* (Great Britain: The Royal Institute of International Affairs, 2000), pp. 9–14. Also see Bilveer Singh, "Singapore's Management of its Security Problems", *Asia Pacific Community* 29 (Summer 1985): 77–79.

[113] Rahim, *Singapore in the Malay World*, p. 149.

[114] Liow, *The Politics of Indonesia–Malaysia Relations*, p. 115. Also see Leifer, *Indonesia's Foreign Policy*, p. 123.

[115] "What Comes After Confrontation", *Canberra Times*, 5 July 1966, quoted in Liow, *The Politics of Indonesia–Malaysia Relations*, p. 105.

very difficult if I found myself between Malaysia and Indonesia."[116] Singapore was worried about being encircled by its two immediate Malay neighbours.[117] It viewed the two Malay states as its primary security concerns.[118] Singapore was not convinced that the newly formed ASEAN was meant to ensure the friendly coexistence of its member states.[119] War-like tensions occasionally emerged between Singapore and Malaysia, and between Singapore and Indonesia in the early years of ASEAN.[120] Only low-level Singaporean officials had been sent to attend ASEAN meetings during these years.[121]

Singapore, meanwhile, began to develop its armed forces based on the model of the Israel Defence Forces — a model which emphasized on air superiority, armour and pre-emptive defence.[122] The Singapore Armed Forces (SAF) was always in a high state of combat-readiness.[123] By 1972, Prime Minister Lee declared: Singapore "had made the transition from military impotence to combat-readiness, thus achieving the goal of a defence state".[124]

A few decades later — on Singapore's National Day (9 August 1991) — Malaysia and Indonesia jointly conducted a military exercise code named "Total Wipe Out" which ended with paratroopers' landing in southern Johor.[125] The landing site was Malaysia's territory 18 km north of Singapore.[126] Singapore immediately executed its highly publicized "Operation Trojan", aiming to deter the Malaysian and Indonesian armed

---

[116] *The Observer*, 15 August 1965, quoted in Michael Leifer, *Singapore's Foreign Policy: Coping with Vulnerability* (London: Routledge, 2000), p. 58.

[117] Rahim, *Singapore in the Malay World*, p. 149.

[118] Singh, "Singapore's Management of its Security Problems", pp. 77–79.

[119] Antolik, *ASEAN and the Diplomacy of Accommodation*, p. 35.

[120] Acharya, *Constructing a Security Community in Southeast Asia*, p. 48.

[121] Seah Chee Meow, "Singapore's Position in ASEAN Co-operation", in *Singapore's Position in ASEAN Cooperation,* edited by Lim Chong Yah, Seah Chee Meow and Shaw K.E. (Tokyo: Institute of Developing Economies, 1979), p. 62, quoted in Antolik, *ASEAN and the Diplomacy of Accommodation*, p. 35.

[122] Tan, *Intra-ASEAN Tensions*, pp. 9–14.

[123] Ibid.

[124] Ibid.

[125] Ibid., p. 22.

[126] Ibid.

forces.[127] The SAF was put on full alert and Singapore's reserve forces had been mobilized.[128]

The Philippines continued to challenge Malaysia's sovereignty over Sabah after the formation of ASEAN. It was found in March 1968 that the Philippines had been training a group of militants tasked to infiltrate into Sabah.[129] The mission was a part of the Philippines' plan to take over Sabah by force.[130] Meanwhile, a bill was signed into law in the Philippines declaring that Sabah belonged to the Philippines.

Malaysia responded with a show of force. Six British Hunter jets — upon Malaysia's request under AMDA — flew over Sabah's capital, Kota Kinabalu, while on their way back to Singapore from Hong Kong.[131] The British warships around the same period sailed through the Sibutu Passage — the territorial waters of the Philippines.[132] The British Commander-in-Chief Far East, General Sir Michael Carver, declared in September 1968:[133]

> The British Government fully supports Malaysia's view that Sabah is a part of Malaysia and I affirm that Britain will honour its obligations under AMDA if fighting breaks out.

Malaysia and the Philippines suspended their diplomatic ties by the end of 1968 as a result of the Sabah dispute. The dispute continues to plague the relationship between the two states till this day.

The Malaysia–Thailand relations, on the other hand, were strained by their rivalries, and the activities of the Communist Party of Malaya

---

[127] Ibid.

[128] Ibid.

[129] Abdullah Ahmad, *Tengku Abdul Rahman and Malaysia's Foreign Policy 1963–1970*, pp. 73–74. Also see Anwar, *Indonesia in ASEAN*, p. 169.

[130] Ibid.

[131] Abdullah Ahmad, *Tengku Abdul Rahman and Malaysia's Foreign Policy 1963–1970*, pp. 133–34.

[132] Ibid. Also see Anwar, *Indonesia in ASEAN*, p. 169.

[133] *The Times*, 20 September 1968, quoted in Abdullah Ahmad, *Tengku Abdul Rahman and Malaysia's Foreign Policy 1963–1970*, p. 134.

(CPM) and Muslim separatists in Southern Thailand.[134] Thailand was always worried that Malaysia might have the intention to acquire the Malay territories in Southern Thailand.[135] Malaysia, meanwhile, was uneasy about its supposed Thai toleration of the CPM rebels operating in Southern Thailand.[136] A certain degree of arms race existed between Thailand and Malaysia.[137]

It was therefore apparent that the war avoidance norms of ASEAN were largely a consequence of the existence of a security regime between Indonesia and Malaysia. The two states' commitment to defuse their defence against each other served as an established norm within ASEAN which shaped, and was shaped by, the conception of self of the ASEAN member states. The shared war avoidance norms of Indonesia and Malaysia spawned the ASEAN-Five's habit to avoid violent conflicts among them. Overtime, ASEAN war avoidance norms became established, which had a life of their own.[138]

By 1976, it was the intersubjective recognition of the five ASEAN member states that they formed a common region which was peaceful and stable.[139] There was no armed conflict in the region since the formation of ASEAN in 1967. Confronted with the communist victory in Indochina, especially a military powerful and potentially hostile Vietnam, the five ASEAN states organized their first summit in Bali in February 1976. The summit was to demonstrate the solidarity of the ASEAN member states and their determination to preserve the peace and stability of the ASEAN region.[140] The five states came to view

---

[134] Acharya, *Constructing a Security Community in Southeast Asia*, pp. 59–60, 199.

[135] Christopher B. Roberts, *ASEAN Regionalism: Cooperation, Values and Institutionalization* (London and New York: Routledge, 2012), p. 44.

[136] Acharya, *Constructing a Security Community in Southeast Asia*, pp. 59–60, 199.

[137] Ibid.

[138] Antolik, *ASEAN and the Diplomacy of Accommodation*, p. 159.

[139] Leifer, *Indonesia's Foreign Policy*, pp. 160–64. Also see Antolik, *ASEAN and the Diplomacy of Accommodation*, p. 159; and Ghazali Shafie, *Malaysia, ASEAN and the New World Order*, pp. 151–53, 159–61.

[140] Leifer, *Indonesia's Foreign Policy*, pp. 160–64. Also see Anwar, *Indonesia in ASEAN*, p. 152; and Ghazali Shafie, *Malaysia, ASEAN and the New World Order*, pp. 151–53, 159–61.

that the security of any of their counterpart directly affected that of their own.[141]

While the Indonesia–Malaysia special relationship was essential to the existence of ASEAN as a security regime, the two states did not possess the power that would result in their dominance in ASEAN. The strategic cooperation of Indonesia and Malaysia ensured the friendly coexistence of the states within ASEAN. Indonesia and Malaysia, however, were unable to establish their preferred autonomous regional order of Southeast Asia through their strategic partnership.

The two states declared their "Kuantan Principle" in March 1980, aiming to bring an end to Vietnam's occupation of Cambodia that took place since December 1978. "Kuantan Principle" stressed that "for Southeast Asia to be a region of peace, Vietnam must be freed from Soviet and Chinese influence".[142] Indonesia and Malaysia deemed that Vietnam's aggression was a reaction against China's dominance, and sustained by the rivalries between two extraregional great powers — the Soviet Union and China.[143] The exclusion of external influence, that was the creation of Southeast Asia's regional autonomy — as Indonesia and Malaysia saw it — would be the way to end Vietnam's occupation of Cambodia.[144]

Indonesia–Malaysia strategic cooperation expressed through their declaration of Kuantan Principle carried no impact on the development of the crisis in Indochina. Thailand went ahead to consolidate its informal alliance with China in the face of the direct military threat from Vietnam.[145] ASEAN's policy towards the Vietnamese invasion was dominated by Thailand, which was dealing with an existential threat

---

[141] Anwar, *Indonesia in ASEAN*, p. 152. Also see Saravanamuttu, *Malaysia's Foreign Policy, the First Fifty Years*, p. 175; and Weatherbee, *International Relations in Southeast Asia*, pp. 80–81.

[142] Liow, *The Politics of Indonesia–Malaysia Relations*, pp. 129–31. Also see Leifer, *Indonesia's Foreign Policy*, pp. 166–69; and Saravanamuttu, *Malaysia's Foreign Policy, the First Fifty Years*, pp. 174–75.

[143] Ibid.

[144] Ibid.

[145] Ibid.

from Vietnam.[146] ASEAN chose to stand up against Vietnam. It forged a partnership with China, aiming to force Vietnam out of Cambodia. Indonesia and Malaysia had to follow suit to prevent the disintegration of ASEAN.[147]

THE WIDTH AND THE DEPTH OF THE INDONESIA– MALAYSIA SPECIAL RELATIONSHIP

Indonesia and Malaysia began to share a relationship with various special characters after the abortive movement in Indonesia in September 1965. They had worked together to claim ownership of the Straits of Malacca.

Shortly after the end of Confrontation, Malaysia decided to adopt Indonesia's measurement of territorial waters, which was codified in Indonesia's Archipelago Doctrine. A bill was introduced by the Tunku administration in 1967 stipulating the extension of Malaysia's territorial waters based upon Indonesia's measurement — that was the adoption of the straight baseline system, and the extension of Malaysia's territorial waters from 3 to 12 miles. The bill was passed by Malaysia's parliament in 1969, paving the way for an agreement reached between Indonesia and Malaysia in March 1970.[148] The agreement delimited the continental shelves between the two states.

Indonesia and Malaysia had essentially declared their sovereignty over the Straits of Malacca through the signing of the 1970 agreement. The 12 miles delimitation of territorial sea meant that the two states possessed the jurisdictions over the straits. Indonesia and Malaysia sought to revoke the existing international status of the straits. Both — in a joint public statement on 16 November 1971 — asserted that the Straits of Malacca were "not international straits, while fully recognising

---

[146] Ibid. Also see Anwar, *Indonesia in ASEAN*, p. 188; and Weatherbee, *International Relations in Southeast Asia*, pp. 80–81.

[147] Ibid.

[148] Liow, *The Politics of Indonesia–Malaysia Relations*, pp. 122–23. Also see Dino Patti Djalal, *The Geopolitics of Indonesia's Maritime Territorial Policy* (Jakarta: Centre for Strategic and International Studies, 1996), p. 29.

their use for international shipping in accordance with the principle of innocent passage".[149]

Claiming ownership of the Straits of Malacca was an effort of Indonesia and Malaysia to strengthen the presence of the Malay world in archipelagic Southeast Asia. In the two states' strategic thinking of the Malay world, waters always unite them. For Indonesia and Malaysia, the Straits of Malacca is not a divider between them, but a bridge that unites them.[150] Tun Dr Ismail, in his capacity as Malaysia's Deputy Prime Minister, said in July 1972:

> ...we have the Straits of Malacca as our common border. Even though the straits separates the two countries physically but in my view, the straits is a bridge that ties up the two nations of *serumpun*. In order to safeguard this bridge, both countries have agreed to defend it, not just to ensure that it is freed from threats, but also to enhance our cooperation and to protect national sovereignty.[151]

In the eyes of Indonesia and Malaysia, the Straits of Malacca was a part of the Malay world which bound them together; both needed to own and protect the straits, so that their existence as states built around the Malay way of life would be secured.

Singapore did not recognize Indonesia's and Malaysia's statement that denied the international status of the Straits of Malacca. It suspected that such a move was the two Malay states' attempt to corner Singapore.[152] Indonesian and Malaysian officials had been reported to have been trying to omit Singapore from negotiations over the legal status of the Straits of Malacca.[153]

The two superpowers firmly opposed Indonesia's and Malaysia's challenge to the existing status of the Straits of Malacca. The U.S. and the Soviet navies sailed through the straits to affirm the longstanding

---

[149] Leifer, *Indonesia's Foreign Policy*, p. 144.
[150] Interview 919, Kuala Lumpur, 19 September 2012.
[151] Government of Malaysia and Government of Indonesia, *GBC MALINDO Malaysia–Indonesia*, p. 5.
[152] Liow, *The Politics of Indonesia–Malaysia Relations*, pp. 122–23.
[153] Ibid.

international status of the straits.[154] Consequently, Indonesia's and Malaysia's assertion of their sovereignty over the Straits of Malacca was nothing more than a declaration.[155]

On 13 May 1969, clashes broke out between Malays and Chinese in Malaysia following the general election held in Malaysia two days before. The racial riots were a result of the belief among the Malays that their supremacy in Malaysia was being threatened by the Chinese.[156] The setback of the Alliance led by UMNO — the Malay nationalist ruling party — in the general election was a trigger for the clashes. It was the first time since independence that the Alliance lost its two-thirds majority in Malaysia's parliament. The Alliance also lost two states — Penang and Kelantan — in the state-level election. Violence began to spread when the Malays reacted to the Chinese-based opposition party's celebrations of its achievements in the 1969 general election.

In the midst of the racial riots, General Yoga of Indonesia was sent by President Suharto to meet with Ghazali Shafie — Permanent Secretary of Malaysia's Ministry of Foreign Affairs — informing him that Indonesia was ready to help the Malaysian government.[157] General Tjokropranolo — a close aide to Suharto — indicated that Indonesia felt obliged to assist the Malays in Malaysia in their struggle against the Chinese.[158] The Malays, meanwhile, believed that Indonesia would always have their back in fighting the Chinese.[159] Ghazali Shafie was moved by Indonesia's support expressed through General Yoga's visit. He revealed years later, "it was an extraordinary gesture which I can never forget".[160]

The chaotic situation in Malaysia was quickly brought under control. The Tunku had to step down from power as a consequence of the

---

[154] Leifer, *Indonesia's Foreign Policy*, p. 145.

[155] Ibid.

[156] Cheah Boon Keng, *Malaysia: The Making of a Nation* (Singapore: Institute of Southeast Asian Studies, 2002), 105-p. 106. Also see Liow, *The Politics of Indonesia–Malaysia Relations*, p. 115.

[157] Ghazali Shafie, *Malaysia, ASEAN and the New World Order*, p. 394.

[158] Liow, *The Politics of Indonesia–Malaysia Relations*, p. 116.

[159] Ibid.

[160] Ghazali Shafie, *Malaysia, ASEAN and the New World Order*, p. 394.

13 May racial riots.[161] He was succeeded by Tun Abdul Razak, who had been in power few days after the start of the riots.[162] The new Razak administration had brought about a fundamental change to Malaysia's domestic politics. It worked vigorously to consolidate the Malay supremacy in Malaysia.[163] The administration implemented the New Economic Policy, aiming to uplift the social economic position of the Malays. The Malays were entitled to massive government assistance under the new policy.[164] The Razak administration also introduced its National Culture policy. The policy was to create a Malaysian culture based upon Malay culture, Islam and suitable elements from other cultures. In 1970, Razak made a decision that the Malay language would replace English as the main medium of instruction in Malaysia's education system.

The Razak administration, on the other hand, began to encourage Indonesians to migrate to Malaysia.[165] The move was to expand the Malay population, while being the largest ethnic group in Malaysia.[166] Such an expansion would underpin the Malay supremacy in Malaysia.[167] The policy of making the Malay language as the main medium of instruction in Malaysia's education system further enhanced the closeness between Indonesia and Malaysia. Indonesia supplied Malaysia with teachers and lecturers to help mitigate Malaysia's difficulties in implementing its language policy.[168] Malaysia did not have the volume of teachers and

---

[161] Cheah, *Malaysia*, pp. 106, 130–31, 136–37.

[162] Ibid. Also see Nik Anuar Nik Mahmud, Muhammad Haji Salleh, Abd. Ghapa Harun, *A Biography of Tun Abdul Razak: Statesman and Patriot* (Bangi: Universiti Kebangsaan Malaysia Press, 2012), p. 258.

[163] Cheah, *Malaysia*, pp. 126–27, 138.

[164] Ibid., pp. 123, 127, 141–44.

[165] Ahmad Nizar Yaakub, "Malaysia and Indonesia: A Study of Foreign Policies with Special Reference to Bilateral Relations", PhD dissertation, The University of Western Australia, 2009, p. 103. Also see Liow, *The Politics of Indonesia–Malaysia Relations*, p. 48.

[166] Ibid.

[167] Ibid.

[168] Interview 926-001, Kuala Lumpur, 26 September 2012. Interview 1011, Jakarta, 11 October 2012. Also see Yaakub, "Malaysia and Indonesia", pp. 110–11, 120, 152; and Nik Mahmud et el., *A Biography of Tun Abdul Razak*, p. 293.

experts needed for the creation of a nationwide education system that used the Malay language as its main medium of instruction.[169] Meanwhile, the textbooks in Malaysia were still not all written in Malay. Indonesia assisted Malaysia to overcome the challenge by providing Malaysia with its expertise in producing textbooks in Malay.[170] Abdul Rahman Yaakub — Malaysia's Education Minister in the Razak administration — confided that, without Indonesia's assistance, the implementation of the National Education Policy and the introduction of the Malay language into Malaysia's schools and universities would have failed.[171]

The Razak administration provided firm support for Indonesia's decision to annex East Timor in 1975. The prospect of East Timor's emergence as an independent state began to surface following Portugal's move to decolonize its possession of East Timor that took place since 1974. The New Order Regime in Indonesia was alarmed by such a prospect. It could not tolerate an independent East Timor.[172] In the eyes of the regime, an independent state situated at the periphery of the Indonesian archipelago constituted a threat to the integrity of Indonesia.[173] The regime believed that East Timor which was independent might become a base for hostile forces to spread separatist movements in Indonesia.[174] Most importantly, the possibility of East Timor becoming a democracy posed a direct threat to the New Order Regime, which was undemocratic.[175] The Indonesian public would be exposed to a democratic alternative functioning within the sphere of the Indonesian archipelago if East Timor had eventually become a democracy.[176]

---

[169] Ibid.

[170] Ibid.

[171] K. Muniandy, *Malaysia–Indonesia Relations 1957–1970* (Kuala Lumpur: Dewan Bahasa dan Pustaka, 1996), p. 267, quoted in Yaakub, "Malaysia and Indonesia", PhD dissertation, The University of Western Australia, 2009, pp. 110–11. Also see Cheah, *Malaysia*, pp. 128–29.

[172] Leifer, *Indonesia's Foreign Policy*, pp. 154–56, 159.

[173] Ibid.

[174] Ibid.

[175] Clinton Fernandes, *Reluctant Saviour: Australia, Indonesia and the Independence of East Timor* (Australia: Scribe Publications, 2004), p. 14.

[176] Ibid.

Indonesia annexed East Timor in December 1975 to prevent it from becoming an independent state.[177] Malaysia provided full diplomatic support for Indonesia's invasion of East Timor. The integrity of Indonesia as an archipelagic state was crucial to Malaysia's security. Malaysia needed the existence of Indonesia as together they formed the Malay world — a shield that protected Malaysia's existence as a Malay nation-state. Shortly before the invasion, Prime Minister Razak publicly declared Malaysia's support for the integration of East Timor into Indonesia.[178] He also told the Australian media that "he did not see how Portuguese Timor could survive as an independent country and criticized Portugal for not being sensitive enough to Indonesia's feelings on the Timor issue".[179] Malaysia voted against a UN resolution that called for Indonesia's withdrawal from East Timor. When Indonesia was confronted with an increasingly harsh international criticism of its military operations in East Timor, Prime Minister Razak publicly asserted that "the obvious future for Portuguese Timor is for the territory to become part of Indonesia".[180]

After six years of their border security cooperation, Indonesia and Malaysia moved to establish a General Border Committee (GBC) on 23 July 1972. The two states broadened and deepened their existing border security cooperation through GBC. The committee was co-chaired by Indonesia's and Malaysia's security officers at the highest level — either Minister of Defence or Minister of Home Affairs.[181] Previously, it was the Indonesian and Malaysian brigade commanders that were taking charge of the two states' border security cooperation.[182]

Indonesia–Malaysia security cooperation was to be expanded as a result of the forming of GBC. Apart from their common border in Borneo, the two states would also undertake their security cooperation

---

[177] Leifer, *Indonesia's Foreign Policy*, pp. 154–58.
[178] Fernandes, *The Independence of East Timor*, p. 41.
[179] Ibid.
[180] Liow, *The Politics of Indonesia–Malaysia Relations*, p. 127.
[181] Government of Malaysia and Government of Indonesia, *GBC MALINDO Malaysia–Indonesia*, pp. 31, 39.
[182] Ibid.

along their shared borders at the Straits of Malacca and the South China Sea.[183] GBC was the principal body that oversaw Indonesia–Malaysia security cooperation at these three border regions.[184]

The newly-established committee inherited the two defining roles of the existing border security cooperation of Indonesia and Malaysia in Borneo. The committee was an outcome of the two states' war avoidance norms. GBC functioned as a mechanism between Indonesia and Malaysia that allowed them to sort out their border disputes via negotiations.[185] From 1973 onwards, Indonesia and Malaysia made use of the committee to jointly measure and delimit their common border in Borneo.[186] GBC was also the body tasked to carry out development projects in areas around this shared border.[187] The attempt to develop the border areas was meant to avoid war between Indonesia and Malaysia by generating socio-economic progress in these areas for the common good of the two states.[188] Such an idea of avoiding war was originated from the proposal put forward by OPSUS and its Malaysian counterparts back then in the final years of Confrontation.

GBC, on the other hand, furnished a framework for the military cooperation between Indonesia and Malaysia. One of the main tasks of GBC is to handle Indonesia–Malaysia military operations along their shared borders against their common enemy.[189] The committee has the authority to form a joint task force that involves the armies, navies and air forces of the two states.[190]

The immediate task of GBC was to organize joint military operations of Indonesia and Malaysia to eradicate the communist insurgents operated along the two states' common border in Borneo.[191] The committee also

---

[183] Ibid., pp. 29, 31, 39, 45, 51–52.
[184] Ibid.
[185] Ibid., pp. 140–43, 166, 173–74, 179.
[186] Ibid.
[187] Ibid., pp. 16, 69, 105, 150, 170, 174.
[188] Ibid.
[189] Ibid., p. 23.
[190] Anwar, *Indonesia in ASEAN*, p. 144.
[191] Government of Malaysia and Government of Indonesia, *GBC MALINDO Malaysia–Indonesia*, pp. 31, 41, 57, 75.

worked to establish coordinated patrols of the navies and air forces of Indonesia and Malaysia in their respective territories along the Straits of Malacca.[192] Through GBC, Indonesia and Malaysia had jointly developed plans to conduct surveillance on the movements of foreign ships in the Straits of Malacca.[193] The patrols and the surveillance plans were meant to assert Indonesia's and Malaysia's ownership over the Straits of Malacca, which both the Malay states regarded as a vital part of the Malay world. A decision had been made by GBC that any problem or dispute in the Straits of Malacca should and will be resolved by the sovereign states bordering the straits without the interventions of outsiders.[194]

GBC over time had put in place nearly all of the regular joint military exercises that existed between Indonesia and Malaysia.[195] These exercises involved the armies, navies and air forces of the two states.[196] A joint exercise code named "Elang Malindo IV" was performed by the Indonesian and Malaysian air forces in November 1978. It was an exercise organized by GBC.[197] The exercise pretended that the Indonesian army in Natuna Island was confronted with attacks from enemy forces and had retreated into the jungle of the island.[198] The air forces of Indonesia and Malaysia quickly formed an Air Joint Task Force to recapture the airport in Natuna Island.[199]

"Elang Malindo IV" had crucial meaning for both Indonesia and Malaysia. It indicated the two states' determination to execute their strategic thinking — that of the Malay world functioned as a shield for their respective existence. Natuna is an Indonesian island in the South

---

[192] Ibid., pp. 51–52, 77.

[193] Ibid., p. 159.

[194] Ibid., p. 102.

[195] Ibid., p. 125. Also see Anwar, *Indonesia in ASEAN*, pp. 143–46; Liow, *The Politics of Indonesia–Malaysia Relations*, p. 129; and Acharya, *Constructing a Security Community in Southeast Asia*, p. 148.

[196] Ibid.

[197] Anwar, *Indonesia in ASEAN*, pp. 144–45. Also see Government of Malaysia and Government of Indonesia, *GBC MALINDO Malaysia–Indonesia*, p. 125.

[198] Ibid.

[199] Ibid.

China Sea located between East and West Malaysia. It is the strategic frontline of the perceived Malay world. In December 1984 — at the 13th GBC meeting — it was decided that Indonesia and Malaysia would jointly use the facilities at Natuna Island for training and emergency purposes.[200]

The Indonesian and Malaysia air forces performed their Elang Malindo series joint exercises every year.[201] In these exercises, the two air forces practised air defence, combat air patrol, tactical and photographic reconnaissance, pre-planned air strikes, close air support and search-and-rescue operations on land and at sea.[202] The Indonesian and Malaysian air forces managed to familiarize themselves with each other's operating procedures through the Elang Malindo series joint exercises.[203]

In 1978, the Indonesian and Malaysian armies carried out for the first time their combined command-post exercises.[204] The exercises were designed to familiarize the two armies with each other's doctrine, tactics and staff procedures.[205] The Indonesian and Malaysian navies, on the other hand, regularly performed their Malindo series joint exercises, which was organized by GBC.[206] They too from time to time carried out their combined patrol, minesweeping and amphibious exercises in the northern part of the Straits of Malacca.[207]

GBC had succeeded in institutionalizing the military cooperation between Indonesia and Malaysia. The two states had come to identify their regular joint military exercises as a norm that they share. The communist insurgents in Borneo were no longer a credible threat to Indonesia and Malaysia by the early 1980s.[208] They had been eliminated

---

[200] Government of Malaysia and Government of Indonesia, *GBC MALINDO Malaysia–Indonesia*, p. 122.

[201] JIO Study No. 12/76 issued November 1979.

[202] Ibid.

[203] Ibid.

[204] Ibid.

[205] Ibid.

[206] Ibid. Also see Government of Malaysia and Government of Indonesia, *GBC MALINDO Malaysia–Indonesia*, p. 125.

[207] JIO Study No. 12/76 issued November 1979.

[208] Government of Malaysia and Government of Indonesia, *GBC MALINDO Malaysia–Indonesia*, pp. 35, 103, 107, 142, 169–70.

by Indonesia–Malaysia military operations, which were performed within the framework of GBC.[209] Regular joint exercises of the Indonesian and Malaysian armed forces since then served to sustain the military cooperation between the two states.[210] GBC had been able to ensure the continuous implementation of these exercises.[211]

The military ties between Indonesia and Malaysia became the most intimate one among the bilateral security ties that existed within ASEAN.[212] It was in fact the Indonesia–Malaysia *de facto* security alliance that formed the core of ASEAN security cooperation, which was characterized by a series of bilateral military cooperation between ASEAN member states.[213] The ties between the Indonesian and Malaysian armed forces were remarkably close. The two together could easily form a single command and control structure for a military mission if necessary.[214] Crucially, Malaysia featured prominently in Indonesian defence thinking.[215] Indonesia's participation in defensive operations in Malaysia was openly discussed at the Indonesian Army Command and Staff College.[216] Indonesia and Malaysia also cooperated closely in military trainings.[217] The Indonesian armed forces provided training for their Malaysian counterparts, which included the training of parachutists, commandos, frogmen, special forces, infantries and pilots.[218] Each year Malaysia's military officers were enrolled in various Indonesia's staff colleges.[219] The Malaysian armed forces, on the other

---

[209] Ibid.

[210] Ibid., pp. 107, 125, 142, 169–70. Also see "Indonesia, Malaysia to Increase Security Maintenance in Border", *Antara News*, 5 July 2011, available at <http://www.tniad. mil.id/?p=2063> (accessed 4 February 2014).

[211] Ibid.

[212] Donald E. Weatherbee, "ASEAN Security Cooperation and Resource Protection", in *The Invisible Nexus Energy and ASEAN's Security*, edited by Kusuma Snitwongse and Sukhumbhand Paribatra (Singapore: Executive Publications, 1984), pp. 119–21. Also see Anwar, *Indonesia in ASEAN*, pp. 142–51, 158–59.

[213] Ibid.

[214] Ghazali Shafie, *Malaysia, ASEAN and the New World Order*, p. 393.

[215] JIO Study No. 12/76 issued November 1979.

[216] Ibid.

[217] Ibid.

[218] Ibid.

[219] Ibid.

hand, provided training for Indonesian helicopter pilots and air traffic control personnel.[220] It had become a belief that Indonesia–Malaysia security relations had the potential of advancing "from *de facto* alliance to *de jure* alliance".[221]

Indonesia's and Malaysia's assertions of their sentimental bonds were salient throughout the course of the military cooperation between them. The Indonesian Joint-Chairman of GBC (1972–77), General Maraden Panggabean, described his experience of cooperating with Malaysia: "it is felt as if Malaysia is part of us as much as we are a part of them...I can say that Malaysia is a member of our family..."[222] Two decades later, the Malaysian Joint-Chairman of GBC, Najib Razak, asserted that the abilities of the Indonesian and Malaysian armed forces to operate together served to showcase to other Southeast Asian states, as well as to the world, the brotherhood and the unity between Indonesia and Malaysia.[223]

General Benny Murdani — the Commander of the Indonesian Armed Forces — announced in November 1983 that Indonesia was ready to provide military assistance to Malaysia if the latter was being attacked.[224] The announcement was made during the 12th GBC meeting held in Kuala Lumpur. Specifically, General Murdani promised that the Indonesian armed forces would come to Malaysia's assistance if Layang-Layang Island was under attack.[225] Layang-Layang is an island of Malaysia which both China and Vietnam have also claimed to be theirs. It is an island of the disputed Spratly Islands group situated in the South China Sea. General Murdani was firm on his pledge. He emphasized, "When Malaysia is pinched, Indonesia feels the pain."[226]

---

[220] Ibid.
[221] Weatherbee, "ASEAN Security Cooperation and Resource Protection", p. 121.
[222] Government of Malaysia and Government of Indonesia, *GBC MALINDO Malaysia–Indonesia*, p. 136.
[223] Ibid., p. 175.
[224] Anwar, *Indonesia in ASEAN*, pp. 145–46. Also see Government of Malaysia and Government of Indonesia, *GBC MALINDO Malaysia–Indonesia*, pp. 46–47, 152–57.
[225] Ibid.
[226] Ibid.

Indonesia's readiness to help defend Malaysia revealed the mutual strategic dependence between the two states. The Indonesia–Malaysia strategic cooperation was rooted in the idea that together they constituted a shield — that was the Malay world — which safeguarded their existence as states built around the Malay way of life. An attack on Malaysia — as Indonesia saw it — would thus mean an attack on the shield that was protecting Indonesia's survival. Indonesia was bound to throw its weight behind Malaysia if Malaysia was being attacked.

Malaysia's strategic judgement, on the other hand, was no different from that of Indonesia. Ghazali Shafie — as the Malaysian Joint-Chairman of GBC — declared at a GBC meeting:[227]

> It is a fact that whatever serves as a threat to any of the two countries [Indonesia and Malaysia] will also be regarded as so by the other...Let the understanding and cooperation now closely binding the two countries serve as a warning to any power that has ill intentions towards us. We will act together to oppose this threat completely and we shall never tolerate any nonsense from anywhere ...Let this joint stand of ours be understood by all, particularly by those who have designs on us.

The institutionalization of Indonesia–Malaysia military cooperation, in the meantime, strengthened the war avoidance norms shared by the two states. Through the collaborations between the Indonesian and Malaysian armed forces — mainly in the form of regular joint exercises — contacts and friendships had been established between military officers of the two states at all levels.[228] These collaborations were carried out within the framework of GBC.[229] Leaders of Indonesia and Malaysia described the nurturing of the friendships between Indonesian and Malaysian military officers as confidence building measures.[230]

---

[227] *Utusan Melayu*, 18 September 1979, quoted in Liow, *The Politics of Indonesia–Malaysia Relations*, p. 131.

[228] Government of Malaysia and Government of Indonesia, *GBC MALINDO Malaysia–Indonesia*, pp. 65, 107, 125, 142, 173. Also see Interview 920, Kuala Lumpur, 20 September 2012.

[229] Ibid.

[230] Government of Malaysia and Government of Indonesia, *GBC MALINDO Malaysia–Indonesia*, pp. 142–43, 148–49, 173–75, 179.

The basic purpose of ASEAN was to promote harmonious ties among its member states through regional cooperation.[94] The 1967 Bangkok Declaration — which established ASEAN — meanwhile, stated that Southeast Asian states were determined to ensure the stability and security of their region with no external interference. ASEAN was to embrace the notion of regional autonomy.

While the creation of a friendly regional climate in ASEAN was to allow its member states to immerse in their internal developments, the creation was also prompted by the surge of communism in Indochina.[95] The United States had escalated its war against the communists in Vietnam since 1965 with an increasing cost and casualties. Communism was a common threat to the five non-communist ASEAN member states. The creation of a peaceful and stable ASEAN served to demonstrate its member states' solidarity against the communists in Indochina.

Essentially, ASEAN is a security regime with its social and economic functions remain un-definitive.[96] The behaviours of ASEAN member states are restrained by a set of norms aims at avoiding armed conflicts between the states concerned.[97] The member states refrain from the use of force to resolve their disputes.[98] They strive not to interfere in their counterparts' domestic affairs, so that they would not become a threat to their counterparts' internal security.[99] Central to these war avoidance norms

---

[94] "The ASEAN Declaration (Bangkok Declaration) Bangkok, 8 August 1967", available at <http://asean.org/the-asean-declaration-bangkok-declaration-bangkok-8-august-1967/> (accessed 5 December 2013).

[95] Donald E. Weatherbee, *International Relations in Southeast Asia: The Struggle for Autonomy* (Singapore: Institute of Southeast Asian Studies, 2010), pp. 68–69, 72, 74.

[96] Ibid., pp. 99, 105–9, 304. Also see Amitav Acharya, "A Regional Security Community in Southeast Asia?" in *The Transformation of Security in the Asia Pacific Region*, edited by Desmond Ball (London: Frank Cass, 1996), p. 191; and Donald K. Emmerson, "Indonesia, Malaysia, Singapore: A Regional Security Core?" in *Southeast Asian Security in the New Millennium*, edited by Richard J. Ellings and Sheldon W. Simon (New York and London, England: NBR: Armonk, 1996), p. 34.

[97] Amitav Acharya, *Constructing a Security Community in Southeast Asia: ASEAN and the Problem of Regional Order* (London and New York: Routledge, 2001), p. 47. Also see Acharya, "A Regional Security Community in Southeast Asia?", pp. 185–86.

[98] Acharya, *Constructing a Security Community in Southeast Asia*, pp. 48–51.

[99] Ibid., pp. 57–60. Also see Anwar, *Indonesia in ASEAN*, p. 134.

Positive identifications as well as the mutual understanding between the Indonesian and Malaysian armed forces were being enhanced as a result of these personal friendships.[231] These friendships, consequently, contributed to the two states' commitment to adhere to their war avoidance norms. Indonesia and Malaysia were able to resolve several of their border disputes peacefully through GBC largely due to the good rapport that existed between the armed forces of the two states.[232]

It was the shared understanding of Indonesia and Malaysia that both played a central role in ensuring a friendly regional environment in ASEAN.[233] Both were aware that they were the only two states within ASEAN that had eased their defence against each other through their security cooperation implemented in the form of GBC.[234] Both understood, the existence of such cooperation sustained the essence of ASEAN as a security regime — that was the friendly coexistence of the ASEAN member states.[235]

ZOPFAN — COMPETITIVE COOPERATION FOR REGIONAL AUTONOMY

A special relationship between Indonesia and Malaysia was undoubtedly in place. Both intersubjectively recognized that they shared a close relation — closer than other bilateral ties that either of them enjoyed. Both, however, did not share a collective-self understanding. They were entrenched in egoistic understanding of each other. The reordering of the strategic landscape in Southeast Asia revealed such basic qualities of Indonesia–Malaysia relations.

In February 1966, the British government published its Defence White Paper declaring Britain's intention to reduce its military commitments east of Suez. A final decision was made in January 1968. Britain would withdraw its military presence from east of Suez, which

---

[231] Ibid., pp. 148–49, 173, 179.

[232] Ibid., pp. 166, 173–74, 179.

[233] Ibid., pp. 14, 33, 150, 172, 179.

[234] Ibid.

[235] Ibid.

included its military bases in Singapore and Malaysia. The withdrawal would be completed by the mid-1970s. On the other hand, President Nixon introduced his Guam Doctrine in July 1969, signalling the impending U.S. withdrawal from its war in Vietnam.[236] The implementation of the Guam Doctrine would allow the United States — Britain's closest ally — to reduce its military presence in Southeast Asia. The doctrine ruled out the involvement of U.S. ground forces in any future armed conflict in Asia.

The military disengagement of Britain and the United States from Southeast Asia meant that Malaysia would lose its security umbrella provided by the two great powers.[237] Britain's military bases in Singapore and Malaysia were crucial to Malaysia's fight against Indonesia during the years of Confrontation.

Malaysia was to make fundamental adjustments so that it could still survive without Britain's protection. The Tunku began to seek ways to ensure that a certain degree of AMDA would remain in place even after the British armed forces had left Southeast Asia. He lobbied for a five-Commonwealth nation conference since July 1967.[238] A Five Power Defence Arrangement (FPDA) was reached between Malaysia, Singapore, Britain, Australia and New Zealand in April 1971 as a result of the conference. FPDA would replace the existing AMDA by November 1971. The essential aim of FPDA — from Malaysia's point of view — was to check any possible ill intention that Indonesia had on Malaysia.[239] Malaysia continued to be apprehensive of Indonesia's armed attacks

---

[236] Dick Wilson, *The Neutralization of Southeast Asia* (New York: Praeger Publishers, 1975), pp. xvii, 3. Also see Heiner Hanggi, *ASEAN and the ZOPFAN Concept* (Singapore: Institute of Southeast Asian Studies, 1991), p. 12.

[237] Hanggi, *ASEAN and the ZOPFAN Concept*, p. 12. Also see Wilson, *The Neutralization of Southeast Asia*, pp. xvi, 65.

[238] Abdullah Ahmad, *Tengku Abdul Rahman and Malaysia's Foreign Policy 1963–1970* (Kuala Lumpur: Berita Publishing, 1985), p. 132.

[239] Saravanamuttu, *Malaysia's Foreign Policy, the First Fifty Years*, pp. 92, 159–60. Also see Ian Storey, Ralf Emmers, and Daljit Singh, "Introduction", in *Five Power Defence Arrangements at Forty*, edited by Ian Storey, Ralf Emmers, and Daljit Singh (Singapore: Institute of Southeast Asian Studies, 2011), p. xvi; and Rahim, *Singapore in the Malay World*, p. 148.

because of Confrontation that happened in the past.[240] It wanted to prevent such armed incursions from happening again. FPDA stipulated that in the event of an external attack or the threat of such attack on Malaysia and Singapore, the five powers concerned would immediately consult together, deciding on measures that should be taken jointly or separately with regard to the attack or threat.[241]

Malaysia, in the meantime, proposed the neutralization of Southeast Asia. In September 1970 — shortly before becoming the new Prime Minister of Malaysia — Tun Razak revealed Malaysia's proposal of neutralization at the Non-Aligned Movement meeting held in Lusaka. He stated:[242]

> It is my hope that in reaffirming the right of self-determination and non-interference in the Indo-China area, the Non-Aligned Group would at the same time take a positive stand in endorsing the neutralization of the area and possibly of the entire region of Southeast Asia, guaranteed by the three major powers, the People's Republic of China, the Soviet Union and the United States.

Embracing neutralism was to become Malaysia's central response to the West's massive detachment from Southeast Asia.[243] Malaysia was confronted with the hard reality that it could no longer rely on Britain — and Britain's allies in general — for basic security. It realized that regional autonomy was the ultimate solution for Malaysia's long-term survival.[244] The apprehension was derived from the notion of the Malay world. Malaysia perceived Southeast Asia as basically one entity, which was rooted in the Malay way of life, constituting a protection for Malaysia's existence as a Malay nation-state. Malaysia sought to

---

[240] Ibid.

[241] Saravanamuttu, *Malaysia's Foreign Policy, the First Fifty Years*, pp. 159–60.

[242] "Speech by Tun Abdul Razak, Deputy Prime Minister and Leader of the Malaysian Delegation, at the Third Summit Conference of Non-Aligned Countries in Lusaka, Zambia on 9 September 1970", *Foreign Affairs Malaysia* 3, no. 2 (December 1970): 16, quoted in Hanggi, *ASEAN and the ZOPFAN Concept*, p. 14.

[243] Saravanamuttu, *Malaysia's Foreign Policy, the First Fifty Years*, pp. 91–93, 105, 119–20, 143, 149, 154–55.

[244] Ibid., pp. 91–93, 119–20, 144, 149, 155, 158, 167.

establish an autonomous Southeast Asia through neutralization. Malaysia's idea of neutralization was a result of the Cold War. It was derived from the concept of non-alignment, which meant a state would not choose sides between the West and the Communist camps.[245]

The neutralization of Southeast Asia — as proposed by Malaysia — entailed both internal and external levels.[246] It first addressed the relations among the states within Southeast Asia. The proposal called for Southeast Asian states to agree on non-aggression and non-interference among them, which were premised on respect for one another's sovereignty and territorial integrity.[247] Also, foreign powers should be excluded from Southeast Asia, and the states in the region should cooperate with one another to ensure peace of the region.[248]

As for the external level, Malaysia proposed that the neutrality of Southeast Asia should be guaranteed by three major external powers — the United States, the Soviet Union and China.[249] Malaysia's idea of neutralization essentially contained two key purposes. It aimed for the establishment of an autonomous Southeast Asia while seeking to secure Malaysia from the threat of being attacked by its neighbouring states, notably Indonesia.

Malaysia believed that a neutral Southeast Asia guaranteed by the three great powers would ensure the absence of foreign powers in the region. Under the guarantee, any external power would be barred from struggling for power in Southeast Asia.[250] In the event that a Southeast Asian state was being attacked by a power — hence its neutral status

---

[245] Ibid., p. 122.

[246] Ghazali Shafie, "The Neutralization of Southeast Asia", *Pacific Community* 3, no. 1 (October 1971): 110–17, quoted in Hanggi, *ASEAN and the ZOPFAN Concept*, pp. 14–15. Also see Saravanamuttu, *Malaysia's Foreign Policy, the First Fifty Years*, pp. 119–20; Liow, *The Politics of Indonesia–Malaysia Relations*, pp. 124–25; Hanggi, *ASEAN and the ZOPFAN Concept*, pp. 12–15; and Wilson, *The Neutralization of Southeast Asia*, pp. 3–6.

[247] Ibid.

[248] Ibid.

[249] Ibid.

[250] Ghazali Shafie, "The Neutralization of Southeast Asia", *Pacific Community* 3, no. 1 (October 1971): 110–17, quoted in Hanggi, *ASEAN and the ZOPFAN Concept*, pp. 14–15. Also see Wilson, *The Neutralization of Southeast Asia*, pp. 5–6.

being violated — either of the three guarantor states would have to come to the state's assistance to defend its neutral status and territorial integrity.[251] On the other hand, the neutralized Southeast Asian states were not obliged to be an ally of other states and should not host foreign military facilities on their soils.[252] Put simply, such neutralization of Southeast Asia — as Malaysia saw it — would lead to an autonomous order of the region.

The three great powers' guarantee of Southeast Asia's neutrality as well as the peace deal — non-aggression and non-interference — among Southeast Asian states would, in the meantime, serve as Malaysia's insurance against any possible attack from Indonesia. It was an established suspicion of Malaysia that Indonesia — as the largest state in Southeast Asia — might want to dominate its neighbouring states.[253] The suspicion was reinforced by Malaysia's memory of Confrontation.[254]

Malaysia adamantly spearheaded the move to neutralize Southeast Asia following Razak's introduction of the idea in Lusaka. It launched a series of diplomatic efforts striving to secure the widest possible support for its neutralization proposal.[255] Malaysia met with the UN members, talked to the Third World states, discussed with its Commonwealth partners, and consulted with its ASEAN colleagues, lobbying for their support for the proposal.[256] Of all these actors, ASEAN was the key to the success of Southeast Asia's neutralization.

Malaysia was confronted with the push back from Indonesia while pressing for the neutralization of ASEAN. Indonesia interpreted Malaysia's proposal of neutralization as an attempt to dominate ASEAN.[257] Specifically, it was a challenge to Indonesia's aspiration — to become the strategic centre for regional security.[258] The three great powers would be the

---

[251] Wilson, *The Neutralization of Southeast Asia*, pp. 10–15.
[252] Ibid.
[253] Anwar, *Indonesia in ASEAN*, pp. 48, 136, 174–75, 180, 182.
[254] Ibid.
[255] Wilson, *The Neutralization of Southeast Asia*, pp. 19, 22–25, 66–67. Also see Hanggi, *ASEAN and the ZOPFAN Concept*, p. 15.
[256] Ibid.
[257] Leifer, *Indonesia's Foreign Policy*, pp. xiv–xv, 149.
[258] Ibid. Also see Weatherbee, *International Relations in Southeast Asia*, p. 105. Also see Liow, *The Politics of Indonesia–Malaysia Relations*, p. 125.

ultimate guarantors of Southeast Asia's security if the region was being neutralized based upon Malaysia's proposal. Indonesia was determined to curb Malaysia's press for Southeast Asia's neutralization.

Adam Malik — Indonesia's Foreign Minister — expressed Indonesia's rejection of Malaysia's neutralization proposal in September 1971:[259]

> ...neutralization that is the product of "one-way" benevolence on the part of the big Powers, at this stage, would perhaps prove as brittle and unstable as the interrelationship between the major Powers themselves...
>
> I strongly believe that it is only through developing among ourselves an area of internal cohesion and stability, based on *indigenous* socio-political and economic strength, that we can ever hope to *assist in the early stabilization of a new equilibrium in the region* that would not be the exclusive "diktat" of the major Powers...I think there is and there should be scope for an *indigenous* Southeast Asian component in the *new, emerging power balance of the region*...
>
> It is only through such *a Southeast Asian presence in the power equation* that we can ever hope to persuade the major Powers to take into account our wishes and aspirations and the directions and forms in which we want to develop. *At this transitional stage, in which the international constellation of forces is moving towards new balances of accommodation, we are afforded an opportunity to contribute our concepts into the mainstream of the thinking and searching that is going on...*
>
> ...the nations of Southeast Asia should consciously work towards the day when security in their own region will be the primary responsibility of the Southeast Asian nations themselves. Not through big Power alignments, not through the build up of contending military pacts or military arsenals...
>
> It is here that the importance of such an organization as ASEAN comes to the fore, as basically reflecting *the determination of its member countries to take charge of their own future and to reject the assumption that the fate of their region is to continue to be determined by outside Powers.* (Author's emphasis)

---

[259] *Far Eastern Economic Review*, 25 September 1971, pp. 32–33, quoted in Wilson, *The Neutralization of Southeast Asia*, pp. 52–55.

Just like Malaysia, Indonesia believed that regional autonomy was the answer for its basic security. Indonesia's strategic thinking of the Malay world — which was a region-wide existence — formed the basis of its understanding of regional autonomy. Both Indonesia and Malaysia — either called for neutralization or rejected it — respectively stressed that their proposed autonomous order of Southeast Asia was in essence indigenous.[260]

Nonetheless, Indonesia's desire to become the strategic centre of an autonomous Southeast Asia was palpable. It was apparent in Malik's statement that he repeatedly emphasized the need for Southeast Asia's indigenous forces to fill the power vacuum created by the vast reduction of Western military presence in the region. Indonesia was well aware that it was the largest and most populous state in Southeast Asia. Militarily, it was the most powerful one in ASEAN, if there was no foreign military presence in the region.[261] Indonesia would be a dominant force in Southeast Asia with the said power vacuum filled by the indigenous forces of the region. That was why it rejected the great powers' guarantee and called for a Southeast Asian presence in the new emerging power balance of the region.

Meanwhile, Indonesia saw the presence of foreign powers in Southeast Asia as a threat to its survival.[262] It was just a recent memory for Indonesia that the PRRI rebel movement had been supported by foreign powers. Indonesia was not convinced that Malaysia would commit to neutrality.[263] Malaysia was advocating the neutralization of Southeast Asia and at the same time working with its Commonwealth partners to put in place the FPDA. The FPDA was basically a military alliance. It was well understood that the purpose of the alliance was to check

---

[260] Ibid. Also see "Speech by Tun Dr. Ismail, Deputy Prime Minister of Malaysia, in Bonn on 9 December 1971", *Foreign Affairs Malaysia* 4, no. 4 (December 1971): 82–83, quoted in Wilson, *The Neutralization of Southeast Asia*, pp. 6–7.

[261] Anwar, *Indonesia in ASEAN*, pp. 174–75.

[262] Ibid., pp. 134–35. Also see Antolik, *ASEAN and the Diplomacy of Accommodation*, p. 8.

[263] Liow, *The Politics of Indonesia–Malaysia Relations*, p. 125. Also see Saravanamuttu, *Malaysia's Foreign Policy, the First Fifty Years*, p. 122.

Indonesia. A neutralized state was not allowed to forge any military alliance with any state.

The general withdrawal of the West from Southeast Asia had put Indonesia and Malaysia into a paradoxical situation. On the one hand, they would need each other's cooperation to create an autonomous Southeast Asia that ensured their basic security. On the other hand, they wanted to balance against one another to safeguard their respective survival. Indonesia and Malaysia were entangled in a situation of competitive cooperation.

A meeting was held between the five ASEAN Foreign Ministers in Kuala Lumpur two months after Indonesia's declaration of its rejection of Malaysia's call for neutralization. The ministers had to meet in Kuala Lumpur to discuss ASEAN's response to the changing strategic landscape in Southeast Asia, which was illuminated by U.S. President Nixon's announcement of his visit to China and the impending admission of China — replacing Taiwan — to the UN.[264]

Malaysia pressed hard for the acceptance of its neutralization proposal by ASEAN during the meeting.[265] Thailand and the Philippines would not even consider to forswear their military alliances with the United States.[266] Singapore remained steadfast in its support for the U.S. military presence in Southeast Asia.[267] The three states did not support Malaysia's call for neutralization.[268] They rallied around Indonesia to reject the neutralization proposal.[269]

Indonesia, nevertheless, was restrained by its special ties with Malaysia. It after all understood that Malaysia was its only ASEAN partner that

---

[264] Wilson, *The Neutralization of Southeast Asia*, pp. 24–25, 65. Also see Anwar, *Indonesia in ASEAN*, pp. 176–77; and Hanggi, *ASEAN and the ZOPFAN Concept*, pp. 12–17.

[265] Hanggi, *ASEAN and the ZOPFAN Concept*, pp. 16–17.

[266] Ibid., p. 15. Also see Wilson, *The Neutralization of Southeast Asia*, pp. 69, 71, 73.

[267] Wilson, *The Neutralization of Southeast Asia*, pp. 83–84. Also see Hanggi, *ASEAN and the ZOPFAN Concept*, p. 15.

[268] Leifer, *Indonesia's Foreign Policy*, pp. 149–50. Also see Wilson, *The Neutralization of Southeast Asia*, pp. 68–75, 78–84; and Hanggi, *ASEAN and the ZOPFAN Concept*, pp. 15–17.

[269] Ibid.

aspired for regional autonomy. Malaysia no longer sought to host foreign military bases after the withdrawal of British armed forces from its territory which took place since 1968. Indonesia essentially needed Malaysia — and vice versa — to strive for a Southeast Asia that was truly autonomous. The two states' aspiration for regional autonomy was rooted in their strategic understanding of the Malay world — a shield that protected their survival. Understandably, Indonesia was to accommodate Malaysia while pressing for an end to its move to neutralize Southeast Asia.

Indonesia made a stand in the meeting that a neutral Southeast Asia as proposed by Malaysia was a long-term objective.[270] Consequently, under the leadership of Indonesia — with the backing of Thailand, the Philippines and Singapore — the five ASEAN Foreign Ministers issued a Kuala Lumpur Declaration:[271]

> We...Agreeing that the neutralization of Southeast Asia is a desirable objective and that we should explore ways and means of bringing about its realization...Do hereby state:
>
> 1. That Indonesia, Malaysia, the Philippines, Singapore and Thailand are determined to exert initially necessary efforts to secure the recognition of, and respect for, Southeast Asia as Zone of Peace, Freedom and Neutrality, free from any form or manner of interference by outside Powers...

The declaration was a compromise reached among the ASEAN states; at the core of it, it was the competitive cooperation between Indonesia and Malaysia. Malaysia was forced to give up its idea of great powers' guarantee in the face of the opposition of all its ASEAN partners to the idea, with Indonesia in command of the opposition.[272]

---

[270] Hanggi, *ASEAN and the ZOPFAN Concept*, p. 17. Also see Liow, *The Politics of Indonesia–Malaysia Relations*, p. 126.

[271] Leifer, *Indonesia's Foreign Policy*, pp. 149–50. Also see Kuala Lumpur Declaration, 1971, quoted in Saravanamuttu, *Malaysia's Foreign Policy, the First Fifty Years*, pp. 161–62.

[272] Ibid.

In the meantime, Indonesia worked with Malaysia to incorporate some elements of Malaysia's idea of neutrality into the declaration amidst strong objection from Singapore and the Philippines.[273] The concept of neutrality in the declaration had come to mean a zone free from any form or manner of interference by outside powers, which was the notion of regional autonomy stated in the 1967 Bangkok Declaration — the founding document of ASEAN. [274] Thereafter, the concept of Zone of Peace, Freedom and Neutrality (ZOPFAN) became the framework for ASEAN's strive for regional autonomy.[275]

Malaysia remained adamant despite being forced to forswear its idea of great powers' guarantee in its proposal to neutralize Southeast Asia. Shortly after the issuing of the Kuala Lumpur Declaration, Malaysia embarked on its plan to establish diplomatic ties with China.[276] Malaysia had erstwhile voted in support of China's membership in the UN while Indonesia abstained. In May 1974, Prime Minister Razak made his landmark visit to Beijing to officially establish Malaysia's diplomatic ties with China. Malaysia was the first ASEAN state to establish official ties with China.

By establishing diplomatic relations with China, Malaysia aimed to associate China with the idea that Southeast Asia was a ZOPFAN.[277] China was one of three great powers in which Malaysia had proposed for their guarantee of Southeast Asia's neutrality. China had voiced its support for the concept of ZOPFAN after it was being introduced by ASEAN.[278] The other two great powers — the United States and the

---

[273] Liow, *The Politics of Indonesia–Malaysia Relations*, p. 126. Also see Hanggi, *ASEAN and the ZOPFAN Concept*, p. 17.

[274] Hanggi, *ASEAN and the ZOPFAN Concept*, p. 18. Also see Weatherbee, *International Relations in Southeast Asia*, p. 93; and "The ASEAN Declaration (Bangkok Declaration) Bangkok, 8 August 1967", available at <http://asean.org/the-asean-declaration-bangkok-declaration-bangkok-8-august-1967/> (accessed 5 December 2013).

[275] Ibid. Also see Anwar, *Indonesia in ASEAN*, pp. 177–80.

[276] Jeshurun, *Malaysia*, pp. 125–26.

[277] R.S. Milne and Diane K. Mauzy, *Malaysian Politics Under Mahathir* (London and New York: Routledge, 1999), p. 123. Also see Wilson, *The Neutralization of Southeast Asia*, p. 67.

[278] Saravanamuttu, *Malaysia's Foreign Policy, the First Fifty Years*, p. 120. Also see Hanggi, *ASEAN and the ZOPFAN Concept*, p. 40.

Soviet — did not officially respond to the idea.[279] Indonesia was irritated by Malaysia's move to establish diplomatic ties with China.[280] The New Order Regime had suspended Indonesia's diplomatic relations with China since October 1967 due to alleged China's complicity in the abortive movement of September 1965 in Indonesia. The regime remained deeply suspicious of China.[281]

The elements of Malaysia's neutralization proposal had been further integrated into the regional cooperation of ASEAN in the subsequent years. At their first summit in 1976, the five ASEAN member states endorsed several historic documents in response to the communist threat from the north. Most important of all, the five states signed their first ever treaty since the formation of ASEAN — the Treaty of Amity and Cooperation in Southeast Asia (TAC). The treaty was in essence founded on a crucial part of the neutrality proposal of Malaysia — that was the states in Southeast Asia should agree on non-aggression and non-interference, which were premised on respect for each other's sovereignty and territorial integrity. By signing the treaty, ASEAN member states had agreed to respect one another's sovereignty and territorial integrity.[282] They had agreed not to interfere in one another's internal affairs.[283] They too had agreed to renounce threat or the use of force, and settle their disputes via peaceful means.[284] In other words, an agreement of non-aggression and non-interference — previously introduced by Malaysia to prevent Indonesia's armed attacks — had been reached between ASEAN member states through the signing of the TAC. The treaty provides a legal basis for ASEAN war avoidance norms.[285] It therefore strengthened the existing war avoidance norms shared among ASEAN member states in general, and shared by Indonesia and Malaysia in particular.

---

[279] Ibid.
[280] Leifer, *Indonesia's Foreign Policy*, p. 153.
[281] Liow, *The Politics of Indonesia–Malaysia Relations*, p. 127.
[282] <http://www.asean.org/news/item/treaty-of-amity-and-cooperation-in-southeast-asia-indonesia-24-february-1976-3> (accessed 25 February 2014).
[283] Ibid.
[284] Ibid.
[285] Acharya, "A Regional Security Community in Southeast Asia?", p. 186. Also see Weatherbee, *International Relations in Southeast Asia*, pp. 129–30.

The signing of the TAC was aimed at institutionalizing the friendly coexistence among the ASEAN member states.[286] It was enshrined in the treaty that the ASEAN member states "shall endeavour to cooperate in all fields for the promotion of regional resilience…which will constitute the foundation for a strong and viable community of nations in Southeast Asia".[287] The ASEAN member states had come together as a region in the face of a potentially hostile and military powerful communist Vietnam, which had just won the Vietnam War.[288] They intended to adopt TAC as a basis to engage with Vietnam.[289] The signing of TAC was being understood as "the first step towards the realization of ZOPFAN".[290]

THE PRESENCE OF POWER BALANCE AND THE ABSENCE OF A SECURITY COMMUNITY

The hypothesis of this study has been confirmed by Indonesia–Malaysia relations from 1966–84. The presence of power balance between Indonesia and Malaysia furnished a basis of order between them which resulted in them coexisting peacefully. The power balance also led to the establishment of a special relationship between Indonesia and Malaysia, which was also a security regime between them.

However, while Indonesia and Malaysia identified positively with each other due to their special ties, their understanding of one another remained fundamentally egoistic. The presence of power balance between Indonesia and Malaysia meant that no one was in a dominant position vis-à-vis the other. Both, as a consequence, competed with each other for dominance while aiming to balance against one another, all of which to safeguard their respective survival. Such a state of relationship was

---

[286] Leifer, *Indonesia's Foreign Policy*, pp. 160–63. Also see Liow, *The Politics of Indonesia–Malaysia Relations*, pp. 129–30; and Anwar, *Indonesia in ASEAN*, p. 297.

[287] <http://www.asean.org/news/item/treaty-of-amity-and-cooperation-in-southeast-asia-indonesia-24-february-1976-3> (accessed 25 February 2014).

[288] Leifer, *Indonesia's Foreign Policy*, pp. 160–63. Also see Ghazali Shafie, *Malaysia, ASEAN and the New World Order*, pp. 151–53, 159–61.

[289] Ibid. Also see Liow, *The Politics of Indonesia–Malaysia Relations*, pp. 129–30.

[290] Hanggi, *ASEAN and the ZOPFAN Concept*, pp. 39–40.

evidenced by Malaysia's press for Southeast Asia's neutralization and Indonesia's efforts to put an end to the move. It was also evidenced by Malaysia's embrace of the FPDA, which was to prevent Indonesia's armed incursions.

In other words, Indonesia's and Malaysia's egoistic understanding of each other had been sustained by the power competition between them. The presence of power balance between the two states was a cause for their competition. Despite the establishment of a special relationship between Indonesia and Malaysia — in which they began to be bound by their intimate ties — the two states did not share a collective-self understanding. That said, Indonesia and Malaysia did not constitute a pluralistic security community, they were at most a security regime. War between them was unlikely, not unthinkable.

7

NO MORE *SERUMPUN?*
INDONESIA–MALAYSIA
RELATIONS, 1985–2017

This chapter reveals the double-edged effects of the Indonesia–Malaysia special relationship. By the mid-1980s, a solid foundation had been established in Indonesia's and Malaysia's domestic politics as well as in their regional affairs. The unmistakable political supremacy of the indigenous people over the Chinese in Indonesia and Malaysia, as well as ASEAN's proven ability to function as a shield for its member states, revealed that the Malay world had taken root in archipelagic Southeast Asia. In other words, the strategic cooperation of Indonesia and Malaysia — forming the Malay world — was well established. Indonesia's and Malaysia's respective nationhoods too had become entrenched. Consequently, the two states each began to venture into a new stage of economic development that would transform their respective economy and national identity.

By the late 1980s, the transformation of Indonesia's and Malaysia's economies had ushered in an era of high economic growth in the two states. With their new found economic might, Indonesia and Malaysia were looking beyond ASEAN, striving to expand the space for their respective survival. Indonesia and Malaysia competed with each other amidst their endeavours to expand their respective influence abroad. The competition was enhanced by the mismatch of expectation between them; and mutually reinforced with their respective assertion of their superiority over the culturally similar counterpart.

The intertwined three sources of conflicts were also embedded in the territorial disputes between Indonesia and Malaysia and the issue of Indonesian migrant workers in Malaysia. The three sources of conflicts reinforced one another. Anti-Malaysia sentiments emerged in Indonesian society as a result — which were the substantial conflicts between Indonesia and Malaysia.

Because of the war avoidance norms that existed in the Indonesia–Malaysia special relationship, the substantial conflicts between them had not been able to turn into violent ones. The absence of power imbalance in the Indonesia–Malaysia special relationship means that the relationship remains as a security regime, not a security community. Indonesia–Malaysia relations are fundamentally competitive. The two states continue to understand each other in egoistic terms. War between them is unlikely, yet it remains possible.

THE SOLID PRESENCE OF THE MALAY WORLD AND THE NEW STAGE OF ECONOMIC DEVELOPMENT

By the mid-1980s, it was evident that a solid foundation had been established in Indonesia's and Malaysia's domestic politics as well as in the regional affairs of ASEAN.

The political supremacy of the indigenous people in Indonesia and Malaysia over the ethnic Chinese in the two states was obvious and robust.[1] The political and economic power of the Indonesian and

---

[1] Leo Suryadinata, *Indonesia's Foreign Policy Under Suharto: Aspiring to International Leadership* (Singapore: Times Academic Press, 1996), p. 108. Also see Robert E. Elson, *Suharto: A Political Biography* (Cambridge: Cambridge University Press, 2001), pp. 161–62; and Cheah Boon Keng, *Malaysia: The Making of a Nation* (Singapore: Institute of Southeast Asian Studies, 2002), pp. 193, 238.

Malaysian Chinese had been effectively subdued by the policies of the two states.[2] The Indonesian and Malaysian indigenous people by then no longer perceived the local Chinese as a credible threat to their survival.[3] Malaysian Prime Minister, Dr Mahathir Mohamad — who had been in power since 1981 — wrote in 1986 that the Malays had emerged from a long period of backwardness.[4] Mahathir's writing implied that the political and economic status of the Malays in Malaysia had been secured. In other words, in the eyes of the Malays, the perceived Chinese economic hegemony in Malaysia had been overcome.[5] Back in the 1960s and 1970s, Mahathir was a strong advocate that the Malays' backwardness was largely caused by the Chinese domination of Malaysia's economy.[6]

The concern for the local Chinese was further weakened by a steady decline of China's interest to exert its influence on the overseas Chinese in Southeast Asia.[7] By the late 1980s, China's dwindling support for the Chinese-led communist insurgencies in Malaysia and Indonesia had come to an end with the end of the Cold War. In 1989, China had officially severed its political ties with the overseas Chinese through the passing of the Law on Citizenship.

The dissipation of the perceived threat of the domestic Chinese meant that the presence of the Malay world was well in place in archipelagic Southeast Asia. Consequently, while keeping in check the Chinese

---

2   Ibid.
3   Ibid. Also see Joseph Chinyong Liow, *The Politics of Indonesia–Malaysia Relations: One Kin, Two Nations* (London and New York: Routledge, 2005*b*), pp. 155–56; and Karminder Singh Dhillon, *Malaysian Foreign Policy in the Mahathir Era 1981–2003: Dilemmas of Development* (Singapore: NUS Press, 2009), pp. 33–34.
4   Mahathir Mohamad, *The Challenge* (Petaling Jaya: Pelanduk Publications, 1986), Introduction.
5   Dhillon, *Malaysian Foreign Policy in the Mahathir Era 1981–2003*, pp. 26–34.
6   Ibid.
7   Joseph Chinyong Liow, "Balancing, Banwagoning, or Hedging?: Strategic and Security Patterns in Malaysia's Relations with China, 1981–2003", in *China and Southeast Asia: Global Changes and Regional Challenges*, edited by Ho Khai Leong and Samuel C.Y. Ku (Singapore: Institute of Southeast Asian Studies and Center for Southeast Asian Studies, 2005*a*), pp. 287, 302. Also see Suryadinata, *Indonesia's Foreign Policy Under Suharto*, p. 108.

influence in their respective communities, the Indonesian and Malaysian indigenous people had shifted their attention away from stressing the dominance of the Malay world over the ethnic Chinese in Indonesia and Malaysia.[8]

Externally, Indonesia and Malaysia had jointly created a friendly regional climate in the form of ASEAN, which essentially functioned as a shield that secured the two states from external threats. Since the first ASEAN summit held in 1976, it had become clear that the ASEAN member states saw themselves as constituting a common region that was peaceful and stable. They were determined to preserve such a climate of ASEAN.

ASEAN's solidarity had effectively prevented Vietnam's invasion of Thailand after Vietnam's occupation of Cambodia since December 1978.[9] Vietnam launched repeated cross-border incursions into Thailand following its occupation of Cambodia. ASEAN was quick to declare that such incursions directly affected the security of the ASEAN member states.[10] To confront the military threat of Vietnam, ASEAN sponsored the anti-Vietnamese forces in Cambodia and forged a *de facto* alliance with China. ASEAN, meanwhile, became a political force in the international arena that pressed for Vietnam's withdrawal from Cambodia. Because of the increasing cost of occupying Cambodia largely resulted from sustained international pressure, Vietnam had declared in 1985 that it would withdraw its troops from Cambodia by 1990.[11]

---

[8] Liow, *The Politics of Indonesia–Malaysia Relations*, pp. 155–56. Also see Suryadinata, *Indonesia's Foreign Policy Under Suharto*, p. 108; and Cheah, *Malaysia*, p. 238.

[9] Donald E. Weatherbee, *International Relations in Southeast Asia: The Struggle for Autonomy* (Singapore: Institute of Southeast Asian Studies, 2010), pp. 79–83. Also see Dewi Fortuna Anwar, *Indonesia in ASEAN: Foreign Policy and Regionalism* (Singapore: Institute of Southeast Asian Studies, 1994), p. 188.

[10] Ibid.

[11] Ibid. Also see Amitav Acharya, *Constructing a Security Community in Southeast Asia: ASEAN and the Problem of Regional Order* (London and New York: Routledge, 2001), p. 90.

The dwindling of Soviet economic and military aid to Vietnam prompted by the deterioration of the Soviet Union's economy as well as the Sino–Soviet rapprochment in fact played a key role in forcing Vietnam to withdraw completely from Cambodia. Yet, it should be pointed out that Vietnam's decision to withdraw from Cambodia too reflected ASEAN's ability in ensuring the peace and stability of its region. The decision illuminated the fact that ASEAN functioned as a shield for all its member states. The security of an ASEAN member state had been viewed by its counterparts as directly affecting that of their own. At the core of the shield, however, lay the Indonesia–Malaysia special relationship. The friendly regional climate of ASEAN was created and sustained by the special relationship between Indonesia and Malaysia. The two states created their friendly coexistence to ensure their strategic cooperation in constituting the Malay world — a shield that secured their existence as states built around the Malay way of life. In other words, by the mid-1980s, the Malay world's function as a shield for Indonesia and Malaysia was soundly in place manifested in the form of ASEAN.

The unmistakable political supremacy of the indigenous people over the Chinese in Indonesia and Malaysia, as well as ASEAN's proven ability to function as a shield for its member states, revealed that the Malay world had taken root in archipelagic Southeast Asia. The strategic cooperation of Indonesia and Malaysia was well established. The two states by the mid-1980s no longer needed to allocate much of their attention in emphasizing the presence of the Malay world.

While having solidified the presence of the Malay world in archipelagic Southeast Asia, Indonesia and Malaysia had also succeeded in consolidating their respective nationhood after decades of independence. By the mid-1980s, Indonesia and Malaysia each had emerged as a stable sovereign state with sound economic foundations. The respective GDP per capita of Indonesia and Malaysia had increased substantially in the past one and a half decade (see Figure 7.1). Most notably, people living below the poverty line in Indonesia had reduced from 40 per cent of its

FIGURE 7.1
GDP per capita of Indonesia and Malaysia, 1970–85

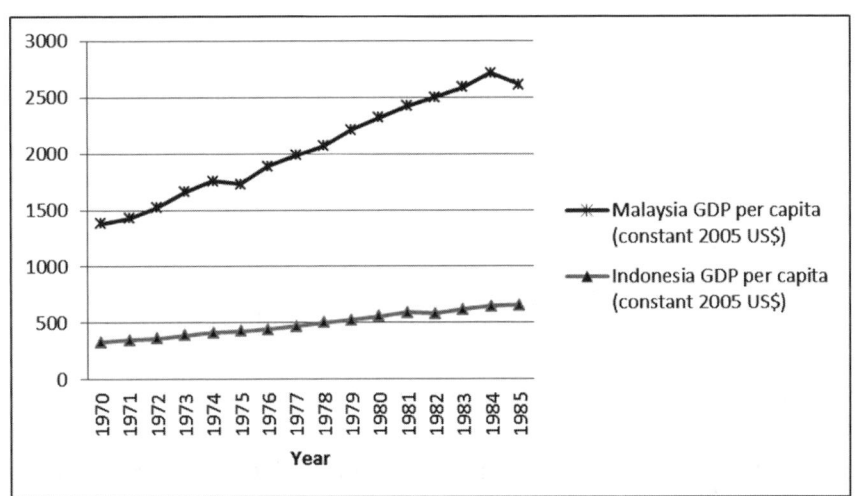

Source: World Development Indicators.

population in 1980 to 21 per cent in 1987.[12] Indonesia was one of the most populous states in the world.

As their respective nationhood had become entrenched and the Malay world was well in place, Indonesia and Malaysia each was confident enough to venture into a new stage of economic development that would transform their respective economy and national identity.

By 1981, oil and gas accounted for 82 per cent of Indonesia's total export revenue.[13] Indonesia's economy was heavily dependent on its oil and gas exports.[14] Largely fuelled by the earnings from oil and gas, Indonesia's annual GDP growth rate was as high as 8.1 per cent in

---

[12] Michael R.J. Vatikiotis, *Indonesian Politics Under Suharto: Order, Development and Pressure for Change* (London and New York: Routledge, 1993*a*), p. 58.

[13] Vatikiotis, *Indonesian Politics Under Suharto*, pp. 34–35.

[14] Ibid. Also see Elson, *Suharto*, p. 246.

1981.[15] The plummeting of oil price which began to take place from 1982 revealed the fundamental weakness of Indonesia's economy.[16] Indonesia's export revenue had fallen sharply because of the oil price crisis. By 1985, the annual GDP growth rate of Indonesia had dropped to 3.5 per cent.[17] Indonesia was forced to embrace reforms in order to sustain its economic growth.

In 1986, Indonesia began to diversify the range of its exports and move to liberalize its tightly state-controlled economy.[18] The economic reforms — which were essentially aimed to ensure Indonesia's economic growth — were to serve two key purposes: to ensure the survival of the New Order regime in Indonesia; and to allow Indonesia to expand its influence abroad.

Ensuring continuous economic development was the source of legitimacy for Suharto's New Order regime.[19] Suharto had to ensure Indonesia's economic growth through economic reforms to perpetuate his political survival in Indonesia. Furthermore, the economic reforms were linked to Suharto's broader strategy of ensuring his political survival. Suharto intended to promote himself as an international statesman by positioning Indonesia as a leader of the Third World.[20] The leadership claim was based on the idea that Indonesia was a model of development for the developing states.[21]

For Suharto, his role as an international statesman was characterized by the New Order regime's ability in delivering impressive economic

---

[15] Ibid. Also see <http://data.worldbank.org/indicator/NY.GDP.MKTP.KD.ZG?page=6> (accessed 28 March 2014).

[16] Elson, *Suharto*, p. 246. Also see Vatikiotis, *Indonesian Politics Under Suharto*, pp. 38–39.

[17] Vatikiotis, *Indonesian Politics Under Suharto*, p. 38. Also see <http://data.worldbank.org/indicator/NY.GDP.MKTP.KD.ZG?page=5> (accessed 28 March 2014).

[18] Vatikiotis, *Indonesian Politics Under Suharto*, pp. 38–40. Also see Elson, *Suharto*, pp. 246–47.

[19] Vatikiotis, *Indonesian Politics Under Suharto*, p. 45. Also see Elson, *Suharto*, pp. 246, 253.

[20] Vatikiotis, *Indonesian Politics Under Suharto*, pp. 34–35, 180–84. Also see Elson, *Suharto*, pp. 235, 254; and Suryadinata, *Indonesia's Foreign Policy Under Suharto*, pp. 174–77.

[21] Ibid.

progress in one of the largest and most populous states in the world — Indonesia — coupled with a degree of openness exhibited by Indonesia.[22] By the mid-1980s, the New Order regime had begun to face the rise of the new social forces that sought for political change in Indonesia. The call for a change of leadership in Indonesia had also started to emerge. Suharto was already in power for nearly two decades. Making use of his political dominance in Indonesia, Suharto had been preparing the grounds for his re-election as Indonesia's five-year term President for the fifth time.[23] The largely symbolic presidential election would be held in 1988. The New Order regime attempted to demonstrate its openness to change, aiming to address the demand for political change in Indonesia.[24] It therefore partially liberalized Indonesia's economy and began to tolerate a certain degree of political debate in Indonesia.

More profoundly, Suharto needed nationalism to strengthen his power base in Indonesia.[25] By projecting himself as an international statesman, Suharto attempted to instil a belief among Indonesians that Indonesia was a leader of the Third World, underpinned by Indonesia being a model of development for the developing states.[26] The sense of national pride was a continuation of Indonesia's nationalism advanced by Sukarno during his time as President of Indonesia. Both Sukarno and Suharto believed that Indonesia was a leader of the Third World, only that the justification for that leadership had changed from Indonesia being a champion for the worldwide revolutionary struggles against colonialism-imperialism to Indonesia being a model of development for the Third World states. In either case, the conviction that Indonesia was an international leader had its roots in the enduring sense of greatness held by Indonesians.

---

[22] Vatikiotis, *Indonesian Politics Under Suharto*, pp. 34–36, 165, 174, 180–83. Also see Elson, *Suharto*, pp. 234–35, 254, 258, 262.

[23] Elson, *Suharto*, pp. 234, 236, 245, 256–58, 262. Also see Vatikiotis, *Indonesian Politics Under Suharto*, p. 25.

[24] Vatikiotis, *Indonesian Politics Under Suharto*, p. 165. Also see Elson, *Suharto*, pp. 234, 258.

[25] Vatikiotis, *Indonesian Politics Under Suharto*, pp. 182–84.

[26] Ibid., pp. 180–81.

Scholars and a senior advisor to Malaysia's government had pointed out that the souls of Indonesians were bound by their shared conviction that Indonesia was a great nation.[27] It was great because it was huge — a wide archipelago — and it was a civilization that had lasted for two thousand years.[28] The civilization was underpinned by Javanese culture which viewed Java as the centre of the world.[29] The greatness of Indonesia — as Indonesians saw it — was evidenced by its ability to become a history maker. In the Malay world — Indonesians would argue — Indonesia was the first and only nation-state that had achieved an independence which was truly authentic. It was authentic because Indonesians had fought for it through a bloody revolution against Dutch colonial rule. In the international arena, Indonesia was a founder of the 1955 Asian-African conference, which marked the rise of the Third World as a stand-alone force in global politics. Indonesia was also a founder of the Non-Aligned Movement (NAM), a movement that represented the Third World, a movement that was built on the Third World solidarity brought about during the 1955 Asian-African conference. In short, Indonesia saw itself as a creator of the Third World unity.

The image of Suharto as an international statesman who was full of wisdom was directly linked to Indonesians' sense of greatness, that Indonesia was a leader of the Third World.[30] In other words, by establishing his status as an international statesman, Suharto evoked the sense of national pride among Indonesians. The domestic support for Suharto as the President of Indonesia, therefore, had been enhanced, because supporting him meant illuminating the greatness of Indonesia.[31]

---

[27] Interview 924-001, Kuala Lumpur, 24 September 2012. Also see Vatikiotis, *Indonesian Politics Under Suharto*, p. 181; and Anwar, *Indonesia in ASEAN*, p. 284.

[28] Ibid. Also see "Build the World Anew", in *The New Emerging Forces: Documents on the Ideology of Indonesian Foreign Policy*, edited by George Modelski (Australia: The Australian National University, 1963), p. 19. Also see John D. Legge, *Sukarno: A Political Biography* (Great Britain: Allen Lane The Penguin Press, 1972), pp. 184–85.

[29] Ibid. Also see Suryadinata, *Indonesia's Foreign Policy Under Suharto*, p. 37.

[30] Elson, *Suharto*, pp. 265, 268.

[31] Vatikiotis, *Indonesian Politics Under Suharto*, p. 184.

On the other hand, the New Order regime's attempt to sustain Indonesia's economic growth through economic reforms served to maintain and strengthen Indonesia's existing sound economic foundations. The regime needed the foundations to function as the basis for it to strive for Indonesia's leadership role in the Third World, aiming to expand Indonesia's political and economic influence abroad.[32] Indonesia's aim to become a leader of the Third World boosted, and was boosted by, the nationalist sentiments of Indonesia.

Indonesia's success in doubling its rice production within fifteen years and achieving the goal of rice self-sufficiency by 1984 had attracted worldwide recognition. The UN Food and Agriculture Organization (FAO) invited Suharto to address its fortieth anniversary commemoration held in Rome in November 1985 to honour Indonesia for its achievement of rice self-sufficiency. It was an important achievement considering that Indonesia was one of the most populous states in the world.

Suharto took great pride in being recognized by FAO.[33] The invitation strengthened his conviction that Indonesia was a leader of the Third World. He spoke of the event years later:

> Out of all the developing countries, Indonesia was chosen to relate its experiences…I spoke at the meeting as a representative of the South in the context of the North–South Dialogue…Our knowledge of agricultural development was sought after by a number of other countries…they had voluntarily collected 100,000 tons of unmilled rice. I was requested by the Indonesian farmers to donate this rice to the FAO for distribution among fellow farmers in countries suffering from famine, especially those on the African continent.[34]

---

[32] Michael R.J. Vatikiotis, "Indonesia's Foreign Policy in the 1990s", *Contemporary Southeast Asia* 14, no. 4 (March 1993*b*): 357. Also see Suryadinata, *Indonesia's Foreign Policy Under Suharto*, pp. 174–79.

[33] Elson, *Suharto*, p. 235. Also see Soeharto, *My Thoughts, Words and Deeds: An Autobiography as Told to G. Dwipayana and Ramadhan K.H.* (Jakarta: Citra Lamtoro Gung Persada, 1991), pp. 1–4; and Vatikiotis, *Indonesian Politics Under Suharto*, p. 182.

[34] Soeharto, *My Thoughts, Words and Deeds*, pp. 1–3.

Obviously, Suharto during the FAO commemoration saw Indonesia as representing the force of the Third World, capable of providing its expertise and material assistance to fellow members of the Third World.

In July 1986, the director-general of FAO visited Jakarta. He presented Suharto with two gold medals to pay tribute to Indonesia's success in achieving rice self-sufficiency. The director-general announced that President Suharto was the symbol of international agricultural progress. One of the medals bore an image of Suharto, inscribed with the words, "President Soeharto, Indonesia".[35] The medals had been replicated. It was clear for Indonesians: Suharto was an international statesman; he was the embodiment of Indonesia — a leader of the Third World.

The sense of being a leader of the Third World bolstered Indonesia's resolve to acquire the leadership position in the Third World. From September 1986 onwards, Indonesia began to vie for the chairmanship of NAM.[36] The New Order regime had made it clear that Indonesia's role was "to help solve world problems based on the spirit of the Bandung Principles".[37] Bandung Principles were produced by the 1955 Asian-African conference held in Bandung, Indonesia — the conference that marked the rise of Indonesia as a Third World leader.

As in Malaysia, the Malaysian government was beginning to work relentlessly towards achieving its goal of transforming Malaysia into a fully developed nation-state. Dr Mahathir came to power as the fourth Prime Minister of Malaysia in July 1981. His thought was crystal clear right from the start of his tenure. He wanted to turn Malaysia from being a developing state into a developed one in the shortest time possible.[38] Mahathir described the early days of his prime ministership: "Malaysia was beginning to experience a swift and sharp change

---

[35] Ibid.

[36] Suryadinata, *Indonesia's Foreign Policy Under Suharto*, pp. 174–75.

[37] Arnicun Aziz, ed., Empat GBHN: 1973, 1978, 1983, 1988 (Jakarta: Bumi Aksara, 1990), quoted in Suryadinata, *Indonesia's Foreign Policy Under Suharto*, p. 177.

[38] Mahathir Mohamad, *A Doctor in the House: The Memoirs of Tun Dr Mahathir Mohamad* (Malaysia: MPH Group Publishing, 2011), pp. 326–28. Also see Karminder Singh Dhillon, *Malaysian Foreign Policy in the Mahathir Era 1981–2003: Dilemmas of Development* (Singapore: NUS Press, 2009), p. 276.

from an agricultural to an industrial economy."[39] The recounting reflected Mahathir's determination to make Malaysia a developed state. Immediately after becoming Prime Minister, Mahathir went ahead to establish Malaysia's own heavy industries. He asserted that possessing such industries was "a necessary step towards becoming a developed country".[40]

Mahathir's obsession with turning Malaysia into a fully developed state was meant to achieve a more fundamental goal: to modernize the Malays in Malaysia in particular, and the Malaysian people in general.[41] The Mahathir administration was to transform Malaysians' national identity as a result of this goal.

Through the process of developing Malaysia on a massive scale and at a demanding pace, Mahathir sought to instil a belief among the Malays in Malaysia that they were a group of people defined by their capability.[42] The Malays as capable people — Mahathir argues — is evidenced by their skills in administering and developing a multiracial state — Malaysia — which is peaceful and stable buttressed by sustained economic progress.[43] Mahathir believes that it is a historical tradition of the Malays that they are capable, a tradition dates back to the pre-colonial Malay sultanates.[44] Building the national car serves to demonstrate the capabilities of the Malays. It was the most important heavy industry which the Mahathir administration had chosen to develop. Malaysia's heavy industries were mostly run by the Malays — a design of the Malaysian government in compliance with the New Economic Policy.[45]

The Mahathir administration, in the meantime, introduced its "Look East" policy, which looked to Japan as the main model of development

---

[39] Mahathir Mohamad, *A Doctor in the House*, p. 328

[40] Ibid., p. 328.

[41] Cheah, *Malaysia*, pp. 72, 186, 201, 207. Also see Dhillon, *Malaysian Foreign Policy in the Mahathir Era 1981–2003*, pp. 32–35.

[42] Cheah, *Malaysia*, pp. 189, 192–93. Also see Dhillon, *Malaysian Foreign Policy in the Mahathir Era 1981–2003*, pp. 186, 276. Also see Mahathir Mohamad, *A Doctor in the House*, pp. 29–30, 38.

[43] Mahathir Mohamad, *A Doctor in the House*, pp. 29–30, 38.

[44] Ibid.

[45] Ibid., pp. 328–33.

for Malaysia. Malaysia under the Look East policy would emulate the Japanese way of industrialization to achieve its own industrialization. Japan would become the main source of technology, managerial expertise and investment for Malaysia.

The central purpose of looking East was to ensure that Malaysia would become a developed state in its own way.[46] Not only did Malaysia aim to become a fully developed state, it also wanted to be truly independent.[47] By emulating and cooperating with Japan, Malaysia sought to reduce its traditional economic reliance on the West, aiming to move towards becoming a developed state on its own terms.[48] As Mahathir had made it clear to Malaysia's senior government officials in June 1983:[49]

> Looking East does not mean begging from the East or shifting the responsibility for developing Malaysia to them. Responsibility towards our country is our own and not that of others.

Henceforth, Malaysians' national identity was characterized by the belief that Malaysia — which specifically meant Malays — was capable, competent of becoming a developed nation-state in its own way. Having the only national car industry in Southeast Asia and possessing the third longest bridge in the world — the Penang Bridge — were concrete evidence that Malaysia was on course to become a developed state in its own way.[50] Years later, Mahathir introduced a nationalist slogan: "*Malaysia Boleh*" — Malaysia is Able. "*Malaysia Boleh*" had instilled a real sense of confidence among Malaysians.

To further strengthen the conviction that Malaysia was capable, the Mahathir administration strived to make Malaysia a leader of the

---

[46] Dhillon, *Malaysian Foreign Policy in the Mahathir Era 1981–2003*, pp. 180, 184, 194–95. Also see Mahathir Mohamad, *A Doctor in the House*, pp. 369–71.

[47] Ibid.

[48] Dhillon, *Malaysian Foreign Policy in the Mahathir Era 1981–2003*, pp. 161, 175–76, 184.

[49] Johan Saravanamuttu, *Malaysia's Foreign Policy, the First Fifty Years: Alignment, Neutralism, Islamism* (Singapore: Institute of Southeast Asian Studies, 2010), p. 188.

[50] Dhillon, *Malaysian Foreign Policy in the Mahathir Era 1981–2003*, p. 186. Also see Cheah, *Malaysia*, p. 211.

Third World. Malaysia was a leader of the Third World — the Mahathir administration believed — because Malaysia was a model of development for the developing world, vindicated by its ability — as being a developing state — to put itself on track towards becoming a developed state on its own terms.[51] To become truly independent, free from any form of hegemony, was always the goal of the Third World.

Apart from transforming Malaysia's national identity, Mahathir simultaneously made use of that new identity to consolidate his standing within his party — UMNO — and among the Malaysian people as a whole.[52] In other words, Mahathir used nationalism to solidify his power base at home.

Generating economic growth through extensive economic development was essential in ensuring Mahathir's political survival in successive party as well as general elections. However, the discernible advancement of Malaysia under Mahathir's leadership manifested in the form of new industries and massive scale of new infrastructures induced a sense of national pride among Malaysians which enhanced the domestic support for Mahathir as a result.[53] Mahathir, in the meantime, consistently criticized the hegemony of the West and pursued anti-Western policies — such as Buy British Last — making him being widely recognized as a champion of the causes of the Third World.[54] By ensuring robust developments in Malaysia and by daring to stand up against Western dominance, Mahathir triggered Malaysians' sense of pride and patriotism.[55] They embraced Mahathir's leadership, because he was being perceived as leading Malaysia towards becoming a developed state in a truly independent way.

---

[51] Dhillon, *Malaysian Foreign Policy in the Mahathir Era 1981–2003*, pp. 184, 195, 213.

[52] Ibid., pp. 171–72, 175, 186, 213.

[53] Ibid. Also see Cheah, *Malaysia*, pp. 189, 193.

[54] Dhillon, *Malaysian Foreign Policy in the Mahathir Era 1981–2003*, pp. 34, 160–63, 195, 202, 205–8. Also see Saravanamuttu, *Malaysia's Foreign Policy, the First Fifty Years*, p. 202. Also see Cheah, *Malaysia*, pp. 211–12.

[55] Cheah, *Malaysia*, pp. 189, 193, 206–7. Also see Dhillon, *Malaysian Foreign Policy in the Mahathir Era 1981–2003*, p. 34.

Malaysia's nationalist sentiments mutually reinforced with its will to expand its political and economic influence abroad by claiming the leadership role of the Third World. The desired expansion was to serve the goal of transforming Malaysia into a developed state.[56] Malaysia's sense of being a leader of the Third World — a model of development to be followed by other developing states — bolstered its determination to play a leadership role in the Third World. Malaysia attempted to champion the causes of the developing world by speaking up against the perceived Western hegemony.[57] It strived to become a leader in the Third World organizations — such as NAM and OIC (Organisation of Islamic Cooperation) — by setting the agenda of these bodies.[58] Malaysia, meanwhile, spearheaded the establishment of new Third World bodies such as the G-15. Overtime, Malaysia had won the reputation as the "Hero of the South" and "Champion of the Poor". Such resolve to become a leader of the Third World simultaneously boosted the conviction among Malaysians that they were capable.[59] Mahathir later proclaimed that: "Malaysia is modestly proud to be regarded as a model for economic development..."[60]

After the mid-1980s, the transformation of Indonesia's and Malaysia's economy had ushered in an era of high economic growth in the two states. From 1988 to 1990, the average annual GDP growth rate of Indonesia and Malaysia was as high as 8.1 per cent and 9.3 per cent respectively.[61]

By the late 1980s, Malaysia under the leadership of Mahathir had succeeded in transforming from an agricultural economy into a

---

[56] Dhillon, *Malaysian Foreign Policy in the Mahathir Era 1981–2003*, pp. 74, 195, 199, 202, 205–8, 210–11, 249, 251.

[57] Ibid., pp. 198–99, 202, 208.

[58] Ibid., pp. 195–99.

[59] Ibid., p. 204.

[60] Mahathir Mohamad, speech titled "Regional Business Collaboration" delivered at the opening of the Pacific Rim Business Collaboration Symposium at Kuala Lumpur on 5 December 1994, quoted in Dhillon, *Malaysian Foreign Policy in the Mahathir Era 1981–2003*, p. 209.

[61] <http://databank.worldbank.org/data/views/reports/tableview.aspx#> (accessed 15 April 2014).

manufacturing-based and export-oriented one. In 1981, the manufacturing sector accounted for 20.9 per cent of Malaysia's GDP and the agricultural sector at 21.4 per cent. By 1990, the manufacturing sector's share in Malaysia's GDP had increased to 24.2 per cent while that of the agricultural sector had reduced to 15.2 per cent (see Figure 7.2). From 1981 to 1990, Malaysia's exports had increased from 52 per cent to 74.5 per cent of its GDP.[62] By 1990, Malaysia had earned the status as a Newly Industrializing Country (NIC).

FIGURE 7.2
Contribution of Manufacturing and Agricultural Sectors to Malaysia's GDP in 1981 and 1990

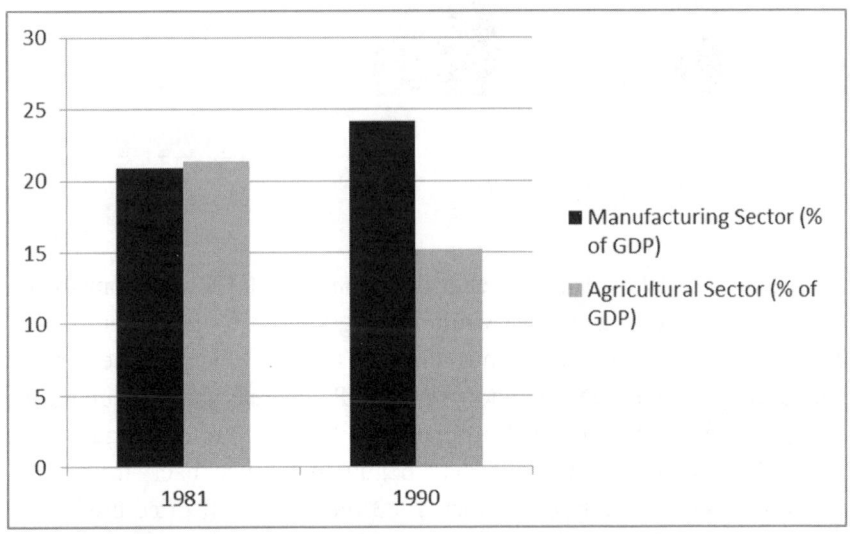

Source: World Development Indicators.

Indonesia, on the other hand, had been recognized as a nascent NIC since the late 1980s. The New Order regime had succeeded in diversifying the range of Indonesia's exports. The economic reforms launched by the regime had led to the creation of a substantial manufacturing base in

---

[62] Ibid.

FIGURE 7.3
Contribution of Manufacturing and Agricultural Sectors to Indonesia's GDP in 1986 and 1990

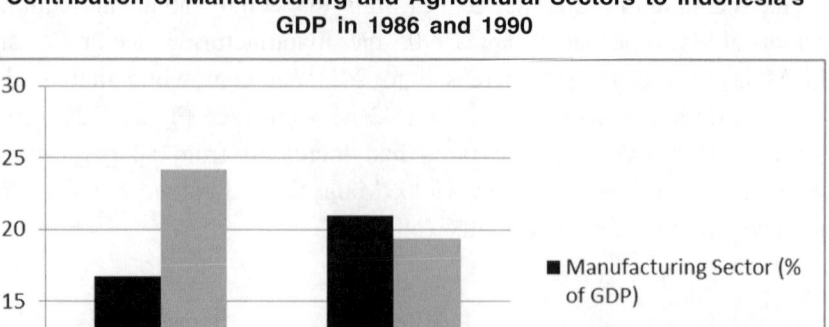

Source: World Development Indicators.

Indonesia.[63] In 1986, 16.7 per cent of Indonesia's GDP was contributed by its manufacturing sector, while the agricultural sector contributed 24.2 per cent. By 1990, the contribution of the manufacturing sector had increased to 21 per cent of Indonesia's GDP, whereas that accounted for by the agricultural sector had dropped to 19.4 per cent (see Figure 7.3). Meanwhile, Indonesia's export had begun to bounce back from 1987 onwards after its steady drop since 1983 due to the oil price crisis.[64] In 1986, Indonesia's export was at its record low since 1973 — 19.5 per cent of Indonesia's GDP.[65] It had then begun to increase up to 25.3 per cent in 1990.[66] Such a rise was largely attributed to the expansion of

---

[63] Vatikiotis, *Indonesian Politics Under Suharto*, pp. 45–46, 174–75.
[64] <http://databank.worldbank.org/data/views/reports/tableview.aspx#> (accessed 15 April 2014).
[65] Ibid.
[66] Ibid.

Indonesia's non-oil exports, within which the manufactures export had continued to grow substantially.[67]

Because of their significant economic success, Indonesia and Malaysia each became more determined to expand their respective political and economic influence abroad by aiming to lead the Third World. Indonesia was more confident than ever before that it was a model of development for the Third World. Its vibrant economy stood in stark contrast to the ailing economies of many of the Third World states, especially those in Latin America.[68] Suharto confidently declared in August 1990: "Indonesia was economically strong enough to begin playing a responsible role in world affairs."[69] Malaysia, on the other hand, began to view ASEAN in economic terms.[70] As it was now an export-oriented economy, Malaysia needed as big a market as possible for its products. It actively involved itself in international affairs, aiming to expand its market in ASEAN and beyond.[71]

Indonesia's and Malaysia's focus had been well beyond ASEAN.[72] The friendly regional climate of ASEAN was well established. The respective nationhood of Indonesia and Malaysia had taken root. The political supremacy of the indigenous people in Indonesia and Malaysia over the local Chinese, meanwhile, remained unchallenged. These were the basis upon which Indonesia and Malaysia began to shift their attention from viewing their region in terms of security to seeing it as related to their economies.[73] It was as if the solid presence of the Malay

---

[67] Vatikiotis, *Indonesian Politics Under Suharto*, pp. 40–41, 45–46. Also see John Paxton, ed., "Indonesia", in *The Statesman's Year-Book: Statistical and Historical Annual of the States of the World for the Year 1990–1991* (Great Britain: The Macmillan Press, 1990), p. 705; and <http://databank.worldbank.org/data/views/reports/tableview.aspx#> (accessed 15 April 2014).

[68] Vatikiotis, *Indonesian Politics Under Suharto*, p. 45.

[69] Ibid., p. 182.

[70] Dhillon, *Malaysian Foreign Policy in the Mahathir Era 1981–2003*, pp. 214–15, 218, 266.

[71] Ibid., pp. 210–11, 214–15, 218, 266.

[72] Suryadinata, *Indonesia's Foreign Policy Under Suharto*, pp. 177, 187. Also see Dhillon, *Malaysian Foreign Policy in the Mahathir Era 1981–2003*, pp. 195, 199, 210–11, 215, 218.

[73] Dhillon, *Malaysian Foreign Policy in the Mahathir Era 1981–2003*, pp. 214–15, 218, 226, 266. Also see Interview 1002, Singapore, 2 October 2012.

world in archipelagic Southeast Asia had become a given for both Indonesia and Malaysia. While the Malay world continued to function as a shield that safeguarded the existence of Indonesia and Malaysia, the two states, with their new found economic might, were looking beyond ASEAN, striving to expand the space for their respective survival.

LOOKING BEYOND SOUTHEAST ASIA

On 28 February 1991, Mahathir presented a policy speech titled "Malaysia: The Way Forward" at the first meeting of the Malaysian Business Council. This speech was to have a decisive impact on the future of Malaysia. Mahathir revealed in the speech the "ultimate" goal for Malaysia.[74] He declared that Malaysia would aim to become a fully developed country by the year 2020. The goal was later known as the Vision 2020 — *Wawasan 2020* — of Malaysia. To realize this vision — Mahathir explained — Malaysia's GDP by the year 2020 should become eight times larger than that in 1990. Such an expansion would require Malaysia to grow at an average annual GDP growth rate of 7 per cent for the next thirty years. During the speech, Mahathir once again reaffirmed Malaysia's commitment to become a developed nation-state in its own way:[75]

> Do we want to be like any particular country of the present 19 countries that are generally regarded as 'developed countries'? ...Without being a duplicate of any of them we can still be developed. We should be a developed country in our own mould.

Aiming at realizing Vision 2020 necessitated Malaysia to maximize its reach to overseas markets in order to sell its products as well as to seek for sources of investments, technologies and expertise which were crucial for advancing Malaysia's economy. Malaysia was faced with real challenges amidst its attempt to extend its reach to the markets abroad.

---

[74] Mahathir Mohamad, "Malaysia: The Way Forward", available at <http://www.pmo.gov.my/?menu=page&page=1904> (accessed 25 April 2014).
[75] Ibid.

The emergence of the North American Free Trade Agreement (NAFTA) and the European Community (EC) at the turn of the 1980s increasingly signified the existence of trade blocs in these regions.[76] Because of the preferential treatments that each of these agreements provided to its members, the states in the two regions had shown a growing tendency to trade and invest among themselves. The reunification of Germany that began to take place in 1989 pointed to the possibility that the states of Eastern Europe might also join the EC.[77] NAFTA and EC, therefore, posed a serious challenge to Malaysia's economy. They would weaken Malaysia's exports to Europe and North America and divert the investments from the two regions away from Malaysia.[78] In 1990, the United States was the second largest export market for Malaysia, which accounted for 16.9 per cent of Malaysia's total export.[79]

Apart from NAFTA and EC, Malaysia's economic expansion abroad was also restrained by the failure of the GATT (General Agreement on Tariffs and Trade) negotiations and the ASEAN member states' inability to forge substantial economic cooperation between them.[80] Because of Vision 2020, the Mahathir administration viewed this combination of restrictions as a matter of survival for Malaysia.[81] Shortly before announcing Malaysia's Vision 2020, Prime Minister Mahathir introduced Malaysia's response to the restrictions that it faced in international trade.

---

[76] Linda Low, "The East Asian Economic Grouping", *The Pacific Review* 4, no. 4 (1991): 375, 377. Also see Chandran Jeshurun, *Malaysia: Fifty Years of Diplomacy 1957–2007* (Singapore: Talisman Publishing, 2007), pp. 219–20.

[77] Mahathir Mohamad, "The Impact of a Changing World on ASEAN–European Community Relations", in *Reflections on ASEAN: Selected Speeches of Dr Mahathir Mohamad, Prime Minister of Malaysia*, edited by Hashim Makaruddin (Malaysia: Pelanduk Publications, 2004*d*), pp. 102–3. Also see Mahathir Mohamad, "ASEAN in the 1990s and Beyond", in *Reflections on ASEAN*, pp. 150–52; Low, "The East Asian Economic Grouping", p. 375; and Jeshurun, *Malaysia*, p. 215.

[78] Mahathir Mohamad, "ASEAN in the 1990s and Beyond", pp. 147–48, 151–52.

[79] "Exports by Country of Destination, 1990–1999", available at <http://www.epu.gov.my/en/external-trade> (accessed 25 April 2014).

[80] Low, "The East Asian Economic Grouping", p. 375. Also see Saravanamuttu, *Malaysia's Foreign Policy, the First Fifty Years*, p. 190.

[81] Ibid. Also see Dhillon, *Malaysian Foreign Policy in the Mahathir Era 1981–2003*, pp. 179, 192. Also see Jeshurun, *Malaysia*, pp. 232–33.

During the state banquet held on 10 December 1990 for the visiting Chinese Premier Li Peng, Mahathir announced that "the countries of the region should strengthen further their economic and market ties so that eventually an economic bloc would be formed to countervail the other economic blocs".[82] The proposed economic grouping was known as the East Asian Economic Group (EAEG) which should include Japan, South Korea, China, Taiwan, Hong Kong, the Indo-China states and ASEAN.

A combination of factors led to Mahathir's proposal of the EAEG. While the United States and Europe each alone was one of Malaysia's largest export markets, the East Asian states combined, on the other hand, constituted the largest export market for Malaysia.[83] In 1990, the East Asian states — Japan, South Korea, China, Taiwan, Hong Kong and the five ASEAN partners — together accounted for 56.9 per cent of Malaysia's total export.[84] Further, the intra-regional trade in East Asia was growing faster than its extra-regional trade, and that expansion of trade within East Asia would accelerate in the coming years.[85] Crucially, the top investors in Malaysia since the mid-1980s had been from the East Asian states. In 1990, the East Asian states — Taiwan, Japan, Hong Kong, Singapore and South Korea — combined was the largest investor in Malaysia, which accounted for 67 per cent of the total foreign direct investments in Malaysia.[86] It was therefore clear for the Mahathir administration that the future of Malaysia's economy lay in the region of East Asia. Malaysia proposed the creation of the EAEG

---

[82] Mahathir Mohamad, speech presented at state banquet for the visiting Chinese Prime Minister Li Peng, Kuala Lumpur, 10 December 1990, quoted in Liow, *The Politics of Indonesia–Malaysia Relations*, p. 140.

[83] "Exports by Country of Destination, 1990–1999", available at <http://www.epu.gov.my/en/external-trade> (accessed 25 April 2014).

[84] Ibid.

[85] Jeshurun, *Malaysia*, p. 220. Also see Low, "The East Asian Economic Grouping", pp. 378–79, 382.

[86] International Centre for the Study of East Asian Development (ICSEAD) Symposium, Kitakyushu, 1990, p. 93, quoted in Low, "The East Asian Economic Grouping", p. 378.

as a trade bloc, aiming to secure a huge market — comparable to the size of NAFTA and EC — for Malaysia's economy.[87] The EAEG as an economic grouping — Malaysia maintained — could, in the meantime, work to balance against Western dominance expressed in the form of NAFTA and EC, ensuring a free multilateral trading system worldwide, hence enabling Malaysia to maximize its reach to the markets across the globe.[88]

Malaysia's determination to ensure its economic space by proposing the EAEG boosted, and was boosted by, its sense of nationalism. Prime Minister Mahathir believed that Malaysia should stand up against Western hegemony by embracing the EAEG so that Malaysia could become a fully developed nation-state on its own terms.[89] Years later, when discussing about the issue of the EAEG, Mahathir expressed his discontent at Indonesia and Singapore for being — he alleged — "influenced by the Americans" in the face of Western dominance.[90] "I don't want to be influenced by anybody", he asserted.[91] Mahathir intended to affirm Malaysia's credentials as a Third World leader by introducing the EAEG. Having a group of developing states in a powerful economic grouping like EAEG — Mahathir argued — would serve to uplift the economic status of the developing world as a whole.[92]

Mahathir announced his proposal of the formation of the EAEG without consulting his ASEAN partners. Several reasons led to his decision to do so. Given the steady increase of trade within East Asia,

---

[87] Low, "The East Asian Economic Grouping", pp. 375–77. Also see Mahathir Mohamad, "ASEAN and the World Economy: The Challenge of Change", in *Reflections on ASEAN*, p. 122; Mahathir Mohamad, "ASEAN: Good Return of Growth and Stability", in *Reflections on ASEAN*, pp. 126–27; Mahathir Mohamad, "ASEAN in the 1990s and Beyond", p. 156; and Saravanamuttu, *Malaysia's Foreign Policy, the First Fifty Years*, p. 190.

[88] Ibid. Also see R.S. Milne and Diane K. Mauzy, *Malaysian Politics Under Mahathir* (London and New York: Routledge, 1999), p. 130.

[89] Jeshurun, *Malaysia*, pp. 232–33. Also see Milne and Mauzy, *Malaysian Politics Under Mahathir*, p. 130; and Weatherbee, *International Relations in Southeast Asia*, p. 209.

[90] Ibid. Also see Interview with Dr Mahathir Mohamad, 9 May 2007, quoted in Jeshurun, *Malaysia*, p. 233.

[91] Ibid.

[92] Mahathir Mohamad, "ASEAN and the World Economy", p. 122.

Malaysia believed that East Asia becoming a *de facto* trading group was inevitable.[93] It thus made no difference — Malaysia concluded — if Malaysia chose to discuss the EAEG concept with its ASEAN counterparts before officially calling for its formation.[94] The EAEG, on the other hand, was a matter of survival for Malaysia. East Asia — with its sizeable market, considerable technologies and knowledge, its capacity to invest, and the continued expansion of its intra-regional trade — was the key market for Malaysia, if it was to transform into a developed state by the year 2020, especially in the face of the emerging trade blocs in Europe and North America.[95] Malaysia, as a consequence, lost its patience to consult its ASEAN partners about the EAEG as it needed the East Asian market dearly so as to realize its Vision 2020. Mahathir years later explained why he went ahead to propose the forming of the EAEG without consulting his ASEAN counterparts: "there was really no diplomatic way of facing up to the inequalities that loomed ahead", Mahathir argued.[96]

Malaysia decided to take the lead in forming the EAEG after it had officially introduced this concept. The EAEG proposal was immediately opposed by the United States. The forming of the EAEG would pose a direct challenge to the U.S. dominance in East Asia, particularly in view of the fact that it had been excluded from the grouping.[97] The United States exerted pressure on Japan to prevent Japan from joining the grouping.[98] Within its immediate neighbourhood, Malaysia was faced with Indonesia's opposition to the creation of the EAEG.

---

[93] Low, "The East Asian Economic Grouping", p. 377.

[94] Ibid.

[95] Mahathir Mohamad, "ASEAN and the World Economy", p. 122. Also see Mahathir Mohamad, "ASEAN in the 1990s and Beyond", p. 156; and Dhillon, *Malaysian Foreign Policy in the Mahathir Era 1981–2003*, pp. 179, 192.

[96] Jeshurun, *Malaysia*, p. 232. Also see Interview with Dr Mahathir Mohamad, 9 May 2007, quoted in Jeshurun, *Malaysia*, pp. 232–33.

[97] Saravanamuttu, *Malaysia's Foreign Policy, the First Fifty Years*, p. 191. Also see Liow, *The Politics of Indonesia–Malaysia Relations*, p. 141; and Low, "The East Asian Economic Grouping", p. 377.

[98] Ibid. Also see Weatherbee, *International Relations in Southeast Asia*, p. 209.

Forming the EAEG had the effects of weakening the power of Indonesia. Malaysia's proposal of the EAEG and its decision to spearhead the formation of the grouping posed a challenge to Indonesia's perceived leadership status in ASEAN.[99] Indonesia viewed itself as the *primus inter pares* in ASEAN.[100] Crucially, the creation of the EAEG would threaten the growth of Indonesia's economy. Half of Indonesia's development budget was financed by the aid from Western states and Japan.[101] It was the influence of the United States that had ensured the flow of this aid to Indonesia.[102] This foreign aid played a vital role in stabilizing Indonesian currency in the face of the massive debt that Indonesia had incurred.[103] Indonesia's economy was largely dependent on its foreign aid. Supporting the EAEG would antagonize the United States hence might lead to the reduction of foreign aid to Indonesia.[104]

Also, Malaysia's call for the formation of the EAEG ran counter to Indonesia's expectation. In Indonesia's understanding, any regional initiative that involved ASEAN was a matter of strategic partnership between Indonesia and Malaysia. When the idea of APEC (Asia-Pacific Economic Cooperation) was first proposed by Australia in 1989, it was Indonesia and Malaysia that had together resisted the proposal due to the fear that ASEAN might be dominated by the United States and Japan through APEC.[105] Such a concerted resistance — as Indonesia saw it — was the strategic cooperation of Indonesia and Malaysia. They

---

[99] Liow, *The Politics of Indonesia–Malaysia Relations*, pp. 141, 164. Also see Interview 1017, Jakarta, 17 October 2012; Interview 1002, Singapore, 2 October 2012; Michael Vatikiotis, "Stormy Weather: Tension Behind the Smiles at Mahathir–Suharto Talks", *Far Eastern Economic Review* (29 July 1993c): 18–19; and Suryadinata, *Indonesia's Foreign Policy Under Suharto*, p. 73.

[100] Ibid.

[101] Vatikiotis, *Indonesian Politics Under Suharto*, pp. 46–47, 188.

[102] Ibid.

[103] Ibid.

[104] Lily Zubaidah Rahim, *Singapore in the Malay World: Building and Breaching Regional Bridges* (Oxon: Routledge, 2009), pp. 156–57.

[105] APEC is a consultative, non-negotiating economic body first consisting of the United States, Australia, Canada, Japan, New Zealand, South Korea, and the ASEAN-6. Weatherbee, *International Relations in Southeast Asia*, pp. 208–9. Also see Milne and Mauzy, *Malaysian Politics Under Mahathir*, p. 128.

had worked together, striving to uphold an autonomous ASEAN — an aspiration rooted in their strategic thinking of the Malay world. Indonesia, therefore, expected Malaysia to consult with Indonesia when it came to the matter of the EAEG, as indicated by both a former Malaysian policy advisor and a former Indonesian diplomat.[106] The EAEG was similar to APEC. It would have an impact on ASEAN on a scale similar to that of APEC. The forming of the EAEG — Indonesia would think — without doubt entailed the strategic cooperation between Indonesia and Malaysia. Malaysia's unilateral move to push for the creation of the EAEG did not match with Indonesia's expectation that it should be consulted. President Suharto felt insulted because of the mismatch of expectation.[107]

Meanwhile, it was clear that Malaysia's endeavour in proposing and creating the EAEG served to showcase Malaysia's ability in making an international impact, enabling its transformation into a developed state with no capitulation to Western dominance.[108] Malaysia was putting itself on the world map. Because of the close similarities between Indonesia and Malaysia owing to their common identities — the Malay way of life — Indonesia had been provoked to stress its difference vis-à-vis Malaysia, so as to illuminate its existence in the world of nations amidst Malaysia's activism in international politics.

The differentiation was expressed in superiority sense — an outcome of the combination of Indonesia's sense of uniqueness in relation to Malaysia, and its power politics with Malaysia, in which power politics equipped the two states with a mindset of comparison. Indonesia asserted its superiority over Malaysia in the form of the big-little brothers complex. In the eyes of Indonesians, they were the big brother of Malaysia.[109] Indonesians believed that Indonesia was a great nation.

---

[106] Interview 1017, Jakarta, 17 October 2012. Also see Interview 917, Kuala Lumpur, 17 September 2012.

[107] Weatherbee, *International Relations in Southeast Asia*, pp. 208–9.

[108] Vatikiotis, "Stormy Weather", pp. 18–19.

[109] Suryadinata, *Indonesia's Foreign Policy Under Suharto*, p. 69. Also see Interview 1011, Jakarta, 11 October 2012; Interview 920, Kuala Lumpur, 20 September 2012; Interview 926-001, Kuala Lumpur, 26 September 2012; and Interview 924-001, Kuala Lumpur, 24 September 2012.

The sense of greatness was derived from the understanding of the sheer size of Indonesia and a few thousand years of existence of its culture. Scholars have pointed out, in view of the fact that most of the Malays in Malaysia had their roots in Indonesia, Indonesians would think that Malaysia's culture was provided by Indonesia.[110] Indonesians believed that their culture was superior when compared to Malaysia's, a former Malaysian policy advisor noted.[111] Indonesians expressed their disdain for the perceived shallowness of Malaysia. As indicated by a senior policy advisor of Malaysia, Indonesians for example would argue that Malaysia had no Borobudur — a ninth-century Buddhist temple located in Central Java, Indonesia — and that Malaysia had not fought for its independence.[112] Indonesians were proud of their culture, when they thought of Malaysia, the advisor maintained.[113] A former Indonesian diplomat too stressed the cultural pride of Indonesians when discussing about the issue of Indonesia–Malaysia common culture with the author.[114] Because Indonesia perceived itself as the provider of culture to Malaysia, it thus saw itself as the big brother of Malaysia.

Owing to its big brother sentiment, Indonesia was always helpful to Malaysia, a former Malaysian Foreign Minister explained.[115] Indonesia was keen to supply Malaysia with its teachers, lecturers and expertise to help establish a Malay language-based national education system in Malaysia during the 1970s.[116] "We [Indonesia] sent many of our teachers and lecturers to Malaysia. Indonesia was helping Malaysia like a big brother. Being Indonesia's younger sibling, Malaysia was learning from

---

[110] Interview 917, Kuala Lumpur, 17 September 2012. Also see Khadijah Md. Khalid and Shakila Yacob, "Managing Malaysia–Indonesia Relations in the Context of Democratization: The Emergence of Non-State Actors", *International Relations of the Asia-Pacific* 12, no. 3 (2012): 356, 360. Liow has stated that most Malays in Malaysia have their roots in Sumatra, Indonesia. See Liow, *The Politics of Indonesia–Malaysia Relations*, p. 40.

[111] Interview 917, Kuala Lumpur, 17 September 2012.

[112] Interview 924-001, Kuala Lumpur, 24 September 2012.

[113] Ibid.

[114] Interview 1016, Jakarta, 16 October 2012

[115] Interview 926-001, Kuala Lumpur, 26 September 2012.

[116] Interview 1011, Jakarta, 11 October 2012.

us", said one prominent Indonesian journalist.[117] The efforts to supply Malaysia with teachers, lecturers and expertise strengthened Indonesia's sense of superiority as Malaysia's big brother. The big brother sentiment is also reinforced by the fact that the Malays in Malaysia look to Indonesia as a source of inspiration.[118] The Malays' nationalism and their political thinking had been and continued to be inspired by Indonesia.[119]

Indonesia affirmed its status as the big brother of Malaysia, believing that Malaysia should show deference to Indonesia by consulting with Indonesia first before it went ahead to introduce and spearhead the formation of the EAEG.[120]

The mutual reinforcements of the three sources of conflict — the challenge to Indonesia's power; the mismatch of expectation; and Indonesia's assertion of its status as Malaysia's big brother — resulted in Indonesia's decision to oppose Malaysia's attempt to establish the EAEG.

At the ASEAN Senior Economic Officials' Meeting held in February 1991, the Indonesian delegation had moved to block Malaysia's motion to include the EAEG proposal on the agenda of the meeting. They had succeeded in doing so. One month later, during his speech at the ASEAN conference held in Bali, President Suharto essentially declared Indonesia's opposition to the forming of the EAEG.[121] Suharto in his speech stressed that Indonesia was not in favour of a closed trade bloc.

Malaysia was confronted with the opposition from Indonesia and several Western powers — the United States, Australia and Canada — to

---

[117] Ibid.
[118] Interview 920, Kuala Lumpur, 20 September 2012. Also see Interview 926-001, Kuala Lumpur, 26 September 2012; and Franklin B. Weinstein, *Indonesian Foreign Policy and the Dilemma of Dependence: From Sukarno to Soeharto* (Ithaca and London: Cornell University Press, 1976), p. 199.
[119] Ibid.
[120] Interview 1002, Singapore, 2 October 2012. Also see Interview 924-001, Kuala Lumpur, 24 September 2012; Liow, *The Politics of Indonesia–Malaysia Relations*, p. 132; and Suryadinata, *Indonesia's Foreign Policy Under Suharto*, p. 69.
[121] Suryadinata, *Indonesia's Foreign Policy Under Suharto*, p. 73. Also see Mahathir Mohamad, "ASEAN and the World Economy", p. 111.

its idea of EAEG.[122] It moved to refine the concept, attempting to defuse the opposition. Prime Minister Mahathir emphasized in his speech at the same ASEAN conference that the EAEG was "not intended to be a trade bloc".[123] The EAEG, he argued, would be a formal grouping that facilitated consultation and consensus between the states of East Asia, allowing them to speak with one voice to preserve a worldwide free trade system.[124] Mahathir, nevertheless, remained steadfast to strive for the formation of the EAEG. Such a determination was toughened by Malaysia's sense of superiority over Indonesia.

Malaysia emphasized its difference from Indonesia based on their commonalities to confirm its unique existence in the world. The differentiation was expressed in superiority sense as it entailed Malaysia's power politics with Indonesia which led them to compare with each other. Malaysia's superiority over Indonesia — Malaysians opined — was evidenced by the fact that Malaysia was sophisticated. Malaysia believed that it was sophisticated when compared to Indonesia even though Malaysia was a small nation-state vis-à-vis Indonesia.[125] The defining feature of Malaysia being sophisticated — Malaysians would think — was that it was economically more superior than Indonesia.[126] Since independence, Malaysia's GDP per capita was evidently higher than that of Indonesia.

Malaysia's sense of being sophisticated vis-à-vis Indonesia was a continuation of its erstwhile sense of wisdom in relation to Indonesia. Unlike previous administrations, the Mahathir administration's nation-building programme involved modernization on a big scale which was characterized by Malaysia's technological and industrial advancement. Such advancement would become more obvious in the following years. Malaysia, for example, began to possess the world's tallest buildings — Petronas Twin Towers — in the mid-1990s. It meanwhile began to embark on developing its IT industry by creating a high-tech area —

---

[122] Ibid. Also see Low, "The East Asian Economic Grouping", p. 377.

[123] Mahathir Mohamad, "ASEAN and the World Economy", p. 120.

[124] Ibid., pp. 121–23.

[125] Vatikiotis, "Stormy Weather", pp. 18–19.

[126] Interview 917, Kuala Lumpur, 17 September 2012. Also see Interview 1016, Jakarta, 16 October 2012; and Rahim, *Singapore in the Malay World*, p. 157.

Multimedia Super Corridor — aiming to turn Malaysia into a global IT hub. The evident technological and industrial advancement of Malaysia transformed Malaysians' sense of wisdom into their belief that they were sophisticated, when they were to think of Indonesia. Mahathir expressed his sense of superiority — that Malaysia was sophisticated vis-à-vis Indonesia — decades later:[127]

> Of all the ethnic Malays in the region [Southeast Asia], the Malays in this country [Malaysia] are today widely recognised as the most successful...Today there is a Malay presence everywhere in the world...They have expanded their skills so greatly that now Malays drill for and produce oil, build roads and power plants, and manage multinational corporations and industries, including those involved with sophisticated engineering and high technological content all over the world.

In the meantime, the fact that Indonesians had been and continued to be inspired by Malaysia's economic advancement strengthened the conviction of Malaysians that Malaysia was sophisticated when compared to Indonesia.[128]

Mahathir later apologized to President Suharto for not consulting with Indonesia before introducing the idea of EAEG. He apologized to Suharto for being "a little bit brash on this matter", "a little less controlled, less Javanese" and less "indirect than Suharto".[129] Mahathir's apology perhaps reflected his sense of superiority over Indonesia. Compared to Indonesia — as might have implied by Mahathir — Malaysia was forthright and straight to the point — an indication that Malaysia was sophisticated. Mahathir subsequently made plain Malaysia's determination to spearhead the establishment of the EAEG. He declared in his speech in September 1991: "Malaysia and ASEAN will press on for the formation of the EAEG. We assure you that we have no intention of becoming a trade bloc or to commit economic

---

[127] Mahathir Mohamad, *A Doctor in the House*, pp. 27–30.

[128] Interview 926-001, Kuala Lumpur, 26 September 2012. Also see Rahim, *Singapore in the Malay World*, p. 157.

[129] Vatikiotis, "Stormy Weather", p. 19.

suicide."[130] Malaysia lobbied vigorously for the support of its ASEAN partners for the formation of the EAEG.

Indonesia would not budge in its opposition to the creation of the EAEG.[131] Under Indonesia's leadership, ASEAN during its summit held in Singapore in January 1992 had officially espoused Indonesia's recommendation about the EAEG. The EAEG had been downgraded to the status of a caucus — East Asia Economic Caucus (EAEC) — functioning as a forum within APEC. It was a victory for Indonesia. Malaysia had failed to create an East Asian economic grouping which would be a stand-alone body rather than a unit within APEC.

Creating the EAEC within APEC was an insult to Malaysia. One of the proposed purposes of the EAEG was to confront the hegemony of the West. Regionally, EAEG was to be the alternative to APEC.[132] Malaysia was always worried about being dominated by the United States through APEC.[133] ASEAN's decision to downgrade the EAEG to a caucus within APEC triggered Malaysia's anti-Western sentiments. Prime Minister Mahathir as a result decided not to attend the first APEC summit which would be hosted by the United States in Seattle in November 1993.[134] The decision boosted Malaysia's sense of superiority over Indonesia. Malaysia asserted that Indonesia should accept and tolerate the fact that Malaysia had something more to offer — namely the idea of the EAEG.[135]

Indonesia on the contrary chose to embrace APEC. President Suharto had attended the APEC summit in Seattle. Meanwhile, Indonesia would

---

[130] Mahathir Mohamad, "ASEAN in the 1990s and Beyond", pp. 145, 157.

[131] Suryadinata, *Indonesia's Foreign Policy Under Suharto*, p. 73. Also see Liow, *The Politics of Indonesia–Malaysia Relations*, p. 141.

[132] Weatherbee, *International Relations in Southeast Asia*, p. 209. Also see Liow, *The Politics of Indonesia–Malaysia Relations*, pp. 141–42; Interview 1017, Jakarta, 17 October 2012; Suryadinata, *Indonesia's Foreign Policy Under Suharto*, p. 73; and Milne and Mauzy, *Malaysian Politics Under Mahathir*, p. 129.

[133] Ibid. Also see Dhillon, *Malaysian Foreign Policy in the Mahathir Era 1981–2003*, p. 220.

[134] Suryadinata, *Indonesia's Foreign Policy Under Suharto*, p. 180. Also see Milne and Mauzy, *Malaysian Politics Under Mahathir*, p. 130; and Weatherbee, *International Relations in Southeast Asia*, p. 209.

[135] Interview 926-001, Kuala Lumpur, 26 September 2012.

take up the chairmanship of APEC for the year 1994. The decision to become APEC chairman was part of Indonesia's efforts to expand its economic and political influence abroad by striving to represent the Third World.[136] Indonesia had been actively promoting the cause of the Third World in the international arena since becoming the Chairman of NAM in 1992.[137] Representing the NAM, President Suharto proposed in the UN the restructuring of the UN Security Council in which the Third World would have representations in the new Security Council. Suharto met with the Japanese Prime Minister and the U.S. President, attempting to promote the North–South dialogue — a dialogue aiming at preventing the economic marginalization of the Third World. By holding the chairmanship of APEC, Indonesia's influence as a Third World leader would understandably be enhanced.[138] In the meantime, the chairmanship consolidated Suharto's standing as an international statesman at home.[139] Being the chairman of APEC strengthened Indonesians' conviction that Indonesia had been widely recognized as a model of development for the developing states — hence a Third World leader — because of its openness and impressive economic performance delivered by President Suharto.[140]

Indonesia had committed itself to host the second APEC summit in Bogor in November 1994. Indonesia's outright support for APEC and its decision to bring the summit to Southeast Asia constituted a rebuff to Malaysia's antagonism towards APEC.[141] Malaysia had been put under pressure to choose whether to challenge the unity of ASEAN or to attend the APEC summit in Bogor.[142]

Indonesia's decision to host the APEC summit boosted its sense of superiority over Malaysia. President Suharto made clear that he "expected"

---

[136] Suryadinata, *Indonesia's Foreign Policy Under Suharto*, pp. 179–81.
[137] Ibid.
[138] Ibid.
[139] Ibid.
[140] Ibid. Also see Elson, *Suharto*, p. 283.
[141] Ibid. Also see Weatherbee, *International Relations in Southeast Asia*, pp. 209–10.
[142] Ibid. Also see Milne and Mauzy, *Malaysian Politics Under Mahathir*, p. 130.

Mahathir to attend the summit.[143] It was essentially a gesture of being the big brother of Malaysia: the little brother — Malaysia — should show deference to Indonesia — the big brother — by taking part in the APEC summit. Prime Minister Mahathir attended the APEC summit in Bogor. Mahathir, however, emphasized decades later that his decision to attend the summit had little to do with Indonesia's supposed big brother status. "…I went [APEC Summit in Bogor] because I felt it was a decision made by the group [APEC], not just by President Suharto", Mahathir wrote.[144]

The rivalries between Indonesia and Malaysia amidst their endeavours to expand their respective influence abroad were also evident in other areas of international politics which involved the Third World. While Indonesia had succeeded in being elected as the Chairman of NAM from 1992 to 1995, Malaysia had been at the forefront in shaping the agenda of the movement, aiming to create a new basis for the movement's existence in the post-Cold War era.[145] Malaysia in consequence had won the recognition as the "new voice for the Third World".[146] Indonesia was particularly irritated by Prime Minister Mahathir stealing "much of the thunder" at the 1992 NAM conference held in Jakarta.[147] Indonesians described Mahathir as "a little Sukarno" because of Mahathir's outspokenness and assertiveness that defined his endeavours in championing the causes of the Third World.[148]

---

[143] Peter Searle, "Recalcitrant or Realpolitik? The Politics of Culture in Australia's Relations with Malaysia", in *Pathways to Asia: The Politics of Engagement*, edited by Richard Robison (Australia: Allen & Unwin, 1996), p. 67.

[144] Mahathir Mohamad, *A Doctor in the House*, p. 615.

[145] Suryadinata, *Indonesia's Foreign Policy Under Suharto*, p. 176. Also see Dhillon, *Malaysian Foreign Policy in the Mahathir Era 1981–2003*, p. 204; and Liow, *The Politics of Indonesia–Malaysia Relations*, p. 137.

[146] *Far Eastern Economic Review*, 20 August 1992.

[147] Liow, *The Politics of Indonesia–Malaysia Relations*, p. 137. Also see Dhillon, *Malaysian Foreign Policy in the Mahathir Era 1981–2003*, p. 204.

[148] Liow, *The Politics of Indonesia–Malaysia Relations*, p. 137. Also see Michael Vatikiotis, "Clash of Styles: High Profile Diplomacy Upsets Neighbours", *Far Eastern Economic Review* (20 August 1992): 19; and Dhillon, *Malaysian Foreign Policy in the Mahathir Era 1981–2003*, pp. 202–4.

Calling Mahathir "a little Sukarno" was a consequence of Indonesia's sense of superiority over Malaysia. For Indonesians, Sukarno — their first President — was a founding father and a pioneer of the Third World movement. It was Sukarno's charismatic personalities and great oratory skills that distinguished his leadership role in the Third World. Such qualities had become an example of the leadership style of a Third World leader. Mahathir the "little" brother — as Indonesians saw it — was indeed learning from Sukarno — Indonesia, the big brother — in how to lead the Third World.

Malaysia's attempt to play a leadership role in OIC was being perceived by Indonesia as a challenge to its standing in the Muslim World.[149] Indonesia's standing — as Indonesians saw it — was based on the fact that Indonesia was the state with the largest Muslim population in the world.[150] Indonesia believed that its status in the Muslim World was also being challenged by Malaysia's activism in calling for international action to halt the atrocities committed against Bosnian Muslims.[151] Indonesia and Malaysia were the only Southeast Asian states that had participated in the UN Protection Force in Bosnia-Herzegovina. Malaysian troops in Bosnia — 1,500 men — however, clearly outnumbered that of Indonesia — 200 men. In October 1993, President Suharto surprised the world by having a meeting with Israeli Prime Minister Yitzhak Rabin in Jakarta in his capacity as the chairman of NAM. One month earlier, it was Yasser Arafat that had met with President Suharto in Jakarta to brief him about the peace accord reached between the Palestine Liberation Organization and Israel. Suharto's meeting with Israeli Prime Minister served to weaken Malaysia's influence in the Palestinian issue. Malaysia had been trying

---

[149] Interview 926-001, Kuala Lumpur, 26 September 2012. Also see Karminder Singh Dhillon, *Malaysian Foreign Policy in the Mahathir Era 1981–2003*, p. 195.
[150] Ibid. Also see Interview 1016, Jakarta, 16 October 2012; Interview 1011, Jakarta, 11 October 2012; and Liow, *The Politics of Indonesia–Malaysia Relations*, p. 138.
[151] Dhillon, *Malaysian Foreign Policy in the Mahathir Era 1981–2003*, pp. 230–31. Also see Jeshurun, *Malaysia*, pp. 240–41; and Liow, *The Politics of Indonesia–Malaysia Relations*, pp. 138, 209.

to involve itself in the Palestinian issue. It was the second state in the world — after Pakistan — to accord full diplomatic status to the Palestine Liberation Organization.[152] The organization had established its embassy in Kuala Lumpur in 1981. Malaysia, meanwhile, was well known for its anti-Zionist and anti-Western stands along its support for the Palestinian cause.[153] It had no diplomatic relations with Israel. Malaysia had made clear that it treated the 1993 Palestinian-Israeli Peace Agreement with caution.[154]

The competition between Indonesia and Malaysia in the international arena — which was enhanced by the mismatch of expectation between them; and mutually reinforced by their respective assertion of their superiority over the culturally similar counterpart — resulted in Indonesia's move to balance against Malaysia in the area of security. Indonesia forged closer military ties with Singapore, aiming to curtail Malaysia's regional as well as international influence.[155] Singapore had been allowed to maintain its military training facilities in Sumatra since 1988. It was the only state that had a military presence in Indonesia. The deepening of military cooperation between Indonesia and Singapore contradicted with Malaysia's expectation. Malaysia expected that its relations with Indonesia should be closer when compared to their respective ties with Singapore, since Indonesia and Malaysia shared a special relationship. Malaysia's main newspaper expressed its disgruntlement towards Indonesia owing to the mismatch of expectation:[156]

Although Indonesia had the right to establish relations with another country, it should take into account the special ties between Kuala Lumpur and Jakarta which encompassed all aspects of life.

---

[152] Shanti Nair, *Islam in Malaysian Foreign Policy* (London: Routledge, 1997), pp. 206–7.
[153] Dhillon, *Malaysian Foreign Policy in the Mahathir Era 1981–2003*, pp. 227–29.
[154] Ibid.
[155] Rahim, *Singapore in the Malay World*, pp. 155–56.
[156] *Utusan Melayu*, 10 February 1990, quoted in Liow, *The Politics of Indonesia–Malaysia Relations*, p. 140.

The Malaysian government too indicated its discontent with Indonesia, stressing that it regarded Singapore's military presence in Sumatra as a threat to Malaysia.[157]

The bad feelings towards Indonesia served to strengthen Malaysia's resolve to enhance its own military standing. From 1988 to 1991, the military expenditure of Malaysia had been on an upward trend.[158] In 1988, Malaysia's military expenditure accounted for 2.43 per cent of its GDP.[159] In 1991, it was at 3.2 per cent.[160] Such an expansion in military spending was also driven by the need to replace the aging military equipments of the Malaysian armed forces, and fostered by the changing of Malaysia's perception of threat which began to view neighbouring states as its main threat following the end of communist insurgency in Malaysia.[161]

Despite the conspicuous rivalries between Indonesia and Malaysia since the late 1980s, strategic cooperation between the two states, however, remained well in place. Indonesia and Malaysia had protested against Singapore's decision in 1990 to offer itself as the military hub for the U.S. military in Southeast Asia. Both Indonesia and Malaysia viewed the U.S. military presence in Singapore as a challenge to their desired autonomous order of Southeast Asia, which was in essence a threat to the presence of the Malay world in archipelagic Southeast Asia.[162] Both the Malay states conducted their largest ever joint military exercise shortly after.[163] The exercise was conducted in August 1991 in the state of Johor of Malaysia. It ended with the landing of paratroopers

---

[157] Suryadinata, *Indonesia's Foreign Policy Under Suharto*, p. 71.
[158] <http://databank.worldbank.org/data/views/reports/tableview.aspx#> (accessed 15 May 2014).
[159] Ibid.
[160] Ibid.
[161] Aaron Karp, "Military Procurement and Regional Security in Southeast Asia", *Contemporary Southeast Asia* 11, no. 4 (1990): 334–35. Also see N. Ganesan, "Rethinking ASEAN as a Security Community in Southeast Asia", *Asian Affairs* 21, no. 4 (1995): 218.
[162] Michael Antolik, *ASEAN and the Diplomacy of Accommodation* (New York: An East Gate Book, 1990), p. 162. Also see Rahim, *Singapore in the Malay World*, pp. 100–1.
[163] Rahim, *Singapore in the Malay World*, p. 157.

in southern Johor — 18 km north of Singapore — on 9 August 1991. The code name of the landing was "Total Wipe Out" and the day of the landing was on Singapore's National Day. Apparently, the joint military exercise was meant to send a message to Singapore: do not challenge the fact that archipelagic Southeast Asia is the Malay world. Together Indonesia and Malaysia formed the Malay world — a shield that protected their existence as states built around the Malay way of life. Singapore in response launched a large scale military exercise, aiming to deter both the Indonesian and Malaysian armed forces.[164]

The Indonesia–Malaysia special relationship produced double-edged effects between them. The joint military exercise revealed the substantial cooperation that existed between the two Malay states. They had maintained their strategic cooperation to protect their respective survival. Such cooperation were salient when Indonesia and Malaysia deemed that they were confronted with a threat posed by culturally different others.

On the other hand, Indonesia's move to forge close military ties with Singapore represented a substantial conflict between Indonesia and Malaysia. The move was designed specifically to weaken Malaysia's military standing in response to the obvious power competition between Indonesia and Malaysia in the international arena.

The intertwined three sources of conflict that were embedded in the Indonesia–Malaysia special relationship — power competition; the assertion of the superiority of national identity; and the mismatch of expectation — bred and enhanced the negative identifications between the two states. Indonesia and Malaysia were entrenched in their egoistic understanding of each other as a consequence.

Indonesia was well aware that Malaysia needed the Five Power Defence Arrangement (FPDA) to prevent Indonesia's armed attacks on Malaysia.[165] Indonesia proposed in 1990 a Three Power Defence

---

[164] Ibid., p. 157. Also see Jeshurun, *Malaysia*, pp. 234–35. For more discussion see Chapter 6, pp. 251–52.

[165] Donald K. Emmerson, "Indonesia, Malaysia, Singapore: A Regional Security Core?" in *Southeast Asian Security in the New Millennium*, edited by Richard J. Ellings and Sheldon W. Simon (New York and London, England: NBR: Armonk, 1996), pp. 71–72. Also see Liow, *The Politics of Indonesia–Malaysia Relations*, p. 139.

Arrangement (TPDA) between Indonesia, Malaysia and Singapore to replace the existing FPDA. It was suspected that Indonesia intended to establish its military dominance over Malaysia through the TPDA.[166] Malaysia rejected such a proposal and continued to embrace the FPDA.

SIPADAN AND LIGITAN

Shortly after Mahathir came into office, he made a decision that Malaysia would claim sovereignty over the Layang-Layang Island — a submerged reef 300 km northwest of Kota Kinabalu, Sabah.[167] Layang-Layang is part of the Spratly Islands located in the South China Sea. These islands are well known for their unexplored oil and gas reserves. In 1983, Prime Minister Mahathir together with senior officers from the Malaysian navy visited the Layang-Layang Island after a makeshift hut had been built on that island.[168]

Mahathir later described that claiming the Layang-Layang Island was one of the most important decisions he had made as the Prime Minister of Malaysia.[169] He explained: "In the past Malay states lost many islands simply because they had no means to survey and oversee their domains...islands such as these are very important as their natural beauty or access to resources may generate income."[170] Oil and gas had been the main source of income for the Malaysian government.[171] Owing to its goal of turning Malaysia into a developed state in the shortest time frame, the Mahathir administration had been obliged to seek for more resources to finance Malaysia's expansion into a developed state.

---

[166] Ibid.
[167] Mahathir Mohamad, *A Doctor in the House*, pp. 343–44.
[168] Ibid.
[169] Ibid.
[170] Ibid., pp. 344–45.
[171] In 2005, oil-related revenue accounted for RM 30.8 billion, or 29.1 per cent of the total revenue of Malaysia's Federal Government. In 2006, this had increased to RM 45 billion, or 37.3 per cent. See "Stronger Revenue from Oil-related Activities", *The Star*, 2 September 2006.

It was against this background that rumours had emerged in Indonesia in 1982 that Malaysia had stationed troops on Sipadan Island.[172] Sipadan and nearby Ligitan are two small islands located near Sabah's northeastern coast, off the land border between the Malaysian state of Sabah and Indonesia's East Kalimantan province. It was understood that there were potential oil and gas reserves in areas around the two islands. The issue of sovereignty over Sipadan and Ligitan emerged in 1969 when Indonesia and Malaysia were negotiating on the delimitation of the continental shelves between the two states.[173] Indonesia and Malaysia had decided to put aside their dispute over the two islands during the negotiations.[174]

Tension arose between Indonesia and Malaysia as a result of the rumour about Sipadan Island.[175] The two states' response to each other, however, had been anchored around their shared war avoidance norms. To avoid escalation of tension, both parties reaffirmed their commitment to preserving peaceful ties between them, in the belief that the counterpart would reciprocate. Indonesia and Malaysia decided to start discussing their sovereignty disputes over Sipadan and Ligitan in GBC (General Border Committee) — the existing mechanism that allowed Indonesia and Malaysia to talk through their territorial disputes.

Tensions over Sipadan and Ligitan re-emerged in June 1991 when Indonesia discovered that Malaysia had been building tourists facilities on Sipadan Island.[176] Malaysia subsequently assured Indonesia that no more development projects would be carried out on the island until the ownership of Sipadan and Ligitan was determined.[177]

---

[172] Liow, *The Politics of Indonesia–Malaysia Relations*, p. 144.
[173] Weatherbee, *International Relations in Southeast Asia*, p. 139.
[174] Liow, *The Politics of Indonesia–Malaysia Relations*, p. 144.
[175] Ibid.
[176] Ibid., pp. 144–45. Also see Renate Haller-Trost, *Boundary and Territory Briefing – The Territorial Dispute Between Indonesia and Malaysia over Pulau Sipadan and Pulau Ligitan in the Celebes Sea: A Study in International Law* (UK: International Boundaries Research Unit, 1995), p. 4.
[177] Ibid.

The two states' respective assertion of sovereignty over Sipadan and Ligitan was firm. Malaysian government officials visited the islands in June 1991 and publicly declared that "for all intents and purposes, they are Malaysian islands".[178] Indonesian air force planes made low passes over Sipadan and Ligitan which usually coincided with senior Malaysian officials' visit to the islands.[179] A flotilla of Indonesian naval warships circled Sipadan from time to time.[180] The Indonesian army had conducted several landings on the island.[181] Malaysia in turn stepped up its military presence in southeastern Sabah.[182]

It appeared that the use of force had become an option for Indonesia and Malaysia to resolve their dispute over Sipadan and Ligitan. Flexing their military muscles, however, illuminated the presence of power balance between them. A basis of order remained firmly established between Indonesia and Malaysia. Each of them did not have the military capacity to prevail over one another, yet each was able to defend itself against the attack of the counterpart. When discussing about the issue of Sipadan and Ligitan, Malaysian Defence Minister Najib Razak maintained: "We are not too worried when the Indonesians sail their ships in the area."[183] Indonesia and Malaysia each was determined to defend their respective sovereignty over the contested Sipadan and Ligitan islands through the show of force, yet both were not ready to resolve their dispute over the islands by using force.

It had become clear that the GBC was unable to defuse the growing tension between Indonesia and Malaysia that arose from their contestation over Sipadan and Ligitan.[184] Malaysia — which occupied Sipadan — refused to accept Indonesia's recommendation that the two states could

---

[178] Liow, *The Politics of Indonesia–Malaysia Relations*, p. 145.

[179] Michael Vatikiotis, "Isle of Contention: Tiny Sipadan Becomes an Object of Rival Claims", *Far Eastern Economic Review* (17 March 1994): 32.

[180] Ibid.

[181] Ibid.

[182] Weatherbee, *International Relations in Southeast Asia*, p. 139.

[183] Vatikiotis, "Isle of Contention", p. 32.

[184] Michael Vatikiotis, "Let's Clear the Air", *Far Eastern Economic Review* (1 August 1991*b*): 10–11. Also see Liow, *The Politics of Indonesia–Malaysia Relations*, p. 145.

jointly develop the islands.[185] Malaysia's refusal in effect had decided on the outcome of the dispute over Sipadan and Ligitan. It would be a zero-sum outcome — either Malaysia or Indonesia would own the two islands. As tension continued to rise, Indonesia and Malaysia nevertheless remained restrained by their tendency to avoid war between them. The two states had decided to set up a joint commission in October 1991 to resolve the Sipadan and Ligitan disputes. More intense talks at the political level about the two islands would be carried out in the joint commission.

A joint commission had already been established between Malaysia and Thailand earlier on. It was created in response to a series of violent incidents involving Malaysia's and Thailand's security forces that had erupted along the common land and maritime border of the two states.[186] These incidents were usually related to the territorial disputes between Malaysia and Thailand.[187] The two states needed the commission to sort out their border disputes that were intertwined with violence.[188] The decision of Indonesia and Malaysia to create their joint commission therefore indicated the deterioration of the ties between them. They needed the commission to prevent an armed conflict between them which seemed increasingly likely.

Still, despite having a joint commission, Indonesia and Malaysia had not been able to call off their combat readiness posture directed at each other in areas around Sipadan and Ligitan. The Indonesian and Malaysian naval fleets continued to routinely carry out their respective patrols around the two islands even though the two states were conducting talks in their joint commission.[189] Malaysia staged a series of military exercises in the vicinity of the two islands.[190] In 1994, the Indonesian

---

[185] Suryadinata, *Indonesia's Foreign Policy Under Suharto*, p. 87. Also see Vatikiotis, "Isle of Contention", p. 32.

[186] Liow, *The Politics of Indonesia–Malaysia Relations*, p. 145. Also see Vatikiotis, "Let's Clear the Air", pp. 10–11; and Acharya, *Constructing a Security Community in Southeast Asia*, p. 199.

[187] Ibid.

[188] Ibid. Also see Jeshurun, *Malaysia*, p. 260.

[189] Liow, *The Politics of Indonesia–Malaysia Relations*, p. 146.

[190] Ibid.

navy launched a large-scale exercise involving 40 naval vessels and 7,000 troops in areas near the two islands.[191]

While each side had been trying to exert pressure on the other through the show of force, both parties remained convinced that they would not go to war over Sipadan and Ligitan. President Suharto in fact had issued an order to his administration to settle the Sipadan and Ligitan disputes through "negotiations between two brothers".[192] Suharto was convinced that Indonesia and Malaysia as special partners — that of two brothers — would want to resolve their differences via peaceful means.

After six consecutive meetings of the joint commission, Indonesia and Malaysia remained unable to agree on a solution for the issue of Sipadan and Ligitan. In September 1994, during their Four-Eyes Meeting, Mahathir suggested to Suharto that Indonesia and Malaysia should refer their disputes over the two islands to the International Court of Justice (ICJ). It was an attempt to put an end to the possibility of a military clash between Indonesia and Malaysia in areas around Sipadan and Ligitan, considering that the disputes over the two islands had not been able to be resolved through the joint commission of the two states.[193] Suharto had rejected Mahathir's proposal. Malaysia, meanwhile, would not accept Indonesia's idea that they could let the ASEAN High Council to rule on the sovereignty of Sipadan and Ligitan.[194] The High Council is a mechanism provided for in the Treaty of Amity and Cooperation of ASEAN. It would be made up of representatives from all the ASEAN member states. There were unresolved territorial disputes between Malaysia and all its other ASEAN partners. Malaysia therefore would think that representatives in the ASEAN High Council were bound to have conflict of interests in the judgment to be made on Sipadan and Ligitan.[195]

---

[191] Saravanamuttu, *Malaysia's Foreign Policy, the First Fifty Years*, p. 280.
[192] Interview 1016, Jakarta, 16 October 2012.
[193] Jeshurun, *Malaysia*, p. 286.
[194] Ibid., p. 269. Also see Suryadinata, *Indonesia's Foreign Policy Under Suharto*, p. 72.
[195] Ibid.

Once again, President Suharto and Prime Minister Mahathir met in October 1996 for their Four-Eyes Meeting. Suharto during the meeting had at last accepted the proposal of resolving the Sipadan and Ligitan disputes once and for all through the ICJ. Both the heads of government agreed that the ICJ's verdict on the two islands would be final and binding.[196]

The joint decision to bring the case of Sipadan and Ligitan to the ICJ reflected the strength of Indonesia–Malaysia war avoidance norms. Despite the growing likelihood that armed clashes might break out between the two states because of their contested claims over the two islands, the commitment to avoid war prevailed in relations between Indonesia and Malaysia. When the disputes over Sipadan and Ligitan began to strain their relationship, Indonesia and Malaysia sought to de-escalate their tension by making use of the GBC to start discussing about the disputes. When GBC proved unable to ease their respective drive to compete for sovereignty over Sipadan and Ligitan through the show of force, the two states created a joint commission, aiming to resolve the disputes via more intense talks. As the commission too was unable to resolve their differences over the two islands, which seemed growingly likely to be the cause of a military clash between them, Indonesia and Malaysia decided to permanently end the conflict by letting the ICJ to decide on the sovereignty of the two islands. Both parties had consistently adhered to their shared war avoidance norms. A possible armed conflict between them had been avoided.

The decision to bring their disputes to the ICJ, meanwhile, was the strategic cooperation of Indonesia and Malaysia. It was the first time in Southeast Asia's history that two states had agreed to peacefully resolve their territorial disputes through the verdict of a third party.[197] Such a

---

[196] Weatherbee, *International Relations in Southeast Asia*, p. 139. Also see Kadir Mohamad, *Malaysia's Territorial Disputes – Two Cases at the ICJ: Batu Puteh, Middle Rocks and South Ledge (Malaysia/Singapore) & Ligitan and Sipadan [and the Sabah Claim] (Malaysia/Indonesia/Philippines)* (Kuala Lumpur: Institute of Diplomacy and Foreign Relations, 2009), pp. 36–37. Also see Liow, *The Politics of Indonesia–Malaysia Relations*, p. 146.

[197] Kadir Mohamad, *Malaysia's Territorial Disputes – Two Cases at the ICJ*, pp. 35, 49.

move strengthened the existing friendly regional climate of ASEAN — the shield that protected the existence of Indonesia and Malaysia. It represented Indonesia's and Malaysia's determination to preserve the friendly climate of their region.[198] It also became a new model of peaceful settlement of disputes for ASEAN as well as the world.[199]

Strong leadership, however, had been a key factor that underpinned Indonesia's and Malaysia's ability to embrace ICJ as a way to resolve their dispute. The New Order regime was essentially an authoritarian regime. The Mahathir administration, on the other hand, had converted Malaysia into a semi-democracy by the late 1980s.[200] Power in Indonesia and Malaysia was centralized in the hands of the head of government.[201] It was effectively the personal decision of Suharto and Mahathir that had resulted in Indonesia and Malaysia willing to refer the Sipadan and Ligitan disputes to the ICJ.[202]

The government of Indonesia and Malaysia were well aware of the consequence of resorting to the ICJ. The verdict of the ICJ would be a zero-sum one. One would win, and the other would lose. Either Indonesia or Malaysia would own the two islands. The two governments had agreed that no one would celebrate for being the winner of the court case.[203] It was to prevent triggering the anger of the losing party.[204] Both would accept the decision of the ICJ in silence.[205]

TERRITORIAL DISPUTES IN THE SULAWESI SEA

The 1997–98 Asian financial crisis had led to the collapse of the New Order Regime in Indonesia. The ruling coalition led by UMNO in Malaysia, however, had survived the crisis and continued to be in power.

---

[198] Ibid. Also see Interview 917, Kuala Lumpur, 17 September 2012.
[199] Ibid.
[200] Dhillon, *Malaysian Foreign Policy in the Mahathir Era 1981–2003*, pp. 40–48.
[201] Ibid. Also see Elson, *Suharto*, pp. 275–77.
[202] Ibid. Also see Interview 1016, Jakarta, 16 October 2012.
[203] Interview 1016, Jakarta, 16 October 2012.
[204] Ibid.
[205] Ibid.

Indonesia began to democratize after the fall of Suharto and had transformed into a liberal democracy. In 1999, Indonesia held its first free and fair parliamentary election since 1955. It was followed by Indonesia's first direct presidential election held in 2004. From 2005 onwards, all the governors, bupatis and mayors in Indonesia had to be directly elected by the people. In 2006, Indonesia was the only Southeast Asian state that had been ranked by Freedom House as a free state.[206] While Freedom House had since 2014 downgraded Indonesia to a partly free state, it was still significantly freer than Malaysia, which — according to Freedom House — was also a partly free state. In 2016, based on the assessment of Freedom House, Indonesia's and Malaysia's aggregate score of freedom was 65 and 45 respectively.[207]

The steady democratization of Indonesia had created a sense of pride among Indonesians that Indonesia was the most advanced democracy in Southeast Asia. The newfound self-esteem further promoted Indonesians' sense of being the big brother of Malaysia — that Malaysia as the little brother was characterized by its shallowness, and should be learning from Indonesia in realizing its political reforms. In fact, it was widely known that the *reformasi* movement in Malaysia launched by Anwar Ibrahim — Malaysia's opposition leader — had been drawing inspiration from the campaign to overthrow Suharto in Indonesia, which was also termed as *reformasi* movement. Such turn of events only solidified Indonesians' belief that Malaysians had been learning from their big brother — Indonesia.

Indonesia's superiority complex in the face of Malaysia was discernible when the editor of the *Indonesian Observer* commented on Ghafar Baba's harsh reply to a hostile Indonesian press corps about the sacking of Anwar Ibrahim as Malaysia's Deputy Prime Minister, and

---

[206] Marcus Mietzner, *Military Politics, Islam, and the State in Indonesia: From Turbulent Transition to Democratic Consolidation* (Singapore: Institute of Southeast Asian Studies, 2009), p. 303.

[207] <https://freedomhouse.org/report/freedom-world/2016/indonesia> (accessed 6 June 2017). Also see <https://freedomhouse.org/report/freedom-world/2016/malaysia> (accessed 6 June 2017).

his subsequent arrest in late 1998.[208] Ghafar Baba — former Malaysia's Deputy Prime Minister — was in Indonesia with a mission given by Prime Minister Mahathir. He was charged to defuse tensions between Indonesia and Malaysia arising from Indonesia's concern over the treatments of Anwar. The editor wrote:[209]

> ...We must therefore have patience with the likes of Mr. Baba who comes from a country which, despite its modern appearance, is actually a feudal society, which received independence on a golden platter. This puts us in a different category from Malaysia because we are Revolutionaries who fought and died to achieve our independence. It is now the beginning of the end for feudalistic establishments which will be swept away by the new wave of reform initiated by Anwar Ibrahim.

From Indonesia's perspective, Indonesia was qualitatively more superior than Malaysia, as evidenced by its supposition that Malaysia's independence was obtained without a bloody fight against colonial rule. Such inferior characters of Malaysia — Indonesia believed — would be eliminated by political reforms similar to those experienced by Indonesia.

Likewise, Indonesia demonstrated its big brother sentiment in response to the powerful *Bersih* movement faced by the UMNO-led Malaysia's government around two decades later. *Bersih* is a movement calling for thorough reforms of Malaysia's electoral system.[210] On 29 August 2015, the movement was able to draw tens of thousands of supporters to its street rallies in Kuala Lumpur. The *Jakarta Post*'s editor had been quick to express an opinion on the rallies:[211]

> This is the perfect time for Malaysians to prepare a new direction for their nation. Like it or not, they have to embrace fully fledged democracy. Malaysia can only adopt a true democracy if its constitution

---

[208] Ann Marie Murphy, "Indonesia and the World", in *Indonesia: The Great Transition*, edited by John Bresnan (U.S.: Rowman & Littlefield Publishers, 2005), p. 263.

[209] Ibid.

[210] "What You Need to Know About Malaysia's *Bersih* Movement", *The Straits Times*, 27 August 2015.

[211] "Time for Najib to Go?: The Jakarta Post", *The Straits Times*, 1 September 2015.

guarantees equal rights and responsibilities for all citizens, regardless of their ethnicity or religion. As long as the nation resists this revolutionary mindset it will remain a segregated nation.

For Indonesia, its perceived inability of Malaysia to become a fully fledged democracy was an evidence of Malaysia's shallowness. Being the little brother of Indonesia — as Indonesia saw it — Malaysia had to learn from Indonesia in transforming itself into a true democracy. In the eyes of Indonesia, Malaysia's democracy would not be authentic if it did not embrace the spirit of egalitarianism, which was a spirit regarded by Indonesians as one of their defining revolutionary qualities.

After experiencing a severe economic downturn brought about by the 1997–98 Asian financial crisis, the economies of Indonesia and Malaysia had begun to bounce back since around 1999 and 2000 (see Table 7.1).

TABLE 7.1
GDP per capita of Indonesia and Malaysia, 1997–2002

Year	Indonesia GDP per capita (constant 2005 US$)	Malaysia GDP per capita (constant 2005 US$)
1997	1,235	4,879
1998	1,057	4,409
1999	1,050	4,569
2000	1,086	4,862
2001	1,110	4,784
2002	1,143	4,941

Source: World Development Indicators.

The ICJ delivered its judgment on the ownership of Sipadan and Ligitan on 17 December 2002. The court had decided that the sovereignty over the two islands belonged to Malaysia based upon the fact that the islands had been controlled and administered by Malaysia.

Losing the ownership of Sipadan and Ligitan was a serious blow to Indonesian national pride.[212] It was especially humiliating for Indonesia to have lost the two islands to its supposed little brother — Malaysia.[213] In the eyes of Indonesia, Malaysia all along had been learning from Indonesia. Meanwhile, Indonesians' sense of weakness which stemmed from the separation of East Timor was reinforced by the loss of Sipadan and Ligitan.[214] East Timor had just separated from Indonesia in 1999. The ICJ's granting of the ownership of Sipadan and Ligitan to Malaysia was at odds with Indonesians' expectation. A senior policy advisor of Malaysia had pointed out, many Indonesians believed that Malaysia had chosen to take away the two islands of Indonesia at a time when Indonesia was weak.[215] Malaysia should not take advantage of a weak Indonesia since they share a special relationship, many Indonesians would think. The anger triggered by the loss of Sipadan and Ligitan had been deepened by this mismatch of expectation. Indonesians, as a result, accused Malaysia of "stealing" Sipadan and Ligitan from Indonesia or maintained that Malaysia "robbed" Indonesia of the two islands.[216] Since then, Indonesians generally shared a perception that Malaysia intended to extend its territory into Indonesian soil.[217]

The Indonesian government was confronted with a nationalist backlash at home after the ICJ had announced its verdict on Sipadan and Ligitan. The Indonesian Parliament — DPR (Dewan Perwakilan Rakyat) — quickly demanded an explanation from Indonesia's

---

[212] Marshall Clark and Juliet Pietsch, *Indonesia–Malaysia Relations: Cultural Heritage, Politics and Labour Migration* (London and New York: Routledge, 2014), p. 35. Also see Ahmad Nizar Yaakub, "Malaysia and Indonesia: A Study of Foreign Policies with Special Reference to Bilateral Relations", PhD dissertation, The University of Western Australia, 2009, p. 147.

[213] Yaakub, "Malaysia and Indonesia", p. 145.

[214] Ibid. Also see Yang Razali Kassim, *ASEAN Cohesion: Making Sense of Indonesian Reactions to Bilateral Disputes* (IDSS Commentaries, 15/2005) (Singapore: Institute of Defence and Strategic Studies, Nanyang Technological University), pp. 2–3. Also see Interview 924-001, Kuala Lumpur, 24 September 2012.

[215] Interview 924-001, Kuala Lumpur, 24 September 2012.

[216] Ibid. Also see Yaakub, "Malaysia and Indonesia", p. 145.

[217] Interview 926-001, Kuala Lumpur, 26 September 2012.

President, Megawati Soekarnoputri, on the loss of the two islands.[218] House Speaker Akbar Tandjung declared: "We are all shocked and disappointed by the results [the decision of the ICJ]."[219] The Indonesian government immediately moved to strengthen Indonesia's presence at the remaining disputed islands situated along its borders.

A few years later, the relationship between Indonesia and Malaysia was once again strained by their territorial disputes. In February 2005, Malaysia granted oil exploration concessions in two deep-water blocks known by Malaysia as ND6 and ND7. The two blocks are close to Sipadan and Ligitan, situated in the region south of the two islands. The possession of the ownership of Sipadan and Ligitan undoubtedly served as a basis for Malaysia to justify its sovereignty over the two deep-water blocks.[220]

ND6 and ND7, however, are part of the maritime area known by Indonesians as Ambalat, which Indonesia claims to be its territory. It is an oil and gas-rich area located in the Sulawesi Sea, off the eastern coast of Kalimantan. Indonesia had earlier on awarded exploration concessions in Ambalat. Essentially, Malaysia's claim over ND6 and ND7 was based on its official territorial sea and continental shelf map published in 1979.[221] Indonesia's claim over Ambalat, on the other hand, was based on the Anglo-Dutch Convention of 1891.[222] The claims of both sides were equally strong.[223]

The Indonesian government immediately lodged a protest against Malaysia's decision to grant exploration concessions in ND6 and ND7.[224]

---

[218] "House Asks Government to Explain 'Loss of Islands' to Public", *The Jakarta Post*, 19 December 2002. Also see "DPR Akan Panggil Presiden Soal Pulau Sipadan-Ligitan", *Tempo*, 24 June 2003.

[219] Ibid.

[220] Kassim, *ASEAN Cohesion*, p. 1

[221] Weatherbee, *International Relations in Southeast Asia*, p. 141. Also see Yaakub, *Malaysia and Indonesia*, p. 147.

[222] Ibid.

[223] "Borneo Maritime Territorial Dispute Tests Indonesian–Malaysian Ties", *WikiLeaks*, 1 June 2009, available at <http://wikileaks.org/cable/2009/06/09JAKARTA929.html> (accessed 9 June 2014).

[224] Clark and Pietsch, *Indonesia–Malaysia Relations*, p. 35. Also see "RI Awaits Shell's Response Over Ambalat", *The Jakarta Post*, 26 March 2005; and Jeshurun, *Malaysia*, p. 343.

It insisted that such a move had violated Indonesia's sovereignty.[225] The Indonesian navy sent three warships to the disputed area — ND6 and ND7 — to assert Indonesia's sovereignty over Ambalat.[226] Four F-16 fighter jets of Indonesia had also been sent to Ambalat a few days later to join the Indonesian warships in patrolling the area.[227] On 8 March 2005, Indonesia's President, Susilo Bambang Yudhoyono, visited Sebatik Island — an Indonesian island near Ambalat. He declared that the purpose of the visit was to inspect the readiness of the Indonesian armed forces in protecting Indonesia's borders with Malaysia.[228] Malaysia in response strengthened its military presence in the areas around ND6 and ND7/Ambalat.[229]

In early April 2005, minor skirmishes broke out between the Indonesian and Malaysian navies in ND6 and ND7/Ambalat. Indonesian warship *KRI Tedung Naga* collided with Malaysian warship *KD Rencong* when *KD Rencong* was trying to disrupt Indonesia's efforts to build a lighthouse on Malaysia's Karang Unarang reef — a reef situated within ND6 and ND7.[230] Since the collision the free media in

---

[225] Ibid.

[226] "Warships Deployed Close to Disputed Territory", *The Jakarta Post*, 2 March 2005.

[227] "F-16s Deployed Ahead of Susilo's Visit to Sebatik", *The Jakarta Post*, 7 March 2005.

[228] Ibid. Also see "Presiden Mambantah Berkonfrontasi Dengan Malaysia", *Liputan 6*, 8 March 2005, available at <http://news.liputan6.com/read/97134/presiden-membantah-berkonfrontasi-dengan-malaysia> (accessed 8 June 2014); and "Presiden Bertolak Ke Blok Ambalat Kaltim", *Indosiar*, 8 March 2005, available at <http://www.indosiar.com/fokus/presiden-bertolak-ke-blok-ambalat-kaltim_30180.html> (accessed 8 June 2014).

[229] Yaakub, "Malaysia and Indonesia", p. 149. Also see Weatherbee, *International Relations in Southeast Asia*, p. 141; and Jeshurun, *Malaysia*, p. 343.

[230] "RI, Malaysia Navies Make Peace Following Ambalat Incident", *The Jakarta Post*, 16 April 2005. Also see "RI, KL Warships Collide in Ambalat", *The Jakarta Post*, 10 April 2005; "Close Encounters of the Worrying Kind in Sulawesi Sea", *Singapore Institute of International Affairs* (12 April 2005), available at <http://www.siiaonline.org/page/insightsDetails/id/2833/ArticleCategoryId/KeepSessionAlive.aspx#.U5a8x8x--70> (accessed 9 June 2014); "Pembinaan Di Laut Sulawesi Jejaskan Rundingan 22 Mac", *Utusan Malaysia*, 12 March 2005; and Weatherbee, *International Relations in Southeast Asia*, p. 142.

Indonesia reported extensively on the Ambalat dispute.[231] Very quickly, Ambalat became an issue of nationalism for Indonesians which was suffused with their anger.[232] Street protests against Malaysia's claim on ND6 and ND7/Ambalat erupted in many Indonesian cities which involved the burnings of Malaysian flags.[233] Such protests had also been staged outside the Malaysian Embassy in Jakarta.[234] The Indonesian media termed the Ambalat dispute as "Kofrontasi 2.0".[235] Some Indonesians had initiated a movement titled "Front Ganyang Malaysia" — Crush Malaysia Front — to recruit volunteers across Indonesia, aiming to launch the Confrontation 2.0 against Malaysia.[236]

The situation in Malaysia by contrast had been calm owing to the restrain observed by the Malaysian media.[237] The government-controlled Malaysian media were following the official order that they should not provoke further tension between Indonesia and Malaysia.[238]

It appeared that Indonesia had become ever more nationalistic and assertive in the face of territorial disputes with Malaysia.[239] Such responses were attributable to a combination of factors.

After the fall of Suharto, Indonesia was facing serious challenges in maintaining its territorial integrity. It had lost East Timor and was

---

[231] Yaakub, "Malaysia and Indonesia", p. 148. Also see Kassim, *ASEAN Cohesion*, pp. 1–2; and Khalid and Yacob, "Managing Malaysia–Indonesia Relations in the Context of Democratization", pp. 369–71.

[232] Ibid.

[233] Ibid.

[234] Jeshurun, *Malaysia*, p. 343.

[235] Kassim, *ASEAN Cohesion*, p. 2.

[236] Yaakub, "Malaysia and Indonesia", p. 148. Also see Khalid and Yacob, "Managing Malaysia–Indonesia Relations in the Context of Democratization", p. 371; and "Makassar Bentuk Front Ganyang Malaysia", *Tempo*, 5 March 2005.

[237] Yaakub, "Malaysia and Indonesia", pp. 148–49. Also see Khalid and Yacob, "Managing Malaysia–Indonesia Relations in the Context of Democratization", pp. 358, 372–73; and "Malaysians Downplay Maritime Tensions with Indonesia", *Cable Gate Search*, 15 June 2009, available at <http://www.cablegatesearch.net/cable.php?id=09KUALALUMPUR483&q=kuala%20lumpur> (accessed 9 June 2014).

[238] Ibid.

[239] "Malaysians Downplay Maritime Tensions with Indonesia", *Cable Gate Search*, 15 June 2009, available at <http://www.cablegatesearch.net/cable.php?id=09KUALALUMPUR483&q=kuala%20lumpur> (accessed 9 June 2014).

plagued by the independent movements in West Papua and Aceh. In the meantime, Indonesia had failed to defend its claim over Sipadan and Ligitan in the ICJ. Indonesians had become highly sensitive to the issue of territorial integrity of Indonesia.[240] They were afraid of losing more territories.[241] As a result, Indonesia was adamant that it would not lose its supposed territory — ND6 and ND7/Ambalat — this time around.[242] Such resolve was reinforced by Indonesians' shared perception that Malaysia intended to expand into their soil.

Most importantly, Indonesia wanted to secure its access to the untapped oil and gas resources in ND6 and ND7/Ambalat.[243] Petroleum was vital for financing Indonesia's development. Indonesia's oil and gas production had been in consistent decline. By 2008, Indonesia was no longer qualified to be a member of the Organization of the Petroleum Exporting Countries (OPEC).

Ambalat, in the meantime, was an issue of national pride for Indonesia.[244] In the eyes of Indonesians, the issue of Ambalat was inextricably intertwined with their loss of Sipadan and Ligitan.[245] It was humiliating to have lost the two islands to Indonesia's little brother — Malaysia. Indonesia as Malaysia's big brother — Indonesians maintained — had provided all the assistance that Malaysia needed for its nation building, and Malaysia in return had taken away Sipadan and Ligitan that belonged to Indonesia.[246] The humiliations which stemmed from the loss of Sipadan and Ligitan fortified Indonesia's determination to defend its

---

[240] Yaakub, "Malaysia and Indonesia", p. 146. Also see Kassim, *ASEAN Cohesion*, p. 3; and Rizal Sukma, "Domestic Politics and International Posture: Constraints and Possibilities", in *Indonesia Rising: The Repositioning of Asia's Third Giant*, edited by Anthony Reid (Singapore: Institute of Southeast Asian Studies, 2012), p. 88.

[241] Ibid.

[242] Ibid.

[243] "Indonesia to Fight Malaysia's Ambalat Oil Claims", *Jakarta Globe*, 22 October 2009.

[244] Interview 1008, Jakarta, 8 October 2012. Also see Interview 920, Kuala Lumpur, 20 September 2012.

[245] Interview 1011, Jakarta, 11 October 2012. Also see Clark and Pietsch, *Indonesia–Malaysia Relations*, p. 35; and "Indonesian Political Tensions Surge in Border Disputes with Malaysia", *WikiLeaks*, 8 June 2009, available at <http://wikileaks.org/cable/2009/06/09JAKARTA974.html> (accessed 9 June 2014).

[246] Interview 926-001, Kuala Lumpur, 26 September 2012. Also see Interview 1011, Jakarta, 11 October 2012.

alleged sovereignty over ND6 and ND7/Ambalat. Indonesians asserted that Malaysia had seized Sipadan and Ligitan from Indonesia, it would not again lose Ambalat to Malaysia.[247]

The nature of Indonesia's domestic politics led to a further intensification of nationalist sentiments in Indonesia over the issue of Ambalat. Politicians in the new democracy of Indonesia constantly sought to establish their nationalist credentials by stirring up nationalist sentiments in order to win popular support at home.[248] Indonesian politicians therefore saw the need to foment the Indonesian public's nationalist feelings towards the Ambalat dispute, aiming to translate such emotions into their respective domestic support.[249]

Meanwhile, the free media in Indonesia had been liberally expressing strong nationalist sentiments through their reporting, which included the reporting of the Ambalat dispute.[250] The press freedom in Indonesia — which came into being after the fall of Suharto — had engendered the emergence of a highly competitive media industry in Indonesia. The Indonesian media in consequence embraced the nationalistic style of reporting, aiming to stimulate the demand for their papers or programmes.[251] The nationalist feelings of the Indonesian public therefore had always been evoked and intensified by the reporting of the local media.

The Indonesian military also made use of nationalism to promote its own interests. In the midst of the talks between the DPR and Indonesia's government on the budget for possible military operations in ND6 and ND7/Ambalat, Indonesia's Defense Minister intentionally

---

[247] Interview 1011, Jakarta, 11 October 2012.

[248] Interview 924-001, Kuala Lumpur, 24 September 2012. Also see Interview 1008, Jakarta, 8 October 2012; "Indonesian Political Tensions Surge in Border Disputes with Malaysia", *WikiLeaks*, 8 June 2009, available at <http://wikileaks.org/cable/2009/06/09JAKARTA974.html> (accessed 9 June 2014); and "Borneo Maritime Territorial Dispute Tests Indonesian–Malaysian Ties", *WikiLeaks*, 1 June 2009, available at <http://wikileaks.org/cable/2009/06/09JAKARTA929.html> (accessed 9 June 2014).

[249] Ibid.

[250] Khalid and Yacob, "Managing Malaysia–Indonesia Relations in the Context of Democratization", pp. 369–71. Also see Kassim, *ASEAN Cohesion*, pp. 1–2; and Yaakub, "Malaysia and Indonesia", p. 148.

[251] Ibid.

revealed the proposed amount of the budget to the media, understandably trying to create public pressure on the DPR to ensure that it would ratify the proposed budget.[252] Indonesian legislators had criticized the Defence Minister for making such a move, arguing that the talks were meant to be confidential.[253]

On the other hand, the Indonesian military had been trying to instigate Indonesians' nationalist emotions through the media. It had reported to the local media about the "aggressiveness" of the Malaysian navy, claiming that Malaysia's warships had frequently intruded into Indonesian waters in Ambalat, and Indonesia's navy was moments away from firing on a Malaysian warship which had encroached deep into Ambalat.[254] The revelation triggered Indonesians' anger against Malaysia.[255] Malaysia was surprised by the Indonesian military's tendency to escalate their navies' routine encounters in ND6 and ND7/Ambalat into a crisis in Indonesia.[256] It was an exaggeration that Indonesia's navy was on the brink of firing at a Malaysian warship.[257] The two navies had been adhering to their agreed upon standard operating procedures during their encounters in the disputed Ambalat waters.[258] It was understood that Indonesia's military had been trying to foment Indonesians' patriotic sentiments as it needed popular support

---

[252] "Legislators Criticize Juwono Over Ambalat Disclosure", *The Jakarta Post*, 20 March 2005. Also see Patrick Ziegenhain, *The Indonesian Parliament and Democratization* (Singapore: Institute of Southeast Asian Studies, 2008), p. 182; and Mietzner, *Military Politics, Islam, and the State in Indonesia*, p. 318.

[253] Ibid.

[254] "Ambalat Waters Row Must Be Resolved", *Jakarta Globe*, 31 May 2009. Also see "Malaysia Enters Ambalat Again", *Jakarta Globe*, 4 June 2009.

[255] "Malaysians Downplay Maritime Tensions with Indonesia", *Cable Gate Search*, 15 June 2009, available at <http://www.cablegatesearch.net/cable.php?id= 09KUALALUMPUR483&q=kuala%20lumpur> (accessed 9 June 2014).

[256] Ibid. Also see "Borneo Maritime Territorial Dispute Tests Indonesian–Malaysian Ties", *WikiLeaks*, 1 June 2009, available at <http://wikileaks.org/cable/2009/06/ 09JAKARTA929.html> (accessed 9 June 2014).

[257] "Borneo Maritime Territorial Dispute Tests Indonesian–Malaysian Ties", *WikiLeaks*, 1 June 2009, available at <http://wikileaks.org/cable/2009/06/09JAKARTA929.html> (accessed 9 June 2014).

[258] Ibid.

for the increase in Indonesia's defence budget.[259] The increase was needed for the modernization of Indonesian armed forces. Since 2004, the Indonesian military had been lobbying for a substantial increase in Indonesia's defence budget.[260]

In a nutshell, the democratization of Indonesia gave rise to strong nationalism in its society, which in turn intensified Indonesians' nationalist emotions towards the issue of Ambalat. The Indonesian government in consequence had to be nationalistic if it was to secure its popular support at home.

Indonesia's resolve to defend its supposed sovereignty over ND6 and ND7/Ambalat was further toughened by its resentments towards Malaysia, which stemmed from its loss of Sipadan and Ligitan. Indonesia's officials had revealed to their Malaysian counterparts about why Indonesians were emotional about Ambalat. It was because Indonesians were bound by a sentiment: they would not forgive Malaysia for taking away Sipadan and Ligitan.[261] This sentiment was an outcome of the mismatch of expectation. Indonesia and Malaysia shared a special relationship. Malaysia — as Indonesians saw it — hence should not choose to take possession of Sipadan and Ligitan when Indonesia was weak.

The exploration activities in ND6 and ND7/Ambalat had to be suspended as both Indonesia and Malaysia were regularly flexing their respective military muscles in the disputed waters.[262] It was clear that Indonesia's and Malaysia's sovereignty disputes over ND6 and ND7/Ambalat were more intense than their territorial disputes in the past. Nonetheless, the war avoidance norms shared by the two states remained strong enough to prevent them from plunging into an armed conflict between them. Shortly after the surface of the Ambalat dispute, Indonesia and Malaysia reaffirmed their commitment to preserving their friendly coexistence by creating a joint technical committee and

---

[259] Interview 920, Kuala Lumpur, 20 September 2012. Also see Mietzner, *Military Politics, Islam, and the State in Indonesia*, p. 312.

[260] Mietzner, *Military Politics, Islam, and the State in Indonesia*, p. 312.

[261] Interview 926-001, Kuala Lumpur, 26 September 2012.

[262] Weatherbee, *International Relations in Southeast Asia*, p. 141. Also see "Petronas Urges Governments to Solve Ambalat Issue", *Bernama*, 8 June 2009; and "Indonesia To Fight Malaysia's Ambalat Oil Claims", *Jakarta Globe*, 22 October 2009.

begin to negotiate for a solution to the disputes.[263] Both parties had reassured each other that the Ambalat dispute would be resolved through discussions.[264]

When minor skirmishes broke out between Indonesian and Malaysian warships in ND6 and ND7/Ambalat in early April 2005, top political and military leaders of the two states intervened immediately to put an end to the skirmishes.[265] President Yudhoyono expressed Indonesia's aspiration for peace with Malaysia, asserting that such clashes should not happen again in the future.[266] The two states had pledged better communications to prevent a clash in ND6 and ND7/Ambalat between their armed forces from happening again.[267] The two armed forces subsequently established their standard operating procedures, designed to prevent any physical clashes between them during their encounters in the disputed area of Ambalat.[268] Once again — like the disputes of Sipadan and Ligitan — Indonesia and Malaysia each was determined to defend their overlapping claims over a maritime zone in the Sulawesi Sea through the show of force, yet they were not ready to take possession of the territory by using force.

However, Indonesia's utter rejection to refer the Ambalat dispute to the ICJ reflected its intense resolve in defending its claim over the disputed waters. Malaysia had proposed to let the ICJ to decide on the sovereignty of ND6 and ND7/Ambalat. Indonesia was perfectly clear:

---

[263] "Malaysia and Indonesia Agree to Continue Talks", *The Star*, 7 May 2005. Also see "No Talks on Ambalat Block At Malindo Meeting", *The Star*, 11 December 2008; "KL and Jakarta Will Do More To Fight Transborder Crime", *Asiaone*, 12 December 2008, available at <http://news.asiaone.com/News/AsiaOne+News/Malaysia/Story/A1Story20081212-107220.html> (accessed 13 June 2014); and "Ambalat Issue: 'No Official Protest From Indonesia'", *The Star*, 15 June 2009.

[264] "DPM: Don't Retaliate Against Anti-Malaysia Protests", *The Star*, 10 May 2005.

[265] "RI, KL Warships Collide in Ambalat", *The Jakarta Post*, 10 April 2005. Also see "RI, Malaysia Navies Make Peace Following Ambalat Incident", *The Jakarta Post*, 16 April 2005.

[266] Ibid.

[267] Ibid.

[268] Interview 924-001, Kuala Lumpur, 24 September 2012.

it would never bring the disputes to the ICJ or any other third-party arbitration.[269]

Such vigorous resolve boosted Indonesians' sense of superiority over Malaysia. The Chief of Malaysian Armed Forces, Abdul Aziz Zainal, visited Jakarta in June 2009. It was at a time when extensive reporting had been given by the Indonesian media about an allegation that Indonesia's navy was moments away from firing on a Malaysian warship that had intruded deep into Ambalat.[270] The Indonesian media perceived Zainal's visit as a Malaysian representative rushing to Jakarta to deal with the reported crisis.[271] Indonesians deemed that Malaysia was trying to pay deference to its big brother — Indonesia — in an effort to resolve the recent crisis between them in Ambalat. In fact, Zainal's visit to Jakarta had already been scheduled long before the date of the reported crisis.[272] He was scheduled to be there to attend a conference.[273] Zainal, however, did meet with his Indonesian counterpart during the visit to discuss about the Ambalat issue.[274]

It should be noted that the observations on the Indonesian media's perception of Malaysia and its way of reporting with regard to the alleged crisis that had erupted in Ambalat were made by the American diplomats based in Jakarta and Kuala Lumpur. The diplomats put on

---

[269] Interview 1011, Jakarta, 11 October 2012. Also see Interview 926-001, Kuala Lumpur, 26 September 2012; and Weatherbee, *International Relations in Southeast Asia*, p. 142.

[270] "Borneo Maritime Territorial Dispute Tests Indonesian–Malaysian Ties", *WikiLeaks*, 1 June 2009, available at <http://wikileaks.org/cable/2009/06/09JAKARTA929. html> (accessed 9 June 2014). Also see "Malaysians Downplay Maritime Tensions with Indonesia", *Cable Gate Search*, 15 June 2009, available at <http://www. cablegatesearch.net/cable.php?id=09KUALALUMPUR483&q=kuala%20lumpur> (accessed 9 June 2014).

[271] "Malaysians Downplay Maritime Tensions with Indonesia", *Cable Gate Search*, 15 June 2009, available at <http://www.cablegatesearch.net/cable. php?id=09KUALALUMPUR483&q=kuala%20lumpur> (accessed 9 June 2014).

[272] Ibid.

[273] Ibid.

[274] Ibid. Also see "KL Confident Over Ambalat", *The Star*, 10 June 2009. Also see "Ambalat Dispute and Manohara Saga Not Related, Indonesian Media Told", *The Star*, 13 June 2009.

record the observations in classified cables that had been sent to the U.S. State Department. WikiLeaks had recently disclosed the cables. As can be observed from the cables, apart from their own understandings — which were a third party's perspective — the American diplomats' confidential communications with the policymakers of Southeast Asian states formed a critical basis of their observations on the Indonesian media. Hence, the observations of the American diplomats perhaps provide an accurate insight into how the Indonesian media viewed Malaysia with regard to the Ambalat dispute.

Indonesia and Malaysia remained unable to work out a solution for their sovereignty disputes over ND6 and ND7/Ambalat. Both sides' dealings with the disputes, nevertheless, were effectively restrained by their shared war avoidance norms. Intense and regular negotiations had been going on between the two states, aiming to resolve the disputes.[275] Both sides were of the view that armed conflict between them over ND6 and ND7/Ambalat would not occur.[276] They recognized that peace prevailed in their relationship.[277] Both shared an understanding that their talks over the Ambalat dispute could go on indefinitely, until they had reached an agreement.[278] "We have achieved a level of sophistication in solving our disputes peacefully", said one former top level Malaysian diplomat.[279]

In other words, Indonesia and Malaysia shared reasonable expectations of peaceful change. Each was convinced that the counterpart will not use force to settle their disputes, yet no one was certain about it. Indonesia's and Malaysia's navies continued to conduct their respective

---

[275] Interview 1008, Jakarta, 8 October 2012.

[276] Ibid. Also see Interview 1011, Jakarta, 11 October 2012. Also see Interview 920, Kuala Lumpur, 20 September 2012; and Interview 924-001, Kuala Lumpur, 24 September 2012.

[277] Interview 920, Kuala Lumpur, 20 September 2012. Also see Interview 1011, Jakarta, 11 October 2012.

[278] Interview 1008, Jakarta, 8 October 2012. Also see Interview 920, Kuala Lumpur, 20 September 2012.

[279] Interview 920, Kuala Lumpur, 20 September 2012.

patrols in the disputed waters in Ambalat.[280] War between the two states was unlikely, not unthinkable.

MIGRANT WORKERS

The sustained expansion of Malaysia's economy and its rapid industrialization since the early 1980s resulted in the dramatic increase of Indonesian labour migration to Malaysia.[281] Malaysia's absorption of Indonesian workers was an outcome of the mutual dependence between the two states. As most of the Malaysian workers had moved to industrial sectors amidst Malaysia's industrialization, Malaysia needed to import foreign workers especially Indonesian workers to address the problem of labour shortage in its plantation sectors.[282] Given the proximity of Indonesia to Malaysia and the Malay way of life shared by the two states, it had been most cost effective to recruit Indonesian workers when compared to foreign workers of other nationalities.[283] It was very easy for Malaysia's employers to communicate with Indonesian workers.[284] Crucially, Indonesian workers could easily be converted into Malays in Malaysia hence ensured the Malays' supreme electoral power vis-à-vis the non-Malays in Malaysia.[285]

Indonesia, on the other hand, due to its huge population and chronic poverty, had always wanted to export its workforce, aiming to reduce the unemployment rate at home and promote its economic growth through the inflow of remittances.[286] Malaysia became the most appropriate place for Indonesian migrant workers to seek for employment

---

[280] Weatherbee, *International Relations in Southeast Asia*, p. 142. Also see "Zahid's Trip to Ease Ambalat Tension", *The Star*, 1 July 2009.

[281] Alexander R. Arifianto, "The Securitization of Transnational Labor Migration: The Case of Malaysia and Indonesia", *Asian Politics & Policy* 1, no. 4 (2009): 619. Also see Joseph Chinyong Liow, "Malaysia's Illegal Indonesian Migrant Labour Problem: In Search of Solutions", *Contemporary Southeast Asia* 25, no. 1 (April 2003): 47.

[282] Ibid. Yaakub, "Malaysia and Indonesia", pp. 152–53.

[283] Arifianto, "The Securitization of Transnational Labor Migration", pp. 617–19. Also see Liow, "Malaysia's Illegal Indonesian Migrant Labour Problem", p. 47; and Interview 926-001, Kuala Lumpur, 26 September 2012.

[284] Ibid.

[285] Liow, "Malaysia's Illegal Indonesian Migrant Labour Problem", pp. 46–47.

[286] Arifianto, "The Securitization of Transnational Labor Migration", p. 619.

as it was evidently wealthier than Indonesia and also because of geographical proximity and their cultural commonalities.[287] Specifically, Indonesian labour working in Malaysia was an economic cooperation between the two states. It mainly served the respective economic interests of Indonesia and Malaysia.

Because of Malaysia's high economic growth, the number of Indonesian migrant workers in Malaysia had continued to rise in the 1990s. Indonesian labour by the 1990s had also entered into the construction and domestic service sectors in Malaysia. Overtime, the construction and plantation sectors in Malaysia had become heavily dependent on workers from Indonesia.[288] By the late 1990s, Indonesian workers accounted for 63.9 per cent of the total number of documented migrant workers in Malaysia.[289] By 1997, Malaysia became the main destination for Indonesian migrant workers which accounted for 63.2 per cent of the total Indonesian workers working overseas.[290]

The majority of Indonesian workers, however, chose to migrate to Malaysia through illegal channels.[291] By 1997, there were around 1.9 million Indonesian migrants working in Malaysia.[292] More than half of them were illegal.[293] The sheer size of illegal Indonesian workers in Malaysia had created a series of challenges for Malaysia. One of them was the presence of illegal Acehnese migrants in Malaysia.

Facilitated by porous maritime borders and weak law enforcement, the rebels of the Acehnese independent movement and Acehnese refugees had been able to flee to the peninsula of Malaysia illegally

---

[287] Ibid., p. 617. Also see Liow, "Malaysia's Illegal Indonesian Migrant Labour Problem", p. 47.

[288] Liow, "Malaysia's Illegal Indonesian Migrant Labour Problem", p. 52. Also see Interview 926-001, Kuala Lumpur, 26 September 2012.

[289] P. Ramasamy, "International Migration and Conflict: Foreign Labour in Malaysia", in *International Migration in Southeast Asia*, edited by Aris Ananta and Evi Nurvidya Arifin (Singapore: Institute of Southeast Asian Studies, 2004), p. 275.

[290] Sukamdi, Elan Satriawan and Abdul Haris, "Impact of Remittances on the Indonesian Economy", in *International Migration in Southeast Asia*, pp. 144–45.

[291] Arifianto, "The Securitization of Transnational Labor Migration", p. 619.

[292] Ibid.

[293] Ibid.

throughout the unrest that broke out in Aceh since 1989.[294] Malaysia had become a place of asylum and hideout for Acehnese.[295] Malaysia's government did not provide political asylum for the rebels from Aceh and had upheld its policy of non-involvement in Indonesia's domestic affairs. Indonesian authorities did not suggest that Malaysia's government was involved in the separatist movement in Aceh. Nonetheless, Acehnese rebels — as illegal migrants — had been able to operate in Malaysia and occasionally conduct underground military trainings in Malaysia.[296] The ties between Indonesia and Malaysia in consequence were sometimes strained by the presence of Acehnese rebels and refugees in Malaysia.[297] With the signing of a peace accord between Indonesia's government and the GAM (Aceh Independence Movement) in August 2005, Aceh unrest was no more an issue between Indonesia and Malaysia.[298]

The huge inflow of illegal Indonesian migrants to Malaysia had also contributed to the increase of crime rates in Malaysia.[299] It was found that undocumented Indonesian migrants were often engaged in serious criminal activities — rape, robberies and murders — in Malaysia.[300] In 1987, around 36 per cent of prison inmates in Malaysia were Indonesian illegals.[301] Meanwhile, between 1985 and 1991 — as indicated in the unpublished records of Malaysia's police — illegal foreign workers were responsible for between 14.7 per cent and

---

[294] Liow, *The Politics of Indonesia–Malaysia Relations*, pp. 150–51, 212. Also see Yaakub, "Malaysia and Indonesia", pp. 154–55; Saravanamuttu, *Malaysia's Foreign Policy, the First Fifty Years*, p. 280; and "Indonesia Keeps Troops in Rioting Province", *The New York Times*, 3 September 1998.

[295] Ibid. Also see Michael R.J. Vatikiotis, "Aceh Unrest Leads to Mounting Death Toll: Troubled Province", *Far Eastern Economic Review* (24 January 1991*a*): 20.

[296] Vatikiotis, "Aceh Unrest Leads to Mounting Death Toll", p. 20. Also see Liow, *The Politics of Indonesia–Malaysia Relations*, pp. 150–51.

[297] Saravanamuttu, *Malaysia's Foreign Policy, the First Fifty Years*, p. 280. Also see Liow, *The Politics of Indonesia–Malaysia Relations*, pp. 150–51.

[298] Mietzner, *Military Politics, Islam, and the State in Indonesia*, p. 300. Also see Saravanamuttu, *Malaysia's Foreign Policy, the First Fifty Years*, p. 280.

[299] Liow, "Malaysia's Illegal Indonesian Migrant Labour Problem", pp. 48–49.

[300] Ibid.

[301] Liow, *The Politics of Indonesia–Malaysia Relations*, p. 148.

18.2 per cent of all murders committed in Malaysia, and between 32.7 per cent and 48.2 per cent of all robberies occurred in Malaysia.[302] This pattern of criminal activities persisted well into the mid-1990s.[303]

Despite the challenges brought about by the presence of illegal Indonesian workers, Malaysia's handling of Indonesian illegals was largely shaped by an understanding of cooperation between two brothers. It perceived the large influx of Indonesians to Malaysia as cousins coming from the archipelago.[304] Legalizing the status of the undocumented Indonesian migrants had been the main approach of Malaysia's government in regulating illegal immigration from Indonesia.[305] From 1992 to 1995, around 147,000 illegal Indonesian migrants had been deported from Malaysia.[306] Yet, around 403,500 Indonesian illegals had obtained their legal status from Malaysia's government during the same period, which was more than double the number of those who had been deported.[307] The comment made by the Indonesian Army Daily in September 1994 reflected the cooperative sentiments that existed between Indonesia and Malaysia with regard to Indonesian migrant workers: "Perhaps in Malaysia there are still a lot of illegal immigrants. If this is true, it will be very good should these people be recruited and are given the legal status. If more is needed, then Malaysia could recruit directly from Indonesia."[308]

Confronted with economic recession following the 1997–98 Asian financial crisis, Malaysia began to take a tougher action in reducing the number of illegal migrants, aiming to mitigate the pressure of local

---

[302] Azizah Kassim, "Illegal Alien Labour in Malaysia: Its Influx, Utilization, and Ramifications", *Indonesia and the Malay World* 25, no. 71 (1997): 73.

[303] Ibid.

[304] Liow, *The Politics of Indonesia–Malaysia Relations*, p. 149.

[305] Arifianto, "The Securitization of Transnational Labor Migration", pp. 619–20, 623.

[306] Ibid.

[307] Ibid.

[308] "Tajuk Rencana", *Angkatan Bersenjata*, 19 September 1994, quoted in Suryadinata, *Indonesia's Foreign Policy Under Suharto*, p. 72.

unemployment in Malaysia.[309] Indonesian illegals in Malaysia would no longer be legalized; they would have to leave Malaysia immediately.[310] Large-scale deportations of illegal migrants — mainly Indonesian workers — were regularly conducted by Malaysia's authorities since 1998.[311]

The deportation campaign was also encouraged by the Malay communities' call for the repatriation of Indonesian illegals in Malaysia.[312] Since the mid-1990s, the Malays in Malaysia had begun to realize that Indonesian migrants were basically different from them.[313] It was difficult to assimilate these migrants into Malay society.[314] Indonesian migrants had established their own communities throughout Malaysia which were separated from the local Malays. The Malays in Malaysia as a result began to view Indonesian migrants as undoubtedly Indonesians.[315] They thought that Indonesian illegals had to be repatriated to prevent Indonesian migrants — a huge presence in Malaysia — from becoming a threat to the Malays' existence in Malaysia.[316] The Malaysian government had to deport illegal Indonesian migrants to address the concern of the Malay communities.[317] In the meantime, Indonesian illegals continued to undertake serious criminal activities in Malaysia.[318] Most disturbing was that weapons had been discovered by Malaysia's authorities in illegal immigrant squatters throughout Malaysia.[319]

---

[309] Arifianto, "The Securitization of Transnational Labor Migration", p. 620. Also see Yaakub, "Malaysia and Indonesia", p. 157; Patrick Pillai, "The Malaysian State's Response to Migration", *Sojourn* 14, no. 1 (1999): 187; and Liow, "Malaysia's Illegal Indonesian Migrant Labour Problem", p. 52.

[310] Arifianto, "The Securitization of Transnational Labor Migration", pp. 619–20, 623.

[311] Ibid. Also see Liow, "Malaysia's Illegal Indonesian Migrant Labour Problem", pp. 50–51. Also see Khalid and Yacob, "Managing Malaysia–Indonesia Relations in the Context of Democratization", p. 366.

[312] Azizah Kassim, "Illegal Alien Labour in Malaysia", pp. 74–75.

[313] Ibid. Also see Arifianto, "The Securitization of Transnational Labor Migration", p. 622.

[314] Ibid.

[315] Ibid.

[316] Ibid.

[317] Ibid.

[318] Liow, "Malaysia's Illegal Indonesian Migrant Labour Problem", p. 49.

[319] Ibid.

The combination of three factors — the need to reduce the local unemployment in Malaysia; the resolve to ensure Malaysia's existence as a Malay nation-state; and the need to curb the serious crimes committed by Indonesian illegals — resulted in Malaysia's decision to amend its Immigration Act, aiming to eradicate the presence of illegal migrants in Malaysia. In March 2001, Malaysia's government began its move to amend the existing Immigration Act in Malaysia. The Act's amendments involved the incorporation of harsh punishments against illegal migrants which included large fines, a mandatory jail term, and caning.

Successive large-scale riots launched by Indonesian workers in different parts of Malaysia between October 2001 and January 2002 only hardened Malaysia's determination to expulse illegal migrants from Malaysia.[320] Malaysia embarked on a large-scale deportation of illegals — in which most of them were Indonesians — in response to the riots.[321] It temporarily halted the recruitment of Indonesian workers and announced a "Hire Indonesians Last" policy. From August 2002 onwards, Malaysia began to enforce its newly amended Immigration Act. During the four months of amnesty provided for illegals before the enforcement of the Act, around 400,000 Indonesian migrant workers had left Malaysia.[322] The enforcement of the new Immigration Act marked the end of an era where the issue of Indonesian migrant workers was predominantly characterized by the cooperation between Indonesia and Malaysia.

Malaysia's resolve to expulse Indonesian illegals from Malaysia boosted, and was boosted by, its sense of superiority over Indonesia. The mutually reinforcing dynamics were manifested through the mass repatriation of illegal migrants carried out by Malaysia's authorities.

A few decades of interactions with Indonesian migrant workers — who were mainly plantation and construction workers or household maids — had further consolidated Malaysians' sense of being sophisticated

---

[320] Ibid., pp. 49–52.

[321] Ibid.

[322] Ibid. Also see Arifianto, "The Securitization of Transnational Labor Migration", pp. 620–21.

vis-à-vis Indonesia. Because of the superior–subordinate relationship between Malaysians and Indonesian migrants, coupled with the fact that Indonesian migrants were working in sectors that were dirty, dangerous and demeaning, Malaysians — especially the Malays — had over time begun to refer to Indonesians as *Indon*.[323] *Indon* was a derogatory term.[324] It carried the hidden meaning that Indonesians were inferior when compared to the Malays, who were economically more superior.[325]

On 24 August 2007, at around 2 a.m., an Indonesian karate coach was confronted by four plain clothes Malaysian policemen near the hostel of Universiti Sains Islam Malaysia in Nilai, Malaysia. The policemen were in an operation hunting for illegal migrants.[326] Meanwhile, Donald Peter Luther Kolopitha — the Indonesian karate coach — together with his Indonesian team were in Malaysia to participate in the Eighth Asian Karate Championship held in Nilai.

The four Malaysian policemen had decided to arrest Kolopitha. The arrest was made notwithstanding the fact that Kolopitha as a professional karate coach was in Malaysia with an official duty. He had been appointed as a referee in the international karate contest held in Nilai, representing the Indonesian team. Having involved in the operation to arrest illegals seemed to have cemented the likely perception of the policemen that Kolopitha as an Indonesian was indeed an *Indon*. Presumably driven by such a sense of superiority in the face of a supposed *Indon*, the policemen had been steadfast in deciding to detain Kolopitha even though he was not an illegal, but a legal visitor to Malaysia. As if to confirm their perceived superiority over Indonesians, the four Malaysian policemen used excessive force on Kolopitha when he resisted their attempt to arrest him and continued to beat him even after he was handcuffed.[327] Kolopitha suffered

---

[323] Khalid and Yacob, "Managing Malaysia–Indonesia Relations in the Context of Democratization", p. 367. Also see Arifianto, "The Securitization of Transnational Labor Migration", p. 629.

[324] Ibid.

[325] Ibid.

[326] "Love, Hate Thy Neighbour", *My Sinchew*, 19 September 2007, available at <http://www.mysinchew.com/node/829> (accessed 18 June 2017).

[327] "Six Months' Jail For Cops", *The Star*, 22 October 2010.

serious injuries as a consequence. He had to be admitted to a hospital later on.

Indonesians protested strongly against the assault with the Indonesian team deciding to withdraw from the karate championship followed by successive demonstrations against Malaysia in several cities of Indonesia. A lecturer from the University of Indonesia expressed his view on the assault on Kolopitha: "Malays in Malaysia always think of Javanese [Indonesians] as ethnically inferior compared to them..."[328]

Malaysian Prime Minister, Abdullah Ahmad Badawi, had to apologize to the President of Indonesia, Susilo Bambang Yudhoyono, as a consequence of the obvious misconduct of the four Malaysian policemen. Three years later, the four policemen were each sentenced to six months in prison for assaulting Kolopitha.

Meanwhile, in October 2007, members of RELA — Malaysia's volunteer security force — had the brazenness to detain the wife of the Indonesian Embassy's Education and Culture attaché amidst their operation to arrest illegal migrants in Kuala Lumpur.[329] Perhaps, in the eyes of the RELA members, Muslianah Nurdin — the name of the lady — was an *Indon*, who was inferior; and their resolve to detain her had been strengthened as a result.[330] The RELA members reportedly refused to recognize Muslianah's diplomatic identity card — which had been presented to them — and remained adamant in their decision to detain her.[331] Muslianah had been detained for two hours.[332] She was being arrested while shopping in Kuala Lumpur.[333]

---

[328] "Love, Hate Thy Neighbour", *My Sinchew*, 19 September 2007, available at <http://www.mysinchew.com/node/829> (accessed 18 June 2017).

[329] Ooi Kee Beng, *Lost in Transition: Malaysia Under Abdullah* (Singapore: Institute of Southeast Asian Studies, 2008), p. 68. Also see "Indonesia, Malaysia Row Over Diplomat's Wife 'Detention'", *Asiaone*, 10 October 2007, available at <http://snews.asiaone.com/News/Latest+News/Story/A1Story20071011-29499.html> (accessed 25 June 2014).

[330] Ibid.

[331] Ibid.

[332] Ibid.

[333] Ibid.

RELA was Malaysia's volunteer security force with approximately 500,000 members.[334] Since February 2005, Malaysia's government had made use of RELA — together with Malaysia's police and immigration department — to enforce the newly amended Immigration Act.[335] In 2006, RELA had arrested a total of 25,000 illegal migrants.[336]

Indonesia was surprised by the major shift in Malaysia's treatment of Indonesian illegal migrants.[337] Malaysia's harsh policy against Indonesian workers — mass deportations of Indonesian illegals; Hire Indonesians Last policy; the new Immigration Act — resulted in intense anger among Indonesians towards Malaysia.[338]

Indonesia and Malaysia shared a special relationship. Migration from the Indonesian archipelago to Malaysia had always been a symbol of closeness between the two states.[339] Indonesians therefore expected Malaysia to always treat Indonesian migrant workers with friendly measures, let alone becoming the main reason for Malaysia to enact harsh immigration policies, and being the prime target of such policies. This mismatch of expectation resulted in Indonesians' resentments towards Malaysia. The chairman of Indonesian People's Consultative Assembly (MPR), Amien Rais, stressed that Malaysia's decision to cane Indonesian illegals had hurt Indonesia deeply.[340] "Frankly, I feel disappointed, angry, and unable to accept the fact that Malaysia, a modern country which belongs to the same Malay ethnic group (as Indonesia), has resorted to punishing Indonesian illegal workers in a way that is really inhuman", he said.[341]

---

[334] Christine B.N. Chin, "'Diversification' and 'Privatisation': Securing Insecurities in the Receiving Country of Malaysia", *The Asia Pacific Journal of Anthropology* 9, no. 4 (December 2008): 294–95. Also see "Volunteer Security Force Defies Critics in Malaysia", *Asiaone*, 10 October 2007, available at <http://news.asiaone.com/News/Latest+News/Story/A1Story20071011-29537.html> (accessed 25 June 2014).

[335] Ibid. Also see Pranom Somwong and Marie Huberlant, *Undocumented Migrants and Refugees in Malaysia: Raids, Detention, and Discrimination* (Kuala Lumpur and Paris: FIDH-Suaram, 2008), p. 11.

[336] Ibid.

[337] Arifianto, "The Securitization of Transnational Labor Migration", p. 624.

[338] Liow, "Malaysia's Illegal Indonesian Migrant Labour Problem", p. 54.

[339] Ibid., p. 45.

[340] "Amien Warns KL Not to Play with Fire", *The Jakarta Post*, 19 August 2002.

[341] Ibid.

In the meantime, the implementation of Malaysia's new policy against Indonesian illegals constituted a direct challenge to Indonesians' pride. The media and politicians in Malaysia had been trying to associate Indonesian illegal migrants with violence and crime.[342] The Malaysian authorities' crackdown on illegal migrants received wide media coverage in Malaysia with photos showing large groups of illegal Indonesian migrants being forced to squat down with security personnels standing around them.[343] The Indonesian illegals were being detained in unhygienic environments and being shipped back to Indonesia in overcrowded vessels.[344]

Obviously, the mass ill treatment of Indonesians illegals that came with the execution of Malaysia's new immigration policies hurt Indonesians' dignity as humans. Yet, fundamentally, it offended Indonesians' national pride. In the eyes of Indonesians, Malaysia was Indonesia's little brother, which was culturally inferior, when compared to Indonesia. It was difficult for Indonesians to accept that their people — the Indonesian illegals — had been treated poorly by Malaysians whom they considered as inferior in relation to Indonesia.[345] The perceived challenge to Indonesians' sense of superiority over Malaysia stirred up Indonesians' will to confront Malaysia, which was suffused with resentments. Amien Rais criticized Malaysia's stern punishment on Indonesian illegals as "inhumane", asserted that it was an insult to Indonesia.[346] He warned Malaysia "not to play with fire by caning illegal Indonesian workers".[347] Leaders of the DPR — the Indonesian Parliament — urged President Megawati "to withdraw all Indonesian workers, both

---

[342] Liow, "Malaysia's Illegal Indonesian Migrant Labour Problem", pp. 50, 54. Also see Arifianto, "The Securitization of Transnational Labor Migration", pp. 622, 624–25; and Frederik Holst, *(Dis-) Connected History: The Indonesia–Malaysia Relationship* (Germany: Regiospectra, 2007), pp. 334–35.

[343] Ibid. Also see Interview 924-002, Kuala Lumpur, 24 September 2012. Also see Interview 926-002, Kuala Lumpur, 26 September 2012.

[344] Liow, "Malaysia's Illegal Indonesian Migrant Labour Problem", p. 48.

[345] Ibid., p. 54. Also see Interview 924-001, Kuala Lumpur, 24 September 2012.

[346] "Government to Pay for Lawyers for Workers in Malaysia", *The Jakarta Post*, 23 August 2002.

[347] "Amien Warns KL Not to Play with Fire", *The Jakarta Post*, 19 August 2002.

legal and illegal, from Malaysia to teach Malaysia a lesson over its harsh treatment of Indonesian workers".[348]

The Indonesian people launched a series of street protests against Malaysia in response to Malaysia's harsh action against Indonesian illegals that had taken place since early 2002. Indonesia's politicians, in the meantime, issued strong political statements to protest against such new measures on Indonesian illegals. The attempt of the Indonesian media and politicians to foment nationalist sentiments in Indonesia's society further exacerbated Indonesians' anger against Malaysia.[349] A demonstration had been staged in front of Malaysia's embassy in Jakarta shortly after Malaysia began to enforce its new immigration law. The protestors burned the Malaysian flag as a reaction to Malaysia's decision to cane and deport Indonesian illegals.[350] They broke down the gate of the embassy.[351] The Indonesian police did not take action to stop the protesters from doing so.[352]

It was unmistakable that Indonesians' resentments towards Malaysia prompted by Malaysia's crackdown on illegals were evidently more intense than that expressed by other states, in which their people were also part of the illegals.[353] Migrants of other nationalities — such as Indians, Bangladeshis and Filipinos — accounted for roughly less than 20 per cent of the total number of illegals in Malaysia.[354] Such higher intensity of resentments were the results of the perceived challenge to Indonesia's superiority over Malaysia, and the mismatch between Indonesians' expectation and Malaysia's action. Other states did not

---

[348] "60,000 Indonesian Workers Have Returned to Malaysia", *The Jakarta Post*, 30 August 2002.

[349] Khalid and Yacob, "Managing Malaysia–Indonesia Relations in the Context of Democratization", p. 371. Also see Marshall Clark, "The Politics of Heritage: Indonesia–Malaysia Cultural Contestations", *Indonesia and the Malay World* 41, no. 121 (2013): 397.

[350] "Stop Political Row with Malaysia: Megawati", *The Jakarta Post*, 28 August 2002. Also see Yaakub, "Malaysia and Indonesia", p. 158.

[351] Ibid.

[352] Ibid.

[353] Liow, "Malaysia's Illegal Indonesian Migrant Labour Problem", p. 54.

[354] Saravanamuttu, *Malaysia's Foreign Policy, the First Fifty Years*, p. 282.

share common identities with Malaysia, and they did not have a special relationship with Malaysia.

The subsequent repeated cases of ill treatment of Indonesian workers by Malaysian employers, especially the abuses of Indonesian maids, only served to reinforce Indonesians' resentments towards Malaysia. These abuses involved serious inhumane tortures. The Indonesian media reported extensively on these maid abuse cases, stirring up Indonesians' nationalist sentiments.[355] The people throughout Indonesia were infuriated by the abuses.[356] They reacted by launching furious demonstrations against Malaysia with the burning of Malaysian flags.[357] Indonesia's President issued strong representations, protesting against these abuses.[358]

Observers from both states acknowledged that while Indonesians were also enraged by the abuses of Indonesian maids happening in other states, the degree of their anger expressed towards these states was always lesser than that expressed towards Malaysia when it came to

---

[355] Khalid and Yacob, *Managing Malaysia–Indonesia Relations in the Context of Democratization*, p. 371. Also see Clark, "The Politics of Heritage", p. 397; "Indonesian President Yudhoyono's Visit to Malaysia", 19 November 2009, available at <http://wikileaks.org/cable/2009/11/09KUALALUMPUR935.html> (accessed 28 June 2014); "Death of Indonesian Maid Highlights Continuing Migrant Worker Problems in Malaysia", 10 November 2009, available at <http://www.wikileaks.org/plusd/cables/09KUALALUMPUR908_a.html> (accessed 28 June 2014); and Lim Jiet, "Maid Abuse in Malaysia: A Legal Analysis", *Academia.edu* (n.d.): 12, available at <http://www.academia.edu/3437442/Maid_Abuse_In_Malaysia_-_A_Legal_Analysis> (accessed 28 June 2014).

[356] Lisa Thomas, "Indonesia Pushes for Better Migrant-Worker Protection", *Time*, 28 July 2009, available at <http://content.time.com/time/world/article/0,8599,1913134,00.html> (accessed 28 June 2014). Also see Matthew Moore, "Vow of Protection for Mistreated Indonesian Maids", *The Sydney Morning Herald*, 22 July 2004, available at <http://www.smh.com.au/articles/2004/07/21/1090089223202.html?from=storyrhs> (accessed 28 June 2014).

[357] Yaakub, "Malaysia and Indonesia", p. 159. Also see *Antara News*, 2007, quoted in Mario Pandu Dewano, "Non-Traditional Security Issue and International Conflict: A Case Study of Indonesian Migrant Labor in Malaysia", Master dissertation, Lund University, 2007, p. 28; Saravanamuttu, *Malaysia's Foreign Policy, the First Fifty Years*, p. 282; and Lim, "Maid Abuse in Malaysia", p. 12.

[358] Ibid.

such abuses.[359] The abuses of Indonesian maids occured in Saudi Arabia, for example, did not result in Indonesians burning the Saudi flag. The greater degree of anger towards Malaysia was attributable to Indonesians' expectation not being met by Malaysia, and the sense that Indonesia's status as Malaysia's big brother was being challenged by Malaysia. In the minds of Indonesians, it was a daring act for Malaysians — Indonesia's little brother — to abuse Indonesian maids — the people of Malaysia's big brother.[360] Also, Indonesians expected Malaysia to treat the maids like family members — rather than abusing them — since the two states shared a special relationship.[361]

The issue of Indonesian migrant workers in Malaysia had experienced a transformation since 2002. It had transformed from an issue that largely reflected the close cooperation between Indonesia and Malaysia into one that exhibited the double-edged effects of Indonesia–Malaysia special ties. The migration of Indonesia's labour to Malaysia became a manifestation of cooperation as well as conflicts between the two states.

Indonesian labour working in Malaysia persisted as a crucial economic cooperation between the two states. The construction and plantation sectors in Malaysia were unable to continue their operations once Malaysia had begun enforcing its new immigration law in 2002.[362] They had to suspend their operations because of labour shortage.[363] The Malaysian government had to expedite the recruitment of more than 300,000 legal foreign workers to address the shortage.[364] In fact, Malaysia had to quickly call off its "Hire Indonesians Last" policy as its construction sector was heavily dependent on Indonesia's workforce.[365]

---

[359] Interview 926-001, Kuala Lumpur, 26 September 2012. Also see Interview 924-001, Kuala Lumpur, 24 September 2012; Interview 1019, Jakarta, 19 October 2012; and Interview 1011, Jakarta, 11 October 2012.

[360] Interview 924-001, Kuala Lumpur, 24 September 2012.

[361] Interview 1019, Jakarta, 19 October 2012. Also see Interview 1011, Jakarta, 11 October 2012.

[362] Holst, *(Dis-) Connected History*, pp. 333–34.

[363] Ibid.

[364] Ibid.

[365] Liow, *The Politics of Indonesia–Malaysia Relations*, p. 212. Also see Liow, "Malaysia's Illegal Indonesian Migrant Labour Problem", p. 52.

Indonesia too had to endure great economic cost as a consequence of Malaysia's crackdown on illegals. The enforcement of the new immigration law in Malaysia — which took place since 2002 — had contributed to the increase of unemployment in Indonesia. Indonesia's unemployment rate had risen from 9 per cent in 2002 to 11 per cent in 2005.[366]

It was clear for Indonesia and Malaysia that they were relying on each other with regard to Indonesian migrant workers. The two states since 2004 had come together to establish clearer and more comprehensive rules and procedures for recruiting Indonesian migrant workers.[367] One-stop processing centres were set up in Indonesia to speed up the process of recruiting legal Indonesian workers for jobs in Malaysia.[368] Meanwhile, in March 2006, Indonesia and Malaysia had jointly signed a memorandum of understanding (MOU) in response to the recurrent abuses of Indonesian maids in Malaysia.[369] The MOU provided legal protection for Indonesian workers in Malaysia, protecting them from being abused by their employers.[370] In November 2008, the Malaysian court had sentenced the former employer of Nirmala Bornat to 18 years in jail after she was found guilty of inflicting horrific wounds on Nirmala. Nirmala Bornat — an Indonesian maid — was tortured by her Malaysian employer in 2004. The Malaysian police came to her rescue after a security guard had reported the abuse to the police.[371] Nirmala's case received wide media coverage both in Malaysia and Indonesia.[372]

---

[366] <http://databank.worldbank.org/data/views/reports/tableview.aspx#> (accessed 29 June 2014).

[367] Arifianto, "The Securitization of Transnational Labor Migration", p. 625.

[368] Yaakub, "Malaysia and Indonesia", p. 161. Also see "Malaysia Widens Recruitment for Foreign Workers", *Malaysian Trades Union Congress*, 26 May 2005, available at <http://www.mtuc.org.my/msia-widens-recruitment-for-foreign-workers/> (accessed 30 June 2014).

[369] Claudia Derichs, "Malaysia in 2006: An Old Tiger Roars", *Asian Survey* 47, no. 1 (January/February 2007): 153. Also see "RI, Malaysia Ink MOU on Protection Workers", *The Jakarta Post*, 15 May 2006.

[370] Ibid.

[371] "Maid Abuse Case Shocks Malaysia", *BBC News*, 20 May 2004, available at <http://news.bbc.co.uk/2/hi/asia-pacific/3732241.stm> (accessed 28 June 2014).

[372] "Malaysian Maid Abuse Shocks PM", *BBC News*, 21 May 2004, available at <http://news.bbc.co.uk/2/hi/asia-pacific/3734695.stm> (accessed 28 June 2014). Also see Yaakub, "Malaysia and Indonesia", pp. 159–60.

Indonesian migrant workers in Malaysia, on the other hand, almost became a source of Indonesians' resentments towards Malaysia. Indonesians reacted strongly every time Indonesia's media reported extensively on a case of an Indonesian maid being abused by her Malaysian employer. In June 2009, Indonesia's government decided to temporarily ban the sending of Indonesian maids to Malaysia in response to the revelation of an Indonesian maid named Siti Hajar being seriously tortured by her Malaysian employer.[373] Hajar's case sparked outrage throughout Indonesia.[374] Officials from both states had later on begun to negotiate for a new MOU. Indonesia aimed to improve wages and legal protection for Indonesian maids working in Malaysia through the negotiation.[375]

After almost two years of negotiations, an agreement to better protect Indonesian maids in Malaysia had been reached between the two states. Indonesia and Malaysia signed a new MOU on 30 May 2011. Under the new MOU, Indonesian maids working in Malaysia would be allowed to keep their passports, and would be given one day off each week. The minimum wage of the maids, however, was to be determined by market forces.[376]

The signing of the new MOU did not immediately lead to the lifting of the ban on sending Indonesian maids to Malaysia. The issue concerning the forming of a proper mechanism for the implementation of the MOU had prompted Indonesia's government not to lift the ban until the end of November 2011. It was a relief for Malaysian families when Indonesia resumed sending its maids to Malaysia since 1 December 2011. There were around 35,000 Malaysian families waiting for

---

[373] Lisa Thomas, "Indonesia Pushes for Better Migrant-Worker Protection", *Time*, 28 July 2009, available at <http://content.time.com/time/world/article/0,8599,1913134,00. html> (accessed 28 June 2014). Also see "Death of Indonesian Maid Highlights Continuing Migrant Worker Problems in Malaysia", *WikiLeaks*, 10 November 2009, available at <http://www.wikileaks.org/plusd/cables/09KUALALUMPUR908_a.html> (accessed 28 June 2014).

[374] Ibid.

[375] Ibid. Also see "Malaysia, Indonesia Mending Fences Over Maid Abuse", *The Jakarta Post*, 12 November 2009.

[376] "RM900 for Indonesian Maids", *The Star*, 31 October 2015. Also see "More for Maids Under New Deal", *The Star*, 28 May 2011.

Indonesian maids before the sending of the maids to Malaysia had been unfreezed.[377] By the end of 2015, there were about 320,000 foreign maids working in Malaysia; 230,000 of them were from Indonesia, which accounted for around 72 per cent of the total 320,000 foreign maids.[378]

The overall number of legal Indonesian workers in Malaysia had been in decline since the mid-2000s. In 2005, there were around 1.2 million legal Indonesian migrants working in Malaysia.[379] By early 2016, the number of legal Indonesian workers in Malaysia had dropped to 792,571 Indonesians.[380] The reduction was an outcome of Malaysia's efforts to reduce its reliance on Indonesian labour. From 2000 onwards, Malaysia's government had begun to expand its recruitment of migrant workers from other states such as Nepal, Bangladesh, Myanmar and India.[381] Nonetheless, Indonesians were still the largest group of documented foreign workers in Malaysia.[382] They made up about 40 per cent of the total number of legal foreign workers in Malaysia as of February 2016.[383] Legal foreign workers in 2015 accounted for around 15 per cent the total workforce in Malaysia.[384] From 2011 to 2015, among the states which had been sending workers to Malaysia, Indonesia

---

[377] Ibid.

[378] Ibid.

[379] Number of Foreign Workers in Malaysia by Country of Origin, 2000–2015, available at <http://www.epu.gov.my/sites/default/files/1.4.1.pdf> (accessed 30 June 2017).

[380] "Indonesian Still Largest Group of Foreign Workers in Malaysia", *The Jakarta Post*, 30 March 2016.

[381] Blanca Garces-Mascarenas, *Labour Migration in Malaysia and Spain* (Amsterdam: Amsterdam University Press, 2012), p. 67. Also see Number of Foreign Workers in Malaysia by Country of Origin, 2000–2015, available at <http://www.epu.gov.my/sites/default/files/1.4.1.pdf> (accessed 30 June 2017).

[382] "Indonesian Still Largest Group of Foreign Workers in Malaysia", *The Jakarta Post*, 30 March 2016.

[383] Ibid.

[384] Number of Foreign Workers in Malaysia by Country of Origin, 2000–2015, available at <http://www.epu.gov.my/sites/default/files/1.4.1.pdf> (accessed 30 June 2017). Also see <http://databank.worldbank.org/data/reports.aspx?source=2&country=MYS#> (accessed 1 July 2017).

stood as the top recipient of remittances from Malaysia.[385] A total of RM6.2 billion had been remitted from Malaysia to Indonesia in 2015 alone.[386] As late as October 2017, Malaysia remained as the top destination for Indonesians working abroad.[387]

ANTI-MALAYSIA

Three sources of conflict were embedded in the issue of Indonesian migrant workers and the Ambalat dispute — Indonesia's and Malaysia's competitive bahaviours against each other; their respective sense of superiority over the other; and the mismatch of expectation between them. They reinforced one another. Anti-Malaysia sentiments began to emerge in Indonesia's society as a result.

Some Indonesians had chosen to embrace tit-for-tat measures against Malaysia. It was an outcome of Indonesians' intense resentment towards Malaysia, which was produced by the combination of the mismatch of expectation and the perceived challenge to Indonesia's superiority over Malaysia.

The Front Ganyang Malaysia movement that had been created in reaction to the Ambalat dispute was an example of such tit-for-tat measures. The movement sought to recruit volunteers across Indonesia with the goal of launching Confrontation 2.0 against Malaysia. It was a direct response to Malaysia using its volunteer security force (RELA) — apart from using its official security forces — to crackdown on illegals. RELA had been accused of adopting heavy-handed tactics during their large-scale operations to arrest illegals in Malaysia.[388] There were reports

---

[385] "Foreign Workers Send Home RM34.75b from Malaysia in 2015", *Malaysiakini*, 16 March 2016, available at <http://www.malaysiakini.com/news/334083> (accessed 1 July 2017).

[386] Ibid.

[387] The National Council of the Settlement and Protection of Indonesian Labour, "The Data of the Settlement and Protection of Indonesian Labour October 2017", available at <http://www.bnp2tki.go.id/uploads/data/data_10-11-2017_015327_Laporan_Pengolahan_Data_BNP2TKI_2017_(s.d_Oktober_).pdf> (accessed 8 December 2017).

[388] "Indonesia, Malaysia Row Over Diplomat's Wife 'Detention'", *Asiaone*, 10 October 2007, available at <http://news.asiaone.com/News/Latest+News/Story/A1Story 20071011- 29499. html> (accessed 25 June 2014).

which indicated that some migrants had been verbally and physically assaulted by RELA members.[389] Front Ganyang Malaysia entailed the intention to retaliate against the alleged RELA's attacks on Indonesian illegals by using the perceived same tactic — which was to recruit volunteers across Indonesia to confront Malaysia.

Likewise a group called Benteng Demokrasi Rakyat (Bendera) — the People's Democratic Front — was also active in recruiting volunteers in Indonesia and planned to wage a war against Malaysia.[390] Bendera was formed by a small group of Indonesians in 2009.[391] Armed with bamboo spears, Bendera's volunteers set up roadblocks in Jakarta in September 2009 to search for Malaysians passing by and aimed to detain them.[392] "If we had caught them [Malaysians], we would have sent them home", Bendera's coordinator said.[393] It was clear, Bendera's approach was its tit-for-tat response to Malaysia using its volunteer security force to arrest and deport Indonesian illegals. The Indonesian police had removed Bendera's volunteers from the streets.[394] Bendera later alleged that it had 1,500 volunteers who were ready to go to war with Malaysia.[395]

A survey indicated that Indonesians' perception of Malaysia had been moving towards a negative direction. In 2006, Malaysia was ranked by Indonesians as the state that they felt closest to.[396] It had dropped to 11th

---

[389] Chin, "'Diversification' and 'Privatisation'", p. 295.

[390] "Indonesian Vigilantes Prepare For Battle in Malaysia", *Jakarta Globe*, 25 September 2009; and "Malaysia and Indonesia Try to Mend Ties", *BBC News*, 12 November 2009, available at <http://news.bbc.co.uk/2/hi/asia-pacific/8355417.stm> (accessed 30 June 2014).

[391] Ibid.

[392] Ibid. Also see Chong Jinn Winn, "'Mine, Yours or Ours?': The Indonesia–Malaysia Disputes Over Shared Cultural Heritage", *Journal of Social Issues in Southeast Asia* 27, no. 1 (2012): 3.

[393] "Indonesian Vigilantes Prepare For Battle in Malaysia", *Jakarta Globe*, 25 September 2009.

[394] Chong, "Mine, Yours or Ours?", p. 3.

[395] Ibid. Also see "Indonesian Vigilantes Prepare For Battle in Malaysia", *Jakarta Globe*, 25 September 2009.

[396] "Indonesians Grow Cool Towards Malaysia", *ABC Radio Australia*, 21 March 2012, available at <http://www.radioaustralia.net.au/international/2012-03-21/indonesians-grow-cool-towards-malaysia/482528> (accessed 30 June 2014).

position in 2012.[397] A survey conducted in five major Indonesian cities in 2009 revealed that the majority of respondents perceived Malaysia as threatening Indonesia's sovereignty — which was 60.5 per cent of the total number of respondents.[398] This was followed by Singapore, in which only 20.4 per cent of the respondents deemed that Singapore was a threat to Indonesia's sovereignty.[399] There were numerous anti-Malaysia columns and editorials in Indonesia's media.[400] Some Indonesian politicians called for boycotts of Malaysian goods.[401] A prominent Indonesian journalist had pointed out that Indonesians generally chose not to go to Petronas petrol station to refuel their vehicles.[402] Petronas — Malaysia's national oil company — was an obvious symbol of Malaysia, specifically Malay-Malaysia.

With the proliferation of anti-Malaysia sentiments in Indonesia's society, the common culture of Indonesia and Malaysia emerged as a new issue of contention between the two states. Indonesians since 2006 began to assert that Malaysia had been trying to steal Indonesia's cultural heritage.[403] The notion of "steal" had its origins in Indonesia's loss of Sipadan and Ligitan. As Indonesians saw it, Malaysia had "stolen" or "robbed" the two islands from Indonesia. The humiliation and resentments which stemmed from the loss of the two islands almost certainly contributed to Indonesians' view that Malaysia attempted to steal their culture.

Indonesians before long started to call Malaysia as *Malingsia*, meaning "Malaysia thief".[404] *Malingsia* was derived from the word *maling* — a

---

[397] Ibid.
[398] Guido Benny, "The Indonesian Nationalism and Perceived Threats of Neighbouring Countries: Public Opinion Toward the ASEAN Community", *International Journal on Social Science Economics & Art* 2, no. 3 (2012): 40, 43.
[399] Ibid.
[400] Clark, "The Politics of Heritage", p. 397.
[401] "Asia: No Brotherly Love; Indonesia and Malaysia", *The Economist*, 13 October 2007, p. 77.
[402] Interview 1011, Jakarta, 11 October 2012.
[403] Clark, "The Politics of Heritage", p. 406. Also see ibid.
[404] Clark, "The Politics of Heritage", pp. 401, 406.

Javanese word meaning "thief".[405] A series of culture had been stolen by Malaysia from Indonesia, Indonesians maintained.[406] The folk song *Rasa Sayang* — Indonesians argued — was originated from Indonesia's Moluccan Islands; same with the *Reog Ponorogo* dance which was originated from East Java.[407] Indonesians stressed that Malaysia had stolen the two cultural forms from them.[408] *Rasa Sayang* and *Reog Ponorogo* had been featured in Malaysia's tourism commercials as part of its 2007 tourism promotion campaign termed as *Malaysia Truly Asia*.

Later, Indonesians alleged that the melody of *Negaraku* — Malaysia's national anthem — was plagiarized from an Indonesian song called *Terang Bulan*, which was first recorded in Indonesia in 1956.[409] It was later found out that *Negaraku* and *Terang Bulan* were in fact adaptations of a nineteenth-century French composition called La Rosalie.[410]

Indonesians too protested strongly against the alleged stealing of the Balinese temple dance — *pendet* — by Malaysia.[411] In August 2009, Discovery Channel broadcasted a documentary on Malaysia featuring a *pendet* dance performed by two Balinese dancers.[412] Demonstrations were staged in front of Malaysia's embassy in Jakarta to protest against the alleged appropriation with protesters chanting *"Ganjang Malaysia!"*

---

[405] Ibid.
[406] Ibid., pp. 398–400. Also see Chong, "Mine, Yours or Ours?", pp. 2–3.
[407] Ibid.
[408] Clark, "The Politics of Heritage", pp. 398–400, 406. Also see Chong, "Mine, Yours or Ours?", p. 2; and "Hopping Mad Indonesians Demonstrate Against Malaysia", *WikiLeaks*, 30 November 2007, available at <http://www.wikileaks.org/plusd/cables/07JAKARTA3289_a.html> (accessed 30 June 2014).
[409] Clark, "The Politics of Heritage", p. 399. Also see Candra Malik, "Malaysian Anthem Actually Indonesian, Says Record Company", *Jakarta Globe*, 29 August 2009.
[410] Clark, "The Politics of Heritage", p. 399. Also see Chong, "Mine, Yours or Ours?", pp. 11–12.
[411] Clark, "The Politics of Heritage", pp. 399–400. Also see Chong, "Mine, Yours or Ours?", pp. 1–3; and "Hopping Mad Indonesians Demonstrate Against Malaysia", *WikiLeaks*, 30 November 2007, available at <http://www.wikileaks.org/plusd/cables/07JAKARTA3289_a.html> (accessed 30 June 2014).
[412] Ibid.

— Crush Malaysia — and pelting the embassy with rotten eggs and rocks.[413] Discovery Networks Asia-Pacific subsequently issued an official apology to Indonesia, explaining that the *pendet* dance clip used in the documentary was sourced from a third party.[414]

It was essentially a combination of Indonesians' desire to compete with Malaysia and their sense of superiority over Malaysia that prompted Indonesians' assertion that their culture had been stolen by Malaysia. Most of the cultural forms that Indonesians deemed to have been stolen by Malaysia were the ones that had been used to promote Malaysia's tourism industry. Malaysia utilized these cultural forms to generate income. Understandably, Indonesians wanted to prevent Malaysia from doing so as they themselves could make use of these cultural forms to create wealth for Indonesia. In November 2007, around one thousand Indonesians launched a demonstration outside Malaysia's embassy in Jakarta in protest of Malaysia using *Rasa Sayang* and *Reog Ponorogo* in its tourism commercials.[415] "We want the Malaysian government to stop copying our cultural heritage", one of the protesters told the media.[416] In other words, the protesters wanted Malaysia's government to stop using what was supposed to be Indonesia–Malaysia common culture to generate wealth for Malaysians. "Malaysia thief!" the protesters shouted.[417] *Malingsia* — Malaysia thief — could also be understood as "*maling asal Asia*", meaning Asia's thief.[418] Indonesians employed the notion of "Asia's thief", aiming to undermine Malaysia's tourism promotion campaign known as *Malaysia Truly Asia*.[419]

---

[413] Ibid. Also see "Storm Over 'Stealing' of Balinese Dance", *Malaysiakini*, 2 September 2009, available at <http://www.malaysiakini.com/news/111938> (accessed 30 June 2014).

[414] Chong, "Mine, Yours or Ours?", pp. 1–2.

[415] "Hopping Mad Indonesians Demonstrate Against Malaysia", *WikiLeaks*, 30 November 2007, available at <http://www.wikileaks.org/plusd/cables/07JAKARTA3289_a.html> (accessed 30 June 2014). Also see Clark, "The Politics of Heritage", pp. 399–400; and ibid., p. 2.

[416] "Hopping Mad Indonesians Demonstrate Against Malaysia", *WikiLeaks*, 30 November 2007, available at <http://www.wikileaks.org/plusd/cables/07JAKARTA3289_a.html> (accessed 30 June 2014).

[417] Ibid.

[418] Clark, "The Politics of Heritage", p. 406.

[419] Ibid.

Indonesians' desire to prevent Malaysia from using their common culture to promote Malaysia's economic growth strengthened, and was strengthened by, their sense of superiority over Malaysia. In the eyes of Indonesians, Malaysia's culture was provided by Indonesia. Malaysia was culturally inferior, when compared to Indonesia. In response to the issue of *Rasa Sayang* and *Reog Ponorogo*, Indonesians asserted: "Malaysians don't have their own culture so they steal Indonesia's... They should find their own identity!"[420]

Indonesia's assertion of its ownership over batik — a traditional wax-resistant dyeing technique — also reflected the mutually reinforcing dynamics of its will to compete with Malaysia and its sense of superiority over Malaysia. Indonesia accused Malaysia of appropriating batik that belonged to Indonesia.[421] The Indonesian government moved to lodge a claim with UNESCO for batik to be listed as a distinctly Indonesian intangible heritage item, aiming to curb the development of the batik industry in Malaysia, especially Malaysia's efforts to market its batik products abroad.[422] In September 2009, UNESCO announced its decision to recognize batik as a distinctly Indonesian intangible cultural heritage. The decision was being treated as a victory in Indonesia.[423] To celebrate the "victory", President Susilo Bambang Yudhoyono called for all Indonesians to wear batik on 2 October 2009, the day when UNESCO officially announced the recognition.[424]

The success in winning the recognition of UNESCO boosted Indonesians' sense of superiority over Malaysia. Indonesia's Culture and

---

[420] "Hopping Mad Indonesians Demonstrate Against Malaysia", *WikiLeaks*, 30 November 2007, available at <http://www.wikileaks.org/plusd/cables/07JAKARTA3289_a.html> (accessed 30 June 2014).

[421] "Rivals of the East: Battle for Batik", *The Independent*, 28 September 2009. Also see Clark, "The Politics of Heritage", p. 398.

[422] "Indonesians Tell Malaysians 'Hands Off Our Batik'", *The Telegraph*, 5 October 2009. Also see Chong, "Mine, Yours or Ours?", pp. 28–29, 31–32; and Clark, "The Politics of Heritage", p. 411.

[423] "Indonesians Tell Malaysians 'Hands Off Our Batik'", *The Telegraph*, 5 October 2009. Also see Chong, "Mine, Yours or Ours?", pp. 31–32.

[424] "Indonesians Tell Malaysians 'Hands Off Our Batik'", *The Telegraph*, 5 October 2009. Also see "Score One for Indonesia in the War over Batik'", *The New York Times*, 14 September 2009. Also see "Administration Calls for All-in Batik Day This Friday", *The Jarkata Post*, 29 September 2009.

Tourism Minister, Jero Wacik, emphasized: "Malaysia could no longer claim batik as its cultural heritage because Indonesia has proven its case...If Malaysia still wants to challenge UNESCO's decision, go ahead. But, it would be better if it tried its own creation."[425] In the eyes of Indonesians, Malaysia was lacked of culture or at least Malaysia's culture was inferior to Indonesia's.

Indonesians' sense of superiority over Malaysia, in the meantime, toughened their resolve to compete with Malaysia. Jero Wacik asserted: "We will keep fighting for our heritage one tradition at a time."[426] Batik was the third cultural forms that Indonesia had secured UNESCO's recognition as a distinctly Indonesia's cultural heritage after *Wayang Kulit* and *Kris*.[427] All together there were four cultural forms — *Kris, Wayang Kulit, Batik* and *Angklund* — in which Indonesia had brought to UNESCO to seek for its recognition.[428] The four items were all the common culture of Indonesia and Malaysia.

Malaysia's batik industry, however, is not threatened by UNESCO's decision.[429] UNESCO's intangible heritage listing of batik "neither puts a patent on batik's production nor grants intellectual property right protection".[430] An author's comment on Malaysia's batik reflects Malaysians' sense of being sophisticated vis-à-vis Indonesia — that Malaysia was technologically and industrially more advanced than Indonesia:[431]

---

[425] "UNESCO: Batik is Indonesian Heritage", *Waspada Online*, 2 October 2009, available at <http://waspada.co.id/index.php?option=com_content&view=article&id=55879:-unesco-batik-is-indonesian-heritage&catid=30:english-news&Itemid=94> (accessed 3 July 2014).

[426] "Batik Selected for UNESCO Cultural Heritage List", *The Jakarta Post*, 8 September 2009.

[427] Ibid.

[428] Chong, "Mine, Yours or Ours?", pp. 31–32.

[429] Clark, "The Politics of Heritage", p. 407.

[430] "Indonesia Cut From a Different Cloth", *Asia Times Online*, 3 October 2009, available at <http://www.atimes.com/atimes/Southeast_Asia/KJ03Ae02.html> (accessed 3 July 2014).

[431] Azlina Yunus Noor, *Malaysian Batik: Reinventing a Tradition* (Singapore: Tuttle Publishing, 2011), p. 10, quoted in Clark, "The Politics of Heritage", pp. 410–11.

More often they [Malaysia's batik] are creations that display all the characteristics of works of art — originality of composition and design, effective use of colour, a high level of technical expertise and, above all, a flair for working in the medium of batik...the old system of anonymous artisans is giving way before a new style and organization of the batik industry that encourages individual talent and promotes recognized batik designers and artists.

The Malaysian government was actively promoting Malaysia's batik industry.[432] It required all the government servants to wear batik once a week.[433] The Chief Secretary to Malaysia's government, however, issued an order with regard to the wearing of batik: "it will have to be Malaysian batik, of course".[434]

Anti-Malaysia sentiments in Indonesia's society seemed to have reached its peak since around August 2010. On 13 August 2010, five officers from the Indonesian Marine and Fisheries Ministry approached five Malaysian fishing boats during their patrol operation at night-time. They had decided to arrest seven Malaysian fishermen on the fishing boats for allegedly encroaching into Indonesia waters near Bintan Island, Indonesia. When on their way back to a nearby Indonesian island — Batam Island — together with the seven arrested Malaysian fishermen and the five fishing boats, the patrol boat of the Indonesian officers was intercepted by the Malaysian marine police.[435] The marine police failed to capture the Indonesian patrol boat carrying the seven Malaysian fishermen but were able to stop the five Malaysian fishing boats from being brought to Batam Island.[436] Three Indonesian officers were found on the fishing boats. They were arrested by the Malaysian marine police for allegedly trespassing into Malaysian waters near Tanjung Punggai, Malaysia. The three Indonesian officers had been brought to a police station of Malaysia in Kota Tinggi. Whereas the seven Malaysian

---

[432] Clark, "The Politics of Heritage", p. 407.
[433] Ibid.
[434] "Thursday is Batik Day", The Star, 16 January 2008.
[435] Mergawati Zulfakar, "Calming the Waves of Wrath", The Star, 25 August 2010. Also see "M'sian, RI Police Give Different Versions of Bintan Incident", Antara News, 27 August 2010.
[436] Ibid.

fishermen on the Indonesian patrol boat were being sent to a police station of Indonesia in Riau Islands. Malaysia's officials later claimed that their GPS device clearly showed that the arrest of the seven Malaysian fishermen by Indonesia's authority took place in Malaysian territory. Indonesia's officials, in the meantime, stated that their patrol boat's GPS device was broken, hence were unable to indicate where exactly did the arrest take place.[437]

All those who had been detained — the seven Malaysian fishermen and the three Indonesian officers — were released by the respective authority of Indonesia and Malaysia on 17 August 2010. Yet, the double arrest gave rise to unprecedented extreme form of anti-Malaysia protests not seen in Indonesia before. Demonstrations against Malaysia had been staged in several cities of Indonesia to protest against the arrest of the three Indonesian officers by Malaysia's authority. Protesters burnt Malaysian flags during the demonstrations. The demonstration in Jakarta turned out to be the most disturbing one. Not only did the protesters burnt Malaysian flags, they spat on the flags.[438] Worse still, the protesters threw human faeces into the compound of Malaysia's embassy in Jakarta.[439]

The extreme behaviour of the Indonesian protesters was an expression of their sense of humiliation. It was particularly humiliating for Indonesians when knowing that the Malaysian authority had the courage to detain Indonesia's officers in the supposed territory of Indonesia. As Indonesians saw it, the detention of their three officers by Malaysia's authority was almost intelorable in view of Indonesia's status as the big brother of the culturally inferior Malaysia. Further, it was hard to accept because the three Indonesian officers were a representation of the sovereignty of Indonesia as a state, and the arrest was being made in the supposed waters of Indonesia. Sudin — an Indonesian legislator — stressed that the Malaysian marine police's act of detaining Indonesia's

---

[437] Ibid.
[438] "Anti-Malaysian Demonstrators Too Aggressive: Mahathir", *My Sinchew*, 28 August 2010, available at <http://www.mysinchew.com/node/44094> (accessed 13 July 2017).
[439] Ibid. Also see "Anti-Malaysia Sentiment in Indonesia", *BBC Indonesia*, 24 August 2010, available at <http://www.bbc.com/indonesia/forum/2010/08/100824_forum_ri_malaysia.shtml> (accessed 13 July 2017).

officers was indeed "a form of humiliation of Indonesia's sovereignty".[440] "That means that Malaysia has underestimated us [Indonesians]. Who is Malaysia? We are better than Malaysia", he asserted.[441]

Indonesians' sense of humiliation toughened their will to confront Malaysia, which was expressed in the form of radical protest against Malaysia. Indonesia's President, Susilo Bambang Yudhoyono, was compelled to address the whole population of Indonesia via television broadcast to allay the popular anger that had erupted in Indonesia's society following the case of the double arrest.

While there had been no street protest in Malaysia against Indonesia after the arrest of the seven Malaysian fishermen by Indonesia's authority, various quarters in Malaysia were seriously concerned about the extreme form of anti-Malaysia protests that had been staged in Indonesia. Malaysia's government began to demonstrate its discontent over Indonesians' demonstrations against Malaysia especially with regard to the throwing of human faeces at Malaysia's embassy in Jakarta. The Foreign Minister of Malaysia, Anifah Aman, stated that Malaysia was "out of patience" with the anti-Malaysia protests in Indonesia.[442] Indonesia's government was quick to denounce the radical anti-Malaysia protests launched by Indonesians, describing them as threatening the diplomatic ties between the two states.[443]

The intense anti-Malaysia sentiments in Indonesia's society persisted nonetheless. Another fierce protest against Malaysia erupted in Jakarta as a result. Indonesians reacted strongly to yet one more case of abuse against an Indonesian maid, which came to light in Malaysia a month after the episode of the double arrest. Apart from being tortured, the 26-year-old Indonesian maid also accused her employer of raping her repeatedly. Incensed by the maid abuse case, around 500 angry Indonesian protesters with their motorbikes besieged the residence of Malaysia's

[440] "Malaysian Police Arrests Indonesian Maritime Officers, Deny Shooting", *Jakarta Globe*, 15 August 2010.

[441] Ibid.

[442] "Malaysian Says Protests Don't Reflect Relationship with Indonesia", *Jakarta Globe*, 1 September 2010.

[443] "Officials Lambast Malaysia Protests as Over the Top", *Jakarta Globe*, 28 August 2010.

Ambassador to Indonesia. They demanded the Ambassador to leave Indonesia in two days. They too threatened to search for Malaysian tourists in the nearby hotels and shopping malls to demand them to leave Indonesia. The Indonesian police were put on alert, charged to prevent the protesters from causing harm to any Malaysian in Jakarta.

Strong anti-Malaysia sentiments in Indonesia remained unabated even nearly fourteen months later. Indonesia's crowds and officials demonstrated their hostilities towards Malaysia's athletes and their entourage during the November 2011 SEA Games held in Indonesia, reflecting the prevalence of anti-Malaysia sentiments in Indonesia's society.[444] Right before the games' semi-final football match between Malaysia and Myanmar, the bus carrying the Malaysian football team had been surrounded and kicked by hostile Indonesia's supporters. The Malaysian team later had to be escorted by armoured vehicles to and from the Gelora Bung Karno Stadium in Jakarta before and after their SEA Games final football match against Indonesia. More than a hundred thousand Indonesia's supporters were in the stadium watching the final match. The playing of the Malaysian national anthem prior to the start of the match was overwhelmed by the ear-piercing horns, jeers, and shouting of Indonesia's supporters in the stadium.[445] Other Malaysian athletes had been booed by Indonesia's crowds when they were representing Malaysia to compete in the games.[446] An Indonesian official was blunt in expressing his anger towards Malaysia. He shouted at a group of Malaysian reporters while he was on duty at the games' swimming competition: *"Ini semua orang Malaysia! Tak ada otak semua"* — These are all Malaysians! They all don't have brains.[447] He then was confident enough to assert that: "This is our country! If you don't like it, you can get out!"[448]

Rather parodoxically, signs of the dwindling of anti-Malaysia sentiments in Indonesia had surfaced even though Indonesians' resentments towards Malaysia were strong and appeared to be long-lasting. In fact,

---

[444] Clark, "The Politics of Heritage", p. 401.

[445] Ibid. Also see Wong Chun Wai, "Shame on You!", *The Star*, 20 November 2011.

[446] Clark, "The Politics of Heritage", pp. 403–4.

[447] Ibid. Also see Wong, "Shame on You!".

[448] Ibid.

street protest against Malaysia had not erupted in Indonesia since the anti-Malaysia protests that took place in Jakarta in September 2010, which were to protest against the abuse of the 26-year-old Indonesian maid in Malaysia. A series of developments in Indonesia–Malaysia relations had contributed to the weakening of anti-Malaysia sentiments in Indonesia's society.

The establishment of a more comprehensive and responsive way of administrating Indonesian migrant workers in Malaysia played a significant role in easing Indonesians' anger towards Malaysia. The implementation of the new MOU between Indonesia and Malaysia since December 2011 served to further protect Indonesian maids from being abused by their Malaysian employers. Observers have pointed out that while the MOUs are not perfect, they however are better than nothing.[449] In other words — as indicated by the comment – the treatments of Indonesian maids in Malaysia have been substantially improved. Malaysian employers who had been found torturing or abusing their Indonesian workers were subjected to stern punishments in Malaysia. As for the case of Siti Hajar — the maid abuse case in June 2009 — the Malaysian court had first sentenced the Indonesian maid's former Malaysian employer to eight years in prison for torturing her. The court had then decided to extend the jail term for an additional three years — a total of 11 years in prison — after Hajar's former employer had appealed to the court to have her sentence overturned. Also, a Malaysian couple had been sentenced to death in March 2014 for murdering their Indonesian maid — Isti Komariyah — in Malaysia about three years ago by deliberately starving her to death.

The execution of the 6P programme by Malaysia's government since October 2011 had significantly lessen the likelihood of the eruption of conflicts between Indonesia and Malaysia arising from the issues of Indonesian migrant workers. 6P was the acronym for *Pendaftaran* — Registration; *Pemulihan* — Legalization; *Pengusiran* — Deportation; *Pemantauan* — Monitoring; *Penguatkuasaan* — Rehabilitation; *Pengampunan* — Amnesty. Many undocumented Indonesian migrants in Malaysia had obtained their legal status through the 6P programme.

---

[449] Clark and Pietsch, *Indonesia–Malaysia Relations*, p. 185.

Owing to the legalization programme, the total number of legal Indonesian workers in Malaysia had increased from 746,063 workers in 2012 to 1,021,655 workers in 2013, which was an increase of around 37 per cent.[450] Meanwhile, Malaysia's government had granted amnesty to those Indonesian illegals who had decided to leave Malaysia during the implementation of the 6P programme, which ended in 2014. Legalizing the status of a large number of undocumented Indonesian migrants in Malaysia via the 6P programme meant that more Indonesian workers had been protected by the MOUs between Indonesia and Malaysia. In the meantime, the granting of amnesty had led to the further reduction of the number of Indonesian illegals in Malaysia. In other words, because of the overall reduction of the number of Indonesian illegals in Malaysia as a result of the execution of the 6P programme, the possibility of mistreating Indonesian workers in Malaysia had been substantially reduced. The likelihood of the eruption of conflicts between the two states prompted by such mistreatments was also in decline as a consequence. In fact, Indonesia's Foreign Minister, Retno Marsudi, had expressed her gratitude to Malaysia's government for introducing the 6P programme.[451]

Furthermore, the establishment of educational facilities for the children of Indonesian migrants working in the oil palm estates in Sabah and Sarawak — the East Malaysian states — further reflected the improvement of the treatment of Indonesian workers in Malaysia. In response to the request of Indonesia's government, Indonesian schools had been allowed to be built in Sabah since 2008. The schools were built to provide basic education to the children of Indonesian workers in Sabah. They were funded by the Indonesian government and followed Indonesian curriculum. Within around seven years, 50 such schools had been established in Sabah. Malaysia's government in February 2015 accepted another request from Indonesia's government, which was to set up schools for the children of Indonesian workers in the state right next to Sabah — Sarawak. The state government of Sarawak, however,

---

[450] Number of Foreign Workers in Malaysia by Country of Origin, 2000–2015, available at <http://www.epu.gov.my/sites/default/files/1.4.1.pdf> (accessed 18 August 2017).

[451] "Malaysia Will Help Indonesia Solve Illegal Migrant Workers Issue", *Antara News*, 28 January 2015.

decided later that Community Learning Centres (CLCs) — instead of Indonesian schools — would be set up for the children of Indonesian workers in Sarawak. The learning centres were to be owned and operated by Malaysian estate owners in Sarawak. By August 2017, 16 CLCs had already been set up across Sarawak, accommodating a total of 981 students who were Indonesian children. The Sarawak government planned to set up another three CLCs in response to the growing number of Indonesian children in the state.

Apart from the issue of Indonesian migrant workers in Malaysia, the waning of Indonesians' strong nationalist sentiments towards the Ambalat dispute also contributed to the dwindling of anti-Malaysia sentiments in Indonesia's society. Owing to their shared commitment to avoid armed conflicts between them, Indonesia and Malaysia had been able to negotiate indefinitely on their sovereignty disputes over ND6 and ND7/Ambalat as long as both were unable to work out a solution for the dispute. The intense nationalist feelings of Indonesians towards the Ambalat dispute had over time began to deplete as a consequence of the seemingly endless talks between Indonesia and Malaysia over the disputes, which began in 2005. After almost eight years of negotiation, Indonesia and Malaysia in 2013 began to become capable of exploring the possibility of an agreement between them to share the mineral resources in the disputed area of Ambalat.[452] Perhaps facilitated by the decline of the strong nationalist sentiments, the two states by early 2015 began to possess enough flexibility to call for renewed efforts to resolve their sovereignty disputes over ND6 and ND7/Ambalat.

Both Indonesia's President, Joko Widodo, and Malaysia's Prime Minister, Najib Razak, during their first bilateral meeting in February 2015 had agreed that a new mechanism was to be established, charged to accelerate the process of finding a solution for the Ambalat dispute. Two special envoys each representing Indonesia and Malaysia had been appointed to lead exploratory talks on ways to resolve the sovereignty dispute.

---

[452] "Ambalat Border Dispute Ignored for Joint Indonesia/Malaysia Exploration Efforts", *Jakarta Globe*, 17 June 2013.

Because of having more flexibility in dealing with the Ambalat dispute, Indonesia and Malaysia were becoming even more capable of assuring each other their mutual commitment to avoid armed conflicts between them in the disputed region. The Commander of the Indonesian Armed Forces, General Moeldoko, informed the media in June 2015 that both the armed forces of Indonesia and Malaysia had agreed to stop deploying their respective troops to the disputed waters of ND6 and ND7/Ambalat. He stressed that the two states' sovereignty disputes over the martime zone would be resolved via diplomatic means. General Moeldoko expressed Indonesia's aspiration for peace with Malaysia: "I often communicate with the Commander of the Malaysian Armed Forces…We both understand that there is nothing that should be fought for in the region [ND6 and ND7/Ambalat], we are just wasting our energy."[453] About a year later — August 2016 — the two leaders of Indonesia and Malaysia — Joko Widodo and Najib Razak — had come to the conclusion that the two states' sovereignty disputes over ND6 and ND7/Ambalat should be resolved completely. A fresh mandate had been given to the two special envoys. They were to soon figure out a final comprehensive solution for the dispute which both Indonesia and Malaysia would find agreeable.

It had been a common understanding of Indonesia and Malaysia that the issues of Indonesian migrant workers in Malaysia as well as the two states' territorial disputes were among the most important issues in their bilateral ties.[454] It was the real improvement of the treatments of Indonesian workers in Malaysia coupled with the two states' ability to negotiate indefinitely on their sovereignty disputes that had been driving the dwindling of anti-Malaysia sentiments in Indonesia's society. The sense of pride among Indonesians — that they were the big brother of

---

[453] "Indonesia dan Malaysia Sepakat Tidak Akan Turunkan Prajurit di Ambalat", *Kompas*, 16 June 2015, available at <http://nasional.kompas.com/read/2015/06/16/19463091/ Indonesia.dan.Malaysia.Sepakat.Tidak.Akan.Turunkan.Prajurit.di.Ambalat> (accessed 31 August 2017).

[454] "Jokowi Visit Shows Importance of Jakarta–KL Ties, Says Envoy", *The Star*, 2 February 2015. Also see "Improved Indonesia–Malaysia Ties 'Significant' for ASEAN", *Deutsche Welle*, 6 February 2015, available at <http://www.dw.com/en/improved-indonesia-malaysia-ties-significant-for-asean/a-18237917> (accessed 31 August 2017).

Malaysia — had been confirmed by the fact that Indonesian workers in Malaysia were better protected when compared to previously. The authority of Malaysia was becoming rather responsive in dealing with cases of the abuses of Indonesian workers in Malaysia. The quick response coupled with the stern punishments associated with such abuses in Malaysia symbolized the acknowledgment of Indonesians' status in Malaysia. The rise of Indonesians' sense of humiliation triggered by the repeated cases of mistreatments of Indonesian workers in Malaysia therefore had been effectively moderated.

A few days after the death of Isti Komariyah — who had been starved to death by her Malaysian employers — a representative of Malaysia's Ministry of Human Resources had been sent to Indonesia's embassy in Kuala Lumpur. Maznah Mazlan — the representative — expressed Malaysia's condolences and sympathies to Komariyah's family and Indonesia's society on the passing of Komariyah.[455] He stressed that Malaysia was committed to resolve the abuse case completely.[456] Indonesia's Ambassador to Malaysia, Professor Dai Bachtiar, before long applauded the Malaysian police force for being efficient and credible in handling the abuse case of Komariyah.[457] "We [Indonesia] express our appreciation to the Malaysian government because the police [the Malaysian police] had been quick to investigate [the investigation on the abuse of Komariyah]...", he said.[458] In fact, no street protest against Malaysia had been launched in Indonesia following the death of Isti Komariyah. Subsequent cases of Malaysian employers abusing their Indonesian maids — including a possible murder of a maid — too had not prompted Indonesians to launch street protests against Malaysia. As observed by an officer of Indonesia's embassy in Kuala Lumpur, the swift actions taken by Malaysia's authority against the abuses, and the harsh punishments imposed in Malaysia on those convicted of abusing

---

[455] "Malaysia Sampaikan Belasungkawa kepada Isti Komariyah", *Republika*, 8 June 2011. Also see "Malaysia Sampaikan Belasungkawa Atas Tewas Isti Komariyah", *Tempo*, 8 June 2011.

[456] Ibid.

[457] "Indonesian Envoy Praises Malaysia's Handling of Housemaid Abuse Case", *Borneo Post*, 10 June 2011.

[458] Ibid.

Indonesian workers, together played a crucial role in placating the Indonesian public.[459]

Meanwhile, the setting up of educational facilities for the children of Indonesians working in Sabah and Sarawak had served to enhance Indonesians' sense of closeness with Malaysia. The establishment of such facilities in Malaysia based upon Indonesia's request reflected the close ties between the two states. It matched with Indonesia's expectation that Indonesian workers in Malaysia should be treated with care and respect, since the two states shared a special relationship. Also, Indonesians' clear sense of humiliation associated with the Ambalat dispute — which was inextricably tied to Indonesia's loss of Sipadan and Ligitan — was too in decline over the years. It was the lengthy process of the seemingly endless talks between Indonesia and Malaysia over the disputes that had enabled the fading of such a sense of humiliation among Indonesians.

In essence, it was the moving away from the two sources of conflict in Indonesia–Malaysia relations — that of Indonesians' assertion of their sense of superiority as Malaysia's big brother and the mismatch of expectation between the two states — that had led to the easing of Indonesians' resentment towards Malaysia. Anti-Malaysia sentiments in Indonesia's society waned as a result.

In August 2017, the 29th SEA Games was held in Kuala Lumpur. It was planned that the SEA Games souvenir booklets were to be distributed to the guests who would be attending the games' opening ceremony. Indonesia's Youth and Sports Minister, Imam Nahrawi, while watching the ceremony was quick to detect an error in the souvenir booklets. The Indonesian flag in the booklets had been printed upside down.

Indonesia almost immediately demanded an official apology from Malaysia. Malaysia's Youth and Sports Minister, Khairy Jamaluddin, and the Chairman of the Malaysian SEA Games Organising Committee (MASOC) quickly apologized to Indonesia over the blunder. Khairy admitted that the misprint was a mistake of Malaysia which happened

---

[459] Author's conversation with an Indonesian officer of the Embassy of The Republic of Indonesia in Malaysia during a conference, Kuala Lumpur, 23 May 2017.

due to carelessness. He ordered the souvenir booklets to be corrected and reprinted. Malaysia later made a formal apology to the Indonesian government and the people of Indonesia for the misprint of Indonesia's flag. Indonesia's President, Joko Widodo, accepted the apology. Throughout, he had been reminding Indonesians not to overreact to the flag incident.

Still, some Indonesians did not accept Malaysia's public and official apologies. On 21 August 2017, a protest against the flag blunder had been staged outside Malaysia's embassy in Jakarta. It, however, was not a large-scale demonstration. Only dozens of Indonesians had participated in the protest.[460]

NO MORE *SERUMPUN*?

It had become increasingly common for Indonesians to assert that: no more *serumpun* between Indonesia and Malaysia.[461] For decades, people of the two states had been using the *serumpun* concept to describe the Indonesia–Malaysia special relationship. The rise of the anti-Malaysia sentiments in Indonesia since the early 2000s gave birth to Indonesians' willingness to advocate that there was no more special relationship between Indonesia and Malaysia.

The Indonesia–Malaysia special relationship, nonetheless, continues to exist. Anti-Malaysia sentiments in Indonesia reflect precisely the presence of substantial conflicts in a special relationship. The hypothesis of this thesis points out that a special relationship produces substantial cooperation and substantial conflicts between the two states involved. The conflicts are produced by the intertwined three sources of conflict that are embedded in such a relationship.

Indonesia and Malaysia share a sense of a basis that exists between them, which — in their view — emerged after the Confrontation.[462] That basis is the existence of the strategic cooperation — substantial

---

[460] "Insiden bendera RI terbalik: kedubes Malaysia di Jakarta didemo", *BBC Indonesia*, 21 August 2017.

[461] Interview 926-001, Kuala Lumpur, 26 September 2012. Also see Interview 924-001, Kuala Lumpur, 24 September 2012.

[462] Interview 920, Kuala Lumpur, 20 September 2012. Also see Interview 1008, Jakarta, 8 October 2012; and Interview 1011, Jakarta, 11 October 2012.

cooperation — between them. Indonesia and Malaysia rely on each other to ensure that the Malay world continues to function as a shield that protects their existence as states build around the Malay way of life. The shield is manifested in the form of ASEAN. Both Indonesia and Malaysia are of the view that they are the central force in ASEAN.[463]

In his nationally televised address which was to allay Indonesians' anger towards Malaysia following the case of the double arrest — the arrest of seven Malaysian fishermen and three Indonesian officers that occurred in August 2010 — Indonesia's President, Susilo Bambang Yudhoyono, spelt out five reasons to explain why Indonesia–Malaysia relations should be protected. The first two most important reasons concerned the close ties between Indonesia and Malaysia, and the roles of the two states in ASEAN. President Susilo Bambang Yudhoyono explained that, owing to their intimate cultural and social bonds, ties between Indonesia and Malaysia were probably closer than those of other states, and Indonesia–Malaysia relations were important in the "big ASEAN family".[464] "ASEAN may grow more rapidly due to a strong foundation in Malaysia and Indonesian relations", he said.[465] In other words, the intimate ties between the two Malay states — Indonesia and Malaysia — are deemed to be crucial to the well-functioning of ASEAN.

Former Malaysia's Prime Minister, Dr Mahathir, argued in his speech in December 2009: "…both governments [Indonesia and Malaysia] with a combined population of about 280 million, could reach decisions in ASEAN without being questioned".[466] Such a comment once again reflected the view that Indonesia and Malaysia together constitute

---

[463] Interview 926-001, Kuala Lumpur, 26 September 2012. Also see Interview 1011, Jakarta, 11 October 2012.

[464] "Indonesia and Malaysia Need to Resolve Border Issues Immediately – Susilo", *My Sinchew*, 2 September 2010, available at <http://www.mysinchew.com/node/44306> (accessed 18 September 2017).

[465] Ibid.

[466] "Look at Big Picture, Dr. M Advises Both Countries", *New Straits Times*, 9 December 2009.

the central force in ASEAN. In 2011, Indonesia's and Malaysia's governments had joined forces in preparing for a proposal to turn *Bahasa Indonesia–Melayu* — the Malay language — into an ASEAN language.[467] The proposition was based on the fact that *Bahasa Indonesia–Melayu* is used by the majority population in ASEAN.[468] When discussing about the proposal, Malaysia's Information, Communications and Culture Minister, Dr Rais Yatim, emphasized that *Bahasa Indonesia* and *Bahasa Melayu* were "rich and complete just like American English and British English".[469] The Anglo-American special relationship is a famous and prominent bilateral ties in international politics.

The military ties between Indonesia and Malaysia remains the closest among all other bilateral security ties in ASEAN.[470] The Indonesian and Malaysian armed forces maintain all levels of collaboration between them.[471] The two states' armies, navies, and air forces continue to carry out their regular joint exercises within the framework of GBC. The former top level Malaysian diplomat mentioned earlier described the closeness between the Indonesian and Malaysian armed forces: "An Indonesian army general will say 'We must defend Ambalat!'; the next day you will see him enjoying a drink with his Malaysian counterparts in Kota Kinabalu [Sabah, Malaysia]."[472]

Indonesia's and Malaysia's governments continue to emphasize the closeness between the two states. Indonesia's President, Susilo Bambang Yudhoyono, made Malaysia his first official trip abroad after being re-elected as Indonesia's President in 2009. He declared during the visit: "Malaysia is the closest friend to Indonesia."[473] When he came into power in October 2014, the new President of Indonesia, Joko Widodo,

---

[467] "Bahasa Indonesia-Melayu as ASEAN Language", *Bernama*, 17 November 2011.
[468] Ibid.
[469] "Strive for Bahasa Melayu and Indonesia to Become Respected Languages", *Bernama*, 23 September 2011.
[470] Interview 920, Kuala Lumpur, 20 September 2012.
[471] Ibid.
[472] Interview 920, Kuala Lumpur, 20 September 2012.
[473] "Indonesian President Yudhoyono's Visit to Malaysia", *WikiLeaks*, 19 November 2009, available at <http://wikileaks.org/cable/2009/11/09KUALALUMPUR935.html> (accessed 28 June 2014).

too had decided to make Malaysia his first state visit abroad. Likewise, shortly after taking office in April 2009, Najib Razak had choosen Indonesia to be the destination of his first overseas visit as Malaysia's Prime Minister. The top leaders of the two states maintain a very close relationship.[474] When asked which world leaders did he has a good relationship with, former Malaysia's Prime Minister, Abdullah Badawi, said: "I had good relations with everyone. But one of those I was particularly close to was Indonesia's Susilo Bambang Yudhoyono."[475]

Observers from both sides confirmed that there is a special relationship between Indonesia and Malaysia, acknowledging the coexistence of the two sources of closeness — common identities and shared strategic interests — in the relations.[476] When asked whether Indonesia and Malaysia share common strategic interests, the reply of the former top level Malaysian diplomat was: "Definitely, definitely, we [Indonesia and Malaysia] share common strategic interests, just look at how we formed ASEAN."[477] The forming of ASEAN was an expression of the Indonesia–Malaysia special relationship. An Indonesian diplomat, on the other hand, said: "We [Indonesia and Malaysia] are more than neighbours; we are brothers."[478] In fact, in the face of China's growing assertiveness in the South China Sea since 2009, Weatherbee — a prominent scholar on Southeast Asia — has argued for the strategic cooperation among the "core of like-minded maritime states" in Southeast Asia.[479] ASEAN as a whole — the ten member states — has been unable to restrain China's assertive behaviour in the disputed South China Sea. The like-minded maritime ASEAN member states

---

[474] Ibid. Also see Interview 926-001, Kuala Lumpur, 26 September 2012; and "RI, Malaysia Navies Make Peace Following Ambalat Incident", *The Jakarta Post*, 16 April 2005.

[475] Abdullah Badawi, "'Doing the Invisible': A Conversation with Tun Abdullah Ahmad Badawi", in *Awakening: The Abdullah Badawi Years in Malaysia*, edited by Bridget Welsh and James U.H. Chin (Petaling Jaya: SIRD, 2013), p. 20.

[476] Interview 920, Kuala Lumpur, 20 September 2012. Also see Interview 1011, Jakarta, 11 October 2012; and Interview 1008, Jakarta, 8 October 2012.

[477] Interview 920, Kuala Lumpur, 20 September 2012.

[478] Interview 1008, Jakarta, 8 October 2012.

[479] Donald E. Weatherbee, *Indonesia in ASEAN: Vision and Reality* (Singapore: Institute of Southeast Asian Studies, 2013), pp. 86–89.

therefore — Weatherbee argues — should disengage themselves from the framework of ASEAN and establish a strategic consensus among them.[480] Enhanced security cooperation among the maritime states based on their common strategic view coupled with their limited security links with the United States — Weatherbee maintains — would allow them to be better able to deal with the challenge from China.[481] Such cooperation — Weatherbee suggests — would entail treating China's aggregate economic and political interests in the maritime subregion of Southeast Asia as part of China's stakes in its pursuit of territorial claims in the South China Sea.[482] Weatherbee's arguments reflect the presence of the Malay world in archipelagic Southeast Asia. Driven by the existing strategic partnership between Indonesia and Malaysia in forming the Malay world, the like-minded maritime states of Southeast Asia could work together in solidifying the function of the Malay world — that of a shield that safeguards their respective survival.

The observers, however, recognized the importance of power in the Indonesia–Malaysia special relationship. The Indonesian diplomat explained: "It's different from Singapore; the only larger neighbour that we [Indonesia] have is Malaysia. That's why this [ties with Malaysia] is special for us."[483] The prominent Indonesian journalist mentioned earlier, meanwhile, opined: "It is still a special relationship [Indonesia–Malaysia relations]. We are closer than our respective ties with Singapore and Australia. We can't find this kind of relationship [Indonesia–Malaysia relations] with others. Maybe with Brunei, but Brunei is small."[484]

The hypothesis of this thesis indicates that each of the two states sharing common identities needs to own a necessary amount of power before they could share a special relationship. The amount of power owned by Malaysia — unlike that of Singapore and Brunei — has

---

[480] Ibid.
[481] Ibid.
[482] Ibid.
[483] Interview 1008, Jakarta, 8 October 2012
[484] Interview 1011, Jakarta, 11 October 2012.

surpassed a level that secures Indonesia's recognition of its special ties with Malaysia.

In fact, there is no special relationship between Brunei and Indonesia or Brunei and Malaysia even though the three states were bound by their common Malay way of life. Brunei is always wary of being dominated by Indonesia or Malaysia.[485] It maintains a competitive security posture against Malaysia. Brunei forges extremely close military ties with Singapore in the face of the perceived threat from Malaysia.[486] Instead of maintaining a competitive security posture, two states that share a special relationship will defuse their defence against each other, which is an outcome of their shared war avoidance norms that come with the emergence of the relationship.

While Indonesia and Malaysia share a special relationship, each of them, however, has a closer economic ties with Singapore when compared to that between them. In 2016, Singapore accounted for 9.4 per cent of Indonesia's total trade while Malaysia was at 5.1 per cent.[487] In that same year, Singapore accounted for 12.59 per cent of Malaysia's total trade while Indonesia was at 3.85 per cent.[488] Singapore was the largest foreign investor in Indonesia in both 2015 and 2016.[489]

---

[485] Interview 917, Kuala Lumpur, 17 September 2012.

[486] Tim Huxley, "Singapore and Malaysia: A Precarious Balance?" *The Pacific Review* 4, no. 3 (1991): 209–10.

[487] Ministry of Trade, Republic of Indonesia, "Total Balance of Trade of Indonesia, 2012–2017", available at <http://www.kemendag.go.id/en/economic-profile/indonesia-export-import/indonesia-trade-balance> (accessed 23 September 2017). Also see Ministry of Trade, Republic of Indonesia, "Trade Balance – Indonesia and Singapore, 2012–2017", available at <http://www.kemendag.go.id/en/economic-profile/indonesia-export-import/balance-of-trade-with-trade-partner-country?negara=122> (accessed 23 September 2017); and Ministry of Trade, Republic of Indonesia, "Trade Balance – Indonesia and Malaysia, 2012–2017", available at <http://www.kemendag.go.id/en/economic-profile/indonesia-export-import/balance-of-trade-with-trade-partner-country?negara=124> (accessed 23 September 2017).

[488] MATRADE, "Malaysia's Trade Statistics 2016", available at <http://www.matrade.gov.my/en/malaysian-exporters/services-for-exporters/trade-market-information/trade-statistics> (accessed 27 September 2017).

[489] "Singapore, Biggest Investor in Indonesia in 2015", *Antara News*, 22 January 2016. Also see Santander, "Indonesia: Foreign Investment", available at <https://en.portal.santandertrade.com/establish-overseas/indonesia/foreign-investment> (accessed 26 September 2017).

One, however, has to remember that China is Japan's biggest trading partner. Yet, Japan–China relations are characterized by their explicit strategic competition, rather than mutual strategic dependence. In other words, close economic ties between two states do not necessarily mean that the two states are strategically dependent on each other or share a sense of closeness towards one another.

Obviously, Indonesia's and Malaysia's respective relations with Singapore have been defined by their respective strategic competition with Singapore, not strategic cooperation. Singapore had repeatedly made it clear to Malaysia that it would not hesitate to go to war with Malaysia if Malaysia's government threatens to cut off Singapore's water supply from Johor.[490] When enraged by a series of Singapore's behaviours in 2000, Indonesia's President, Abdulrahman Wahid, during his speech at the Indonesian embassy in Singapore accused Singaporeans of underestimating the Malays and suggested that Indonesia and Malaysia could cut off water supplies to Singapore.[491]

The economic ties between Indonesia and Malaysia has become closer over the years. Malaysia's exports to Indonesia, for example, had increased by 85.3 per cent between 2006 and 2016.[492] Malaysia's exports to Singapore during the same period, however, had increased by less than 30 per cent, which was at around 27 per cent.[493] Malaysia, meanwhile, was the second largest foreign investor in Indonesia in 2015.[494] In November 2015, Indonesia and Malaysia had joined forces in founding the Council of Palm Oil Producing Countries (CPOPC), aiming to better protect their respective palm oil industry through cooperation. The two

---

[490] Jeshurun, *Malaysia*, pp. 225–26.

[491] Rahim, *Singapore in the Malay World*, p. 164.

[492] Economic Planning Unit, Prime Minsiter's Department of Malaysia, "Malaysia's Exports by Major Destination, 1990–2016", available at <http://www.epu.gov.my/en/economic-statistics/external-trade> (accessed 26 September 2017).

[493] Ibid.

[494] Ministry of International Trade and Industry, "Media Release: The Second Indonesia–Malaysia Joint Trade and Invesment Committee (JTIC) Meeting, Jakarta, 30 June 2016", available at <http://www.miti.gov.my/index.php/pages/view/3438> (accessed 27 September 2017). Also see "Singapore, Biggest Investor in Indonesia in 2015", *Antara News*, 22 January 2016.

states are the largest palm oil exporters in the world, which account for 85 per cent of the world's palm oil production. Prompted by the European Union's decision to restrict the imports of palm oil — which will be in place in 2020 — Indonesia and Malaysia have come together in leading ASEAN to face up to the challenge. The two states are tightening their cooperation to cope with the mounting allegations that oil palm planting is harming the environment.[495]

The hypothesis of this thesis has pointed out that the presence of power imbalance in a special relationship is necessary, if it is to transform into a pluralistic security community. Because of the absence of an overwhelmingly strong power between the two, the Indonesia–Malaysia special relationship remains as a security regime, not a security community. Indonesia–Malaysia relations are fundamentally competitive. The two states continue to understand each other in egoistic terms. Each of them is convinced that the counterpart will not use force to settle their disputes, yet no one is certain about it. Indonesia and Malaysia had both engaged in the show of force via military exercises and patrols — not the use of force — when dealing with their sovereignty disputes over Sipadan and Ligitan, and also over the disputed waters of ND6 and ND7/Ambalat.

Observers from both sides acknowledged the existence of substantial conflicts in the Indonesia–Malaysia special relationship. "The Indonesia–Malaysia relationship is special because there is conflict. It doesn't happen between Malaysia and Thailand", said the former top level Malaysian diplomat.[496] "Conflict between brothers sometimes is worse than their respective conflict with other people. This is always the case", said the Indonesian diplomat.[497]

The Indonesia–Malaysia special relationship — like other special relationships — produces double-edged effects — substantial cooperation and substantial conflicts. The U.S.–Canada special relationship, on the one hand, is one of the closest military alliances in the world; yet

---

[495] "Malaysia–Indonesia to Jointly Combat Anti-palm Oil Campaigns", *New Straits Times*, 23 December 2016.

[496] Interview 920, Kuala Lumpur, 20 September 2012.

[497] Interview 1008, Jakarta, 8 October 2012.

on the other, anti-Americanism remains as the premise of Canadian nationalism.[498] The Indonesia–Malaysia special relationship has the same quality. A Malaysian commentator described the relationship between Indonesia and Malaysia: "*benci tapi rindu*" — we hate each other yet we miss each other.[499] An Indonesian senior researcher revealed his appreciation of Malaysia: "Sometimes I see Malaysia as my brother; sometimes I see it as my enemy."[500]

---

[498] Srdjan Vucetic, "The Anglosphere: A Genealogy of an Identity in International Relations", PhD dissertation, The Ohio State University, 2008, p. 182.

[499] Noraini Razak, "Hubungan Benci Tapi Rindu Tiada Kesudahan", *Utusan Malaysia*, 26 June 2012.

[500] Interview 1012, Jakarta, 12 October 2012.

8

CONCLUSION

This study seeks to establish an understanding of what is a special relationship, its dynamics, and its transformation into a pluralistic security community. The theoretical understanding is being tested through the examination of Indonesia–Malaysia relations, which in turn serves to foster better appreciation of the special relationship.

The existing literature has revealed that a special relationship between two states emerges when two sources of closeness coexist in their relations — that of the two states' common identities and shared strategic interests. The two states concerned identify positively with each other owing to their two sources of closeness which result in them sharing an understanding that their relationship is *closer* than their other bilateral ties. Yet, certain conditions need to be in place before two states bound by their common identities could share common strategic interests.

As indicated in Chapter 2, while the common identities of the United States and Great Britain gave rise to their similar strategic understandings, they, however, did not see each other as a strategic partner up until the late nineteenth century. The steady growing of American power since 1850s, which eventually matched with Britain's existing power, produced their mutual need for strategic cooperation.

The Anglo-American special relationship subsequently began to emerge; thereafter, the two states rely on each other for survival. They forge strategic partnerships between them to preserve their similar vision of international order, which is rooted in the English concepts of liberty. Likewise, despite the shared values of the United States and Israel render both similarily prefer a Middle East that is compatible with the interests of Western democracy, the United States did not recognize its mutual strategic dependence with Israel up until 1967 when Israel had demonstrated its capacity by decisively defeating its Arab foes in the Six-Day War. Henceforth, the United States forges a special relationship with Israel. The two states work closely with each other to fashion a strategic landscape in the Middle East which both similarly prefer.

In other words, this study has revealed the relationship between identities and power in the creation of the common strategic interests of two states sharing common identities, which subsequently gives rise to their special relationship. As pointed out in Chapter 2, the identities of a state give birth to its strategic understanding. Common identities of two states, therefore, produce their similar strategic understandings. Yet, sharing similar strategic understandings do not mean that the two states are strategically dependent on each other. Each of them needs to own a necessary amount of power so as to shape their similar strategic understandings into their common strategic interests, namely the creation of their mutual strategic dependence. In a special relationship, the common strategic interests of the two states concerned are founded on their similar strategic outlook rooted in their common identities, and created by their necessary amount of power.

The establishment of an appreciation of the creation of a special relationship with theoretical foundations by this study helps clarify the understanding of the Indonesia–Malaysia special relationship. It addresses the fundamental puzzle that has continued to plague the existing studies of Indonesia–Malaysia relations: that of why the supposedly special nature of Indonesia–Malaysia relations did not prevent the two states from plunging into armed conflicts between them during the 1960s?

The existing studies of Indonesia–Malaysia relations hold the view that a special relationship had already existed between the two states even before the outbreak of their violent conflicts happening during their confrontation from 1963 to 1966.[1] These studies are in the realm of the identity school which argues that a special relationship is the natural consequence of the two states concerned sharing common identities.[2] In other words, in the eyes of these studies, Indonesia and Malaysia share a special relationship because they share common identities.

While the attempts to employ the identity school in explaining the Indonesia–Malaysia special relationship reflect the significant scholarly development in the understanding of this special relation, the existing literature, however, is inherently problematic. It is unable to explain why Indonesia and Malaysia did not manage to avoid an armed conflict between them during their confrontation even though they were supposedly bound by their special ties. In fact, states sharing a special relationship will not easily tumble into armed conflicts between them. The U.S.–U.K., U.S.–Canada and U.S.–Israel special relationships, for example, do not lead to war between the respective two parties since the establishment of these special ties.[3]

---

[1] Joseph Chinyong Liow, *The Politics of Indonesia–Malaysia Relations: One Kin, Two Nations* (London and New York: Routledge, 2005), pp. 79–118, 166. Also see Ahmad Nizar Yaakub, "Malaysia and Indonesia: A Study of Foreign Policies with Special Reference to Bilateral Relations", PhD dissertation, The University of Western Australia, 2009, p. 88; and Marshall Clark and Juliet Pietsch, *Indonesia–Malaysia Relations: Cultural Heritage, Politics and Labour Migration* (London and New York: Routledge, 2014), pp. 8, 20.

[2] Liow, *The Politics of Indonesia–Malaysia Relations*, pp. 3, 16–17, 25–26. Also see Khadijah Md. Khalid and Shakila Yacob, "Managing Malaysia–Indonesia Relations in the Context of Democratization: The Emergence of Non-State Actors", *International Relations of the Asia-Pacific* 12 (2012): 358; Yaakub, "Malaysia and Indonesia", pp. 88, 104; and Clark and Pietsch, *Indonesia–Malaysia Relations*, pp. 8, 20.

[3] Jack L. Granatstein and Norman Hillmer, *For Better Or For Worse: Canada and the United States to the 1990s* (Toronto: Copp Clark Pitman Ltd., 1991), p. 54. Also see Sean M. Shore, "No Fences Make Good Neighbors: The Development of the Canadian–US Security Community, 1871–1940", in *Security Communities*, edited by Emanuel Adler and Michael Barnett (Cambridge: Cambridge University Press, 1998), p. 348.

As revealed by this study, armed conflicts broke out between Indonesia and Malaysia during the 1960s simply because there was no special relationship between the two states. Before its expansion into Malaysia, Malaya did not possess the necessary amount of power that would produce Indonesia's strategic reliance on Malaya. As a result, two sources of closeness — common identities and shared strategic interests — did not coexist in Indonesia–Malaya relations. A special relationship therefore did not exist between the two states. While Malaya had expanded into Malaysia in September 1963, Indonesia was not immediately impressed by the power owned by Malaysia up until late 1965, which was followed by the emergence of the Indonesia–Malaysia special relationship.

As pointed out in this study, a special relationship as a security regime is built on the existence of power balance between the two states involved. The presence of power balance furnishes a basis of order between the two states, which hinders them from launching an armed attack against each other, and consequently, able to coexist peacefully. The absence of special ties between Indonesia and Malaya indicated the absence of power balance — hence a basis of order — between them. Indonesia and Malaya in consequence were unable to coexist peacefully. Indonesia had shown no restraint in launching military attacks on Malaya/Malaysia, aiming to prevent Malaya's expansion into Malaysia.

The focus of the existing studies of Indonesia–Malaysia relations on the factor of identity has led them to overlook the crucial role of power in the relations. As a consequence, their understandings of the Indonesia–Malaysia special relationship are bound to be problematic.

This study has also brought to light the dynamics of a special relationship. A special relationship is characterized by its double-edged effects. It produces substantial cooperation and substantial conflicts between the two states involved. It is the interplay of power and common identities in a special relationship that gives birth to its double-edged effects. Such an appreciation of the dynamics of a special relationship enables this study to point out that conflict is not a dominant feature in Indonesia–Malaysia relations, but rather a part of the double-edged effects of this special relationship.

The overall view of the existing studies of Indonesia–Malaysia relations is that the bilateral ties is largely defined by the conflicts between the two states.[4] The theoretical framework of the study, however, reveals that the Indonesia–Malaysia special relationship — like other special relationships — is in fact characterized by its double-edged effects. Not only does the special relationship result in substantial conflicts between Indonesia and Malaysia, it also produces their substantial cooperation. In other words, while there have been apparent conflicts between Indonesia and Malaysia, cooperation between them are also solid. As pointed out in Chapter 7, on the one hand, anti-Malaysia sentiments are prevalent in Indonesia's society; on the other hand, the strategic cooperation between Indonesia and Malaysia in constituting the Malay world manifests in the form of ASEAN remains a central feature of their foreign policies. It is the study's theoretical framework that has prompted one not to overlook the substantial cooperation that exist in the special ties of Indonesia and Malaysia all along.

Paradoxically, while the strategic cooperation — namely, substantial cooperation — in a special relationship is rooted in the common identities of the two states involved, common identities, in the meantime, are a source of conflicts between them. A state's national identity is founded upon its pre-modern cultural identities. Each state needs its own distinctive national identity so as to ensure its existence in the world of nations. The pre-modern cultural identities of a state therefore become its reservoir of culture which allows it to return, rediscover and reinterpret its culture, creating a national identity that is unique and authentic. As indicated in this study, the respective national identity of two states sharing a special relationship is founded on their pre-modern common cultural identities. There are therefore inevitable similarities between the national identities of the two states concerned. The two states as a result are obliged to emphasize their differences based upon their common cultural identities, in order to ensure their respective unique existence vis-à-vis every other nation. In other words, two states in a special relationship are similar; and because they are similar, they need to enhance their difference.

---

[4]   Liow, *The Politics of Indonesia–Malaysia Relations*. Also see Yaakub, "Malaysia and Indonesia", p. 1; and Clark and Pietsch, *Indonesia–Malaysia Relations*, p. 17.

Indonesia and Malaysia, for example, every now and then quarrel over the issue of which among them is the owner of their common culture.

Further, this study has contributed to the understanding of the Indonesia–Malaysia special relationship's essence as a security regime. As explained in Chapter 4, a special relationship constitutes a security regime, that of the war avoidance norms around which expectations of the states involved converge. States in such a regime are bound by their shared commitment to avoid an armed conflict between them.

The existing literature of Indonesia–Malaysia relations acknowledges the two states' commitment to avoid war between them, namely, they are restrained by their war avoidance norms. The literature, however, remains unable to explain why Indonesia and Malaysia share such norms. Clark's and Juliet's study argues that the existence of ASEAN enables the two states to avoid war between them as they aim to preserve the stability of this regional body.[5] The authors nevertheless do not explain why ASEAN has such effects on Indonesia and Malaysia. The theoretical framework of this study has brought forth the under-standing that it is the two sources of closeness — common identities and shared strategic interests — in the Indonesia–Malaysia special relationship that have given rise to the two states' war avoidance norms. The two sources of closeness in a special relationship generate the mutual aspiration for peace between the two states involved, which are strong enough to give birth to their shared war avoidance norms. The commitment of Indonesia and Malaysia in avoiding an armed conflict between them subsequently creates and sustains the war avoidance norms of ASEAN. As explained in Chapter 6, Indonesia's and Malaysia's shared war avoidance norms serve as an established norm within ASEAN, which spawns the ASEAN member states' habit to avoid armed conflicts between them.

Finally, the hypothesis of the study's thereotical framework has further illuminated the fact that the Indonesia–Malaysia special relationship constitutes a security regime — namely they share war

---

[5]   Clark and Pietsch, *Indonesia–Malaysia Relations*, p. 17.

avoidance norms — not a security community. The framework points out that the presence of power imbalance between Indonesia and Malaysia is necessary if this special relationship is to transform into a pluralistic security community.

As explained in Chapter 2, states in a pluralistic security community understand each other in collective terms. Because of the presence of power imbalance in a special relationship, the weaker state in the relationship views its overwhelmingly powerful counterpart as part of self owing to the counterpart's role as its security guarantor. In a special relationship, the strong state's immense power protects its way of life, which also largely protects that of its weaker counterpart. Two states in a special relationship share similar way of life because of them sharing common identities. Their similar way of life continues to be challenged by culturally different powers, which seek to impose their own values in international politics.

The overwhelmingly powerful state in a special relationship, on the other hand, views its counterpart as part of self as it is strategically dependent on its counterpart to form its international strategic preponderance, which ultimately protects its own survival, namely, its way of life. Further, the strong state's possible confrontational behaviours against its weaker counterpart have been prevented, since it is able to express its dominance over its weaker partner owing to its role as the security guarantor in the special relationship.

A special relationship's transformation into a pluralistic security community once again highlights the essential role of power in such a relationship. The special ties between two states are created by the necessary amount of power that each of them owns. While the survival of the weaker state in a special relationship is rested upon the immense power of its overwhelmingly powerful counterpart, the weaker state, nonetheless, continues to possess the necessary amount of power that ensures its strategic status in the understanding of its powerful counterpart. As revealed in Chapter 4, despite being the junior partner in the Anglo-American and U.S.–Canada special relationships, both Britain and Canada respectively continues to retain the amount of power that produces America's recognition of the need to forge strategic partnerships with them. Without such partnerships, America's global preponderance — expresses in the form of an American international system rooted in the English concepts of liberty — will be in jeopardy. Clearly, with the presence of power imbalance in a special relationship, the junior partner in the relationship is much weaker than its powerful counterpart. Yet, because of owning the necessary amount of power, the junior partner remains able to project an amount of cost that can cripple the international strategic preponderance of its powerful counterpart should its counterpart desists from forging strategic cooperation between them. As pointed out in Chapter 4, despite the earlier consideration of ending its nuclear partnership with Britain, the United States at last agreed to provide Britain with its most advanced nuclear weapon system of the time — the Polaris — having confronted with the prospect of losing Britain as its special junior partner.

The absence of power imbalance in the Indonesia–Malaysia special relationship points to the fact that there is no security community between the two states. Because of the presence of power balance between them, Indonesia and Malaysia will continue to compete with each other for dominance. In other words, their relationship is fundamentally competitive. Indonesia and Malaysia do not view each other in collective-self terms; armed conflict between them is unlikely, although not impossible.

The examination of special relationships by this study has also led to a clearer understanding of the meaning of the presence of power imbalance among states. As pointed out in Chapter 3, power imbalance functions as an accelerator of war or a basis of peace between the states involved. A special relationship will transform into a pluralistic security community — this study argues — when power imbalance exists between the two states concerned. In other words, the existence of common identities between states plays an essential role in shaping the function of power imbalance among them.

Power imbalance between states becomes an accelerator of war between them, when they do not share common identities — which also means they do not share similar way of life. China–Vietnam and Russia–Finland — the examples put forward in Chapter 3 — each are two states that do not share common identities. Hostilities among the states with different identities intensify as a result of the presence of power imbalance between them. The weaker states — among the states concerned — see their overwhelmingly powerful counterpart as a threat to their survival — their ways of life — hence are determined to confront the dominance of their counterpart, which has a different way of life. The weaker states need to do so to protect their very survival — their ways of life. The immensely powerful counterpart in response turns its dominant behaviours against the weaker states into confrontational ones. Such intensification of hostilities often leads to wars between the weak states and the strong one. As revealed in Chapter 3, the asymmetric relation between Russia and Finland and that of between China and Vietnam had precipitated the eruption of war between the respective two parties, which do not share common identities. Finland, for instance, had been unyielding in its struggle against Russia — its mighty neighbour — to protect the Finnish way of life.[6] The Finnish and the Russian ways of life were different.[7] Russia was infuriated by Finland's determination to confront its dominance.[8]

On the other hand, power imbalance between states serves as a basis of peace between them, when they are bound by their common identities — that of sharing similar way of life. The weaker states — among the states which share common identities — accept the dominance of their overwhelmingly powerful counterpart and cease their confrontational behaviours against their counterpart, as they need their immensely powerful counterpart to protect their survival, namely, their ways of life, which are similar to that of their powerful counterpart. The overwhelmingly powerful state — among the states concerned — meanwhile, will not confront its weaker counterparts since it is able to express its dominance over its weaker counterparts, and such expressions have been partially defused by its strategic reliance on its weaker counterparts in forming its international strategic preponderance, which is meant to protect its survival, that of its way of life. The

---

[6] Eloise Engle and Lauri Paananen, *The Winter War: The Soviet Attack on Finland 1939–1940* (US: Stackpole Books, 1992), pp. xiv-xv. For more discussion see Chapter 3, pp. 74–76.

[7] Ibid.

[8] Ibid.

power imbalance between the states concerned therefore ensures the absence of confrontation among them, hence serving as a basis of peace between them — as demonstrated by the U.S.–U.K. and U.S.–Canada asymmetric special ties discussed in Chapter 4. The two states in each of the relations share common identities.

Apart from special relationships, the presence of power imbalance among states which share a broader sense of common identities too functions as a basis of peace between them. As discussed in Chapter 3, the power imbalance between America and Western Europe was a basis of peace among them. America and Western Europe are bound by their broad common identities, namely, Western Christianity.[9] They relied on each other to safeguard their survival — that of their similar way of life deriving from Western Christianity.[10] The international order that protected their similar way of life had been challenged by the culturally different superpower — the Soviet Union. Russia's culture is rooted in Orthodox Christianity.[11] The Soviet sought to establish its own version of global order.

As pointed out in Chapter 2, in order to transform into a pluralistic security community, the identities of the states involved have to be peaceful in nature. A state with identities that are in essence violent — such as identities that are brutal, militaristic, expansionist or ideological crusading — will not be able to form a security community with others, as it remains possible for the state to resort to violent means in solving its interstate disputes. The Austria–Germany security community, for example, collapsed after 1932 amidst the rise of Nazis to power in Germany, who had subsequently transformed Germany into a fascist

---

[9]   Samuel P. Huntington, "The Clash of Civilizations?" *Foreign Affairs* 72, no. 3 (1993): 29–30. Also see Samuel P. Huntington, *The Clash of Civilizations and the Remaking of World Order* (UK: The Free Press, 2002), pp. 46–47.

[10] Huntington, "The Clash of Civilizations?", p. 39. Also see Huntington, *The Clash of Civilizations and the Remaking of World Order*, p. 157.

[11] Huntington, "The Clash of Civilizations?", pp. 29–30. Also see Huntington, *The Clash of Civilizations and the Remaking of World Order*, p. 157.

totalitarian state.[12] In other words, despite the presence of power imbalance in a special relationship, the relationship will not evolve into a pluralistic security community if the identities of any of the two states concerned are violent in nature.

---

[12] Karl W. Deutsch et al., *Political Community and the North Atlantic Area: International Organization in the Light of Historical Experience* (Princeton, NJ: Princeton University Press, 1957), p. 65.

BIBLIOGRAPHY

Abdul Rahman, Tunku. *Viewpoints*. Kuala Lumpur: Heinemann Educational Books, 1978.

————. *Lest We Forget*: *Further Candid Reminiscences*. Malaysia: Eastern Universities Press, 1983.

————. *Looking Back: Monday Musings and Memories*. Malaysia: MPH Group Publishing, 2011.

Abdullah Ahmad. *Tengku Abdul Rahman and Malaysia's Foreign Policy 1963–1970*. Kuala Lumpur: Berita Publishing, 1985.

Abdullah Badawi. "'Doing the Invisible': A Conversation with Tun Abdullah Ahmad Badawi". In *Awakening: The Abdullah Badawi Years in Malaysia*, edited by Bridget Welsh and James U.H. Chin. Petaling Jaya: SIRD, 2013, pp. 3–38.

Acharya, Amitav. "A Regional Security Community in Southeast Asia?" In *The Transformation of Security in the Asia Pacific Region*, edited by Desmond Ball. London: Frank Cass, 1996, pp. 175–200.

————. "Collective Identity and Conflict Management in Southeast Asia". In *Security Communities*, edited by Emanuel Adler and Michael Barnett. Cambridge: Cambridge University Press, 1998, pp. 198–227.

————. *Constructing a Security Community in Southeast Asia: ASEAN and the Problem of Regional Order*. London and New York: Routledge, 2001.

Adams, Henry. *The Education of Henry Adams*. USA: Sentry Edition, 1961.

Adler, Emanuel. "Imagined (Security) Communities: Cognitive Regions in International Relations". *Journal of International Studies* 26, no. 2 (1997*a*): 249–77.

————. "Seizing the Middle Ground: Constructivism in World Politics". *European Journal of International Relations* 3, no. 3 (1997*b*): 319–63.

————. "Seeds of Peaceful Change: The OSCE's Security Community-Building Model". In *Security Communities*, edited by Emanuel Adler and Michael Barnett. Cambridge: Cambridge University Press, 1998, pp. 119–60.

Adler, Emanuel and Michael Barnett. "A Framework for the Study of Security Communities". In *Security Communities*, edited by Emanuel Adler and Michael Barnett. Cambridge: Cambridge University Press, 1998*a*, pp. 29–65.

———. "Security Communities in Theoretical Perspective". In *Security Communities*, edited by Emanuel Adler and Michael Barnett. Cambridge: Cambridge University Press, 1998*b*, pp. 3–28.

Ajami, Fouad. "The End of Pan-Arabism". In *Pan-Arabism and Arab Nationalism: The Continuing Debate*, edited by Tawfic E. Farah. Boulder and London: Westview Press, 1987, pp. 96–114.

Allen, Harry C. *Great Britain and the United States: A History of Anglo-American Relations (1783–1952)*. New York: St. Martin's Press Inc., 1955.

Al-Mashat, Abdul-Monem. "Stress and Disintegration in the Arab World". In *Pan-Arabism and Arab Nationalism: The Continuing Debate*, edited by Tawfic E. Farah. Boulder and London: Westview Press, 1987, pp. 165–76.

Anderson, Benedict. *Imagined Communities: Reflections on the Origin and Spread of Nationalism*. London, New York: Verso, 1991.

Antolik, Michael. *ASEAN and the Diplomacy of Accommodation*. New York: An East Gate Book, 1990.

Anwar, Dewi Fortuna. *Indonesia in ASEAN: Foreign Policy and Regionalism*. Singapore: Institute of Southeast Asian Studies, 1994.

———. *Indonesia's Strategic Culture: Ketahanan Nasional, Wawasan Nusantara and Hankamrata*. Australia: Griffith University, 1996.

Arifianto, Alexander R. "The Securitization of Transnational Labor Migration: The Case of Malaysia and Indonesia". *Asian Politics & Policy* 1, no. 4 (2009): 613–30.

Azizah Kassim. "Illegal Alien Labour in Malaysia: Its Influx, Utilization, and Ramifications". *Indonesia and the Malay World* 25, no. 71 (1997): 50–81.

Azubuike, Samuel. "The 'Poodle Theory' and the Anglo-American 'Special Relationship'". *International Studies* 42, no. 2 (2005): 123–39.

Barker, Elisabeth. *Churchill and Eden at War*. London: Macmillan, 1978.

Barnett, Michael. "Social Constructivism". In *The Globalization of World Politics*, edited by John Baylis and Steve Smith. New York: Oxford University Press, 2005, pp. 251–70.

Barnett, Michael and Emanuel Adler. "Studying Security Communities in Theory, Comparison, and History". In *Security Communities*, edited by Emanuel Adler and Michael Barnett. Cambridge: Cambridge University Press, 1998, pp. 413–41.

Baylis, John. "The 'Special Relationship': A Diverting British Myth?" In *Haunted by History: Myths in International Relations,* edited by Cyril Buffet and Beatrice Heuser. Oxford: Berghahn Books, 1998, pp. 117–34.

———. "The Anglo-American Relationship and Alliance Theory". *International Relations* 8, no. 4 (1985): 368–79.

————, ed. *Anglo-American Relations since 1939: The Enduring Alliance*. Manchester and New York: Manchester University Press, 1997.

Benny, Guido. "The Indonesian Nationalism and Perceived Threats of Neighbouring Countries: Public Opinion Toward the ASEAN Community". *International Journal on Social Science Economics & Art* 2, no. 3 (2012): 38–44.

Berenskoetter, Felix. "Friends, There Are No Friends? An Intimate Reframing of the International". *Journal of International Studies* 35, no. 3 (2007): 647–76.

Berger, Thomas U. "Norms, Identity, and National Security in Germany and Japan". In *The Culture of National Security: Norms and Identity in World Politics*, edited by Peter J. Katzenstein, 1996, pp. 317–56.

Bloom, William. *Personal Identity, National Identity and International Relations*. Cambridge: Cambridge University Press, 1990.

Bothwell, Robert. *Canada and the United States: The Politics of Partnership*. Canada: University of Toronto Press, 1992.

————. *Alliance and Illusion: Canada and the World, 1945–1984*. Vancouver and Toronto: UBC Press, 2007.

Bourne, Kenneth. *Britain and the Balance of Power in North America, 1815–1908*. Berkeley: University of California Press, 1967.

Brackman, Arnold C. *Southeast Asia's Second Front: The Power Struggle in the Malay Archipelago*. London: Pall Mall Press, 1966.

Brysk, Alison, Craig Parsons, and Wayne Sandholtz. "After Empire: National Identity and Post-Colonial Families of Nations". *European Journal of International Relations* 8, no. 2 (2002): 267–305.

"Build the World Anew". In *The New Emerging Forces: Documents on the Ideology of Indonesian Foreign Policy*, edited by George Modelski. Australia: The Australian National University, 1963, pp. 1–43.

Bunnell, Frederick P. "Guided Democracy Foreign Policy: 1960–1965 — President Sukarno Moves from Non-Alignment to Confrontation". *Indonesia* 2 (October 1966): 37–76.

Burk, Kathleen. *Old World, New World: The Story of Britain and America*. Great Britain: Abacus, 2009.

Calleo, David P. "Introduction". In *Europe's Franco–German Engine*, edited by David P. Calleo and Eric R. Staal. Washington, D.C.: Brookings Institution Press, 1998, pp. 1–19.

Carey, Peter. "Introduction". In *Born in Fire: The Indonesian Struggle for Independence: An Anthology*, edited by Colin Wild and Peter Carey. Athens: Ohio University Press, 1988, pp. xix–xxviii.

Chalala, Elie. "Arab Nationalism: A Bibliographic Essay". In *Pan-Arabism and Arab Nationalism: The Continuing Debate*, edited by Tawfic E. Farah. Boulder and London: Westview Press, 1987, pp. 18–56.

Cheah Boon Keng. *Malaysia: The Making of a Nation*. Singapore: Institute of Southeast Asian Studies, 2002.

Checkel, Jeffrey T. "The Constructivist Turn in International Relations Theory". *World Politics* 50, no. 2 (1998): 324–48.

Chin, Christine B.N. "'Diversification' and 'Privatisation': Securing Insecurities in the Receiving Country of Malaysia". *The Asia Pacific Journal of Anthropology* 9, no. 4 (December 2008): 285–303.

Chong Jinn Winn. "'Mine, Yours Or Ours?': The Indonesia–Malaysia Disputes Over Shared Cultural Heritage". *Journal of Social Issues in Southeast Asia* 27, no. 1 (2012): 1–53.

Churchill, Randolph S., ed. *The Sinews of Peace, Post-War Speeches by Winston S. Churchill*. London: Cassell, 1948.

Churchill, Winston S. *The Second World War Volume II: Their Finest Hour*. London: Cassell & Co. Ltd., 1949.

———. "The Anglo-American Alliance, November 7, 1945, House of Commons". In *Winston S. Churchill: His Complete Speeches, 1897–1963 Volume VII 1943–1949*, edited by Robert Rhodes James. New York and London: Chelsea House Publishers, 1974*a*, pp. 7241–48.

———. "The Benjamin Franklin Medal". In *Winston S. Churchill: His Complete Speeches 1897–1963, Vol VIII*, edited by Robert Rhodes James. New York: Chelsea House, 1974*b*, p. 8671.

Clark, Marshall. "The Politics of Heritage: Indonesia–Malaysia Cultural Contestations". *Indonesia and the Malay World* 41, no. 121 (2013): 396–417.

Clark, Marshall and Juliet Pietsch. *Indonesia–Malaysia Relations: Cultural Heritage, Politics and Labour Migration*. London and New York: Routledge, 2014.

Coates, David and Joel Krieger. *Blair's War*. Cambridge: Polity Press, 2004.

Costigliola, Frank C. "Anglo-American Financial Rivalry in the 1920s". *The Journal of Economic History* 37, no. 4 (December 1977): 911–34.

Danchev, Alex. "On Specialness". *International Affairs* 72, no. 4 (1996): 737–50.

———. *On Specialness: Essays in Anglo-American Relations*. Great Britain: Macmillan Press Ltd., 1998.

Davis, Forrest. *The Atlantic System: The Story of Anglo-American Control of the Seas*. London: George Allen & Unwin Ltd., 1943.

Dawson, Raymond and Richard Rosecrance. "Theory and Reality in the Anglo-American Alliance". *World Politics* 19, no. 1 (1966): 21–51.

Derichs, Claudia. "Malaysia in 2006: An Old Tiger Roars". *Asian Survey* 47, no. 1 (January/February 2007): 148–54.

Deutsch, Karl W., Sidney A. Burrell, Robert A. Kann, Maurice Lee, Jr., Martin Lichterman, Raymond E. Lindgren, Francis L. Loewenheim, and Richard W. Van Wagenen. *Political Community and the North Atlantic Area: International Organization in the Light of Historical Experience*. Princeton, NJ: Princeton University Press, 1957.

Dewano, Mario Pandu. "Non-Traditional Security Issue and International Conflict: A Case Study of Indonesian Migrant Labor in Malaysia". Master dissertation, Lund University, 2007.

Dhillon, Karminder Singh. *Malaysian Foreign Policy in the Mahathir Era 1981–2003: Dilemmas of Development.* Singapore: NUS Press, 2009.

Dickey, John Sloan. *Canada and the American Presence: The United States Interest in an Independent Canada.* New York: New York University Press, 1975.

Dickie, John. *'Special' No More — Anglo-American Relations: Rhetoric and Reality.* London: Weidenfeld & Nicolson, 1994.

Djalal, Dino Patti. *The Geopolitics of Indonesia's Maritime Territorial Policy.* Jakarta: Centre for Strategic and International Studies, 1996.

Dobson, Alan P. *Anglo-American Relations in the Twentieth Century: Of Friendship, Conflict and the Rise and Decline of Superpowers.* London and New York: Routledge, 1995.

Dumbrell, John. "The US–UK 'Special Relationship' in a World Twice Transformed". *Cambridge Review of International Affairs* 17, no. 3 (2004): 437–50.

———. *A Special Relationship: Anglo-American Relations from the Cold War to Iraq.* New York: Palgrave, 2006.

Dunne, Tim and Brian C. Schmidt. "Realism". In *The Globalization of World Politics*, edited by John Baylis and Steve Smith. New York: Oxford University Press, 2005, pp. 161–83.

Elie, Jerome B. "Many Times Doomed But Still Alive: An Attempt to Understand the Continuity of the Special Relationship". *Journal of Transatlantic Studies* 3, no. 1 (2005): 63–83.

Elson, Robert E. *Suharto: A Political Biography.* Cambridge: Cambridge University Press, 2001.

Emmerson, Donald K. "Indonesia, Malaysia, Singapore: A Regional Security Core?" In *Southeast Asian Security in the New Millennium*, edited by Richard J. Ellings and Sheldon W. Simon. New York and London, England: NBR: Armonk, 1996, pp. 34–88.

Engle, Eloise and Lauri Paananen. *The Winter War: The Soviet Attack on Finland 1939–1940.* US: Stackpole Books, 1992.

Erikson, Erik H. *Identity and the Life Cycle: Volume I.* US: Indiana University Press, 1959.

Fairlie, Henry. *The Kennedy Promise: The Politics of Expectation.* London: Eyre Methuen, 1973.

Federation of Malaya. *Parliamentary Debates, 6th December 1960.* Kuala Lumpur: House of Representatives, 1960.

Feldman, Lily Gardner. *The Special Relationship Between West Germany and Israel.* Boston: George Allen & Unwin, 1984.

Fernandes, Clinton. *Reluctant Saviour: Australia, Indonesia and the Independence of East Timor.* Australia: Scribe Publications, 2004.

———. *Reluctant Indonesians: Australia, Indonesia, and the Future of West Papua.* Australia: Scribe Publications, 2006.

———. *The Independence of East Timor: Multi-Dimensional Perspectives — Occupation, Resistance, and International Political Activism.* Brighton, Portland and Toronto: Sussex Academic Press, 2011.

Friedman, Marilyn. *What Are Friends For?* Ithaca: Cornell University Press, 1993.

Ganesan, N. "Rethinking ASEAN as a Security Community in Southeast Asia". *Asian Affairs* 21, no. 4 (1995): 210–26.

Garces-Mascarenas, Blanca. *Labour Migration in Malaysia and Spain.* Amsterdam: Amsterdam University Press, 2012.

Garver, John W. *Protracted Contest: Sino–Indian Rivalry in the Twentieth Century.* US: University of Washington Press, 2001.

Gelber, Lionel M. *The Rise of Anglo-American Friendship: A Study in World Politics, 1898–1906.* London, New York and Toronto: Oxford University Press, 1938.

Ghazali Shafie. *Malaysia, ASEAN and the New World Order.* Bangi: Universiti Kebangsaan Malaysia Press, 2000.

———. *Malay Rumpun and Malaysia Bangsa towards 2020.* Bangi: Universiti Kebangsaan Malaysia Press, 2009.

Gilbert, Felix. *To the Farewell Address: Ideas of Early American Foreign Policy.* Princeton and New Jersey: Princeton University Press, 1961.

Government of Malaysia. *Malaya–Indonesia Relations 31st August 1957 to 15th September 1963.* Kuala Lumpur: Jabatan Chetak Kerajaan, 1963.

———. *Indonesian Aggression Against Malaysia, Volume I.* Kuala Lumpur: Government Press, 1965.

Government of Malaysia and Government of Indonesia. *GBC MALINDO Malaysia–Indonesia: 25th Anniversary General Border Committee Malaysia–Indonesia.* Kuala Lumpur: Jabatan Perdana Menteri Malaysia, 1997.

Granatstein, Jack L. and Norman Hillmer. *For Better Or For Worse: Canada and the United States to the 1990s.* Toronto: Copp Clark Pitman Ltd., 1991.

Gross Stein, Janice. "Detection and Defection: Security 'Regimes' and the Management of International Conflict". *International Journal* 40, no. 4 (1985): 599–627.

Gwynn, Stephen, ed. "From April 1917 to January 1918". In *The Letters and Friendships of Sir Cecil Spring Rice: A Record, Volume II.* New York: Books For Libraries Press, 1972a, pp. 390–425.

———. "The End of Service". In *The Letters and Friendships of Sir Cecil Spring Rice: A Record, Volume II.* New York: Books For Libraries Press, 1972b, pp. 426–38.

Haggard, Stephan and Beth A. Simmons. "Theories of International Regimes". *International Organization* 41, no. 3 (1987): 491–517.

Haglund, David G. "The US–Canada Relationship: How 'Special' is America's Oldest Unbroken Alliance?" In *America's 'Special Relationships': Foreign and Domestic Aspects of the Politics of Alliance*, edited by John Dumbrell and Axel R. Schäfer. London and New York: Routledge, 2009, pp. 60–75.

Haller-Trost, Renate. *Boundary and Territory Briefing — The Territorial Dispute Between Indonesia and Malaysia Over Pulau Sipadan and Pulau Ligitan in the Celebes Sea: A Study in International Law*. UK: International Boundaries Research Unit, 1995.

Hanggi, Heiner. *ASEAN and the ZOPFAN Concept*. Singapore: Institute of Southeast Asian Studies, 1991.

Hendrick, Burton J. *The Life and Letters of Walter H. Page Volume I*. London: William Heinemann Ltd., 1923*a*.

———. *The Life and Letters of Walter H. Page Volume II*. London: William Heinemann Ltd., 1923*b*.

Hendriks, Gisela and Annette Morgan. *The Franco–German Axis in European Integration*. UK & USA: Edward Elgar Publishing Limited, 2001.

Hensel, Paul R. "The Evolution of the Franco–German Rivalry". In *Great Power Rivalries*, edited by William R. Thompson. US: University of South Carolina Press, 1999, pp. 86–121.

Herman, Robert G. "Identity, Norms, and National Security: The Soviet Foreign Policy Revolution and the End of the Cold War". In *The Culture of National Security: Norms and Identity in World Politics*, edited by Peter J. Katzenstein. New York: Columbia University Press, 1996, pp. 271–316.

Herring, George C. *From Colony to Superpower: U.S. Foreign Relations Since 1776*. New York: Oxford University Press, 2008.

Holst, Frederik. *(Dis-) Connected History: The Indonesia–Malaysia Relationship*. Germany: Regiospectra, 2007.

Hood, Steven J. *Dragons Entangled: Indochina and the China–Vietnam War*. US: An East Gate Book, 1992.

Hopf, Ted. "The Promise of Constructivism in International Relations Theory". *International Security* 23, no. 1 (1998): 171–200.

House, Edward Mandell. *The Intimate Papers of Colonel House Volume I: Behind the Political Curtain, 1912–1915*. London: Ernest Benn Limited, 1926.

Huntington, Samuel P. "The Clash of Civilizations?" *Foreign Affairs* 72, no. 3 (1993): 22–49.

———. *The Clash of Civilizations and the Remaking of World Order*. UK: The Free Press, 2002.

———. *Who Are We? America's Great Debate*. Great Britain: The Free Press, 2005.

Hurrell, Andrew. "An Emerging Security Community in South America?" In *Security Communities*, edited by Emanuel Adler and Michael Barnett. Cambridge: Cambridge University Press, 1998, pp. 228–64.

Huxley, Tim. "Singapore and Malaysia: A Precarious Balance?" *The Pacific Review* 4, no. 3 (1991): 204–13.

Ismail Hussein. "Malay Studies in the Malay World". *Malay Literature* 6, no. 1 (1993): 9–21.

Jepperson, Ronald L., Alexander Wendt, and Peter J. Katzenstein. "Norms, Identity, and Culture in National Security". In *The Culture of National Security: Norms and Identity in World Politics*, edited by Peter J. Katzenstein. New York: Columbia University Press, 1996, pp. 33–75.

Jervis, Robert. "Security Regimes". *International Organization* 36, no. 2 (1982): 357–78.

Jeshurun, Chandran. *Malaysia: Fifty Years of Diplomacy 1957–2007.* Singapore: Talisman Publishing, 2007.

Joffe, Josef. "Europe's American Pacifier". *Foreign Policy*, no. 54 (1984): 64–82.

Kadir Mohamad. *Malaysia's Territorial Disputes — Two Cases at the ICJ: Batu Puteh, Middle Rocks and South Ledge (Malaysia/Singapore) & Ligitan and Sipadan [and the Sabah Claim] (Malaysia/Indonesia/Philippines).* Kuala Lumpur: Institute of Diplomacy and Foreign Relations, 2009.

Kahin, Audrey R. and George McT. Kahin. *Subversion as Foreign Policy: The Secret Eisenhower and Dulles Debacle in Indonesia.* Seattle and London: University of Washington Press, 1997.

Kammen, Douglas and Katharine McGregor. "Introduction: The Contours of Mass Violence in Indonesia, 1965–68". In *The Contours of Mass Violence in Indonesia, 1965–68*, edited by Douglas Kammen and Katharine McGregor. Singapore: NUS Press, 2012, pp. 1–24.

Karp, Aaron. "Military Procurement and Regional Security in Southeast Asia". *Contemporary Southeast Asia* 11, no. 4 (1990): 334–62.

Kassim, Yang Razali. *ASEAN Cohesion: Making Sense of Indonesian Reactions to Bilateral Disputes.* IDSS Commentaries, 15/2005. Singapore: Institute of Defence and Strategic Studies, Nanyang Technological University, 2005.

Katzenstein, Peter J. *Cultural Norms and National Security: Police and Military in Postwar Japan.* Ithaca and London: Cornell University Press, 1996*a*.

———. "Introduction: Alternative Perspectives on National Security". In *The Culture of National Security: Norms and Identity in World Politics*, edited by Peter J. Katzenstein. New York: Columbia University Press, 1996*b*, pp. 1–32.

Khalid, Khadijah Md. and Shakila Yacob. "Managing Malaysia–Indonesia Relations in the Context of Democratization: The Emergence of Non-State Actors". *International Relations of the Asia-Pacific* 12, no. 3 (2012): 355–87.

Kirby, D.G. *Finland in the Twentieth Century.* US: University of Minnesota Press, 1979.

Kissinger, Henry A. "Reflections on a Partnership: British and American Attitudes to Postwar Foreign Policy". *International Affairs* 58, no. 4 (1982): 571–87.

Kondapalli, Srikanth. "Pakistan in China's Security Perceptions". In *China–Pakistan Strategic Cooperation: Indian Perspectives*, edited by Swaran Singh. New Delhi: Manohar Publisher, 2007, pp. 53–75.

Kottman, Richard N. "The Canadian–American Trade Agreement of 1935". *The Journal of American History* 52, no. 2 (1965): 275–96.

Lane, Max. *Unfinished Nation: Indonesia Before and After Suharto*. London & New York: Verso, 2008.

Leahy, James P. *Bridging the Expectation Gap: The Key to Happiness*. US: AuthorHouse, 2006.

Legge, John D. *Sukarno: A Political Biography*. Great Britain: Allen Lane The Penguin Press, 1972.

Leifer, Michael. *Conflict and Regional Order in Southeast Asia*. London: The International Institute for Strategic Studies, 1980.

———. *Indonesia's Foreign Policy*. London: George Allen & Unwin, 1983.

———. *Singapore's Foreign Policy: Coping with Vulnerability*. London: Routledge, 2000.

Liow, Joseph Chinyong. "Malaysia's Illegal Indonesian Migrant Labour Problem: In Search of Solutions". *Contemporary Southeast Asia* 25, no. 1 (April 2003): 44–64.

———. "Balancing, Banwagoning, or Hedging?: Strategic and Security Patterns in Malaysia's Relations with China, 1981–2003". In *China and Southeast Asia: Global Changes and Regional Challenges*, edited by Ho Khai Leong and Samuel C.Y. Ku. Singapore: Institute of Southeast Asian Studies and Center for Southeast Asian Studies, 2005.

———. *The Politics of Indonesia–Malaysia Relations: One Kin, Two Nations*. London and New York: Routledge, 2005.

Low, Linda. "The East Asian Economic Grouping". *The Pacific Review* 4, no. 4 (1991): 375–82.

Mackie, J.A.C. *Konfrontasi: The Indonesia–Malaysia Dispute 1963–1966*. London: Oxford University Press, 1974.

Mahan, A.T. *The Interest of America in Sea Power: Present and Future*. London: Sampson Low, Marston & Company, Limited, 1897.

Mahathir Mohamad. *The Challenge*. Petaling Jaya: Pelanduk Publications, 1986.

———. "ASEAN and the World Economy: The Challenge of Change". In *Reflections on ASEAN: Selected Speeches of Dr Mahathir Mohamad, Prime Minister of Malaysia*, edited by Hashim Makaruddin. Malaysia: Pelanduk Publications, 2004*a*, pp. 111–24.

———. "ASEAN in the 1990s and Beyond". In *Reflections on ASEAN: Selected Speeches of Dr Mahathir Mohamad, Prime Minister of Malaysia*, edited by Hashim Makaruddin. Malaysia: Pelanduk Publications, 2004*b*, pp. 145–57.

———. "ASEAN: Good Return of Growth and Stability". In *Reflections on ASEAN: Selected Speeches of Dr Mahathir Mohamad, Prime Minister of*

Malaysia, edited by Hashim Makaruddin. Malaysia: Pelanduk Publications, 2004c, pp. 125–35.

―――. "The Impact of a Changing World on ASEAN–European Community Relations". In *Reflections on ASEAN: Selected Speeches of Dr Mahathir Mohamad, Prime Minister of Malaysia*, edited by Hashim Makaruddin. Malaysia: Pelanduk Publications, 2004d, pp. 101–10.

―――. *A Doctor in the House: The Memoirs of Tun Dr Mahathir Mohamad*. Malaysia: MPH Group Publishing, 2011.

Majumdar, Anindyo J. "The Changing Imperatives". In *China–Pakistan Strategic Cooperation: Indian Perspectives*, edited by Swaran Singh. New Delhi: Manohar Publishers, 2007, pp. 35–51.

Marsh, Steve and John Baylis. "The Anglo-American 'Special Relationship': The Lazarus of International Relations". *Diplomacy & Statecraft* 17, no. 1 (2006): 173–211.

McKercher, Brian J.C. *Transition of Power: Britain's Loss of Global Pre-Eminence to the United States, 1930–1945*. Cambridge: Cambridge University Press, 1999.

McNeill, William Hardy. *America, Britain, & Russia: Their Co-operation and Conflict, 1941–1946*. New York and London: Johnson Reprint Corporation, 1970.

Mearsheimer, John J. *The Tragedy of Great Power Politics*. US: W.W. Norton & Company, Inc., 2001.

Mergawati Zulfakar. "Calming the Waves of Wrath". *The Star*, 25 August 2010.

Mietzner, Marcus. *Military Politics, Islam, and the State in Indonesia: From Turbulent Transition to Democratic Consolidation*. Singapore: Institute of Southeast Asian Studies, 2009.

Milne, R.S. and Diane K. Mauzy. *Malaysian Politics Under Mahathir*. London and New York: Routledge, 1999.

Milner, Anthony. *The Malays*. United Kingdom: Wiley-Blackwell, 2008.

Modelski, George, ed. "We Are Being Encircled". In *The New Emerging Forces: Documents on the Ideology of Indonesian Foreign Policy*. Australia: The Australian National University, 1963, pp. 74–76.

Momsen, Janet Henshall. "Canada–Caribbean Relations: Wherein the Special Relationship?" *Political Geography* 11, no. 5 (1992): 501–13.

Moore, Matthew. "Vow of Protection for Mistreated Indonesian Maids". *The Sydney Morning Herald*, 22 July 2004. Available at <http://www.smh.com.au/articles/2004/07/21/1090089223202.html?from=storyrhs> (accessed 28 June 2014).

Morgenthau, Hans J. *Scientific Man vs Power Politics*. Chicago & London: University of Chicago Press, 1967.

―――. *Politics Among Nations: The Struggle for Power and Peace*. New York: Alfred A. Knopf, 1978.

Morton, William L. *The Canadian Identity.* Toronto and Buffalo: University of Toronto Press, 1961.

Mowat, Robert Balmain. *The Diplomatic Relations of Great Britain and the United States.* London: Edward Arnold & Co, 1925.

————. *Americans in England.* USA: Houghton Mifflin Company, 1935.

Murphy, Ann Marie. "Indonesia and the World". In *Indonesia: The Great Transition*, edited by John Bresnan. U.S.: Rowman & Littlefield Publishers, 2005, pp. 239–95.

Nair, Shanti. *Islam in Malaysian Foreign Policy.* London: Routledge, 1997.

Nguyen Nam Duong. "Vietnamese Foreign Policy Since *Doi Moi*: The Dialectic of Power and Identity". PhD dissertation, The University of New South Wales, 2010.

Nik Mahmud, Nik Anuar, Muhammad Haji Salleh, and Abd. Ghapa Harun. *A Biography of Tun Abdul Razak: Statesman and Patriot.* Bangi: Universiti Kebangsaan Malaysia Press, 2012.

Noraini Razak. "Hubungan Benci Tapi Rindu Tiada Kesudahan". *Utusan Malaysia*, 26 June 2012.

Nye Jr., Joseph S. "Nuclear Learning and U.S.–Soviet Security Regimes". *International Organization* 41, no. 3 (1987): 371–402.

O'brien, Phillips Payson. *British and American Naval Power: Politics and Policy, 1900–1936.* London: Praeger Publishers, 1998.

Ooi Kee Beng. *The Reluctant Politician: Tun Dr. Ismail and His Time.* Singapore: Institute of Southeast Asian Studies, 2006.

————. *Lost in Transition: Malaysia Under Abdullah.* Singapore: Institute of Southeast Asian Studies, 2008.

Orde, Anne. *The Eclipse of Great Britain: The United States and British Imperial Decline, 1895–1956.* New York: St. Martin's Press, 1996.

Ott, Marvin C. "The Sources and Content of Malaysian Foreign Policy Toward Indonesia and the Philippines: 1957–1965". PhD dissertation, The Johns Hopkins University, 1971.

Otte, Thomas G. "From 'War-in-Sight' to Nearly War: Anglo–French Relations in the Age of High Imperialism, 1875–1898". *Diplomacy & Statecraft* 17, no. 4 (2006): 693–714.

Paxton, John, ed. "Indonesia". In *The Statesman's Year-Book: Statistical and Historical Annual of the States of the World for the Year 1990–1991.* Great Britain: The Macmillan Press, 1990.

Peterson, Horace C. *Propaganda for War: The Campaign Against American Neutrality, 1914–1917.* US: Kennikat Press, 1968.

Pillai, Patrick. "The Malaysian State's Response to Migration". *Sojourn* 14, no. 1 (1999): 178–97.

Porter, Patrick. "Last Charge of the Knights? Iraq, Afghanistan and the Special Relationship". *International Affairs* 86, no. 2 (2010): 355–75.

Poulgrain, Greg. *The Genesis of Konfrontasi: Malaysia Brunei Indonesia 1945–1965.* Australia: Crawford House Publishing, 1998.

———. *The Genesis of Konfrontasi: Malaysia, Brunei and Indonesia, 1945–1965.* Malaysia: SIRD, 2014.

Pouliot, Vincent. "Security Community In and Through Practice: The Power Politics of Russia–NATO Diplomacy". PhD dissertation, University of Toronto, 2008.

Rahim, Lily Zubaidah. *Singapore in the Malay World: Building and Breaching Regional Bridges.* Oxon: Routledge, 2009.

Ramasamy, P. "International Migration and Conflict: Foreign Labour in Malaysia". In *International Migration in Southeast Asia*, edited by Aris Ananta and Evi Nurvidya Arifin. Singapore: Institute of Southeast Asian Studies, 2004, pp. 273–95.

Reich, Bernard. "Reassessing the United States–Israel Special Relationship". *Israel Affairs* 1, no. 1 (1994): 64–83.

Reid, Anthony. "Understanding *Melayu* (Malay) as a Source of Diverse Modern Identities". In *Contesting Malayness: Malay Identity Across Boundaries*, edited by Timothy P. Barnard. Singapore: Singapore University Press, 2004, pp. 1–24.

Reynolds, David. *The Creation of the Anglo-American Alliance 1937–41: A Study in Competitive Co-operation.* London: Europa Publications Limited, 1981.

———. "A 'Special Relationship'? America, Britain and the International Order since the Second World War". *International Affairs* 62, no. 1 (1985–86): 1–20.

———. "Rethinking Anglo-American Relations". *International Affairs* 65, no. 1 (1989): 89–111.

Rittberger, Volker, Manfred Efinger, and Martin Mendler. "Toward an East–West Security Regime: The Case of Confidence- and Security-Building Measures". *Journal of Peace Research* 27, no. 1 (1990): 55–74.

Roberts, Christopher B. "ASEAN's Security Community Project: Challenges and Opportunities in the Pursuit of Comprehensive Integration". PhD dissertation, The University of New South Wales, 2008.

———. *ASEAN Regionalism: Cooperation, Values and Institutionalization.* London and New York: Routledge, 2012.

Rock, Stephen R. *Why Peace Breaks Out: Great Power Rapprochement in Historical Perspective.* Chapel Hill and London: University of North Carolina Press, 1989.

———. *Appeasement in International Politics.* Lexington: University Press of Kentucky, 2000.

Roosa, John. "The September 30th Movement: The Aporias of the Official Narratives". In *The Contours of Mass Violence in Indonesia, 1965–68*, edited by Douglas Kammen and Katharine McGregor. Singapore: NUS Press, 2012, pp. 25–49.

Roussel, Stephane. *The North American Democratic Peace: Absence of War and Security Institution-Building in Canada–US Relations, 1867–1958*. Montreal and Kingston, London, Ithaca: McGill-Queen's University Press, 2004.

Saravanamuttu, Johan. *Malaysia's Foreign Policy, the First Fifty Years: Alignment, Neutralism, Islamism*. Singapore: Institute of Southeast Asian Studies, 2010.

Searle, Peter. "Recalcitrant or Realpolitik? The Politics of Culture in Australia's Relations with Malaysia". In *Pathways to Asia: The Politics of Engagement*, edited by Richard Robison. Australia: Allen & Unwin, 1996, pp. 56–84.

Sheppard, Mubin. *Tunku: His Life and Times*. Malaysia: Pelanduk Publications, 1995.

Shore, Sean M. "No Fences Make Good Neighbors: The Development of the Canadian–US Security Community, 1871–1940". In *Security Communities*, edited by Emanuel Adler and Michael Barnett. Cambridge: Cambridge University Press, 1998, pp. 333–67.

Singh, Bilveer. "Singapore's Management of its Security Problems". *Asia Pacific Community* 29 (Summer 1985): 77–97.

Singh, Swaran. "Introduction". In *China–Pakistan Strategic Cooperation: Indian Perspectives*, edited by Swaran Singh. New Delhi: Manohar Publishers, 2007, pp. 17–34.

Sinha, Satyabrat. "China in Pakistan's Security Perceptions". In *China–Pakistan Strategic Cooperation: Indian Perspectives*, edited by Swaran Singh. New Delhi: Manohar Publishers, 2007, pp. 77–103.

Smith, Anthony D. *National Identity*. London: Penguin Books, 1991.

———. *Nations and Nationalism in a Global Era*. Cambridge: Polity Press, 1995.

———. "Theories of Nationalism: Alternative Models of Nation Formation". In *Asian Nationalism*, edited by Michael Leifer. London and New York: Routledge, 2000, pp. 1–20.

Soeharto. *My Thoughts, Words and Deeds: An Autobiography as Told to G. Dwipayana and Ramadhan K.H.* Jakarta: Citra Lamtoro Gung Persada, 1991.

Somwong, Pranom and Marie Huberlant. *Undocumented Migrants and Refugees in Malaysia: Raids, Detention and Discrimination*. Kuala Lumpur and Paris: FIDH-Suaram, 2008.

Stockwell, Anthony J. "Britain and Brunei, 1945–1963: Imperial Retreat and Royal Ascendancy". *Modern Asian Studies* 38, no. 4 (2004): 785–819.

Storatz, Richard Lawrence. "Anglo-American Relations: A Theory and History of Political Integration". PhD dissertation, Columbia University, 1981.

Storey, Ian, Ralf Emmers, and Daljit Singh. "Introduction". In *Five Power Defence Arragements at Forty*, edited by Ian Storey, Ralf Emmers, and Daljit Singh. Singapore: Institute of Southeast Asian Studies, 2011, pp. xv–xxi.

Sturgis, James. "Learning About Oneself: The Making of Canadian Nationalism, 1867–1914". In *Kith and Kin: Canada, Britain and the United States from the*

Revolution to the Cold War, edited by C.C. Eldridge. Cardiff: University of Wales Press, 1997, pp. 95–146.

Sukamdi, Elan Satriawan and Abdul Haris. "Impact of Remittances on the Indonesian Economy". In *International Migration in Southeast Asia*, edited by Aris Ananta and Evi Nurvidya Arifin. Singapore: Institute of Southeast Asian Studies, 2004, pp. 137–65.

Sukma, Rizal. "Domestic Politics and International Posture: Constraints and Possibilities". In *Indonesia Rising: The Repositioning of Asia's Third Giant*, edited by Anthony Reid. Singapore: Institute of Southeast Asian Studies, 2012, pp. 77–92.

Suryadinata, Leo. *Indonesia's Foreign Policy Under Suharto: Aspiring to International Leadership*. Singapore: Times Academic Press, 1996.

Tan, Andrew. *Intra-ASEAN Tensions*. Great Britain: The Royal Institute of International Affairs, 2000.

Thomas, Laurence. "Friendship and Other Loves". In *Friendship: A Philosophical Reader,* edited by Neera Kapur Badhwar. Cornell: Cornell University Press, 1993, pp. 48–64.

Thomas, Lisa. "Indonesia Pushes for Better Migrant-Worker Protection". *Time*, 28 July 2009. Available at <http://content.time.com/time/world/article/0,8599,1913134,00.html> (accessed 28 June 2014).

Thompson, John Herd and Stephen J. Randall. *Canada and the United States: Ambivalent Allies*. Athens and London: The University of Georgia Press, 1994.

Thompson, William R. "Why Rivalries Matter and What Great Power Rivalries Can Tell Us About World Politics". In *Great Power Rivalries*, edited by William R. Thompson. US: University of South Carolina Press, 1999, pp. 3–28.

Tibi, Bassam. *Conflict and War in the Middle East: From Interstate War to New Security.* New York: St. Martion's Press, 1998.

Trotter, William R. *A Frozen Hell: The Russo–Finnish Winter War of 1939–1940.* US: Algonquin Books of Chapel Hill, 1991.

Van Der Kroef, Justus M. "The Sarawak–Indonesian Border Insurgency". *Modern Asian Studies* 2, no. 3 (1968): 245–65.

Vatikiotis, Michael R.J. "Aceh Unrest Leads to Mounting Death Toll: Troubled Province". *Far Eastern Economic Review* (24 January 1991*a*): 20–21.

———. "Let's Clear the Air". *Far Eastern Economic Review* (1 August 1991*b*): 10–11.

———. "Clash of Styles: High Profile Diplomacy Upsets Neighbours". *Far Eastern Economic Review* (20 August 1992): 19.

———. *Indonesian Politics Under Suharto: Order, Development and Pressure for Change.* London and New York: Routledge, 1993*a*.

———. "Indonesia's Foreign Policy in the 1990s". *Contemporary Southeast Asia* 14, no. 4 (March 1993*b*): 352–67.

————. "Stormy Weather: Tension Behind the Smiles at Mahathir–Suharto Talks". *Far Eastern Economic Review* (29 July 1993*c*): 18–19.

————. "Isle of Contention: Tiny Sipadan Becomes an Object of Rival Claims". *Far Eastern Economic Review* (17 March 1994): 32.

Vucetic, Srdjan. "The Anglosphere: A Genealogy of an Identity in International Relations". PhD dissertation, The Ohio State University, 2008.

Waever, Ole. "Insecurity, Security, and Asecurity in the West European Non-War Community". In *Security Communities*, edited by Emanuel Adler and Michael Barnett. Cambridge: Cambridge University Press, 1998, pp. 69–118.

Wallace, William. "The Collapse of British Foreign Policy". *International Affairs* 82, no. 1 (2005): 53–68.

Wallace, William and Christopher Phillips. "Reassessing the Special Relationship". *International Affairs* 85, no. 2 (2009): 263–84.

Walt, Stephen M. *The Origins of Alliances*. Ithaca and London: Cornell University Press, 1987.

Waltz, Kenneth N. *Theory of International Politics*. Canada: Addison-Wesley Publishing Company, 1979.

————. "The Origins of War in Neorealist Theory". In *The Origin and Prevention of Major Wars*, edited by Robert I. Rotberg and Theodore K. Rabb. Cambridge: Cambridge University Press, 1989, pp. 39–52.

Weatherbee, Donald E. "ASEAN Security Cooperation and Resource Protection". In *The Invisible Nexus Energy and ASEAN's Security*, edited by Kusuma Snitwongse and Sukhumbhand Paribatra. Singapore: Executive Publications, 1984, pp. 116–21.

————. *International Relations in Southeast Asia: The Struggle for Autonomy.* Singapore: Institute of Southeast Asian Studies, 2010.

————. *Indonesia in ASEAN: Vision and Reality.* Singapore: Institute of Southeast Asian Studies, 2013.

Webber, Douglas. "Introduction". In *The Franco–German Relationship in the European Union*, edited by Douglas Webber. USA and Canada: Routledge, 1999, pp. 1–20.

Weinberg, Albert K. *Manifest Destiny: A Study of Nationalist Expansionism in American History.* Chicago: Quadrangle Books, 1963.

Weinstein, Franklin B. *Indonesian Foreign Policy and the Dilemma of Dependence: From Sukarno to Soeharto.* Ithaca and London: Cornell University Press, 1976.

Wendt, Alexander. "The Agent-Structure Problem in International Relations Theory". *International Organization* 41, no. 3 (1987): 335–70.

————. "Anarchy is What States Make of It: The Social Construction of Power Politics". *International Organization* 46, no. 2 (1992): 391–425.

————. "Collective Identity Formation and the International State". *The American Political Science Review* 88, no. 2 (1994): 384–96.

————. "Constructing International Politics". *International Security* 20, no. 1 (1995): 71–81.

Westad, Odd Arne. *The Global Cold War: Third World Interventions and the Making of Our Times.* Cambridge: Cambridge University Press, 2005.

Wilson, Dick. *The Neutralization of Southeast Asia.* New York: Praeger Publishers, 1975.

Womack, Brantly. *China and Vietnam: The Politics of Asymmetry.* New York: Cambridge University Press, 2006.

Wong Chun Wai. "Shame On You!" *The Star*, 20 November 2011.

Yaakub, Ahmad Nizar. "Malaysia and Indonesia: A Study of Foreign Policies with Special Reference to Bilateral Relations". PhD dissertation, The University of Western Australia, 2009.

Zakaria, Fareed. *From Wealth to Power: The Unusual Origins of America's World Role.* Princeton: Princeton University Press, 1998.

Zartman, I. William. "The Quest for Order in World Politics". In *Imbalance of Power: US Hegemony and International Order*, edited by I. William Zartman. US: Lynne Rienner Publishers, 2009, pp. 1–23.

Ziegenhain, Patrick. *The Indonesian Parliament and Democratization.* Singapore: Institute of Southeast Asian Studies, 2008.

ARCHIVAL SOURCES

Tun Dr Ismail A. Rahman Papers,
Drifting into Politics. Unpublished Memoirs Folio 12 (2)
WikiLeaks
JIO – Joint Intelligence Organisation

LIST OF INTERVIEWS

Interviewee	Position	Venue	Date
Interview 917	A former assistant chief official in a prominent Malaysian think-tank that regularly provides policy advice to Malaysia's government; and also an academic who has in-depth knowledge of Indonesia–Malaysia relations.	Kuala Lumpur	17 September 2012
Interview 919	A prominent Malaysian columnist for Malaysia's and Indonesia's mainstream newspapers, who specializes in the study of politics in Indonesia and Malaysia.	Kuala Lumpur	19 September 2012
Interview 920	A former top level Malaysian diplomat	Kuala Lumpur	20 September 2012
Interview 924–001	The chief official in a prominent Malaysian think-tank that regularly provides policy advice to Malaysia's government.	Kuala Lumpur	24 September 2012
Interview 924–002	The chief official in a mainstream newspaper in Malaysia.	Kuala Lumpur	24 September 2012
Interview 925	A former Malaysian diplomat	Kuala Lumpur	25 September 2012
Interview 926–001	A former Malaysian Foreign Minister	Kuala Lumpur	26 September 2012
Interview 926–002	A former Malaysian diplomat	Kuala Lumpur	26 September 2012

Interviewee	Position	Venue	Date
Interview 1002	An academic who specializes in Indonesia–Malaysia relations.	Singapore	2 October 2012
Interview 1008	An Indonesian diplomat	Jakarta	8 October 2012
Interview 1011	A senior editor in a mainstream newspaper in Indonesia	Jakarta	11 October 2012
Interview 1012	A senior researcher in Indonesia's parliament – The House of Representatives of the Republic of Indonesia (DPR-RI).	Jakarta	12 October 2012
Interview 1016	A former Indonesian diplomat	Jakarta	16 October 2012
Interview 1017	A former Indonesian diplomat	Jakarta	17 October 2012
Interview 1019	An Indonesian member of parliament	Jakarta	19 October 2012

NEWSPAPERS AND MAGAZINES

Antara News
Bernama
Borneo Post
Business Insider Australia
Forbes
Jakarta Globe
Jakarta Post
New Straits Times
Republika
Tempo
The Economist
The Independent

The New York Times
The Star
The Straits Times
The Sydney Morning Herald
The Telegraph
Time
Utusan Malaysia

INTERNET SOURCES

Statistics

Economic Planning Unit, Prime Minister's Department of Malaysia,
Malaysia's Exports by Major Destination, 1990–2016,
<http://www.epu.gov.my/en/economic-statistics/external-trade>.

Economic Planning Unit, Prime Minister's Department of Malaysia,
Number of Foreign Workers in Malaysia by Country of Origin, 2000–2015,
<http://www.epu.gov.my/sites/default/files/1.4.1.pdf>.

Malaysia External Trade Development Corporation,
Malaysia's Trade Statistics 2016,
<http://www.matrade.gov.my/en/malaysian-exporters/services-for-exporters/trade-
market-information/trade-statistics>.

Ministry of Trade, Republic of Indonesia,
Indonesia Export/Import,
<http://www.kemendag.go.id/en/economic-profile/indonesia-export-import>.

The National Council of the Settlement and Protection of Indonesian Labour,
The Data of the Settlement and Protection of Indonesian Labour October 2017,
<http://www.bnp2tki.go.id/uploads/data/data_10-11-2017_015327_Laporan_
Pengolahan_Data_BNP2TKI_2017_(s.d_Oktober_).pdf>.

World Development Indicators,
<http://databank.worldbank.org/data/views/reports/tableview.aspx>.

World Economic Forum,
The Global Competitiveness Report 2011–2012,
<http://reports.weforum.org/global-competitiveness-2011-2012/>.

Others

The ASEAN Declaration (Bangkok Declaration) Bangkok, 8 August 1967, <http://asean.org/the-asean-declaration-bangkok-declaration-bangkok-8-august-1967/>.

Lim Jiet, "Maid Abuse in Malaysia: A Legal Analysis", *Academia.edu*: 12, <http://www.academia.edu/3437442/Maid_Abuse_In_Malaysia_-_A_Legal_Analysis>.

Mahathir Mohamad's speech, "Malaysia: The Way Forward", <http://www.pmo.gov.my/?menu=page&page=1904>.

Mitchell G. Bard and Daniel Pipes, "How Special is the US–Israel Relationship?" *Middle East Quarterly* (June 1997), <http://www.meforum.org/349/how-special-is-the-us-israel-relationship>.

Stephen Harper, Statement on the Inauguration of Barack Obama as the 44th President of the United States of America, 20 January 2009, <http://www.pm.gc.ca/eng/media.asp?category=3&id=2391>.

Treaty of Amity and Cooperation in Southeast Asia Indonesia, 24 February 1976, <http://asean.org/treaty-amity-cooperation-southeast-asia-indonesia-24-february-1976/>.

ABC Radio Australia, <http://www.radioaustralia.net.au/international/>.

Aljazeera, <http://www.aljazeera.com/>.

Asiaone, <http://www.asiaone.com/>.

Asia Times Online, <http://www.atimes.com/>.

BBC News, <http://www.bbc.com/news/>.

Deutsche Welle, <http://www.dw.com/en/top-stories/s-9097>.
The Indonesian Army, <http://www.tniad.mil.id/>.

Indosiar, <http://www.indosiar.com/>.

Kompas, <http://www.kompas.com/>.

Liputan 6, <http://www.liputan6.com/>.

Malaysiakini, <http://www.malaysiakini.com/>.

Malaysian Trades Union Congress, <http://www.mtuc.org.my/>.

My Sinchew, <http://www.mysinchew.com/>.

Singapore Institute of International Affairs, <http://siiaonline.org/page/Home>.

Waspada Online, <http://www.waspada.co.id/>.

INDEX

ABOUT THE AUTHOR

HO Ying Chan is an Assistant Professor at the Faculty of Creative Industries, Universiti Tunku Abdul Rahman (UTAR), Malaysia, where he teaches political science. He is also the Chairperson of the Centre for International Studies, UTAR. Ying Chan holds a PhD in International and Political Studies from the University of New South Wales at the Australian Defence Force Academy, Canberra, and a Master's Degree in Public Policy from the Lee Kuan Yew School of Public Policy, National University of Singapore.